5th edition
Headway »

Pre-intermediate Teacher's Guide

Liz & John Soars • Stacey Hughes

with photocopiable activities by Rachel Godfrey

OXFORD
UNIVERSITY PRESS

Contents

Welcome to *Headway* 5th edition.

Headway and its award-winning authors are names that have become synonymous with English Language Teaching and learning. The 5th edition balances *Headway*'s world-renowned methodology with innovative and flexible new material.

This Teacher's Guide has been created for you, with all the lesson preparation, in-class support and resources you need to teach in today's classroom.

Introduction
Course overview	6
What's new for the 5th edition?	8
Why do teachers trust *Headway*?	9
Student's Book contents	10
Speaking skills – from accuracy to fluency	14
Professional Development support	16

Unit 1
Getting to know you — 17

Unit 2
Let's get together — 30

Unit 3
Good news, bad news! — 43

Unit 4
Food for thought — 56

Unit 5
The future's in your hands — 68

Unit 6
History repeats itself — 80

Unit 7
Simply the best — 93

Unit 8
Living dangerously — 106

Unit 9
What a story! — 119

Unit 10
All-time greats — 131

Unit 11
People with a passion — 143

Unit 12
You never know … — 155

Photocopiable activities — 167

Introduction

The *Headway* series

Headway has made a significant contribution to English Language Teaching for more than 30 years.

The *Headway* series has always championed a blend of methodologies:

- traditional methodology: a grammar syllabus with controlled practice, systematic vocabulary work, and reading and writing activities
- a communicative approach: a functional/situational syllabus, personalized practice, real language work in real situations, activities to encourage genuine communication inside and outside the classroom, development of all four skills – especially listening and speaking.

This blend of approaches has proved an excellent combination for English language learning, and has now become a standard for, and indeed expected of, today's ELT coursebooks.

Key features of the Pre-intermediate Student's Book

Unit Opener and Starter

Each unit begins with an opening page which presents the theme of the unit through inspiring images, and questions which generate discussion and encourage students to start thinking about the unit topic. They can also watch the video introduction to the unit by going to **headwayonline.com**.

The first page begins with a Starter section, which launches the grammar and/or the theme of the unit.

Grammar

The upfront, systematic, and effective treatment of grammar is a hallmark of *Headway*. At the Pre-intermediate level, we build students' confidence and knowledge of grammar by introducing new language methodically, comparing and contrasting similar structures, and placing them in context. We introduce learners to:

- tenses and questions
- simple versus continuous aspect
- articles
- verb patterns
- perfect versus non-perfect aspect
- comparative and superlative adjectives
- modal verbs
- active and passive voice
- conditional forms

Grammar spots

There are Grammar spots in the presentation sections, which focus students' attention on the language of the unit. The Grammar spots are cross-referenced to the Grammar reference at the back of the book, where you and your students will find more in-depth explanations of the key structures.

Students are encouraged to go to **headwayonline.com** for further grammar practice.

Vocabulary

Headway has always attached great importance to the acquisition of vocabulary. Its approach can broadly be divided into three areas:

1. an examination of lexical systems such as: phrasal verbs, compound nouns, collocation, dependent prepositions, word building, spelling and pronunciation, synonyms and antonyms.
2. the teaching of new items in lexical sets such as: leisure activities, parts of the body and clothes.
3. the encouragement of good learning habits: using dictionaries, keeping records, reading and working out meaning from context.

Students are encouraged to go to **headwayonline.com** for further vocabulary practice.

Practice

Each unit has a wide variety of practice activities, both controlled and free, mechanical and information gap. These activities allow students to analyse the target language and use it communicatively.

Skills development

We aim to develop the four language skills, Listening, Speaking, Reading, and Writing (with special emphasis on the first two) by providing as much varied practice as the classroom setting can allow with the use of stimulating, relevant material and tasks.

Students are encouraged to go to **headwayonline.com** for further skills practice.

Speaking, Listening, and Everyday English

The communicative emphasis in *Headway* Pre-intermediate gives students plenty of opportunities to put language into practice.

Grammar, Reading, Vocabulary, and Writing sections are combined with speaking and/or listening activities to encourage genuine communication using the target language.

Communicative skills are also given special treatment in their own sections, with Everyday English pages at the end of each unit presenting and practising phrases students can use in social contexts, at the doctor's, to express doubt and certainty, to say thank you and goodbye.

Video

The video material provides revision and extension material through a series of interesting and varied documentary-style videos. The clips are designed to consolidate grammatical, functional and lexical areas covered in the related Student's

Book, and to develop listening comprehension skills. Each video is accompanied by a photocopiable worksheet and a page of teacher's notes. The worksheets are designed to give students exercises and activities that will best prepare them for and help exploit the video.

Writing

Each unit contains a complete writing lesson. Each of these provides a model for students to analyse and imitate. We introduce learners to the structure of discourse (linking words, ordering paragraphs, pronoun reference), and also look at style and register in writing.

Workbook

The Workbook is an important component as it practises, revises, and reinforces the language presented in the Student's Book providing further practice of all of the Grammar, Vocabulary, and Everyday English sections. There is a strong element of progression, from exercises that practise recognition to those that encourage production of the target items. There are also vocabulary exercises and reading texts, as well as a Review section in every unit.

The audio files for the workbook exercises are found at **headwayonline.com**. Students are also encouraged to go online for further practice and to check their progress.

Teacher's Guide

The Teacher's Guide offers the teacher full support both for lesson preparation and in the classroom. It includes:

- Full teaching notes for each section, with answers and audioscripts in the main body of the notes. There are plenty of suggestions, with ideas for exploiting the material with weaker students and/or mixed ability classes, for extending the Student's Book material, and for encouraging students to use English outside the classroom.
- Background notes for the Reading and Listening sections, with information about the people profiled in the texts, historical and geographical notes, and brief explanations about features of the English-speaking world.
- Cross references to relevant exercises in the Workbook.
- Photocopiable activities to accompany units with extra pairwork, group work, and vocabulary revision.

Headway Online

For students

Headway Online Practice is directly linked to each Student's Book unit, and students and teachers are directed to it throughout the unit. Students can access **headwayonline.com** for the first time via the code on the Access Card in their Student's Book. Here they can **Look again** at Student's Book activities that they missed in class or want to try again, do extra **Practice** activities, and **Check progress** on what they have learned so far. They can also get instant feedback on their progress. Students can additionally download all the course audio and video material, and other resources, such as a Language Portfolio.

In **Look again** students can:
- Review every lesson
- Try activities from the unit again
- Watch the videos as many times as they like.

In **Practice** students can:
- Extend their knowledge with extra Reading, Writing, Listening, and Speaking skills practice.

In **Check your Progress** students can:
- Test themselves on the main language from the unit and get instant feedback
- Try an extra challenge.

For teachers

Teachers can use the Access Card in the back of this Teacher's Guide to access the Teacher's Resource Centre in *Online Practice*. In addition to all the students' resources, teachers can access students' work, track their progress and scores in exercises and tests, show/hide tasks, and compare different classes.

As well as getting feedback on progress and practice tasks, students can submit their writing to teachers and record their speaking, e.g. long turns, for assessment and/or comment.

Teachers are also able to access a wide range of resources and materials to support their lessons in the Teacher's Resource Centre. These include:

- Audio files for the Student's Book and Workbook
- Video files
- Full Teacher's Notes and Answer keys
- Photocopiable activities.
- Complete tests, with answers and audio:
  – Entry test for the whole course
  – Unit tests 1–12, in two versions covering the main grammar, vocabulary, and Everyday English syllabus for each Student's Book unit
  – Stop and check tests, in two versions, revising Units 1–4, 5–8, and 9–12
  – Progress tests for mid-year and end-of-year assessment
  – Skills tests covering the four skills of reading, listening, writing, and speaking
  – Optional listening tests 1–12
- Editable audioscripts from the Student's Book and Workbook
- Wordlists from the Student's Book with write-in lines for translations
- CEFR guide for teachers
- Collated answer key.

Finally!

Good luck in your teaching. We hope this new edition helps you in the preparation and execution of your lessons, and that you and your students find it not only useful to learn and practise your language skills, but enjoyable and thought-provoking.

John and Liz Soars

Course overview

For students

Welcome to **Headway** 5th edition. Here's how you can link learning in the classroom with meaningful preparation and practice outside.

Student's Book

All the language and skills your students need to improve their English, with grammar, vocabulary and skills work in every unit. Also available as an e-book.

ACTIVITIES AUDIO VIDEO WORDLISTS

Workbook

Exclusive practice to match the Student's Book, following the grammar, vocabulary, and Everyday English sections for each unit. Students can use their Workbook for homework or for self-study to give them new input and practice.

Online Practice

Extend students' independent learning. They can **Look again** at Student's Book activities, do extra **Practice** activities, and **Check progress** with instant feedback.

headwayonline.com

6   Introduction • Course overview

For teachers

Teacher's Guide

Prepare lessons with full teaching notes and photocopiable activities for each unit. Get ideas on how to adapt and extend the Student's Book material, and how to deal with potential problems.

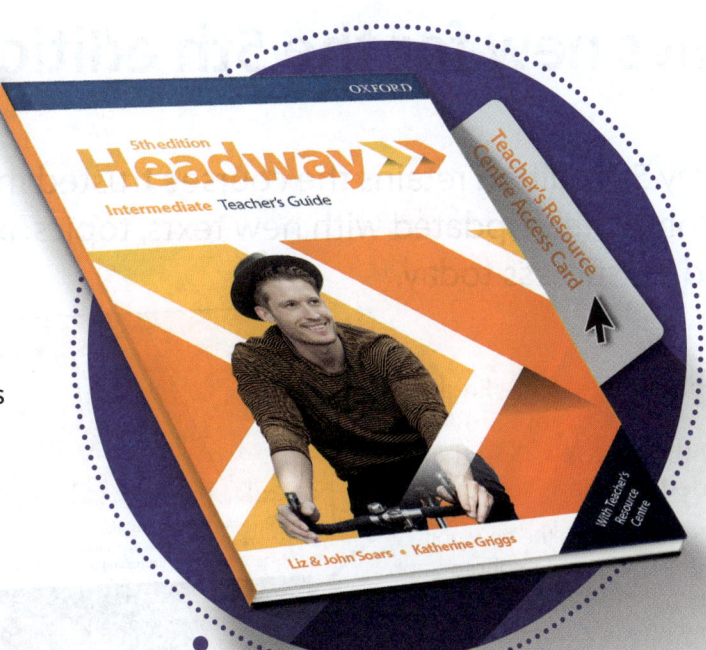

ACTIVITIES   TESTS   TRACKING   RESOURCES

Teacher's Resource Centre

All your *Headway* resources, stored in one place to save you time. Resources include: Student's Book and Workbook audio, videos, audioscripts, answer keys, photocopiable activities, CEFR correlations, teaching notes, tests, wordlists, and more.

Use the Learning Management System to track your students' progress.

To log in for the first time, teachers use the Access Card in the back of the Teacher's Guide for the Teacher's Resource Centre, and students use the Access Card in the back of the Student's Book for Online Practice.

Classroom Presentation Tool

Use in class to deliver heads-up lessons and to engage students. Class audio, video, and answer keys are available online or offline, and updated across your devices.

Class Audio

Full course audio is available on the Teacher's Resource Centre, and on audio CDs.

Introduction • Course overview   7

What's new for the 5th edition?

Headway 5th edition retains the course's trusted methodology and has been completely updated with new texts, topics, and digital resources needed for success today.

From *Headway* 5th edition Pre-intermediate Student's Book.

Teach practical, real life English that is relevant to your students' lives with new topics and themes grounded in today's reality.

Engage students with the new unit opener page. An inspiring photograph with a thought-provoking quote and questions introduce the unit topic and encourage students to think about issues that have an impact on their lives.

Watch the accompanying video introduction in class or set as pre-work to bring the unit topic to life.

Save time with flexible print and digital resources in one place.

Download and adapt material for your students from the Teacher's Resource Centre. Track your students' progress on *Online Practice* using the Learning Management System.

headwayonline.com

Link learning in class with meaningful practice outside class with the powerful blended learning syllabus.

You and your students are all busy. That's why *Headway* 5th edition provides simple, connected materials that seamlessly guide students through learning in class and practising at home for every unit.

After using the **Student's Book** in class, students can get new grammar and vocabulary input and practice with the **Workbook** and look again at each unit, practise all skills, and check their progress with **Online Practice**.

Why do teachers trust *Headway*?

Headway has helped over 100 million students in 127 countries learn English.

Teachers from around the world explain how they have been inspired by *Headway*:

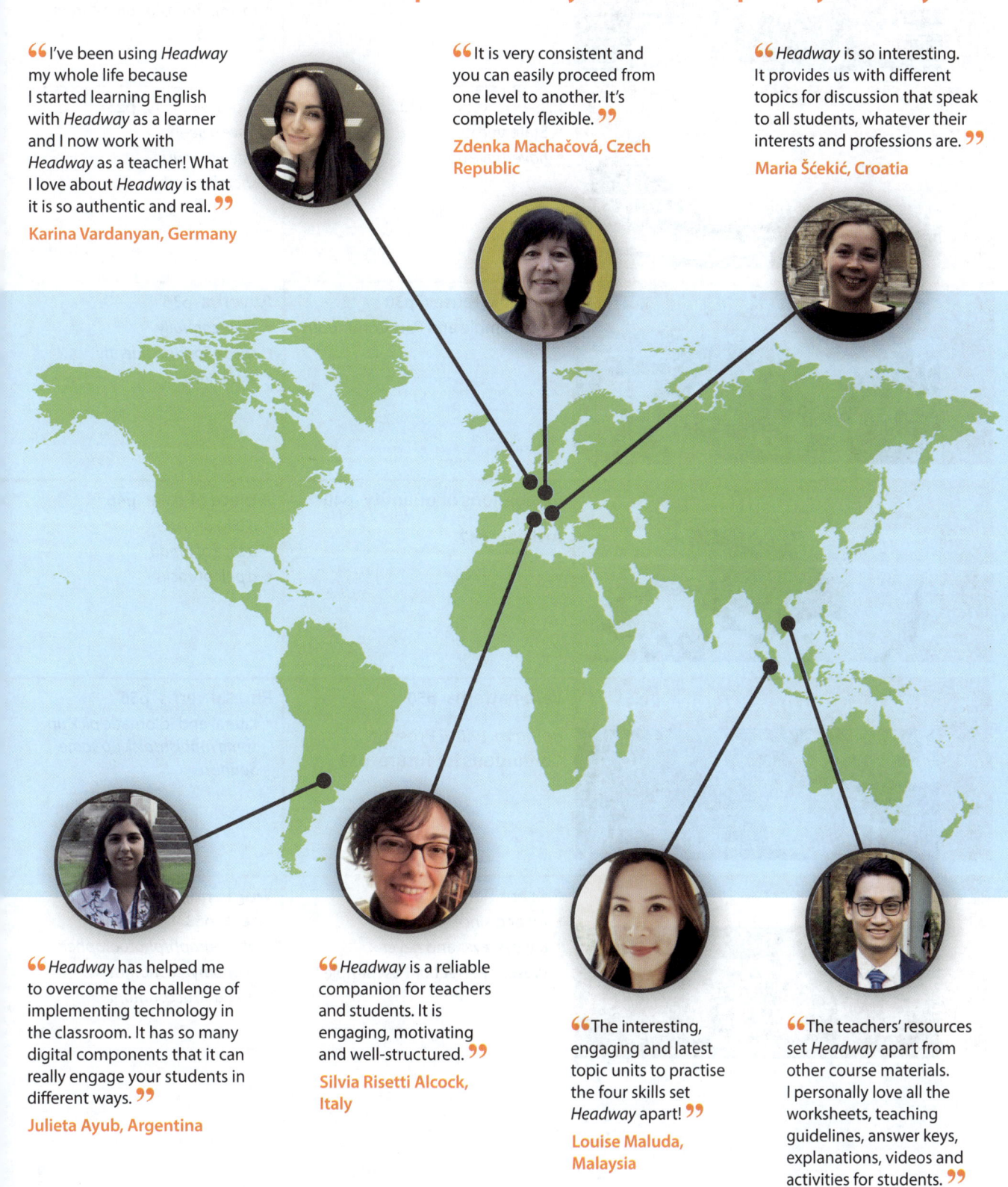

❝I've been using *Headway* my whole life because I started learning English with *Headway* as a learner and I now work with *Headway* as a teacher! What I love about *Headway* is that it is so authentic and real.❞

Karina Vardanyan, Germany

❝It is very consistent and you can easily proceed from one level to another. It's completely flexible.❞

Zdenka Machačová, Czech Republic

❝*Headway* is so interesting. It provides us with different topics for discussion that speak to all students, whatever their interests and professions are.❞

Maria Šćekić, Croatia

❝*Headway* has helped me to overcome the challenge of implementing technology in the classroom. It has so many digital components that it can really engage your students in different ways.❞

Julieta Ayub, Argentina

❝*Headway* is a reliable companion for teachers and students. It is engaging, motivating and well-structured.❞

Silvia Risetti Alcock, Italy

❝The interesting, engaging and latest topic units to practise the four skills set *Headway* apart!❞

Louise Maluda, Malaysia

❝The teachers' resources set *Headway* apart from other course materials. I personally love all the worksheets, teaching guidelines, answer keys, explanations, videos and activities for students.❞

Cao Hong Phat, Vietnam

These teachers are all winners of the *Headway* Scholarship, an initiative set up by John and Liz Soars to give something back to teachers for the trust they have placed in *Headway*. Find out more at **oup.com/elt/headwayscholarship**.

Introduction • Why do teachers trust *Headway*? 9

Student's Book contents: Units 1–6

1 Getting to know you — p9
Tenses and questions p10
- Asking questions
- *Who's* or *Whose*?

Right word, wrong word p16
- *do homework/make a mistake*
- *a high mountain/a tall man*
- *be crazy about/interested in*
- *to train hard/to catch a train*

2 Let's get together — p19
Present tenses p20
- State verbs
- *have/have got*

My perfect day p23
- *have a lie-in*
- *listen to music*
- *shop for clothes*

3 Good news, bad news! — p29
Narrative tenses p30
- Past Simple and Past Continuous

Adverbs p36
- *drive carefully*
- *speak Spanish fluently*
- *work hard*

4 Food for thought — p39
Expressions of quantity p40

Articles p42

A piece of cake p46
- *a bag of crisps*
- *a slice of bread*
- *a pair of socks*

5 The future's in your hands — p49
Verb patterns p50

going to, will & **Present Continuous for future** p52

Phrasal verbs p56
- Literal and idiomatic *pick up some rubbish/pick up some Spanish*

6 History repeats itself — p59
Present Perfect p60
- *for* and *since*
- *always, ever* and *never*
- Present Perfect or Past Simple?

Word endings and word stress p63
- *photograph/photographer*
- *economy/economist*
- *account/accountant*

10 Introduction • Student's Book contents

A blind date p14 • A magazine feature where two readers go on a date	**The *three* types of friends we all need** p13 • Jess describes three friends	• Talking about you p11 & p12 • What do you think? p13 • What happened next? p14 **Everyday English** p17 • Social expressions	**Filling in forms** p18 • Filling in a personal form
The independence quiz p24 • A quiz that tells you how dependent or independent you are	**Getting on with the neighbours** p26 • Two neighbours gossip about each other	• Talking about you p22 & p23 • What do you think? p21 & p25 • Roleplay p26 **Everyday English** p27 • Making conversation	**An email** p28 • Linking words
A spy story p34 • The James Bond story, *The Man with the Golden Gun*	**A spy story** p34 • *The Man with the Golden Gun*	• Talking about you p32 • In your own words p32 & p35 • Project p33 • What do you think? p35 **Everyday English** p37 • Saying when	**Narrative writing** p38 • Position of adjectives and adverbs
Recipes for success p44 • How three popular foods were discovered by accident	**At the shops** p46 • In a café, clothes shop, newsagent's, off-licence, delicatessen and chemist's	• Talking about you p41 & p45 **Everyday English** p47 • Can you come for dinner?	**A postcard** p48 • Style and synonyms
He was only 16 p54 • The possible futures of two teenagers, Joel Kioko and Adam Mudd	**Different generations** p53 • Three people from the same family discuss what they can look forward to	• Talking about you p51, p52 & p56 • What do you think? p53 & p55 • Roleplay p55 **Everyday English** p57 • Expressing doubt and certainty	**Writing for talking** p58 • 'My dreams for the future …'
The not so distant past p64 • How the present can be a reminder of ancient history	**Family history** p66 • David Taylor Bews researches his family history with his grandmother	• Talking about you p61 & p63 • What do you think? p65 & p66 • Project p65 **Everyday English** p67 • Agree with me!	**A biography** p68 • Ordering paragraphs

Student's Book contents: Units 7–12

7 Simply the best → p69
What's it like? p70

Comparatives and superlatives p71

Synonyms and antonyms p76
- scared/frightened
- boring/not very interesting

8 Living dangerously → p79
have to/don't have to p80

should/must p82

Not a thing to wear! p86
- Parts of the body neck/wrist/toes
- Things to wear belt/jumper/leggings

9 What a story! → p89
Past Perfect and narrative tenses p90
- Joining words

Feelings p96
- nervous/upset/homesick

10 All-time greats → p99
Passives p100
- All tenses

Words that go together p103
- Noun + noun business card
- Adverb + past participle well-known

11 People with a passion → p109
Present Perfect Simple and Continuous p110
- Tense review

Life's big moments! p116
- Birth
- Marriage
- Death

12 You never know … → p119
First Conditional p120

Second Conditional p122

bring and take, come and go p126
- Take some suncream on holiday.
- Bring an umbrella with you.

Audioscript → p129   Grammar reference → p142   Extra material → p154

12   Introduction • Student's Book contents

Favourite pictures p74 • A magazine article where readers describe their favourite picture	**The best things in life are free** p73 • Five people talk about the best things in their lives which don't cost anything	• In your own words p71 • General knowledge quiz p72 • Who gets the job? p73 • What do you think? p74 **Everyday English** p77 • What's on?	**Describing my hometown** p78 • Relative pronouns *which*, *that*, *who*, *where*
Two stuntwomen and a stunt man p84 • The tough world of two Hollywood stuntwomen	**A health and fitness quiz** p83 • What should you do to keep fit and stay healthy? **A stuntman's story** p85	• Talking about sports p81 • What do you think? p83 & p85 • Talking about you p83 & p86 • Roleplay p87 **Everyday English** p87 • At the doctor's	**Writing emails** p88 • Comparing formal and informal
The train journey p94 • The Storyteller – a short story by Saki	**Young adult literature** p93 • An interview with a publisher of books for young adults **The story on the train** p95	• In your own words p92 • Talking about you p93 • What do you think? p93 • Telling a story p95 **Everyday English** p97 • Exclamations with *so* and *such*	**Reviewing a book or film** p98 • Referring back in a text
The world's most loved football team! p104 • Manchester United – a football team that has become a world brand	**The world's number one habit!** p106 • A radio programme about chewing gum	• Inventions that changed the world p102 • Project p102 • Talking about you p103 & p104 • What do you think? p106 • Roleplay p107 **Everyday English** p107 • On the phone	**Discussing pros and cons** p108 • Social media sites
The collectors p114 • Three people and their surprising collections	**My kind of thing!** p113 • Three people describe things they love **My life in a nutshell** p116 • Alison talks about her life	• Talking about you p111 • What do you think? p113 & p115 **Everyday English** p117 • Finding the right words!	**Note-taking** p118 • My vision for the 21st century
Risk and chance p124 • An article about the strange world of chance, risk, and probability	**At a crossroads in life** p123 • Three people talk about a big decision they have to make	• What do you think? p123 & p125 **Everyday English** p127 • Thank you and goodbye!	**Correcting common mistakes** p128 • Language review

Go to **headwayonline.com** to download the Wordlist and full Audioscript.

Speaking skills – from accuracy to fluency

The Pre-intermediate level

Pre-intermediate level students will already have a solid foundation in the language. They may have recently completed an elementary course or they may be returning to language learning after a break and need to revise key language before being able to progress further.

Whilst grammar and vocabulary are still a very important part of their development, Pre-intermediate students often find that their receptive skills are more developed than their productive skills. They want to be able to communicate in a wider variety of contexts and can feel frustrated by their current lack of fluency. This is often due to students not yet having a wide enough range of grammar and vocabulary to communicate accurately and fluently, and so it is important that language and skills work is integrated in order to develop students' confidence in using the language.

In *Headway* 5th edition, Pre-intermediate, new language is introduced systematically and at a steady pace, allowing students to increase their knowledge of the language and build their confidence. In the language presentation sections, students have the opportunity to practise the pronunciation and intonation of new language. Practice sections include a variety of controlled activities, which focus on accuracy, and freer speaking activities, where students can focus on their fluency. There are also many speaking activities based around the listening and reading activities, including regular exchanges of opinion and roleplays.

Developing your students' speaking skills

Often the main reason that students are learning English is because they want to be able to *speak* it competently. However, this isn't a simple task. Students need to be able to produce features of grammar, vocabulary, and pronunciation accurately, they need a range of language to be able to communicate, and need to be able to use language in a contextually appropriate way. Furthermore, getting students to speak can be a challenge in itself, and so it is important that we provide engaging and interesting speaking tasks which provide a reason for speaking, and that we allow sufficient planning and thinking time before asking the students to do a speaking task.

Accuracy and fluency

Although the main aim for anybody learning a language is to become more fluent in that language, it is important that students feel confident enough to attempt to use language more freely. Students need to focus on features of language before being able to produce it.

In *Headway* 5th edition, Pre-intermediate, language presentations systematically progress from the controlled, accuracy focused activities to freer, fluency-focused activities. The aim of controlled practice activities is to develop students' accurate use of meaning and form of the target language, but it is also important to focus on pronunciation as part of the presentation and practice of language. In *Headway* 5th edition, Pre-intermediate, we include focus on sounds and intonation as part of language presentations and also by including listening texts which enable students to hear the language being presented.

By providing sufficient controlled practice, it is more likely that students' use of the target language will become more automatic when doing freer speaking activities.

Contextual appropriacy

Often students can use a correct form when producing language, but communication can be seriously impeded if what they have said isn't appropriate in that context. For example, a student who asks for something by saying *Give me some apple juice* is likely to cause offence to the listener even though no grammatical error has occurred, whereas *Could I have some apple juice, please?* would be the appropriate way of making such a request.

In *Headway* 5th edition, Pre-intermediate, the Everyday English sections help students with the language needed for situational contexts and again progress from controlled, accuracy-based activities to freer, fluency-based activities.

Engaging and interesting tasks

We can engage students by providing tasks which build on the context of the lesson and thus are meaningful. This means that students already have opinions and knowledge of topics before being asked to speak about them. We can create interest for the students by providing personalized tasks which allow them to talk about themselves and/or their reactions to the topics in the Student's Book. In *Headway* 5th edition, Pre-intermediate, there are regular sections such as *What do you think?*, *Talking about you*, and *In your own words* which provide freer speaking practice.

Types of communication

It is important to use a variety of communication tasks which encourage fluency-based freer speaking.

In *Headway* 5th edition, Pre-intermediate, there are many different speaking tasks which allow different types of communication. For example, in Unit 2 of the Student's Book you will find:

- Asking and answering questions with a partner (p22)
- Exchanging information/information gap (p22)
- Personalized longer turn speaking (p21, p23)
- Group discussions (p23, p25, p26)
- Pair discussions (p22, p24)
- Roleplay (p26)

Allow planning and thinking time

Most teachers recognize the importance of planning before getting students to write, but less so when it comes to speaking. However, it is equally important to allow a degree of planning time before asking students to perform a speaking task. The planning stage for speaking tasks could be simply allowing thinking time before they start to speak, or could involve making notes about the topic, what they are going to say, or the language structures they may use.

Dealing with spoken errors

It's important to recognize that an error isn't necessarily a mistake, but rather an attempt to use the language. Errors are also evidence that students are taking risks and trying to expand their range of language, and this needs to be encouraged. However, spoken errors do present us with the opportunity to clarify and to further students' exposure to accurate language forms.

What to correct?

The most frequent types of spoken errors students make include:

- **Errors of meaning:** This is when a student has made an error which impacts on successful communication. For example, a student says **I am here for three weeks* when they meant *I have been here for three weeks* – The error may have been caused by L1 transfer, where a student uses the structure they would use in their native language.

  There are also many vocabulary meaning errors which may have been caused by L1 transfer. For example, a student says **My father is a driver*, when in fact they meant *pilot*. This error may have been caused by the same word being used for both words in the student's native language. Other examples may be caused by a *false friend*, which is when the same or a similar word exists in the students' native language but with a significantly different meaning to how it is used in English. For example, a Czech student may say someone is very *sympathetic* when they mean *pleasant* or *friendly* (*sympatický* means 'pleasant' in Czech).

  Teachers who have the same first language as their students are obviously in a better position to recognize typical spoken errors. Teachers who do not speak the same language as their students should try to find out what common errors their students make (a simple Internet search can provide a lot of information on this).

- **Errors of form:** These errors are unlikely to cause problems in communication, but are important to correct as they will affect students' accuracy and fluency. Examples might include the wrong grammatical form being used (**I have been to the cinema yesterday* instead of *I went to the cinema yesterday*), or a wrong collocation (**I did a mistake* instead of *I made a mistake*).

- **Errors of pronunciation:** Students at Pre-intermediate level may have problems with individual sounds, depending on the native language of the students. Typical consonant errors may include /v/ and /w/, /p/ and /b/, or /r/ and /l/. Typical vowel errors often relate to long and short sounds such as in *ship* /ɪ/ or *sheep* /iː/. It is also important to correct word and sentence stress, as well as intonation, as these are features which will affect the fluency of the speaker.

When to correct?

Here are some things to consider when deciding when to correct:

- **Immediate correction:** This is more likely to be done when the focus of the activity is on accuracy and when the error is directly related to the target language. It could be done in open class if drilling new vocabulary or could be done individually whilst the teacher is monitoring an activity.

- **Correcting at the end of the activity:** You may want to do this in a speaking activity in which the focus is on fluency. During the activity you can note down errors to deal with at the end with the whole class. This has the added bonus of correction being more anonymous as the students won't know who made the error, and also that the whole class can benefit from further exposure to problematic target language.

- **Not correcting at all/Recasting:** At Pre-intermediate level, there will be many language structures and vocabulary that students haven't learned yet, and so it may be counter-productive to ask students to correct themselves. You may also decide not to correct if the error has no relevance to the target language of the lesson (for example, if the student makes an article error in a lesson which is focusing on the Present Perfect). One option might be for the teacher to 'recast' – repeat the sentence but using the correct form. This acts as a model and provides exposure to correct forms of language without the need for the students to attempt to self-correct something they have not yet learned.

How to correct?

There are many error correction methods, and of course, each teacher will have his/her own styles. It is important that we use a variety of techniques to encourage the students to self-correct. Below are some suggestions for possible correction techniques for different types of error.

Error	Possible correction techniques
*I am here for three weeks.	Ask concept questions to establish the meaning. For example, *Do you mean you will stay for another three weeks, or you arrived three weeks ago?*
*My father is a driver. (student meant 'pilot')	Ask questions which focus the student on the error. *Does he drive a taxi? A bus? Do we drive a plane?*
*He is very sympathetic. (meant 'pleasant')	Write the error on the board to invite discussion (especially as other students may have the same 'false friend' issue).
*I have been to the cinema yesterday.	Draw a timeline on the board showing *now* and *yesterday*. Ask if the action finished in the past or continues until now (to elicit correct use of Past Simple instead of Present Perfect).
*I go run every Saturday.	Use a gesture to indicate that a longer form of the word is needed.
*I am really boring. (meant 'bored')	Repeat the sentence with a raised intonation to question the error *You're really boring?*
*She did a mistake.	Repeat the sentence but miss out the problem word. *She ___ a mistake.*
*It's fantastic!	Hold up three fingers to show how many syllables and point to the second finger to show that's where the stress should be.
*I am a journalist.	Use the board to draw the stress pattern: Ooo
*I am wery vorried.	Drill the two problem sounds together. You could use a phonemic chart to help.

Professional Development support

Would you like some extra tips and techniques to help your Pre-intermediate students make progress? Here are several useful books we have chosen to help you make the most of *Headway* in the Pre-intermediate classroom.

Teaching at Pre-intermediate level

Motivational Teaching
Nick Thorner

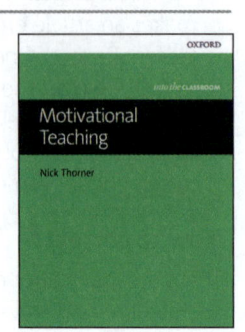

The question of motivation is especially relevant to those learners at Pre-intermediate level, as you support them to revise and extend learning.

This guide provides a clear overview of the factors that affect learner motivation, and connects each of them to innovative teaching ideas and strategies, from choosing materials to closing lessons and giving feedback.

How Vocabulary is Learned
Stuart Webb and Paul Nation

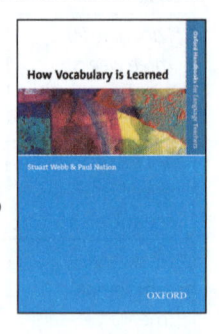

This guide to vocabulary acquisition is essential reading for teachers of Pre-intermediate level students. It presents the major ideas and principles that relate to the teaching and learning of vocabulary and evaluates a wide range of practical activities.

Key questions addressed include:

- How many words should students learn at a time, and how often?
- How much time should be spent teaching vocabulary?
- Why do some students make greater progress than others?

Integrating technology

Mobile Learning
Shaun Wilden

This practical guide provides clear guidance and essential support for teachers who want to use mobile devices in and outside the language classroom. It helps teachers get started with using mobile devices and apps in class. It shows how to make the most of in-built features, such as messaging, photos, and audio recording. It addresses issues such as acceptable use policies and staying safe.

Teaching with Technology
Online Professional Development

This online, self-study professional development course aims to enhance the knowledge and skills needed to successfully implement technology in the classroom. It takes approximately 30 hours to complete and includes input on key concepts, approaches, video, animation and audio clips, discussions, practical tasks, opportunities for reflection, suggestions for further study, and ideas to try out in the classroom.

> 66 The websites, blogs, apps, and other digital tools suggested for class use in this course are great to try in order to reach today's digital natives; our students. 99
> Umit Cebeci, Teacher in Turkey

To find out more about these titles, or additional Professional Development support, visit **oup.com/elt**.

OXFORD TEST OF ENGLISH

The Oxford Test of English: help for teachers

The Oxford Test of English is an online general English proficiency test, which reports at B2, B1, and A2 levels of the CEFR. The test consists of four modules: **Speaking**, **Listening**, **Reading**, and **Writing**.

This course can be used as part of preparation for the Oxford Test of English.

For more information about the Oxford Test of English and how you can help learners prepare for it, visit:
www.oup.com/elt/ote/teachingresources

1 Getting to know you

Introduction to the unit

As you begin *Headway* 5th edition Pre-intermediate, you may well be starting a new course with a new group of students. This is one reason why the theme of this first unit is getting to know people.

The *Grammar* section provides the main grammar focus which is a general revision of key tenses used to talk about past, present, and future. In addition, students review their knowledge of question forms, and the exercises in this unit give you the opportunity to assess your students' strengths and weaknesses. Making questions is an area that often causes problems for students, so there is ample practice on making questions and question words. This is done through a text students listen to and read to put the different aspects of grammar in a natural context. (All the verb forms covered are dealt with in greater depth in later units of the course.)

The *Listening and speaking* section is about friends. Students listen to a woman talking about friends and extract information to complete a chart and answer questions. As with skills sections throughout the Student's Book, there is an opportunity for the class to give their opinions and discuss aspects of the topic.

In the *Reading and speaking* focus, students engage in a jigsaw reading activity for specific information, share information, and predict what happens next. Students listen to find out if their predictions were correct. Adjectives ending in *-ed* and *-ing* from the text are covered in a separate task.

The *Vocabulary* section in this first unit is called *Right word, wrong word* and it covers verbs of similar meaning, adjectives and nouns that go together, prepositions, and words with two meanings.

There is an *Everyday English* section which introduces everyday social expressions, for meeting people, starting and continuing conversations, and saying goodbye.

In the *Writing* section, students learn about form-filling, which is a very practical skill. The section covers the vocabulary for different fields in a form and students also learn common instructions in English for completing forms. Finally, they use their own personal information to complete an application form, which can then be used as a model for when students may need to complete forms in English in real-life situations.

Language aims

Grammar

Tenses and questions
The tenses reviewed are Present Simple, Present Continuous, Past Simple, and *going to* for future plans or intentions. Students practise using first person singular and then third person singular, remembering to change the forms as necessary (e.g. change the auxiliary verbs or add third

person *-s*). The input for grammar work in this unit is related reading and listening texts.

Students revise a wide range of question words and complete questions in all the tenses listed above. They also complete an exercise where they identify which word is missing in a range of questions and use the questions to interview a partner.

Vocabulary

Right word, wrong word
In the vocabulary section, students are encouraged to use their dictionaries efficiently in order to choose from two similar words – *play/go, make/do*, etc. Other activities in the vocabulary section are to practise collocations of adjectives and nouns – *important person, delicious meal*, etc., commonly confused prepositions such as *to, from, about, at*, and words with two meanings such as *train*.

Everyday English

Social expressions
This section covers everyday conversations in social situations. Students match first lines with second lines and there is a focus on continuing the conversations. There are phrases to use for different levels of formality, e.g. *How do you do?*, *Thanks a lot*, and students are asked to identify this aspect of social English interaction.

Additional material

Workbook
Students complete a number of short texts using present, past, and future tenses. There is practice making questions in these tenses, and further work on questions with a focus on using question words accurately. The difference between *who's* and *whose* is practised. There is a reading on Paralympic skiers, with further question and tense practice. There are Vocabulary exercises on verbs of similar meaning, collocations, prepositions, and words with two meanings. The unit provides more work on social English, and there is a Grammar and Vocabulary review.

Photocopiable activities
There are photocopiable activities to review grammar (*A game of past, present, future*), vocabulary (*Find someone who …*), and communication (*Can I help you?*) at the back of the Teacher's Guide as well as on the Teacher's Resource Centre. There is also a worksheet to accompany the video on the Teacher's Resource Centre.

Notes on the unit

Unit opener page
Choose from these activities to engage your students with the topic and target language of this unit:
- Talk about the title
- Talk about the unit goals (*Grammar, Vocabulary, …*)
- Talk about the photo
- Watch the video
- Look at the bottom banner
- Do the activity

Refer students to the photo on p9. Ask the class questions to draw attention to the unit context and elicit vocabulary: *What can you see in the photo? Where are these people? What is happening? Do you think they are friends? What do you think the man is showing to the woman on his phone?*

Refer students to the title, 'Getting to know you'. Ask students what they think the title means. Note that *to get to know someone* is an expression which means *to find out more about them by spending time with them*. Write an example on the board: *I really like you and I would like to get to know you better*. As this is the beginning of term, it would be a good idea at the start of the lesson to do a getting to know you activity with the students (note that the activities on p10 will also help students learn more about each other).

If you don't have time to watch the video introduction to the unit, go through the unit goals below the title: *Grammar, Vocabulary, Everyday English, Reading, Listening, Writing*. Give examples or use translation for unknown words.

Video (2 minutes approximately): The video gives a step-by-step overview of the unit. Play the video, pausing where necessary – especially for students to answer any questions, e.g. *Have you ever been on a blind date?* This makes it a more interactive experience. Highlight the option of practising online.

As shown in the bottom banner, don't forget that there are many exercises to consolidate and practise the target language of the unit in the Workbook as well as online. There are links to these exercises on the relevant pages of the Student's Book and they can be done in class time or you can set them for homework.

Summary: If you're short of time, use the title and the photo to help students understand and engage with the topic, and then move straight on to the activity so that they can discuss the theme in more detail. If you have any more time, try to watch the video together. It is a clear and interesting introduction to the different parts of the unit.

Notes for activity:
Put students in pairs. Ask them to look at the photo and discuss their answers to the questions. Ask them to justify their choices where possible.

> **Suggested answers**
> 1 Probably not; it looks as if they have just met. They probably started talking about their phones; they may have the same one.
> 2 They're probably talking about a photo the boy has on his phone.
> 3 They may go for coffee together, or arrange to meet each other again.

Before you begin
Your main aim over the first few lessons together is to establish a good classroom atmosphere with your new students, in which everyone feels comfortable. Hopefully you will not only work hard, but have fun at the same time. Another of your aims will be to check your students' language abilities. How good are they at using the tense system? Can they form questions in English? What's their vocabulary like? How confident are they in skills work? Do they panic when listening to a recording? All this information will allow you to get a feel for your students' abilities, and will also help you to plan your lessons.

SUGGESTION As this is the first lesson, it's worth starting out with an icebreaker activity to help students find out and memorize each other's names. You will need a soft ball for this game. Introduce yourself clearly and write your name on the board. Students first say their name and then throw the ball to another student. This continues until all students have said their name. Next, students throw a ball to another student and say that student's name as they do so. Finally, if your students are feeling confident, ask them to say, *My name is …* (+ their name), throw the ball and say, *His/Her name is …* (+ the other student's name). Include yourself in the game and encourage students to get faster as they go along.

Grammar SB p10

Tenses and questions
The theme of the unit will help students to get to know each other, and to get to know you. The *Starter* and opening sections revise tenses and question forms, and will help you assess students' strengths and weaknesses in these areas. The general revision of past, present, and future verb forms in this unit is consolidated in greater depth later in the course.

Possible problems
1 The aim of this section is to assess and review students' ability to recognize and use Present Simple and Present Continuous, Past Simple, Present Continuous for Future, and *going to* + infinitive.
2 Some students may simply not have met all the tenses in the unit and you will need to teach them. Others will have difficulty with tricky aspects, including which tense to use for future meaning or with state verbs, remembering all the parts needed in sentences with *going to*, or knowing when Present Continuous has future meaning.
Common mistakes include:
*I am coming from Ireland. (Correction: *I come from Ireland.*)
*He is liking coffee. (Correction: *He likes coffee.*)
*She going to study English. (Correction: *She's going to study English.*)
*Next year I study in Milan. (Correction: *Next year I'm going to study in Milan.*)
*Tomorrow we go to the cinema. (Correction: *Tomorrow we're going to the cinema.*)
3 Question forms in English throw up a lot of problems, especially with the choice and use of auxiliary verbs *do* and *be*. Common mistakes might include:
– Omitting auxiliary verbs completely:

*Where you come from? (Correction: *Where do you come from?*)
*What the children doing? (Correction: *What are the children doing?*)
– Choosing the wrong auxiliary verb:
*Do you married? (Correction: *Are you married?*)
– Word order problems:
*Why she is here? (Correction: *Why is she here?*)
– Question intonation difference in *Yes/No* questions and *wh-* questions:

Where do you live?

Do you like learning English?

4 For all of these possible problems with question forms and tenses, consistent correction is key, including encouraging students to self-correct whenever possible. There are comprehensive Grammar reference sections at the back of the Student's Book which help students check their understanding.

STARTER SB p10

The aim of the first exercise is to test students' ability to recognize and use basic tenses (Present Simple, Present Continuous, and Past Simple). There are also examples of the state verbs *need* and *have*. Students should be familiar with the above tenses and verb forms, but they may still make mistakes.

Lead in to the topic by writing some important numbers about yourself on the board (e.g. your birthday, number of children or pets you have, an important year in your life, when you started teaching, etc.). Ask the students to guess what the numbers are and elicit possible responses from the class. The focus here is to get to know you as a teacher. If you have time, ask students to do the same in pairs, then ask a few students to share information about their partner with the class.

1 Refer students to the *Starter* section. Elicit the answer to the first question with the whole class. Students then work in pairs to match the rest of the questions and answers.

2 **1.1** Play the recording for students to check their answers. Check and drill pronunciation of *born* /bɔːn/ and *twice* /twaɪs/. Play the recording again and ask students to repeat each question with correct intonation. Put students in pairs to ask and answer the questions, giving their own answers.

Answers and audioscript

1.1 Getting to know you

1 A Where were you born?
  B In Hamburg, Germany. (c)
2 A What do you do?
  B I'm a student. (e)
3 A Are you married?
  B No, I'm not. (d)
4 A Why are you learning English?
  B Because I need it for my job. (f)
5 A When did you start learning English?
  B Two years ago. (a)
6 A How often do you have English classes?
  B Twice a week. (b)

My life up to now! SB p10

This section presents Present Simple, Past Simple, and Present Continuous for future in context.

About the text

The text is about a 'busker'. A busker is someone who performs in the street for gratuities – usually in the form of small change from passers-by who stop to listen or watch the performance. Busking is a common way music or drama students earn money while practising their skills!

Covent Garden is in the West End of London – a major theatre, shopping, and dining area, very popular with tourists. It was once called 'Convent Garden' as it was the place where the monks of Westminster Abbey grew their vegetables. Around St Paul's Church is another popular place for buskers to perform in the area.

The Royal College of Music is one of the top schools for Performing Arts in the UK.

1 **1.2** Focus students' attention on the photo of Branna and ask them to say how old they think she is and to give you the name of the musical instrument. Ask them to read the questions and listen to her talking about her life to try to catch the answers. Play the recording through once and elicit answers to the questions. Encourage students to give you other information about her past, present, and future. Drill the pronunciation of the word *busker* /ˈbʌskə(r)/ to make sure they end it in a schwa /ə/ as for many occupation words.

1.2 See SB p10.

SUGGESTION It's a good idea to take opportunities to point out pronunciation patterns to students. In this case, you could ask for other job words which end in *-er* to highlight the typical pronunciation /ə/. Examples: *teacher, driver, writer, police officer, manager, cleaner*, etc.

Answers

She comes from Portrush, Northern Ireland. She is in London now. A 'busker' sings or plays a musical instrument on the streets and people give them money if they like it.

Possible answer for things in her present, past, and future:
She is studying at the Royal College of Music.
She was born in a seaside town in Northern Ireland.
Next year, she is going to study in Milan.

2 Focus attention on the text and make sure students realize that this is the same as they heard in the recording. Point out the example and ask the students which tense it is (Present Simple). Focus their attention on the three boxes containing verbs and give them a moment to find the correct verb for the second gap (*'m living*), but don't go into an explanation of the difference between Present Continuous and Present Simple at this stage – just allow students to work through the task. Let students check their answers in pairs. Get students to read the questions before playing the recording again for a final time. They should check their answers and then answer the questions. Elicit the answers.

Unit 1 • Getting to know you   19

Answers

2	'm living	9	has
3	'm studying	11	left
4	like	12	didn't want
5	don't have	13	won
6	make	14	couldn't say
7	miss	15	'm going to continue
8	have	16	'm going to study

She's working as a busker because it's very expensive to live in London and she doesn't have a job, so she makes a bit of money from busking.
She left home because she won a scholarship to study music.
She's excited because she's going to study at the largest music academy in Italy next year.

In your own words

3 Put students in pairs to talk about Branna and her life. They should take turns saying something about her. Focus them on the example and point out the use of *she*. The aim of this task is to see how well students move between first person singular and third person, i.e. remembering third person *-s* and to change the form of auxiliary verbs (*don't* to *doesn't*, *am* to *is*).

Monitor carefully. If a number of students are having difficulty with this, briefly review the forms on the board.

4 Focus students' attention on the photos and the captions about Conor and Karen where they can find the answers to the questions.

Elicit answers from the class. Check students understand *retired* and *global*. To help them understand the phrase *empty-nester* /ˌempti ˈnestə(r)/, refer students to the photo of the empty bird's nest on p11. Tell them that the nest is like Conor and Karen's home because their children have left.

Answers
They're Branna's parents.
They don't work – they're retired teachers.
An 'empty-nester' is a parent whose grown-up children have left home.
Conor and Karen are now travelling the world.

5 🔊 **1.3** Pre-teach/Check: *teenager, second-hand, camper van, set off, campsite*. Ask students to listen to find out who Brady is. Suggest they take notes about Conor and Karen's life in order to remember information about their past, present, and future. Elicit responses from the class in feedback.

Answers
Brady is their son (Branna's twin brother).

🔊 1.3 Conor and Karen McGrady, retired teachers, empty-nesters, and global travellers

K = Karen   C = Conor

K I think we're typical 'empty-nesters'! We have two children, twins, Branna and Brady, they're 20 now … and when they both left home, just two years ago now, our house felt really big and …
C … and empty – it was just the two of us.
K Yes, it was too quiet. We missed all their noise, their music, and their friends.
C Yeah, we even missed all the mess.
K I'm not so sure about that! Anyway, Branna went to London to study music, and Brady went to South America – he's travelling there with a friend.
C So … I said to Karen, 'Why don't we go travelling, too?'
K Yeah, we're both nearly 60, but we still feel young, and we didn't enjoy teaching any more, … er … teaching teenagers is really tiring …
C So … in just six months we retired from our teaching jobs, rented our house in Portrush.
K … to a nice young couple.
C … yeah – and we bought a second-hand camper van for £4,000 and set off for France.
K Last year, we just toured Europe – we went from campsite to campsite, first in France, then in Spain and Portugal. We loved every minute.
C Yes, we had a great time. Next year, we're going to visit Branna in Italy – she's going to study in Milan. And then we're going to fly to Chile, hire a van there, and meet Brady. We're going to travel with him and his friend for a bit.
K We're really excited about that. We can't wait!

6 🔊 **1.4** Read the instruction as a class and point out the example. Give students time to complete the questions. They could work on this task in pairs or do it individually and then check with a partner. Check answers with the class. Put students in pairs. Student A asks questions 1–4 with Student B answering them. Student B asks questions 5–8 with Student A answering. They can use notes if they made them to help them remember the information. When they've finished, play the recording for them to check their answers. Finally, students practise the questions and answers in pairs. Monitor and check for any grammatical or pronunciation mistakes to correct afterwards.

Answers
2	do, have	6	did, pay
3	did	7	did, do
4	are, doing	8	are, going
5	didn't, enjoy		

🔊 1.4 Questions about Conor and Karen

1 Q How old are they?
   A They're both nearly 60.
2 Q How many children do they have?
   A Two. Twins – a son, Brady, and a daughter, Branna.
3 Q When did their children leave home?
   A Two years ago.
4 Q What are Branna and Brady doing at the moment?
   A Branna's studying in London and Brady is travelling in South America.
5 Q Why didn't Conor and Karen enjoy teaching any more?
   A Because teaching teenagers is very tiring.
6 Q How much money did they pay for the camper van?
   A £4,000.
7 Q What did they do last year?
   A They toured France, Spain, and Portugal.
8 Q Who are they going to visit next year?
   A They going to visit Branna in Italy, and then they're going to fly to Chile to travel with Brady and his friend.

Talking about you

7 Give your own pair of examples (one true and one false), e.g. *I live in a small flat. I have two children.* Ask students if they know which sentence is true. Give them the answer!

Students make their own pairs of sentences about their present, past, and future. Monitor and check they're doing the task as instructed. Assist with any vocabulary they need and to help with any grammar queries.

Focus students on the examples and get two students to read them aloud. Ask students to read out their pairs of sentences to the class so their classmates can guess which are true. If you have a large class, put them in groups for this stage.

Monitor and note any points for correction and elicit these from the class in a whole-class stage using the board as a focus.

SUGGESTION As an extension, ask students to write a short description of themselves, using the text about Branna as a model. You could set this for homework or for students who are quick finishers.

GRAMMAR SPOT SB p11

The *Grammar spot* in each unit aims to get students to think analytically about the language. Ask students to discuss the grammar questions in pairs before feeding back to the whole class, as this encourages peer teaching and builds students' confidence.

1 Draw a table labelled Present, Past, Future on the board and ask students to copy it. Refer students to audioscript 1.3 on p129 of the Student's Book. Put them in pairs to find examples of verb forms with present, past, and future meaning in the script about Branna's parents, and add them to the table. Remind students to include any negative forms they find. Encourage students to work quickly and don't go into detail about the form and use of past and future tenses here, as these will be dealt with in later units. Elicit examples and write them on the board.

Answers

Present	Past	Future
We have two children …	… they both left home …	… we're going to visit Branna in Italy.

2 Ask students to read the example sentences. Elicit the names of the tenses and encourage students to try to explain the difference. If absolutely necessary, with a monolingual class they could use L1 to explain.

Answers
Present Simple and Present Continuous. Present Simple is used for facts or for things that are true all the time. Present Continuous refers to now.

3 Give them a moment to read the example and then continue the matching task. Go through the answers with the class. As an extension, ask students to work in pairs to write the whole question; they can use past, present, or future tense. Elicit questions and answers from the class.

Answers
Who … ? My brother.
Where … ? In a seaside town.
When … ? Last night.
Why … ? Because I wanted to.
How many … ? Four.
How much … ? €10.
How long … ? For two weeks.
Whose … ? It's mine.
Which … ? The blue one.

As this is the first unit in the book, it's worth ensuring students know about the Grammar reference section. Ask them to turn to the Grammar reference on p142 of the Student's Book. Do a short scavenger hunt through the section. Write the following on the board:

1 *What unit will talk about present tenses/past tenses/future forms?*
2 *Find one example of the Present Continuous positive, negative, and question form.*
3 *Find an example of a negative sentence in the past tense.*
4 *What is a Yes/No question?*
5 *How many question words begin with 'W'?*

Students work in pairs to scan the section and write their answers. Encourage them to ask you questions about the section. Elicit responses in feedback. If students have difficulty with Present Continuous for future meaning, point out that this will be practised in Unit 5 of the Student's Book.

Practice SB p12

A student in Canada – asking questions

This section consolidates the question words students covered in the *Grammar spot* on SB p11.

1 Focus attention on the photo of Mehmet. If you have a map, you could get students to identify Toronto in Canada, and Turkey. Explain that Mehmet is studying English in Canada. Ask students what questions they think the interviewer will ask Mehmet.

Pre-teach/Check *improve my English, secondary school, show someone round, Goodness!* (= an exclamation expressing surprise). Ask two students to read the first three exchanges of the conversation and elicit the first missing question word in the fourth line (*Where*). Give students time to complete the task, working individually, and then compare their answers in pairs.

2 🔊 1.5 Play the recording for students to check their answers. If students query the difference between *what* and *which*, explain that *which* is used when there is a limited choice.

Elicit some examples of present, past, and future forms, then let students continue in pairs. Elicit the answers.

Put students in pairs to practise the conversation. If students have problems with pronunciation or intonation, play the recording again as a model and drill key lines chorally and individually.

Answers and audioscript

🔊 **1.5 A student in Canada**
I = Interviewer M = Mehmet
I Hi, nice to meet you Mehmet. Can I ask you one or two questions?
M Yes, of course.
I First of all. **Where** do you come from?
M I'm from Istanbul, in Turkey.
I And **why** are you here in Toronto?
M Well, I'm here mainly because I want to improve my English.
I **How much** English did you know before you came?
M Not a lot. I studied English at school for two years, but I didn't learn much. Now I'm studying in a language school here.
I **Which** school?
M The *Global Village English Centre*.
I Oh *Global Village* – I know it! Your English is very good now. **Who**'s your teacher?
M My teacher's called Andy. He's good.
I And **what** did you do back in Turkey?
M Well, actually, I was a teacher, a secondary school teacher. I taught children from 14 to 18.

> I **How many** children were in your classes?
> M Sometimes as many as 40.
> I Wow, goodness! That's a lot. **How often** do you go back home?
> M Usually, I go back every two months, but this month my brother is coming here. I'm very excited. I'm going to show him round.
> I Well, I hope your brother has a great visit. Thank you for talking to me.

Who's or *Whose*?

This section helps students to resolve the potential confusion between *Who's* and *Whose*. The pronunciation is the same /huːz/, so students need to use the context to help them distinguish the question words.

3 With books closed, write *Who's calling?* on the board. Ask *What is the full form?* (*Who is*). Write *Whose phone is ringing?* on the board. Mime questioning the class and walk around as if listening for a phone. Then go back to your bag and pick it up, again pretending to listen. And give the response with an embarrassed expression *It's mine*. Walk around the classroom, picking up or pointing to the students' belongings and asking *Whose is this pen?*, etc. To elicit a response *It's mine.* or *It's Francesca's.*, etc.

Underline *Who's* and *Whose*, and ask *Is the pronunciation the same or different?* Elicit that the two words sound the same. Ask students to open their books. Read the information about *Whose* and *Who's* with the class, and model the dialogues with a strong student. You could put students in pairs to practise them. This is just to further highlight that the *Who's* and *Whose* sound the same.

Focus on the sentences. Elicit the answer to question 1 as an example (*Whose*). Remind students to read the answer to each question to help them choose the correct word. With weaker students, ask *Which questions ask about possession?* before they do the exercise (sentences 1, 3, 5, and 6).

Students complete the task individually and then check in pairs. Check the answers with the class.

Answers
1 Whose
2 Who's
3 Whose
4 Who's
5 Whose
6 whose

4 🔊 **1.6** This is another discrimination task, but without the support of the text. Tell students they are going to hear six sentences containing *Whose* or *Who's*. Number these respectively 1 and 2 on the board. Use the examples from the blue box to elicit the correct numbers, e.g. *Who's calling?* = 2

Play sentence 1 as an example and encourage all students to make a choice 1 or 2 – loudly if possible! If students disagree on the answer, play it again, writing it on the board and checking the contraction (*Who is*).

Play the rest of the recording, noting on the board if students disagree about the answers. Keep the task fairly brisk to maintain the fun element. Play the sentences again, getting students to spell out the words as a final check.

Answers and audioscript
🔊 **1.6** *Who's* or *whose*
1 **Who's** at the door? Is it the postman? 2
2 I'm going to the pub. **Who's** coming? 2
3 **Whose** coat is this? It's not mine. 1
4 **Whose** are these car keys? They're not ours. 1
5 **Who's** going to Tina's wedding? 2
6 Do you know **whose** umbrella this is? 1

Talking about you

5 🔊 **1.7** Focus attention on the example and ask what tense the question is in (Present Simple). Ask students to correct the questions by adding the missing word in each case. Students check their answers with a partner.

Play the recording to check the answers with the class. Ask students to tell you what tense each question is in.

Play the recording again to model the pronunciation. Get students to repeat chorally and individually. If students sound rather flat, model the questions again yourself.

Answers and audioscript
🔊 **1.7 Questions about you**
1 What **do** you like doing in your free time?
2 Do you like listening **to** music?
3 What sort **of** music do you like?
4 What did you **do** last weekend?
5 What **are** you doing tonight?
6 What are you going **to** do after this lesson?
7 How many languages **does** your teacher speak?
8 What**'s** your teacher wearing today?

6 🔊 **1.8** Read out some of the questions to the class and elicit a range of answers. Give students a few moments to think about how to respond to each question. Divide students into pairs to ask and answer the questions. Monitor and note any common errors (including pronunciation) to feed back on after the pairwork. Ask fast finishers to change one word in questions 2, 3, 4, and 5 to make new questions, e.g. *Do you like listening to podcasts? What kind of films do you like?* As an alternative, do this as a mingling activity so that students can get to know each other better. They stand up and move around the classroom, asking at least three other people the questions. Elicit information about students in whole-class feedback.

Tell students to listen and compare their answers with the ones in the recording. Play the recording, pausing at the end of each conversation to give students time to compare and discuss their version if appropriate. With weaker students, you could refer them to the audioscript on p129 of the Student's Book to read after they have listened.

🔊 **1.8 Listen and compare**
1 A What do you like doing in your free time?
   B I like being with my friends or talking to them on Snapchat.
2 A Do you like listening to music?
   B Yes, of course, especially when I'm doing my homework. It helps me work, but my mum doesn't believe me.
3 A What sort of music do you like?
   B I like all sorts – rock, jazz, pop – I usually listen on Spotify, but I also like playing my dad's old albums. He's got an old-style record player – it's cool.
4 A What did you do last weekend?
   B I went to a music festival in Wales – it was fantastic. I didn't sleep at all.

22 Unit 1 • Getting to know you

5 A What are you doing tonight?
B Nothing much. I want to get an early night before the weekend.
6 A What are you going to do after this lesson?
B I have a bit of shopping to do. Then I'm going home.
7 A How many languages does your teacher speak?
B I think she speaks three – French, German, and a bit of Spanish.
8 A What's your teacher wearing today?
B A very pink jumper and red trousers.

Additional material
For teachers
Photocopiable activity – Grammar: *A game of past, present, future* pp167–8
For students
Online Practice – *Look again*
Workbook pp6–9, exercises 1–11
Online Practice – *Practice*

Listening and speaking SB p13

The *three* types of friends we all need

Lead in to the topic by writing *friend* on the board and eliciting a few collocations from your students, e.g. *make friends, stay friends, keep a friend, a good friend, best friend, oldest friend, close friend, great friend*.

1 Model the activity by writing the names of some of your friends on the board and briefly telling the students about them, including answering the two questions. Put students in pairs to do the same task.

Encourage some students to report on what their partner told them – this is always a good way to practise third person -s.

2 🔊 1.9 Focus attention on the photo of four friends and check the pronunciation of the names of the people: Jess /dʒes/, Jo /dʒəʊ/, Dukey /ˈdjuːki/, Rafferty /ˈræfəti/.

Tell students they are going to hear Jess talking about her three friends shown in the photo. Focus attention on the task. Point out the chart and that they only need to complete the top during this listening. Don't explain the different types of friend as they will work this out from the listening. Play the recording and then check the answers. At this point, you could ask students what they remember about the different types of friends.

Answers
forever friend = Jo
new friend = Dukey
reunited friend = Rafferty.

🔊 1.9 Jess's three friends

This is a very special photo for me. It's me with my three very best friends. Aren't they fabulous!
Jo, on the right, is my oldest friend, my absolutely forever friend. We were both born in the same hospital, on the same day, and Jo's mum and mine became good friends – so Jo and I played together a lot when we were little kids and we went to the same schools. We had other friends of course, but she is the one I can talk to about anything and everything. She was the wild one. I wasn't so much, but I loved her crazy clothes and the way she changed her hair colour every week! After school, I went to university in Newcastle and she went to study fashion in London. There was no need to text and call daily, but we knew we were always there for each other – good times and bad times – and, of course, whenever we meet it's the same as ever. I love Jo.

Dukey is a new friend – a very new friend. We joined the same advertising company on the same day, just a couple of months ago, but already I feel as if he's a best friend. He's a great guy … great fun and very talented. Everyone loves Dukey because he makes us laugh. He's going to go far, I'm sure. His mum and dad are from Barbados, but he was born here. He talks about holidays there – we're all saving like mad so we can go, too. He says his grandparents would love us all! This picture shows the first time Jo met Dukey. You can see how well they get on – two crazy, fun, kind, clever people.
Ah, and then there's Raff, short for Rafferty … 'red-haired Rafferty' we called him at school, but nobody calls him that now. Well Raff … he's not a new friend. In fact, he was my first boyfriend when I was 14. We were really sweet together, so everyone said. But then his family moved to Dubai, his dad got a job there. We emailed for a bit, but then lost touch. Years later, I suddenly saw the name Rafferty Lucas on Facebook – it's an unusual name, so I 'friended' him saying 'are you the Rafferty Lucas who went to … blah blah blah'. And of course he was. Jo was as surprised as I was. Anyway, he's now back in the UK, working near me. Isn't that amazing? He had a girlfriend when we first contacted, but … er … that's finished now. He's my 'friend reunited' and obviously it's different from when we were teenagers, but we still laugh at the same things … Who knows? … maybe we'll get back together. You can see why I love this picture so much.

3 🔊 1.9 Check students understand the questions in the first column of the chart. Play the recording again, pausing after each friend so students have time to write their notes in the chart. With weaker students, you may need to play the recording in shorter sections to allow them to note the details, or ask them to work in pairs with each student answering two of the questions, then sharing the information.

Let students check their answers in pairs before checking with the class. At this stage, you can also ask students if there are any words or phrases they heard in the recording that they would like to clarify with you. Keep this short, though – you can tell them they'll have a chance to read the script afterwards and ask vocabulary questions then.

Answers
Jo
How did they meet? In hospital – they were both born on the same day and their mums were friends.
How long ago? The day they were born.
What do you learn about the friend's life? She was wild at school – she wore crazy clothes and changed her hair a lot. After school, she went to London to study fashion.
Why does Jess like her? They're always there for each other, through good times and bad times. Whenever they meet it's the same as ever.
Dukey
How did they meet? At work – they joined the same advertising company on the same day.
How long ago? A couple of months ago.
What do you learn about the friend's life? He's great fun and talented. His mum and dad are from Barbados, but he was born in the UK. He talks about holidays in Barbados and his grandparents still live there.
Why does Jess like him? He makes her laugh. He's crazy, fun, kind and clever.
Raff
How did they meet? At school.
How long ago? When Jess was 14 – Raff was her first boyfriend.
What do you learn about the friend's life? His family moved to Dubai because his dad got a job there. He's now back in the UK and working near Jess. He had a girlfriend, but they aren't together anymore.
Why does Jess like him? They still laugh at the same things as when they were 14.

Unit 1 • Getting to know you 23

4 Check students understand *nickname*, *laugh*, and *live abroad*. Give students plenty of time to answer the questions. They could do this task in pairs. Then go through the answers together.

> **Answers**
> 1 Dukey's
> 2 Jess and Jo's
> 3 Jess
> 4 Raff
> 5 Raff – Raff is one (short for Rafferty) and 'red-haired Rafferty' is another because of his hair colour.
> 6 Dukey and Raff
> 7 Raff – he lived in Dubai because his dad got a job there.
> 8 Jo – because she wore crazy clothes and changed her hair a lot.

What do you think?

Put students into groups for these discussions. Monitor carefully, and encourage the students to include everyone in their group by asking questions as well as focusing on giving their own opinion. This is a fluency activity so make notes of errors, but try not to interrupt to correct.

When they've had sufficient time in their small groups, conduct whole-class feedback, eliciting information from each group. Do any necessary error correction together.

SUGGESTION This is a good point to do a freer practice activity with questions. Tell students they are going to interview someone in the class they don't know very well. Ask them to write 10–12 questions. Support weaker students by writing a few examples or question frames on the board to get them started: *Do you have a 'forever friend'? Who's your favourite singer? How often do you go on holiday? Where … ? Why … ?*, etc. Students write the questions, then interview another student. The main focus is on communication, so don't interrupt students. Monitor for correct questions, and give general feedback on grammar as a whole class.

Additional material
For students
Online Practice – *Practice*

Reading and speaking SB p14

A blind date

Note

Reading texts are an excellent source of new vocabulary because they introduce words in natural contexts, which allows students to guess or work out what they might mean. Discourage students from using dictionaries or translators too often as they read. They may miss the basic meaning of the text if they spend too much time looking up words. Here are two suggestions for dealing with the unknown vocabulary in the texts in the Student's Book.

- After students have read the text, ask them to underline some of the words they don't know (you could give a limit of five to ten words) and then try to guess what they mean. You could get them to check with a partner before checking their guesses in a dictionary.

- If you know your students and their first language well, you could predict words they don't know, then give students synonyms or definitions and ask them to find matching words in the text, for example: Find an adjective that means 'talks a lot/enjoys conversation' (*chatty*).

About the text

A *blind date* is a meeting with someone you have never met before, in order to find out if you'd like to get to know them better and have a relationship with them. Some magazines and newspapers organize blind dates between people, then interview them to find out about the date, the people's impressions of each other, and whether or not they will go on another date.

1 🔊 **1.10** With books closed, write the word *couple* on the board. Elicit the meaning and that the context it is going to be used in is two people having a romantic relationship. Elicit different ways in which couples can meet. Refer them to the exercise. Ensure they understand *survey*, and know how to talk about percentage, e.g. *three per cent* /pəˈsent/. They work in pairs to match the ways of meeting to the percentages. Elicit an example sentence as a model of what they should say. In weaker classes, write an example sentence on the board to help: *I think 25% meet at work. What do you think? Do you agree?* Check they understand *online dating* and *social media*.

Play the recording. Elicit students' reactions to the figures and establish what they found most surprising. Give a short example of a couple you know and how they met, then elicit a few more examples from the class or put them back in pairs to talk about couples they know.

> **Answers**
> At school or university = 13%
> At work = 18%
> At a bar or club = 6%
> Online dating = 12%
> Social media = 7%
> Through friends = 25%
> Through family = 5%
> A blind date = 3%
> None of these = 11%

🔊 **1.10 How did they meet? A survey**
A survey of over 10,000 couples asked how they first met. The top three were: first, with 25%, 'through friends', second, 'at work', with 18%, and third, 'at school or university', with 13%. Next, 'online dating' is 12% and 'social media' 7% – this means that nowadays about 19% of couples don't actually meet face to face! 6% meet at a bar or club and only 5% through family – that seems surprising. Last of all, 3% meet on a blind date. That leaves 11% who didn't meet in any of these places.

2 Focus attention on the photos of Kitty and Ross, and on the introduction to the article. Check the answers to the questions as a class. Clarify *blind date* if needed.

You could help students understand the use of the verb *go* in the phrase *they answer questions about how it went*. This is a common informal use of the verb in British English which means develop or happen and is used about a situation or event. The question form is *How did it go?* with a similar meaning to *How was it?*

24 Unit 1 • Getting to know you

Answers
A blind date is a meeting with someone you have never met before, where you try to get to know the person and find out if you'd like to have a relationship with them or not.
The people are Kitty Ferry, 22, a festival organizer, and Ross Mayo, 31, a carpenter.
They met in the *Oyster Shack* restaurant in Bigbury-on-Sea, Devon.

3 This is a jigsaw reading exercise – half of the class reads one part of the text, and the other half reads the other. Students collaborate within their reading group to support each other in answering a set of questions. They then pair up with someone who read the other text to share information about the two texts, thus building up the complete picture of what the whole text says.

Jigsaw reading has a number of benefits. Primarily, students have to articulate/summarize what they have read which means they process the information more deeply. It gives them a reason to read and understand because they will have to talk about it. This also makes the reading process more social and more engaging. Finally, it means that everyone has an equal role to play – even weaker students. Sharing information in this way is an authentic communication task, as students can ask follow-up questions to get more information as well. The questions that the students have to answer about their text are the same for each text, and this scaffolding supports students in their reading, understanding, and sharing. Some students will want to read the other text – encourage them to do this for homework.

Put students in two groups, Group A and Group B. (With larger classes, you may need to have multiple sets of the two groups.) Assign a text to each group and remind students to read only their text:

Group A – Kitty
Group B – Ross

Get students to read their text quite quickly. Monitor and help with any queries.

Encourage students to use the context to help them with new vocabulary and to pool knowledge with other students, or use a dictionary when really necessary. Pre-teach/Check some of following vocabulary which is taken from both of the jigsaw texts: *chatty, to wink, a guy* (informal = man), *go on somewhere* (go to another place to continue a date/party), *maybe/definitely, veggie, bubbly*.

Get students to discuss questions 1–8, working in their groups and noting down the answers. Point out that they each have one question which they can't answer from their text (but they will find out the answer when they speak to a partner who has read about the other person). The answers are provided here for reference, but don't check the answers with the whole class at this stage.

Answers
Group A
1 Because Ross saw Kitty on her bike.
2 Kind face with a beard, chatty, and funny.
3 Kitty is, Ross isn't.
4 She'd like to see more of the world.
5 Because it was really hot in the restaurant.
6 He tried to teach her how to wink.
7 They can't answer this question.
8 They went for a walk by the sea in the rain and she fell into the sea – Ross rescued her.

Group B
1 Because they both arrived on bikes.
2 Big smile, crazy clothes, bubbly, a great laugh, funny, interesting, and very pretty.
3 Kitty is, Ross isn't.
4 He travelled the world when he was 21.
5 Because he embarrassed her.
6 They can't answer this question.
7 Ross's flatmate; Kitty isn't going to meet him.
8 They went down to the beach and he rescued her when a wave knocked her over.

4 Pre-teach/Check *have something in common*. Regroup the students, making sure there is a student from Group A and a student from Group B in each pair. Demonstrate the activity by getting a pair of students to start talking about the person in their text. Students continue exchanging the information about their person in closed pairs, working their way through the answers 1–8. Remind them to refer to their notes and answer the questions in their own words, rather than read out sections of the reading text. Monitor and check for correct tense use. Note down any common errors, but feed back on them at a later stage. Bring the whole class together to check what Kitty and Ross have and don't have in common. Tell students to read the text they didn't read in class for homework if they wish.

Answers
In common: they both ride bikes, like travel, love their jobs
Not in common: she's a 'veggie' and he isn't (although they both eat fish), he can wink and she can't

What happened next?

5 Give students a few moments to think individually about the answers to the questions. Elicit a show of hands from students who think they become boyfriend and girlfriend, and then from students who think they won't. Check the result of the vote and encourage students to explain their opinion. Elicit possible problems from the class.

Answers
Possible problem: Kitty wants to travel in the future, but Ross has already done his travelling.

6 🔊 1.11 Read the questions as a class. Explain that students are going to hear Kitty and then Ross in a short recording about their relationship. Play the recording. Let students discuss their answers in pairs before checking with the class. Ask students if they think Kitty and Ross will continue as boyfriend and girlfriend, and why/why not.

Answers
Ross made Kitty a wardrobe. He went to Bristol to see her and they went to a music concert – she liked the music, but he didn't much. He met her friends and she met his flatmate, Mark. She really liked his flatmate. He's hoping this is the beginning of a special relationship and he can see a future together. She's happy at the moment but still wants to travel and maybe work abroad, so that could be a problem for their relationship.

🔊 **1.11 What happened next?**
Kitty
Ross texted the day after we met – I was really pleased! I texted him back immediately. We arranged to meet at his workshop to plan my wardrobe – that was a couple of months ago now, and the wardrobe's nearly finished. It's going to be beautiful. Ross is a wonderful

Unit 1 • Getting to know you   25

carpenter. He came up to Bristol when I was working at a festival there, and we had a great time. All my mates loved him. Oh, and I met his flatmate, Mark. He was nice, too, very nice, in fact – we talked a lot about music. I'm very happy with Ross, but it's early days and I still want to travel and perhaps work abroad – that's a bit of a problem.

Ross
I sent Kitty a text the next day, and she texted back immediately. I like that. She doesn't play games! Pretty soon after that I started work building her wardrobe. She has a really nice flat. She's often away working – she was at a festival in Bristol two weeks ago. I went up there to see it and to see her – it's not far from here. I met some of her friends, and we had a great time, but I didn't like the music very much. I really hope this is the beginning of a special relationship – I can see a future together. Oh, and she finally met Mark. He liked her a lot – I just knew he would.

Vocabulary
Possible problems

1. This section introduces the difference in meaning between adjectives that end in *-ing* and *-ed*. We use adjective + *-ed* ending to talk about our feelings about something, e.g. *I am interested in music*. We use adjective + *-ing* to describe something outside ourselves: *That music is interesting*.

2. Mistakes where students confuse the meaning of the two forms are typical. Common mistakes:
   *I'm boring. instead of *I'm bored.* – It's possible to be boring, of course, but it's unlikely that students mean to say they are boring!
   *I'm interesting in football. (Correction: *I'm interested in football.*)

3. Another less common issue can arise when students over-apply the pattern and create adjectives which don't exist, e.g. *stressing* rather than *stressful*.
   *Exams are stressing. (Correction: *Exams are stressful.*)

4. Students may make mistakes in spelling the adjectives. Remind them to drop the final *-e* when they add *-ed* or *-ing*:
   excite → *excite* + *ed* → *excited*

7. This section uses adjectives from the reading text to highlight the difference between *-ed* and *-ing* endings.
   Focus attention on the examples and elicit the matching lines. Explain that *-ing* adjectives describe a situation, person, or thing; *-ed* adjectives describe how people feel. In feedback, draw students' attention to the collocation *to be interested in something*.

> **Answers**
> Kitty was interested in Ross's job. Kitty was interesting because she was funny and 'bubbly'.

8. Give students time to complete the adjectives, working individually. Students check in pairs before checking with the class. As an extension, give students further pairs of *-ing/-ed* adjectives and ask them to work with a partner to write two sentences which show the difference between them. Examples: *annoyed/annoying, confused/confusing, frightened/frightening, relaxed/relaxing, tired/tiring*. Students share their sentences with another pair. You could collect these up for checking.

> **Answers**
> 1 excited   4 embarrassed
> 2 surprised   5 interesting
> 3 boring

VIDEO In this unit students can watch a video about people moving to another city or country, their reasons for moving, and what they like/don't like about the country they are living in. There's also an interview with a Chilean woman who moved to the UK with her British husband, and another interview with an American woman who decided to start a new life in Barcelona. You can play the video clip on the Classroom Presentation Tool or download it from the Teacher's Resource Centre together with the video script, video worksheet, and accompanying teacher's notes. These notes give full guidance on how to use the worksheets and include a comprehensive answer key to the exercises and activities.

Additional material
For teachers
Photocopiable activity – Video worksheet: *Another country*
For students
Online Practice – *Look again*
Online Practice – *Practice*

Vocabulary SB p16

Right word, wrong word

This section provides an introduction to dictionary work, so if you think your students won't all have their own dictionaries, or if you want students to all use the same edition, you will need to provide a class set for students to work from. Students may also work from an online dictionary (e.g. www.oxfordlearnersdictionaries.com), using computers or handheld devices such as smartphones or tablets.

Dictionaries are, of course, a useful resource in language learning, but most students need help and guidance to get the most out of them. Dictionaries vary greatly in the amount of detail and accuracy of information. The better ones will separate out different meanings, show common collocations, and give plenty of example sentences. With bilingual dictionaries, problems can arise when students look up a word in the L1 to English section and find perhaps three or four words in English to choose from. They need to look at the information carefully to know which one is correct in context. Ideally, they should start using a good learner's dictionary.

The exercises in this section aim to give students controlled practice in distinguishing verbs of similar meaning, adjective + noun collocations, preposition use, and words with more than one meaning.

SUGGESTION Even if students are used to looking up words in dictionaries, it is worth revising the basic skills of dictionary use. Write a range of words starting with different letters on the board and get students to say them in alphabetical order. Also elicit from the class the type of information you can find in a dictionary, e.g. pronunciation, part of speech (= the word type), example of use, other related words, collocations. In a bilingual dictionary, you also get the translation, of course. Ask students to look at their dictionaries and describe the order in which the information is given: the word itself, the phonetic symbols, the part of speech, the translation, etc. If possible, use a projector to show an online dictionary to explain different parts.

Verbs of similar meaning

1 Put students in pairs and make sure they have access to at least one good dictionary. Explain that the first exercise highlights the use of pairs of verbs that are often confused. Focus attention on number 1 as an example. Give the class time to use a dictionary to check their answers even if they think they already know the words. Ask them to find one more collocation for each word. Students complete the task, working in pairs. Check the answers with the class, and elicit other example collocations for each.

> **Answers**
> 1 go, play
> 2 make, do
> 3 speak, say
> 4 teach, learn
> 5 borrow, lend

Adjectives and nouns that go together

2 Explain that this exercise practises choosing the correct adjective + noun collocation. As a demonstration, write the first adjective and three nouns on the board and elicit which two nouns can be used with this adjective (*person, meeting*). NB *important* may be a 'false friend' for some of the students if there is a similar word in their L1 which means *high/considerable*, so don't be surprised if they mistakenly pair it with *price*, but be prepared to explain that it's not correct in English.

Give students time to select the appropriate nouns, working in their pairs. Encourage them to check their answers by looking in their dictionary. They may find the collocation in one of the example sentences and they will also be able to check pronunciation of some of the words – *delicious* /dɪˈlɪʃəs/, *mountain* /ˈmaʊntən/, *journey* /ˈdʒɜːni/, *busy* /ˈbɪzi/ and *heavy* /ˈhevi/ are commonly mispronounced. If possible, project these words from an online dictionary and play the pronunciation. Check the answers with the class, ensuring correct pronunciation.

> **Answers**
> 1 important person/meeting
> 2 delicious cake/meal
> 3 high price/mountain
> 4 long journey/time
> 5 heavy bag/rain
> 6 busy street/person

Prepositions

3 Knowing which preposition to use can cause problems for students. Remind them that the words in the box are prepositions and that they will need to use some of them several times in this exercise. Focus attention on the example. Students complete the task in pairs. Tell them to check their answers in the dictionary if they are not sure.

> **Answers**
> 2 about, in
> 3 to, at, in
> 4 with, in, on
> 5 at
> 6 for, in, for
> 7 of, on, in
> 8 from, for

Words with two meanings

4 Ask students if they can think of any words in English with two meanings. Elicit a few ideas, then focus attention on the examples in the Student's Book. Elicit the two different meanings of *date*.

> **Answer**
> In the first sentence it means *a meeting/meet-up*. In the second sentence it means *a dried fruit*.

5 🔊 **1.12** Elicit possible examples for *left*, e.g. *Turn left at the crossroads. / He left early.* Students work in pairs and use their dictionaries to look up the other words in the table and write sentences to show two meanings of each word. Monitor and help. Point out that the dictionary will also tell them the part of speech (noun, verb, adjective, etc.) which is a very important aspect of understanding how to use a word. For example *left* is an adverb when it is a direction, but the past form of the verb *leave* in the second example. Ask students to share their sentences with another pair, then play the recording so students can compare their sentences with the example answers. As an extension, elicit the parts of speech from the students' own sentences or by looking at the audioscript on p129 of the Student's Book. Use dictionaries if needed.

> **Answers and audioscript**
> 🔊 **1.12 Words with two meanings**
> 1 Turn **left** in the High Street and my house is first on the right.
> She **left** hurriedly to catch her train.
> 2 What **kind** of computer games do you like playing?
> How **kind** of you to bring me some flowers.
> 3 I love travelling by **train**.
> He's going to **train** for the marathon.
> 4 What do you **mean**? I don't understand you.
> He never even buys me a coffee. He's very **mean**.

Additional material

For teachers
Photocopiable activity – Vocabulary: *Find someone who ...* pp169–70

For students
Online Practice – *Look again*
Workbook p10, exercises 1–4
Online Practice – *Practice*

Everyday English SB p17

Social expressions

Possible problems

Everyday social expressions are often formulaic, so this section is useful in helping students sound more natural in English. For example, this section contains the formal social expression *How do you do?* Students often confuse this with *How are you?*, so be prepared to point out that the two are answered differently. *How do you do?* is answered with the same words *How do you do?*, and it is only exchanged once, the first time people meet. It is rather formal. The answer to *How are you?* depends on how you are feeling, e.g. *I'm fine./I'm OK./I'm better.*, etc. It's also important to

Unit 1 • Getting to know you 27

note that English speakers don't expect a long response to the question, *How are you?* – it's a greeting rather than a question to find out more about how the person is.

1 Tell students they are going to practise a range of expressions used in everyday situations. Focus attention on the photos and elicit from the class as much information as possible about the situation and the speakers, e.g. *Do you think they are friends? Where are they?*
Focus their attention on the conversations and word box and do the first example together. Students continue the task individually and then check with a partner.

2 **1.13** Play the recording for them to check their answers. Then play it a second time and get students to repeat. You could mark the main stresses on the sentences to help them. Ask students to practise the conversations in pairs.

Answers and audioscript
1.13 Social expressions
a A Hi, Eva. How are you?
  B Fine, **thanks**. How are you?
b A Thank you so **much**.
  B My pleasure. It's no **trouble** at all.
c A Can I **help** you?
  B No, thank you. I'm just **looking**.
d A Excuse me! Is that **seat** free?
  B No, sorry, I'm **afraid** it isn't.

3 **1.14** Elicit the matching line for conversation 1 as an example. Students work in pairs to match the remaining expressions. Monitor and help as necessary. When they have finished matching, play the recording for students to check their answers.

Discuss as a class where the exchanges might happen and who might be speaking. Elicit which exchanges are the most formal and encourage students to try to explain why. Similarly, elicit which ones are more informal.

Put students in pairs to practise the exchanges. If they have problems, play the recording again, pausing to get them to repeat chorally. Encourage accurate stress and intonation, which are important here in sounding natural.

Answers
1	e	6	b
2	f	7	a
3	i	8	d
4	h	9	b
5	c	10	j

Conversations 3 and 4 are the most formal.

1.14 Social expressions
1 A Good morning!
  B Good morning! Lovely day again.
2 A See you tomorrow!
  B Yeah! About 9.00, in the coffee bar.
3 A How do you do?
  B How do you do. Pleased to meet you.
4 A Thank you very much indeed.
  B You're welcome. It's no trouble at all.
5 A I'm so sorry. I can't come tonight.
  B Never mind. Perhaps another time.
6 A Can you help me with this exercise?
  B Of course. What's the problem?
7 A Bye!
  B Bye! See you later!

8 A Bye! Have a good weekend!
  B Thanks! Same to you.
9 A Sorry I'm late.
  B It doesn't matter. You're here now.
10 A Cheers!
  B Cheers! Here's to your new job!

4 In their pairs, students take turns to test each other on how well they remember the responses. Monitor and ensure they swap roles equally. Ask students how the exchanges compare to what is said in their own languages.

5 **1.15** Focus attention on the list of next lines. Elicit the follow-up for conversation 1 as an example. Students work in pairs to complete the task. Play the recording and let students check their answers.

Answers and audioscript
1.15 Conversations
1 A Good morning!
  B Good morning! Lovely day again.
  A **Yes, it's really warm for the time of year. (b)**
2 A See you tomorrow!
  B Yeah! About 9.00, in the coffee bar.
  A **Fine. Nine is good for me, too. (g)**
3 A How do you do?
  B How do you do. Pleased to meet you.
  A **Pleased to meet you, too. (c)**
4 A Thank you very much indeed.
  B You're welcome. It's no trouble at all.
  A **But it was so kind of you to pay! (e)**
5 A I'm so sorry. I can't come tonight.
  B Never mind. Perhaps another time.
  A **I'm free tomorrow night. What about that? (f)**
6 A Can you help me with this exercise?
  B Of course. What's the problem?
  A **I don't know what this word means. (a)**
7 A Bye!
  B Bye! See you later!
  A **Yes, let's meet after class. (h)**
8 A Bye! Have a good weekend!
  B Thanks! Same to you.
  A **Thanks. Are you doing anything special? (i)**
9 A Sorry I'm late.
  B It doesn't matter. You're here now.
  A **Yeah, I missed the bus. (j)**
10 A Cheers!
  B Cheers! Here's to your new job!
  A **Thanks. I'm really excited about it, but a bit nervous. (d)**

6 Put students in pairs. Give them time to create their extended conversations. Get them to decide who their speakers are and where their conversations take place. This will help them focus on the level of formality, too. Students prepare their short conversations. Monitor and assist as necessary. Allow them time to practise and help them with any pronunciation difficulties. If students are struggling, build up a conversation together on the board as a model:

A *Bye! Have a good weekend!*
B *Thanks! Same to you.*
A *Thanks. Are you doing anything special?*
B *Yes, we're going to a wedding.*
A *Really? Who is getting married?*
B *My sister. She lives in Paris with her boyfriend.*

A *Oh, well have a great time. I hope the weather is good.*
B *Thanks very much. See you next week.*

Encourage students to memorize their conversations, though weaker students may need to rely on written prompts.

Set a challenge – ask students to choose one of the conversations and continue it for one minute. Use a timer or ask students to time themselves. Ask confident pairs to act out their dialogues for the rest of the class.

SUGGESTION Encourage students to use the expressions from this lesson whenever appropriate at the beginning and end of lessons. You could put key phrases on a classroom poster to refer to. Make their use part of class routine.

Additional material
For teachers
Photocopiable activity – Communication: *Can I help you?* pp171–2
For students
Online Practice – *Look again*
Workbook p11
Online Practice – *Practice*

Writing SB p18

Filling in forms

This is the first main writing activity in *Headway* 5th edition, Pre-intermediate. It's a practical task as students will undoubtedly have to complete forms with personal information, on paper and online, in real life.

Students do vocabulary work on the common fields in a form and the information required to complete them.

The final task is to complete an example form with their personal information.

1 Focus students' attention on the form for *The Global School of English*. Elicit that it is a *form* and ask what you do with a form – write the collocations *fill in a form* and *complete a form* on the board.

Brainstorm when, where, and what kind of forms the students have experience of completing. Brainstorm some of the information you might find on a form to elicit/pre-teach *surname, marital status,* etc.

Suggested answers
enrolling at a school or university/on a course; applying for a passport/credit card, etc.; a job application; joining a club; getting married/divorced/registering a birth; registering for a service/account online; setting up a financial/charity transaction; placing an order; giving feedback/completing a survey

2 Pre-teach/Check: *occupation, qualifications, degrees, diplomas, certificates.* Do the first couple of headings and questions together as an example. Students complete the matching, then compare answers in pairs.

When checking as a class, model and drill the words in the first column to ensure good pronunciation and to help students memorize the new vocabulary.

Ask them to take turns in their pairs covering this first column and asking each other the questions from a–k to remember the field name as it appears on a form.

Answers
1 d
2 h
3 g
4 f
5 j
6 a
7 e
8 i
9 b
10 k
11 c

3 Highlight that forms often instruct you to complete the information in a specific way – and sometimes it is a problem if you don't do it as requested. Pre-teach/Check *capital letters, gender, circle, delete, not applicable, country code, postcode, signature.* This could be done by completing the form for yourself on the board as an example. Ask students to follow the instructions 1–7. Highlight that they answer for themselves. When they have finished, they share their answers with a partner.

4 Focus attention on the form and elicit what kind of form it is/what it is for (application for a language school). Pre-teach/Check: *emergency contact, homestay/hostel/student residence, dietary requirements,* and *medical conditions.* Check students have noticed the first instruction below the title. Give students sufficient time to complete as much of the form as possible with their own information. Tell them to leave any sections they don't fully understand. Monitor carefully. There are extra fields in this form which were not in exercise 2 or 3, e.g. *First language* and *level of English.* Allow dictionary use if needed to encourage autonomy.

When students have finished as much as they can, put them in pairs to compare their forms. Then conduct whole-class feedback, going through any of the trickier sections of the form and confirming the kind of information required. Also, make sure they've followed the conventions of using capital letters consistently, deleting where necessary and that they've signed the form.

EXTRA IDEA Using the form as a guide, students could work in new pairs to conduct a roleplay where one person is the receptionist at the language school and the other is the applicant. The receptionist can use questions from exercise 2 or simply read out the field names and the applicant should respond with real information for him/her to write down.

Before doing this, you may wish to do a quick recap of how to say phone numbers and also how to say email addresses (. = *dot,* _ = *underscore,* @ = *at*).

Additional material
For students
Online Practice – *Practice*
Workbook p11, *Review*, exercises 1–2
Online Practice – *Check your progress*

Unit 1 • Getting to know you 29

2 Let's get together

Introduction to the unit

Themes which are explored in this unit include relationships with siblings and with neighbours, things you have/have got and things you like doing.

The main *Grammar* focus is on Present Continuous and Present Simple tenses and how to use them accurately when talking about the present, permanent, or temporary events. In addition, there are exercises on accuracy in using state verbs. Students learn how to use *have* and *have got* correctly in a text about what it's like being an identical twin.

In the *Vocabulary and speaking* section, students learn a range of phrases for talking about what they like doing, such as *have a lie-in, do puzzles, go out for a meal*.

In the *Reading and speaking* section, students learn more vocabulary and phrases to use to talk about themselves in the context of a magazine-type quiz followed by a small group discussion for fluency.

Students listen to two people who are neighbours but don't yet know each other well in the *Listening and speaking* section. This leads to them performing a roleplay of the neighbours getting to know each other. Finally, there is an opportunity for students to talk about their own neighbours.

Students extend their conversational skills in the *Everyday English* section where they learn phrases for starting conversations and making small talk, with phrases such as *What a lovely day it is today!, How's your mother these days?*

The *Writing* section is an email to a friend you haven't heard from for many years. Students have free rein to include any information or news they wish, but the focus is on linking words *but*, *although*, *however*, *so*, and *because* – students are encouraged to include these. Before writing, they do exercises to analyse the function and use of the linking words.

Language aims

Grammar

Present tenses

Students read and listen to texts about identical twins as the context for the present tenses review. The difference between Present Simple and Present Continuous is highlighted, and students practise asking and answering questions using these two tenses. Students are introduced to common state verbs not used in the Present Continuous.

have/have got

Students have already learned the verb *have* for possessions. However, especially in British English, *have got* is often used and is introduced here. At the end of the grammar section, students check their learning with a short assessment.

Vocabulary

My perfect day

Useful verb phrases for talking about what you like doing are introduced, with students matching verbs with phrases that commonly follow, e.g. *chat on the phone*. The final exercise is another opportunity for students to get to know each other and build the class dynamic.

Everyday English

Making conversation

This section extends the conversational English learned in Unit 1. Students learn strategies and phrases for keeping a conversation going. The section builds students' ability to make 'small talk'.

Additional material

Workbook

Students complete a text using Present Simple in positive, negative and question forms. Before students go on to contrast the use of Present Simple and Present Continuous, they practise using state verbs, and revise *have/have got*. All the grammar points are brought together in a text about a Welsh shepherd and his life. In the Vocabulary section, students work on verbs that take the *-ing* form, and this extends to using the *-ing* form in compound nouns. Finally, students get more practice in making conversation and there is a Grammar review to complete the unit.

Photocopiable activities

There are photocopiable activities to review grammar (*Spot the difference*), vocabulary (*Who's like me?*), and communication (*Keep talking*) at the back of the Teacher's Guide as well as on the Teacher's Resource Centre. There is also a worksheet to accompany the video on the Teacher's Resource Centre.

Notes on the unit

Unit opener page

Choose from these activities to engage your students with the topic and target language of this unit:

- Talk about the title
- Talk about the unit goals (*Grammar*, *Vocabulary*, …)
- Talk about the photo
- Watch the video
- Look at the bottom banner
- Do the activity

Refer students to the photo on p19. Ask the class questions to draw attention to the unit context and elicit vocabulary: *Who are the people in the photo? Where are they?*

Refer students to the title, 'Let's get together'. Ask students what they think the title means. Note that *to get together* is an expression which, in this context, means *to meet someone socially*. If you don't have time to watch the video introduction to the unit, go through the unit goals below the title: *Grammar, Vocabulary, Reading, Everyday English, Listening, Writing*. Give examples or use translation for unknown words.

Video (2 minutes approximately): The video gives a step-by-step overview of the unit. Play the video, pausing where necessary – especially for students to answer any questions, e.g. *What's your idea of a perfect day?* This makes it a more interactive experience. Highlight the option of practising online.

As shown in the bottom banner, don't forget that there are many exercises to consolidate and practise the target language of the unit in the Workbook as well as online. There are links to these exercises on the relevant pages of the Student's Book and they can be done in class time or you can set them for homework.

Summary: If you're short of time, use the title and the photo to help students understand and engage with the topic, and then move straight on to the activity so that they can discuss the theme in more detail. If you have any more time, try to watch the video together. It is a clear and interesting introduction to the different parts of the unit.

Notes for activity:

Put students in pairs. Ask them to look at the photo and discuss their answers to the questions. Ask them to justify their choices where possible.

> **Suggested answers**
> 1 They're riding on a tandem. They could be husband and wife, or brother and sister, or just friends.
> 2 fun-loving, crazy, carefree, young at heart
> 3 Students' own answers.

EXTRA IDEA Find out what students like to do when they get together with their friends. Ask students to write down one thing they like doing with friends. Give some examples: *riding bikes, going to see a film, playing games*, etc. They shouldn't show anyone what they have written. On the board, write and practise a mini dialogue, e.g.:

A *Hi. I like riding bikes. What do you like doing?*
B *I like riding bikes, too. Do you want to get together sometime?*
A *Yes …*

Tell students they are going to talk to other students in the room. They should walk around the room greeting people and saying what they like doing. The aim is to find someone who likes the same thing they do. Challenge them to keep the conversation going, e.g. by continuing to talk about the activity or by trying to set up a time to get together!

Grammar SB p20

Present tenses and *have/have got*

Possible problems

1 Students at this level often make mistakes when using present tenses in English. This may be due to differences in the grammar of their L1 with regard to present tense because some languages do not have two forms equivalent to the Present Simple and Present Continuous.

2 Mistakes in form at this level are common:
   – Omission of the third person singular -*s* in Present Simple:
   **He like ice cream*. (Correction: *He likes ice cream*.)
   – Omission of the auxiliary verb *be*:
   **I swimming*. (Correction: *I'm swimming*.)
   – Use of an auxiliary with a Present Simple form:
   **I'm swim*. (Correction: *I'm swimming*.)
   – Use of the wrong auxiliary:
   **It doesn't raining now*. (Correction: *It isn't raining now*.)
   – Use of the wrong form of the auxiliary:
   **Where do he live?* (Correction: *Where does he live?*)
   – Confusion of whether to use Present Simple or Present Continuous:
   **It doesn't rain now*. (Correction: *It isn't raining now*.)
   – Use of a state verb in the continuous form:
   **She's not owning a car*. (Correction: *She doesn't own a car*.)
   – Use of the wrong short answers, or not using them. This can sound too abrupt. The questioner would normally expect more than a simple *Yes/No* answer:
   Are you enjoying the party? **Yes, I do*. (Correction: *Yes, I am*.)
   Do you like cycling? **Yes, I like*. (Correction: *Yes, I do*.)
   These kinds of mistake are to be expected and consistent correction during controlled practice activities will help students consolidate their knowledge and become more accurate.

3 State verbs are usually connected with thinking, opinions, feelings, emotions, and senses. Common state verbs include *think, agree, believe, remember, love, prefer, want, see, hear, taste, smell, feel*. They describe things that are not actions. Although students learn that state verbs are not used in the continuous, it is possible to find examples where they are used in this way: *How are you feeling? I can't believe what I'm seeing!* Sometimes, their use is idiomatic: *I'm not believing this! I'm loving it!* As a result, it's best to treat the stative verb rule as a general one rather than as absolute.

SUGGESTION There will be some new vocabulary in all of the texts in *Headway* 5th edition, Pre-intermediate, including the ones used for grammar presentation, so it is a good idea to develop strategies for this.

If you have a particularly keen and diligent group, you can plan ahead and write a list of vocabulary on the board for students to copy and check at home before the next lesson, using dictionaries or translators.

Alternatively, you can set aside a certain portion of time at the start of the lesson for students to check vocabulary and in this case, you can divide the class into pairs and assign just one or two words to each pair to look up. They can then relay the meanings to the whole class and you can clarify as necessary.

If there isn't an option to have a dedicated vocabulary time, you will just need to pre-teach vocabulary yourself to the whole group. Try to use images on the page if possible or find appropriate images on the Internet. Also be prepared to mime or draw and to think of simple examples which the students can relate to. Translation to L1 is a last resort.

If you choose not to pre-teach, students can of course practise their skills of guessing meaning from context, which is very useful. They may wish to use their dictionaries or translators, which is natural but may slow the pace of the lesson and make it hard to keep students working at a similar pace.

For this lesson, students will need to know these words: *identical twins, personality, competitive, spend time apart, independent, jealous*.

STARTER SB p20

Lead in to the discussion by telling the students about your family – your siblings, who you get on with best, how much time you spend with them, etc. Pass around photos if appropriate.

Ask students to read the questions. Check they understand *get on with*. Put students in small groups to discuss the questions. Assign a group leader who ensures each group member asks one of the questions until all the questions are answered.

Monitor and encourage students to include all members of their groups in the discussions, then conduct whole-class feedback. Find out if there are any twins in the class, and who has the most siblings (brothers and sisters).

Being a twin

1 Focus attention on the photos of Chloe /ˈkləʊiː/ and Leah /ˈliːə/, Liam /ˈliːəm/ and Dylan /ˈdɪlən/. Elicit that these people are *twins* and use the question to go over the meaning and pronunciation of the phrase *identical twins* /aɪˈdentɪkl twɪnz/. If students are interested, teach them the term, *fraternal twins* /frəˌtɜːnl/ (twins that don't look alike). Ask students if they think they like being twins and elicit responses, encouraging students to give reasons for their opinion. Brainstorm some possible reasons twins might like or dislike being a twin.

2 **2.1** Read the questions with the students so that they know what to listen for. Play the recording about the sisters and ask students to read and listen to the texts at the same time to answer the questions. Elicit the answers from the class. Check comprehension of *grown-ups* (= adults).

Answers
Chloe – because they're getting older and they can't live together when they're grown-ups.

2.1 See SB p20.

3 **2.2** Students now read and listen to the text about the twin brothers. Focus the students on the question before you play the recording. Elicit the answer from the class. Check understanding of *competitive, to beat (someone) at sports* (= to be better than them), and *jealous* /ˈdʒeləs/.

Answers
Because they're at different universities.

2.2 See SB p21.

GRAMMAR SPOT SB p21

This *Grammar spot* uses a guided discovery approach to help students notice the forms and meaning of the Present Simple and Present Continuous, *have* and *have got*.

1 Elicit the names of the tenses first. Then give students time to find two examples of each in both of the texts. If possible, ask students to use different coloured highlighters to highlight each of the tenses. Remind them to look for negative forms, too. Students compare their lists in pairs, then compare again with a new pair. In feedback, ask if there are any disagreements about which are Present Simple or Present Continuous, and elicit a few examples. Avoid going through all the possible answers.

Answers
Present Simple and Present Continuous
Present Simple:
We've got similar personalities, and we're very different from Luke and Jessica.
I always want to be with Chloe. I never feel sad when I'm with her – well, not really sad.
I don't like it when I'm not with Leah, but I think it's a good idea to spend a bit more time apart now.
I don't really like being a twin. People see identical twins as special, but they don't see what's different and special about you, on your own.
I think we are different from most twins because we spend more time apart.
We don't feel so competitive now that …
But I still really want to beat him at sports!
I'm happy we're more independent now. I've got a lovely girlfriend in Manchester, and I don't talk to Liam about her – I think he's jealous!
Present Continuous:
People say we're starting to look more different now …
We're getting older …
Dylan's studying Drama in Manchester and I'm doing Physics in Leeds.
… we're living very different lives.

2 Ask a student to read the example sentences aloud. Check/Drill pronunciation of *wear* /weə(r)/ and *jeans* /dʒiːnz/. Give students time to discuss their ideas in pairs before checking with the class. Remember to identify the tenses so that students learn the correct way to refer to them. (It also means that they have the terminology to do further research by themselves if they don't feel they fully understand.)

Unit 2 • Let's get together

Answers
They wear the same clothes. They live in the UK. = all time
They're wearing jeans and a T-shirt. Dylan's living in Manchester. = now

3 Give students time to find examples of *have* and *have got* in the texts. Elicit the answers to the questions from the class. Write examples on the board.

Answers
Examples = We**'ve got** similar personalities, I**'ve got** a best friend, I**'ve got** a lovely girlfriend.
They **have** an older brother …
They **don't have** any other brothers or sisters.
have got is more informal and more spoken than written.

EXTRA IDEA If you think students need more help distinguishing between the use of the Present Simple and Present Continuous, ask students to turn to Grammar reference 2.1–2.2 on pp142–143 for more examples. Tell them to find: three uses for the Present Simple and three uses for the Present Continuous. They should also find three state verbs in section 2.3. In pairs, they write their own sentence to illustrate each. Ask them to compare sentences with another pair. In feedback, elicit an example sentence for each use. Tell students to look at 2.4 to find the meaning of *have/have got* (possession) and one example of when they can't use *have got* (habits/activities). Ask the class to give you an example statement, negative, and question for each and write these on the board.

4 🔊 **2.3** This exercise will help you assess how well students can form questions in the two present tenses. Focus attention on the example.

Put students in pairs to ask and answer the questions. With weaker classes, you could elicit the tenses students need to use before they start the pairwork. Students may also feel more confident if they write out the questions before asking and answering them. This will also give you the opportunity to walk around and spot check for correct tenses. Student A can ask questions about Chloe and Leah with Student B answering. Student B asks questions about Liam and Dylan with Student A answering.

Play the recording for students to check their answers. Play it a second time, if needed, for students to make corrections. Students can also check their answers using the audioscript on p130.

Answers and audioscript
🔊 **2.3 Being a twin**
Chloe and Leah
1 A How **do** they feel when they're together?
    B Much braver.
2 A Why **does** Leah always want to be with Chloe?
    B Because she never feels sad when she's with her.
3 A **Do** they always wear the same clothes?
    B No, not always, but they usually do.
4 A **Are** they starting to look different now?
    B Yes, they are.
5 A How **does** Leah feel about that?
    B She hates it.
6 A Why **does** Chloe think it's good to spend more time apart?
    B Because they're getting older.

Liam and Dylan
7 A Why **doesn't** Dylan like being a twin?
    B Because people don't see what's special about you.
8 A What **does** Dylan never order in a restaurant?
    B The same thing as Liam.
9 A Where **are** Liam and Dylan living?
    B Liam is living in Leeds and Dylan is living in Manchester.
10 A What **are** they studying?
    B Liam is studying Physics and Dylan is studying Drama.
11 A Why **don't** they feel so competitive now?
    B Because they're living different lives.
12 A Which twin **has got** a girlfriend?
    B Dylan.

5 🔊 **2.4** This exercise focuses on Present Simple and Present Continuous forms. Tell students that they are going to hear the twin sisters in an interview. Check understanding of the adjective *scary* /ˈskeəri/. Give students a moment to read the gapped sentences. Play the recording. Students compare answers in pairs. Play the recording again if needed. Check answers as a class, and write *practising* on the board to ensure they have the right spelling. You could check that students fully understand the adjective *nervous* because this is a 'false friend' in some languages and can be confused with *angry*.

Answer
Speaking in front of lots of people.

Answers and audioscript
🔊 **2.4 Talking to Chloe and Leah**
I = Interviewer   L = Leah   C = Chloe
I So, you both say that having a twin sister stops you feeling nervous about things?
L Yes. We**'re practising** for a school play at the moment, and I don't like speaking in front of lots of people, but when I see Chloe, I feel braver.
I **Do** you both sometimes **know** how the other person **is feeling**?
L Yes! Sometimes I'm going to say, 'Let's go to the park', but before I can say it, Chloe says, 'Shall we go to the park?'.
I And I see you**'re wearing** the same clothes today.
C&L Yeah.
I Do you like doing that, Chloe?
C Mmm, not all the time. Leah **likes** wearing dresses, but sometimes I **want** to wear jeans!

6 🔊 **2.5** This second listening gives students further practice with Present Simple and Present Continuous. Again, students read the question and gapped sentences so they know what to listen for. Play the recording and allow students to compare answers before checking as a whole class. Ask students what *think, see, have,* and *want* have in common to elicit that they are state verbs and are not usually used in the continuous.

You could also check students remember the meaning of *competitive* and check other new phrases from the recording: *be good at/be rubbish at*.

Answer
Because they did different subjects.

Unit 2 • Let's get together   33

> **Answers and audioscript**
>
> 🔊 **2.5 Talking to Liam and Dylan**
> I = Interviewer   D = Dylan   L = Liam
> I So, you don't like being a twin, Dylan?
> D Well, sometimes it's good. But I often **think** people only **see** me as a twin – they don't see me as me.
> I You say you're not as similar as other twins, Liam. Why is that?
> L Well, we weren't always in the same class at school because we did different subjects. And we have very different interests now – I like science and Dylan prefers arts and drama. And we**'re living** in different cities, so we **have** different friends.
> I And do you think you're not so competitive now, Dylan?
> D Well, I always **want** to do things better than Liam! But you can't be competitive when you**'re doing** completely different things. I'm no good at science, and he's rubbish at acting!
> L I'm not rubbish! I just don't like it!

What do you think?

7 Check students understand *pros and cons*. You could draw two columns on the board with *pros (+)* on one side and *cons (-)* on the other. Put students in pairs or small groups to discuss the question and make their lists. Monitor and encourage equal participation of all the students in their pairs/groups. You could also encourage them to talk about any twins they know in real life and how being a twin affects them.

Conduct whole-class discussion, encouraging students to use their lists to give reasons for their opinions.

As this is a fluency activity, don't correct much as they speak but note any problems, especially with present tense forms and *have/have got,* to deal with together at the end.

VIDEO In this unit students can watch a video about twins and find out about what life as a twin is like. You can play the video clip on the Classroom Presentation Tool or download it from the Teacher's Resource Centre together with the video script, video worksheet, and accompanying teacher's notes. These notes give full guidance on how to use the worksheets and include a comprehensive answer key to the exercises and activities.

Practice   SB p22

Talking about you

Possible problems

1 This exercise aims to consolidate the differences in form between *have* and *have got*. *Have* and *have got* may both be used for possession. *Have got* is more informal and cannot be used for habits and routines, for example:
I've got a shower every day. (Correction: *I have a shower every day.*)

2 The main problem with *have* is that students may tend to form the negative as *I haven't* rather than *I don't have*. While not grammatically incorrect, the form is archaic. There are fewer problems with *have got* in the negative, but common mistakes include:
 – Mistakes using *haven't* and *don't/doesn't*:
 *I haven't any money. (Correction: *I don't have any money.*)
 *I don't have got any money. (Correction: *I haven't got any money.*)

3 Question forms and short answers are tricky because students practise using auxiliary verbs so much for questions that they overuse them in this case.
 – Confusion of when to use the auxiliary verb *do*:

 *Have you any brothers or sisters? (Correction: *Have you got any brothers and sisters?*)
 *Do you have got a pet? (Correction: *Do you have a pet?*)
 *He doesn't have got a pet. (Correction: *He doesn't have a pet.* or *He hasn't got a pet.*)
 – Wrong choice in the short answer:
 Have you got a car? *Yes, I do. (Correction: *Yes, I have.*)

4 It's worth noting that American English uses *have* instead of *have got*, except when the meaning is *must* (*I've got to go*).

1 🔊 **2.6** Focus attention on the speech bubbles. Remind students that they have already done some work on *have/have got* when they read about it in Grammar reference 2.4. Elicit answers to the question.

Play the recording and ask students to repeat the different forms, chorally and individually. Pay attention to pronunciation, particularly in the answers: the stress on the auxiliary and falling intonation.

> **Answers**
> You don't use the auxiliary *do* in questions, short answers, and negatives with *have got*.

🔊 **2.6** See SB p22.

2 Refer students to the list of things and check comprehension of the items as necessary. Note the change to *we* and *your parents* in the last two items. Tell students to take it in turns, first to ask and then to answer the questions, following the model in exercise 1. They can choose whether they use *have* or *have got* in the question, but the answer must match the chosen verb. Fast finishers can add other things to the list to ask about.

EXTENSION Write the list of things on the board and elicit two more from the class. Ask students to find someone in the class they don't know well, and ask them the questions. Monitor and check carefully for accurate use of *have* and *have got*. Bring the class together again and ask two or three confident students to tell the others about the person they talked to. This also provides practice of the third person after the first and second person practice in the pairwork. Feed back on any common errors and get the students to correct as a class.

Speaking

3 This exercise is a controlled information-gap activity, which brings together practice of the Present Simple and *have/have got*. The final question they need to ask is in Present Continuous so they are also reminded of the difference between the uses of the Present Simple and Present Continuous.

Focus attention on the photos of Candela /kænˈdelə/, Kim and Ethan /ˈiːθən/. Get a pair of students to read the question and answer about Candela in the speech bubbles and another pair to read the ones about Kim and Ethan. Elicit some other questions that students could ask, e.g. *How old are they? What do they do?*

Divide the students into pairs, ask them to find the charts at the back of the Student's Book:
 Student A p154
 Student B p157

34   Unit 2 • Let's get together

Give students time to read the information about their character(s) and deal with any vocabulary queries. Ask two students to model the first question and answer to demonstrate the activity. Remind students not to look at each other's books.

Give students time to ask and answer the questions to complete their missing information. Monitor and check for accurate question formation, especially the difference between the third person singular and plural forms. Note down any common errors to feed back on after the task. When the students have finished, ask individual students to tell the class something they remember about the person they asked questions about. Finally, do any necessary error correction together.

Answers
Questions about Candela
Where does Candela come from?
Where does she live?
Does she have/Has she got a big family?
What does she do?
What does she like doing in her free time?
What is she doing now?
Questions about Kim and Ethan
Where do Kim and Ethan come from?
Where do they live?
Do they have/Have they got a big family?
What do they do?
What do they like doing in their free time?
What are they doing now?
For answers to the questions, see p154 and p157.

State verbs

4 🔊 **2.7** This stage reinforces the use of state verbs. Ask students what they remember about state verbs and elicit some examples. Note that students may be confused about state verbs due to the slogan of a well-known food company: *I'm lovin' it*. You can point out that the English language is ever-changing and that non-standard forms are often found, but as language learners, choosing to use state verbs in this way might lead to listeners thinking they are making a mistake.

Focus on the first sentence as an example. Give students time to complete the sentences, working individually. Allow students to compare their answers in pairs. Play the recording for students to check their answers.

Sentence 10 introduces a new word *solitary* and students will probably want to know the meaning – ask them to use their dictionaries to look it up.

Answers and audioscript

🔊 **2.7 State verbs**
1 **A** Is this the way to the bus station?
  B I **don't know**. Sorry.
2 I **love** your dress! Where did you get it?
3 I'm not good at being on my own. I **need** to be with people.
4 **A** I **think** grammar is really boring.
  B I **don't agree**. I find it interesting.
5 I'm sorry, I **don't understand**. I don't speak French.
6 He's very rich. He **owns** three houses in London.
7 You **look** sad! What's wrong?
8 **A** Sorry, I'm late.
  B Don't worry. It **doesn't matter**.
9 **A** It's my seventieth birthday tomorrow.
  B I **don't believe** you! You don't look a day over 60!
10 I don't know that word, *solitary*. What **does** it **mean**?

Check it

The aim of this activity is to check that students have understood the differences between the Present Simple and the Present Continuous, and *have* and *have got*, in terms of form and meaning.

5 Ask students to work individually or in pairs to choose the correct sentences. When checking the task together, ask a range of students for answers, getting them to explain their choices. This helps students to revise the rules as a class.

Answers
1 Karina lives with her parents.
2 Who do you go walking with?
3 He doesn't see his brother often.
4 I'm at Don's house. I'm waiting for a taxi.
5 She likes black coffee.
6 They haven't got a dog.

SUGGESTION Review tenses with a team competition. You will need a list of 10–20 sentences with mistakes. Ideally, include mistakes that your students typically make with tenses. Divide the class into two to four teams, depending on class size. Draw a tic-tac-toe (noughts and crosses) grid on the board (3x3 grid). Draw two if you have four teams. The object of the competition is to get three squares in a row horizontally, vertically, or diagonally by correcting the grammatical error in the sentence. The rules are that only one person answers (no shouting out by the team), but s/he has to confer with teammates before answering. Set a 30-second time limit and don't allow books or notes! The first team is X and the second team is O. Read a sentence. After conferring, the speaker for team X says the correct sentence. If they are correct, they choose where to put their X in the grid. The turn passes to the next team.

Additional material
For teachers
Photocopiable activity – Grammar: *Spot the difference* pp173–4
For students
Online Practice – *Look again*
Workbook pp12–15, exercises 1–14
Online Practice – *Practice*

Vocabulary and speaking SB p23

My perfect day

Possible problems
1 Students often make collocation mistakes. This may be due to translation from their mother tongue or because they haven't learned the right pairing. Common mistakes can occur between *play, do,* and *go*:
  *I play karate every Saturday. (Correction: *I do karate every Saturday.*)
  *My sister goes exercise. (Correction: *My sister does exercise.*)
  *Can you do guitar? (Correction: *Can you play guitar?*)

Unit 2 • Let's get together   35

As a general rule, *play* is used with sports or competitive games and musical instruments, *do* is for a non-team sport or activity without a ball, *go* is used with *-ing* forms.

2 Students often omit *to* after the verb *listen*:
Do you like listening music? (Correction: *Do you like listening to music?*)

3 *Watch* and *see* are often confused:
I like seeing films. (Correction: *I like watching films.*)
Did you watch that new film yet? (Correction: *Have you seen that new film yet?*)
What are you going to watch at the theatre? (Correction: *What are you going to see at the theatre?*)
Watch is to look at something (usually moving) for a period of time. We use *see* when we talk about being at events:
We watched a film on TV last night (at home).
But:
We saw a film at the cinema last night.
However, when we ask a general question, we use *watch*:
What kinds of films do you like to watch? (in general)

4 *Take a photo* is quite idiomatic and a problem for speakers of Italian or Spanish who would say *do a photo* in their language.

This section revises and extends students' knowledge of verb + noun phrase collocations. The items cover a range of everyday/free-time activities that students will be able to personalize easily.

1 **2.8** Focus attention on the first box of verbs and phrases, and on the example provided. With a weaker group, check they know the phrases in the other boxes – *lie-in, puzzles, drama, barbecue* may be new. Be careful not to say the collocation in any of your explanations though!

Put students in pairs to match the verbs and phrases in the four boxes. Monitor and help at this stage, but don't be tempted to give the complete set of answers. Play the recording so that students can listen and check their answers. Play it again so students can listen and repeat.

Ask students to choose one verb from each section and think of one more phrase that collocates with it (e.g. *play the guitar, do some gardening, take a nap,* etc.). Allow dictionary use. Collect these on the board so that students can add them to their lists.

Answers and audioscript

2.8 Things I like doing

A
play games on my phone
do puzzles
go to the gym
have a lie-in

B
meet friends for a drink
watch dramas on TV
chat on the phone
go out for a meal

C
listen to music
do nothing
take photos
read magazines

D
have a barbecue
go for a long walk
visit other cities
shop for clothes

SUGGESTION This would be a good point to talk to students about keeping a vocabulary notebook. This could be organized by topic or by unit. In the notebook, students should write the new word, a definition or synonym, an example sentence, and any words that go together with the word. An entry might look like this:

barbecue /ˈbɑːbɪkjuː/ (n) – a piece of equipment used to cook food outdoors. *Let's put some more meat on the barbecue.* _____ (= translation)

One section of their notebook could be titled, *Words that go together*. They can add the collocations from Unit 1 to this section, too. Give students a little class time to set up their notebooks. Ask them to look back at the vocabulary learned so far and add the words and phrases to the notebook.

2 Read the questions in exercise 2 as a class and give some true examples about yourself using the phrases from exercise 1, e.g. *I like playing games on my phone when I'm waiting for a bus. I do it on my own. I also like having a barbecue with my family and friends in the garden in the summer.*

Put students in pairs to discuss their answers. Monitor and encourage them to ask follow-up questions to get more information about when and where their partner does the things they like.

In whole-class feedback invite students to report on their partner (which helps to practise third person singular).

Alternatively, if you have a small class, you could conduct the discussion all together.

SUGGESTION You could make the aim of this activity to find other students in the class who like doing the same kind of things as you do. In this case, set it up as a mingle activity and ask students to take notes about anyone they find who does the same things they do. In feedback, students share with the class, e.g. *Both Philipe and I like listening to live music.*, ensuring they use the correct third person plural of the verb.

3 **2.9** Give students time to read the gapped sentences. Pre-teach/Check *headphones, try things on, countryside, crossword*. Do the first sentence together as an example.

Give students time to complete the sentences, working individually. Play the recording for students to listen and check their answers.

Put students into pairs to practise saying the sentences. If necessary, play some sentences again and get students to listen and repeat with the correct stress and intonation. For extra practice with the phrases, ask students to change the sentences in exercise 3 to make them true for themselves or for people they know.

Answers and audioscript

2.9
1 I don't feel like cooking tonight. Shall we **go out for a meal**?
2 I always **listen to music** on headphones when I'm on the train to work.
3 I never **shop for clothes** online – I like to try things on first.
4 I sometimes **do nothing** all day on Sundays – I'm so busy the rest of the week!
5 On Saturdays, I **have a lie-in** – I stay in bed till 11.00 sometimes!
6 It's a lovely day! Let's invite some friends round and **have a barbecue** in the garden.
7 I often **meet friends for a drink** in the pub near my office after work.

8 Let's **go for a long walk** in the countryside this afternoon!
9 You **take** really good **photos**. Do you use a camera, or just your phone?
10 I like **doing** crossword **puzzles** with my wife – I try to get the answers first!

Talking about you

4 Give students time to make notes about their perfect day. Monitor and help with vocabulary as necessary. Encourage students to make the most of this preparation time. Their speaking is likely to be easier and more accurate and they will use more of the target phrases if they have thought about it, rather than just launching in. To add a game element, ask each student to describe their perfect day, but include one false statement. When they tell the other students, they must guess which one is the false statement.

5 Refer students to the example in the Student's Book, or give an additional example yourself of your own perfect Saturday or Sunday. Put students in groups of three or four, and assign a group leader. Students describe their perfect day to their group. The group leader ensures the other students each ask the speaker a question. The main aim here is fluency, but monitor and note down any common errors to feed back on after the task.

Additional material
For teachers
Photocopiable activity – Vocabulary: *Who's like me?* pp175–6
For students
Online Practice – *Look again*
Workbook p16, exercises 1–3
Online Practice – *Practice*

Reading and speaking SB p24

The independence quiz

About the text

The reading text is in the form of an eight-question multiple-choice quiz '*How independent are you?*' This is typical of the quizzes students might find in lifestyle magazines or on some lifestyle websites or social media. Students complete the quiz with their own opinions and responses, check their score, and then read an analysis. This provides a springboard for discussion about quizzes of this kind and the results, and leads into further fluency work which provides an opportunity for students to give their opinions on related topics.

We would normally advise pre-teaching some vocabulary in order for students to be able to work through the reading text quite quickly. However, there is a dedicated vocabulary section after the reading with exercises for students to do in order to work out the meaning of new words and phrases in this quiz. It is better to set the task up as one where students need to use their skills of guessing the meaning of vocabulary in context – then if they have serious problems, you can tell them to use a dictionary/translator or clarify for them yourself. Vocabulary which may be new: *worry, confident, foreign, on my own, pay no attention to, whether,* *view (opinion), recipe, ingredients, explore, takeaway,* and *have a go at.*

1 Focus students' attention on the photos and ask them to read the questions. Put them in pairs to discuss their ideas. Elicit answers from the class. Encourage students to give reasons for their responses as far as possible.

2 Lead in to the quiz by pointing to the title and eliciting the meaning of *independent*. Give them time to read the introduction only.

Find out if anyone in the class can explain *to enjoy your own company* and point out that this noun *company* is also used in the phrase *be in the company of others*. Put them in pairs to decide where they are on the scale. Draw it as a line on the board to help visual learners if necessary.

3 Focus attention on the quiz. Ask students if they have ever done a quiz like this and if they found out anything useful. Read question 1 and give your own answer, *a, b,* or *c* as a reaction. Elicit answers from a few students. Give students sufficient time to read and choose their answers for all eight questions. Monitor and help as necessary. Give students time to calculate their score and get them to note it down.

4 Ask them to guess whether their score indicates they are independent or not before they read the interpretation on p154. Check students understand *doing your own thing* and make sure students understand what their score means overall. Put them in pairs to discuss whether they agree with their score or not. Keep it light-hearted – remind them or elicit that these kinds of quizzes aren't known for being very accurate! Conduct whole-class feedback about the scores and the quiz in general.

Vocabulary

5 Put students in pairs. To demonstrate the task, match the first phrase and meaning together as a class. Students looked at this phrase before doing the quiz so should have a good idea of the meaning. Give students time to complete the task, working together with their partner.

Check answers together. Working in pairs, students help each other learn the phrases. Student A covers up the meanings. Student B says a phrase and Student A tries to remember the meaning. They swap roles after two or three phrases and continue until they can remember all of them.

Answers
1 e 2 f 3 g 4 b 5 h 6 d 7 c 8 a

6 In their pairs, students try to use the new phrases about themselves. To make this activity more conversational, read the examples in the speech bubbles and elicit from students what follow-up questions they might ask: *What do you do when someone tells you a secret?* Tell students to use conversational 'gambits' like these and ask follow-up questions to keep the conversation going. Monitor and encourage the pairs to take turns and note any mistakes to correct afterwards.

SUGGESTION When students are doing speaking activities, especially ones in which they practise fluency, monitor and note down a few errors that you hear, but don't interrupt the students. Write down some good use of language, too.

At the end of the activity, praise the students for their efforts, then say *I heard some good use of language.* Write what you heard on the board and say why it was good. Next tell the students, *I heard a few mistakes. Let's correct them as a class.* It's important to keep it light and formative, so don't mention any names.

What do you think?

Put students in small groups or three or four. Give them time to read the questions before they start discussing so that they can clarify with you if they need to. Assign a group leader who ensures everyone has equal opportunity to speak. To ensure students are giving examples and asking for extra information in their discussion, write some examples on the board: *In my opinion young people are …; For example, they …; I think that people can be … because …; I think that smartphones have …; I mean …; I agree …; I don't agree …; Why do you think that?; What do you think about … ?*

Ask the group to choose a scribe to write down one or two more quiz questions for the last point. Each question should have three possible answers and a score like the ones in the quiz.

When they have discussed in small groups, conduct whole-class feedback, eliciting opinions and examples from the different groups. Encourage students to agree or disagree politely and feed in useful words and phrases they might need to do this. Ask groups to give their question(s) to another group to answer. What do these new questions say about their level of independence?

Additional material
For teachers
Photocopiable activity – Video worksheet: *Twins*
For students
Online Practice – *Look again*
Online Practice – *Practice*

Listening and speaking SB p26

Getting on with the neighbours

The main aim here is to develop students' ability to listen for specific information. The script and questions also revise the use of present tenses and *have got* from earlier in the unit.

1 Focus students on the title of the lesson 'Getting on with the neighbours'. Elicit the meaning and pronunciation of *neighbour* /ˈneɪbə(r)/ and that if you *get on with someone,* you have a good relationship with them. Lead in to the section by saying where you live and how many neighbours you've got, e.g. *I live in a small block of flats. I haven't got many neighbours – maybe about five or six.*

Focus attention on the questions in exercise 1 and answer them about one of your neighbours as an example. Put students in pairs to tell each other about their neighbours. In whole-class feedback, ask a few students for their responses.

2 Read the saying aloud and check that students know the meaning of *fence*. Elicit what they think the saying means. Ask students if they have a similar saying about neighbours in their country.

Answer
It could be interpreted in various ways. One way is to suggest that neighbours should respect each other's property and land, and the boundaries between them. A less literal interpretation would be that you should keep some kind of distance between yourself and your neighbour and not become too friendly with each other.

3 Read the instructions and descriptions of good neighbours with the class. Deal with any vocabulary queries, e.g. *mind your own business* and *chat* may be new to students. Put students into groups of three or four to discuss their ideas. You could ask them to choose the three qualities that they think are the most important in a neighbour. Monitor and help as necessary. Encourage them to give reasons for their opinions and examples from their own experience if possible.

Elicit a range of opinions in the feedback session and find out, sensitively, if any students have had particularly good or bad experiences with neighbours.

4 Focus attention on the photo and ask students to identify Mrs Crumble and Alfie. Pre-teach/Check *above, below, have no manners* (means not be very polite/well brought up), *deaf, unemployed, suspicious.* Ask students what they think the two characters might disagree about, e.g. noise, being polite, etc. Give students time to read through questions 1–9.

5 🔊 2.10 Play the recording of Mrs Crumble through once. Put students in groups of three to check their answers. Be prepared to play the recording of Mrs Crumble again if students have missed a lot of the key information, but don't confirm the answers to the questions at this stage (they are listed below audioscript 2.11).

🔊 2.10 Mrs Crumble

There's a young man living in the flat below me at the moment. I think his name's Alfie Smith – I once got one of his letters by mistake. I gave it back to the postman the next day. I don't talk to Alfie – he never says hello to me.
He hasn't got a job – well, he doesn't go out to work in the morning like most people, that's for sure!
He doesn't get up till the afternoon! And he's never dressed for work – he never wears a suit or anything smart – he wears jeans and a T-shirt all the time. Goodness knows where he gets his money from, but he seems to go out every night. He goes to bed very late – I never see him come home. Tuh! It's all fun and no work for young people these days!
There are people coming in and out of his flat all day long. I've no idea how many people are staying there. Four? Five? Have none of them got jobs to go to?
He's got a girlfriend. She's very pretty. Blonde hair, dyed. She's living with him. I know young people often live together nowadays, but I don't like it, living together and not married. It's not right.
And why does he make so much noise?! Mmm, it's because he doesn't think about me upstairs. Listen! There goes, now – he's listening to loud music again! He listens to it all the time! Oh, young people these days, they live in their own world, and they just don't care about anyone else. They don't even notice old people like me. He probably doesn't even know who I am.

6 🔊 2.11 Get students to look at questions 1–9 again. Play the recording of Alfie through once. Put students in groups of three to check their answers. Be prepared to play the recording of Alfie again if students have missed a lot of the key information.

38 Unit 2 • Let's get together

Ask students to focus on the differences between the answers from Mrs Crumble and those from Alfie.

Check the answers with the class. For the question *What do you think the truth is?* students don't have to agree. However, the point of comparing the viewpoints is that the 'truth' depends to a certain extent on Mrs Crumble and Alfie's interpretations and assumptions based on what they hear about or see of their neighbour.

2.11 Alfie

Things are going well right now! I've got this great new flat – I love it! The only thing is, it's below an old lady, and that's a bit difficult. Her name's Mrs Crumble. I always say hello when I see her in her garden, 'Hello, Mrs Crumble, how are you?' or 'Nice day, Mrs Crumble!', but she never answers – I think she's a bit deaf.
She probably thinks I'm unemployed, 'cos I don't go out to work in the morning, and I don't wear a suit or anything, just jeans and a T-shirt usually. You see, I'm a musician. I play the saxophone, and at the moment I'm playing in a band in a jazz club. I don't start till eight o'clock at night, and I don't finish till 2.00 in the morning, so I sleep from 3.00 till 11.00.
There's only me living here, but some of the other guys in the band are using my flat to keep their instruments in, so they come in and out a lot. I've got a lovely girlfriend – she's the singer in the band. She lives on the other side of town, but she comes here a lot, obviously.
I know I make quite a bit of noise, practising my saxophone. And I'm giving saxophone lessons here at the moment to make some more money. I'm sorry, but what can I do? You can't play the saxophone very quietly!
I know Mrs Crumble watches me all the time. It's sad really – she's got nothing else to do. I'd like to get to know her and maybe offer to help if she needs it, but she's so suspicious of young people. I'm sure she thinks we're all lazy and sit around taking drugs. Ha! I work really hard!

Answers
1 It's below Mrs Crumble's flat.
2 Mrs Crumble says Alfie never says hello. Alfie says he always says hello but she never replies. He thinks she's deaf.
3 Alfie wears jeans and a T-shirt. He doesn't wear a suit. Mrs Crumble says he never looks smart.
4 Mrs Crumble says he hasn't got a job, but Alfie is a musician.
5 Mrs Crumble says he doesn't get up until the afternoon. Alfie says he sleeps from three till eleven.
6 Mrs Crumble says she has no idea how many people are staying, maybe four or five. Alfie says there's only him living in the flat, but his flat's busy because some of the other people in the band keep their instruments there.
7 Yes, he has. She lives on the other side of town.
8 Mrs Crumble says he's very noisy. He's listening to music now. Alfie admits he makes a noise. He's practising his saxophone now.
9 Mrs Crumble says Alfie probably doesn't know who she is. Alfie says he feels sorry for her and that he's really kind to her, but she's suspicious of young people.

Roleplay

Ask students to imagine that Mrs Crumble and Alfie meet at the main door, and they start a conversation. Ask two students to read the start of the conversation aloud.

Put students in pairs to continue the conversation. One student takes the part of Alfie and the other Mrs Crumble. They can decide whether Mrs Crumble warms to Alfie when he explains his lifestyle, or whether she remains rather suspicious. Monitor and help as necessary.

Let students act out their roleplay for the class – with wigs and costumes if possible! If appropriate, students can vote for the one they thought was most entertaining or interesting.

Additional material
For students
Online Practice – *Practice*

Everyday English SB p27

Making conversation

The aim of this section is to get students to think about the techniques involved in starting and keeping a conversation going, and to introduce and practise some phrases which might help them.

1 **2.12** Check students know the meaning of *term*. Lead in by asking students to think back to their first day of term at the language school. Elicit what students and teachers talked about, e.g. names, where people are from, jobs, experiences of learning English, etc. Focus attention on the photos and get students to identify John and Maria, and Maggie and Jean-Jacques.

Ask students *Who is the teacher in each pair?* (John and Maggie). Read the instructions in exercise 1 as a class. Play the recording of conversations 1 and 2 through once. Elicit which conversation is more successful and why.

Answers
The second conversation is more successful because Jean-Jacques asks questions, shows interest, and adds comments of his own. His intonation also expresses interest and invites a reaction from Maggie.

2.12 First days of school

1 John and Maria
J Hello. My name's John. I teach here. What's your name?
M Maria.
J Hi, Maria. Where are you from?
M Italy.
J Ah, OK. Where in Italy are you from?
M Florence.
J Ah, Florence. I love Florence. It's beautiful! So what do you do in Florence?
M I'm a student.
J Ah, I see. What are you studying?
M Psychology.
J That's interesting. And … er … are you enjoying being in London?
M Yes.
J Well, I've got some work to do before I teach my next class. So, nice to talk to you, Maria! See you around, I'm sure!
M Bye.

2 Maggie and Jean-Jacques
M Hello! My name's Maggie. I'm a teacher here. What's your name?
J Hi, I'm Jean-Jacques. Nice to meet you, Maggie!
M And you. Where are you from, Jean-Jacques?
J I'm French. I live in Paris – Paris as you say in English – but I'm from the south, from Provence. Do you know the south of France?
M Yes, I do. It's beautiful.
J It's true, it is! So Maggie, where are you from?
M I'm from Scotland.
J Oh, really! That's interesting! I want to go there while I'm here. Scotland's a beautiful country, too, isn't it?
M Oh, yes, very! Lots of mountains and lakes. And what do you do in France, Jean-Jacques?
J I'm an architect. I design very expensive houses for rich people.

M Wow! That's an interesting job! Are you enjoying being in London – lots of art galleries to look at here!
J Absolutely! I'm having a really good time. There's so much to see here in London – and I want to see more of the UK, too! So what do you do when you're not teaching, Maggie?
M I like going for long walks. There are some lovely ones around here – you should try them.
J I will! What class are you teaching?
M 4F.
J Oh, brilliant! That's my class. You're my teacher!
M Oh, that's nice! Well, it's nearly 9.30. Let's go to class.
J I'll follow you!

2 Read the list of tips with the class. Elicit any other techniques that students can add to the list, e.g. eye contact, open body language, intonation.

Refer students to the audioscript on p130. Put students in pairs to find examples of how Jean-Jacques keeps the conversation going. Check with the class.

Answers
Examples in conversation 2:
Adding comments and not just *yes* or *no* answers
I'm French. I live in Paris – Paris as you say in English – but I'm from the south, from Provence.
It's true, it is!
I'm an architect. I design very expensive houses for rich people.
Absolutely! I'm having a really good time. There's so much to see here in London – and I want to see more of the UK, too!
Asking questions
Do you know the south of France?
So Maggie, where are you from?
So what do you do when you're not teaching, Maggie?
What class are you teaching?
Expressing interest
Oh, really! That's interesting! I want to go there while I'm here.
Oh, brilliant! That's my class. You're my teacher!

3 🔊 **2.13** Refer students to the table. Ask two students to read the example aloud. Ask students to work in pairs to match the rest of the lines with the replies. Monitor and help as necessary. Before they listen, ask students to say whether they think any of the B responses are too short, e.g. f) *Yes, I am.* and i) *Nothing special*. Tell students that the responses in the recording are longer.

Play the recording for students to check their answers to the matching task. Ask *Which strategies did Jean-Jacques use to keep the conversation going?* Tell students to underline the phrases Jean-Jacques used in the audioscript on p130. Play the recording again so they can hear the intonation he uses with each.

Answers
2 f   3 h   4 g   5 i   6 e   7 a   8 d   9 c

🔊 **2.13 Keeping a conversation going**
1 A What a lovely day it is today!
   B Yes, beautiful, isn't it! It's certainly a lot nicer than yesterday!
2 A Are you having a good time in Edinburgh?
   B Yes, I am. It's a really interesting city, and there's so much to do. I love the shops!
3 A Have a good weekend!
   B Thanks. You too! Are you doing anything interesting?
4 A Did you have a nice weekend?
   B Yes, I did – despite the weather! We stayed in and watched nearly all of Netflix! What did you do?
5 A What are you doing tonight?
   B Nothing special. I'm a bit tired, so I think I'll have an early night. What about you?
6 A How's your mother these days?
   B She's OK, thanks. She's feeling a lot better. Thanks for asking.
7 A Did you watch that new crime drama last night?
   B No I didn't. I was out, but I've recorded it though. Was it good?
8 A I like your shoes!
   B Thank you! They're new! I got them last week in a sale. I like your skirt, too!
9 A If you have any problems, just ask.
   B Thanks, that's very kind of you. I will. I'm sure you're very busy though!

---

4 Play the first part of the recording again so that students can focus on the intonation of the speakers. Write the extract on the board and draw a line to indicate the intonation pattern:

1 A *What a lovely day it is today!*

   B *Yes, beautiful, isn't it! It's certainly a lot nicer than yesterday!*

Ask students to emulate the intonation – over exaggeration at this point is useful as it helps clarify the voice range needed to sound interested. Play the rest of the recording, pausing so that students can repeat, imitating the intonation. Put students in pairs to practise the conversations.

They can start by looking at column A, and covering B. They take it in turns to try to remember the replies – cheating if needed! Once they feel confident, Student A picks a conversation starter at random, and Student B replies. Tell them to try to keep the conversation going. Another way to do this exercise is to put all the conversation starters in line A on slips of paper and give each pair a set which they put face down in the middle of the table. They take it in turns to take a slip and start a conversation. Set a challenge to try to keep the conversation going for a full minute. Students can time themselves. In a follow-up lesson, give students a set of conversation starters and next lines on slips of paper. They try to match them up without looking back at their books.

Keeping a conversation going

5 The aim here is to provide some freer practice in keeping a conversation going. Focus attention on the opening lines and elicit a few possible responses.

Demonstrate the activity with two confident students. If you think students might move from one conversation to another very quickly, set a time limit of a minimum of one minute for each one. With weaker students, allow them to plan their conversations more fully, writing down key words as prompts. Students work in pairs on their conversations. Monitor and help. If necessary, remind students that they might sound bored and uninterested if they don't vary their tone when speaking.

Invite student pairs to act out one of the conversations for the class. They shouldn't worry if the conversation isn't exactly as it was the first time they did it, provided they try to keep the conversation going as long as possible.

Praise all efforts and help the class analyse how the pairs that spoke for the longest time managed to keep the conversation going. Refer students back to the techniques listed in exercise 2 if necessary.

Do any necessary error correction with the whole class together, including work on pronunciation.

Additional material

For teachers

Photocopiable activity – Communication: *Keep talking* pp177–8

For students

Online Practice – *Look again*

Workbook p17

Online Practice – *Practice*

Writing SB p28

An email – linking words

NOTE

This writing section focuses on linking ideas to make longer sentences. Students focus on certain linking words: *but, although, however, so,* and *because*. The section covers similarities and differences in meaning and also analyses how these words are used in a sentence, including word order and punctuation.

1 As a lead-in to the section, tell students you received an email from an old friend you haven't seen for seven years. Use the email in the book, but pretend it is to you. The aim is for them to become interested in the details of the email and also start thinking about what kind of information might go into an email to someone they haven't seen for a long time. Tell students some details about your friend's life and how you feel about that, e.g. *She is getting divorced – you are not surprised because you never liked her husband*; *She grows her own vegetables – that's amazing because she never had 'green fingers' before*; *She wants chickens – that makes you glad she doesn't live next to you because chickens make so much noise,* etc.

Get students to read the instruction and check they understand. Give them individual thinking time about what information to include in a reply and encourage them to make notes (but not write full sentences yet).

but, although, however

2 Students read and analyse the structure of sentences with the same meaning, but which use different linking words. Put them in pairs to check their answers. Then elicit the answers from the class. Draw their attention to where the commas are in each sentence. Ensure students note the rules for comma use.

Answers

But, although, and *however* all express contrast.
Although and *however* are more formal than *but*, and are often used in formal writing.
But joins two clauses. It must go before the second clause and has a comma before it.
Although joins two clauses. It can go at the start of the sentence, in which case a comma separates the clauses, as in the example. (It can also go in the middle of the sentence, in which case it is preceded by a comma.) *I use Facebook to keep in touch with friends, although I don't like it.*
Although can express a surprising contrast.
However joins two sentences, and introduces the second sentence. It is preceded by a full stop and followed by a comma.

3 Students work individually to join the pairs of sentences in different ways. Monitor and encourage them to try to use all three of the linkers. Correct as you monitor and also note mistakes which a number of the students are making.

When they have attempted all four sentences, put students in pairs to compare their answers. Then check answers together with the class. It may be easier for students to check answers if you give out the following answers on a handout. When checking, ensure students check their sentences for correct comma use.

Answers

1
I love ice cream, **but** I try not to eat it too often.
Although I love ice cream, I try not to eat it too often.
I try not to eat ice cream too often, **although** I love it.
I love ice cream. **However**, I try not to eat it too often.
2
Alex is a good friend, **but** we don't have a lot in common.
Although Alex is a good friend, we don't have a lot in common.
Alex is a good friend, **although** we don't have a lot in common.
Alex is a good friend. **However**, we don't have a lot in common.
3
I live near Zoe, **but** I don't see her very often.
Although I live near Zoe, I don't see her very often.
I don't see Zoe very often, **although** I live near her.
I live near Zoe. **However**, I don't see her very often.
4
It rained a lot, **but** we had a really good holiday.
Although it rained a lot, we had a really good holiday.
We had a really good holiday, **although** it rained a lot.
It rained a lot. **However**, we had a really good holiday.

so, because

4 Check students understand the words *cause* and *result*. These terms help to explain the function of the linking words. When students have had time to read and think about the sentences and functions, elicit answers from the class. Note that another word to use in sentence 1 is *therefore*. Ask students which word needs a comma and which doesn't.

Answers

Sentence 1 is cause first and then result.
Sentence 2 is result first and then cause.

5 Students work individually as in exercise 3 to link the pairs of sentences using *because* or *so*. When they have finished, put them in pairs to check and then go through the answers together. Ask them to check their work for correct comma use.

Answers

1 I don't like broccoli, **so** I don't eat it.
  I don't eat broccoli **because** I don't like it.
2 She was tired, **so** she went home.
  She went home **because** she was tired.
3 The train was very expensive, **so** we went by bus.
  We went by bus **because** the train was very expensive.
4 It started to rain **so** we had to stop the tennis match.
  We had to stop the tennis match **because** it started to rain.
5 My grandmother's ill **so** I'm going to visit her.
  I'm going to visit my grandmother **because** she's ill.
6 I really like the teacher **so** I enjoy history lessons.
  I enjoy history lessons **because** I really like the teacher.

Unit 2 • Let's get together   41

6 This exercise consolidates all the linking words practised so far. Pre-teach vocabulary from the email: *Time flies!, realize, divorced, a bit of a handful, a spare room, pub, keep in touch*. Alternatively, ask students to read the email first and then write these words and phrases on the board to encourage students to guess the meaning from the context.

Elicit the answers to the questions about who is writing and why, then give students time to complete the email with the linking words.

> **Answers**
> Amber is writing to Grace. She is replying to Grace's email. Grace has recently written to Amber after nearly seven years. Amber tells Grace about her marriage and divorce, her two children, her farmhouse in Clent, and her life in the country.
> 1 although
> 2 but
> 3 so
> 4 so
> 5 However
> 6 because
> 7 although
> 8 because
> 9 although
> 10 so
> 11 but
> 12 because
> 13 However
> 14 so

7 Students read the instruction. Focus attention on the highlighted phrases in the email which can help them to structure their emails. Remind them that they thought about this task in exercise 1 and wrote notes. Give students plenty of time to work individually on their emails. If possible, give students an email template to write into. Monitor carefully and refer them to the model text for ideas. Point out places in their emails where they could join sentences or ideas using the linking words.

If appropriate, students could swap these first drafts in pairs and give each other feedback on the most effective sentences and places where they think corrections could be made or linking words could be used.

It is motivating to choose some of the best sentences which display good use of the linking words and write them on the board to give positive feedback. You don't need to say which students wrote them. In the case of *so* and *because*, you could elicit the result and the cause to consolidate their understanding of the function of these linkers.

You could take their first drafts in for marking and return them for correction. Final emails could be displayed to enable students to read each other's work.

SUGGESTION Try this activity as a way to encourage fluency in writing with a focus on real communication. Prepare this activity by first deciding who will write to whom. Pair up students who don't know each other very well or who don't usually work together. If you have an odd number, then A writes to B and B writes to C. C replies to B and B replies to A. (Choose faster finishing students for the ABC grouping.) In class, ask everyone to take out a sheet of paper. At the top they write:

TO: (+ the name of the person you have told them to write to)
FROM: (+ their name)

Tell them to write an email introducing themselves and asking a few questions about the other person. They should use themes and expressions from the unit – write a prompt on the board if needed to help them get started, e.g. *Hi … I am writing to tell you more about myself. I like listening to podcasts, but …* Give students about ten minutes to write their email, then ask them to 'send' it to the recipient who then responds. Tell students to try to keep the conversation going by asking questions, showing interest and adding comments. They continue replying to each other's emails as long as class time allows.

Additional material
For students
Online Practice – *Practice*
Workbook p17, *Review*, exercises 1–3
Online Practice – *Check your progress*

3 Good news, bad news!

Introduction to the unit

The focus of this unit is on retelling stories and ways of reporting news.

The *Grammar* section introduces narrative tenses, in a true story, and the main grammar aim is to help students become accurate in their formation and use of narrative tenses: Past Simple and Past Continuous. These tenses are introduced and contextualized in good news stories, which are all unusual in some way. There is practice in the formation and use, the spelling, and the pronunciation of both tenses.

The *Reading and listening* section focuses on predicting, and listening and reading for specific information. Using a scene from a James Bond story, it also provides a further way for students to see narrative tenses in context and use them to tell their own story.

The *Vocabulary and speaking* section focuses on how to use adverbs in stories to add meaning and make them more interesting, including how to make adverbs from adjectives and the position of adverbs in sentences.

In the *Everyday English* section, students consolidate and extend their knowledge of how to refer to time and practise saying dates and choosing prepositions to accurately complete a set of time expressions.

In the *Writing* section, students engage in the creative task of producing stories from a series of pictures. This relates back to the idea of news stories and practises the narrative tenses from the unit. There is a strong focus on including adjectives and adverbs to bring their stories alive.

Everyday English

Saying when

This section aims to focus students on talking about dates, years, and using time expressions correctly with prepositions *on/at/in* or no preposition. They go on to practise using time expressions with prepositions to discuss national holidays and important personal dates.

Additional material

Workbook

Students complete a text using regular and irregular Past Simple verbs and practise making Past Simple questions. There is further work on the Past Simple with tasks which include ordering, writing sentences from prompts, and completing and answering questions about a text. Students also do work on time expressions and extend their understanding of how to use *ago*. Adverbs are also practised. The unit ends with further practice of dates and times, and a Grammar and Vocabulary review.

Photocopiable activities

There are photocopiable activities to review grammar (*The birthday present*), vocabulary (*Think of …*), and communication (*Guess when …*) at the back of the Teacher's Guide as well as on the Teacher's Resource Centre. There is also a worksheet to accompany the video on the Teacher's Resource Centre.

Language aims

Grammar

Narrative tenses

Students read news stories and analyse the tenses used. They work on the spelling and pronunciation of Past Simple regular and irregular verbs, and also practise the weak forms of *was* and *were* as they are used in Past Continuous. The uses of the Past Simple and Past Continuous are contrasted in news stories. Practice exercises include making questions from prompts and answering them, finding the correct place in the text for lines which have been removed and completing gaps in texts. Students make up their own stories from prompts using both tenses.

Vocabulary

Adverbs

Students are encouraged to practise making adverbs from adjectives and also discuss a number of irregular adverbs where the form remains the same as the adjective, e.g. *fast*. Students learn where to put adverbs in sentences. They read a poem to see how the use of adverbs can express emotions.

Notes on the unit

Unit opener page
Choose from these activities to engage your students with the topic and target language of this unit:
- Talk about the title
- Talk about the unit goals (*Grammar, Vocabulary, …*)
- Talk about the photo
- Watch the video
- Look at the bottom banner
- Do the activity

Refer students to the photo on p29. Ask students what they can see and how the photo relates to the topic of the unit. (People behind cameras. They might be taking photos or filming a news story.)

Refer students to the unit title, 'Good news, bad news!'. Elicit examples of each, e.g. *I passed my exam!* (good news); *My friend lost her phone.* (bad news) Ask students what to say if someone gives you good/bad news.

If you don't have time to watch the video introduction to the unit, go through the unit goals below the title: *Grammar, Vocabulary, Everyday English, Reading, Listening, Writing*. Give examples or use translation for unknown words.

Video (2 minutes approximately): The video gives a step-by-step overview of the unit. Play the video, pausing where necessary – especially for students to answer any questions, e.g. *Have you ever seen a James Bond film?* This makes it a more interactive experience. Highlight the option of practising online.

As shown in the bottom banner, don't forget that there are many exercises to consolidate and practise the target language of the unit in the Workbook as well as online. There are links to these exercises on the relevant pages of the Student's Book and they can be done in class time or you can set them for homework.

Summary: If you're short of time, use the title and the photo to help students understand and engage with the topic, and then move straight on to the activity so that they can discuss the theme in more detail. If you have any more time, try to watch the video together. It is a clear and interesting introduction to the different parts of the unit.

Notes for activity:
Put students in pairs. Ask them to look at the photo and discuss their answers to the questions. Ask them to justify their choices where possible.

> **Suggested answers**
> 1 Photographers and journalists.
> 2 a celebrity could be arriving somewhere, a press conference, a politician could be speaking
> 3 Students' own answers.

Grammar SB p30

Narrative tenses – Past Simple and Past Continuous

Possible problems

Past Simple

1 The majority of Pre-intermediate students will already be familiar with the Past Simple, but they are likely to need help with the following areas:
   – Pronunciation of *-ed* endings with regular verbs:
   Students may find it confusing that there are three possible endings: /t/, /d/, and /ɪd/. There is a specific exercise on the pronunciation of regular verb *-ed* endings to help with this on p31 of the Student's Book.
   – Irregular verb forms:
   Students will be familiar with some of the higher-frequency irregular verbs, e.g. *came, went, saw, met,* and *took,* but there are still quite a few more to learn! Remind students that there is a list of irregular verbs on p158 of the Student's Book. You could ask them to learn five new irregular verbs every week.
   – The use of the auxiliary *did/didn't*:
   Students forget to use it, or use both the auxiliary and the past form, e.g.
   *What time you got up? (Correction: *What time did you get up?*)
   *Where you went last night? (Correction: *Where did you go last night?*)
   *I didn't went to the cinema. (Correction: *I didn't go to the cinema.*)
   *Did you watched the football? (Correction: *Did you watch the football?*)

2 There are a number of spelling rules students need to learn. These are introduced in the Grammar reference on p144. Common mistakes include:
   – adding *-ed* to words ending in an *-e*: **liveed, *loveed* (Correction: *lived, loved*)
   – not doubling the consonant: **planed, *stoped* (Correction: *planned, stopped*)
   – when to change the *-y* to *-i*: **studyed, *carryed,* but **plaied, *enjoied.* (Correction: *studied, carried, played, enjoyed*)

Past Continuous

1 Past Simple and Past Continuous are contrasted in this unit. The main aim is to show students that the key events of the story are expressed by the Past Simple, while the background information and description is expressed using the Past Continuous. For some students, this tense will be relatively new at this level.

2 Mistakes in use are common. For example, students may not see the difference between:
   *It rained yesterday. (an action completed in the past)
   *It was raining when I got up. (an ongoing action in the past that was interrupted)

3 The form of the Past Continuous does not generally cause a problem, though students need to learn not to use the auxiliary *do/does*:
   *What did she doing? (Correction: *What was she doing?*)

4 Students may need help with the pronunciation of *was* and *were*. They tend to overstress them when they are usually weak forms in normal context.

/wəz/   /wə/

I was working. They were waiting for hours.

There is an exercise on the pronunciation of *was* and *were* on p31 of the Student's Book.

STARTER SB p30

This *Starter* section checks students' knowledge of Past Simple forms, both regular and irregular.

1 Elicit the Past Simple form of *become* (*became*) and ask *regular or irregular?* (irregular). Do the same for *clean* (*cleaned* – regular). Elicit from students that regular verbs add *-d* or *-ed* to the infinitive to form the Past Simple.

Ask students to work in pairs to go through the rest of the verbs. If necessary, refer students to the list of irregular verbs on p158 of the Student's Book. Check the answers as a class, drilling any past tenses that students find difficult to pronounce.

Answers

Regular verbs		Irregular verbs	
clean	cleaned	become	became
die	died	feed	fed
hope	hoped	feel	felt
pass	passed	find	found
stay	stayed	give	gave
try	tried	go	went
want	wanted	grow	grew
		hear	heard
		take	took

2 **3.1** Focus attention on the examples. Then get students to continue saying the verbs and past forms around the class. Then play the recording for students to check their answers. If necessary, play it again, pausing appropriately for students to repeat chorally.

3.1

Regular verbs	Irregular verbs
clean/cleaned	become/became
die/died	feed/fed
hope/hoped	feel/felt
pass/passed	find/found
stay/stayed	give/gave
try/tried	go/went
want/wanted	grow/grew
	hear/heard
	take/took

Put students in pairs to test each other. Ask them to take turns pointing quickly to one of the verbs in the box for their partner to say the Past Simple form. Monitor to make sure they are correct.

A good news story

About the text

The text is an article and it is a true news story, set in Brazil. The main human character is João Pereira de Souza who rescued a sick penguin covered in oil. The penguin survived and spends most of his time with João, but makes an incredible journey of 2,500 miles twice each year between João's home and penguin breeding grounds. (If students are unfamiliar with miles, convert to kilometres: 2,500 miles = 4,023 km/5,000 miles = 8,047 km approx.)

Unknown vocabulary you may wish to pre-teach includes: *retired bricklayer, part-time fisherman, penguin, feathers, sardines, seashore, disappear, honking.*

1 Ask students to look at pp30–31, and focus on the photos, map, and title of the article. Elicit answers to the question. Don't give them time to read any of the article yet. It is good for students to practise the skill of predicting the content based on the title and visual cues as this is what we tend to do when reading a newspaper or online news.

Answers

Because a man helped to save a penguin and the penguin travels back to see him.

2 Give students time to read the three questions. Tell students not to worry about the gaps in the text, but just read quickly to find the information they need. Put students in pairs to compare answers and then elicit from the class.

Answers

João Pereira de Souza is a retired bricklayer who still works part-time as a fisherman. Dindim is a penguin. João found Dindim on the beach near his home. Dindim swims to visit João every year.

3 Focus attention on the example and then give students time to read and complete the text using ten verbs from the box in the *Starter* section.

Answers

2	felt	7	went
3	took	8	tried
4	fed	9	grew
5	gave	10	heard
6	became		

4 **3.2** Ask students to read the instructions for the task and the lines. Point out the symbol which is used to indicate a missing line. Ask students to circle these in the text.

You could ask students to find the correct place in the story for the first line as an example. Elicit the answer from the class. Give students plenty of time to read the article again and find places where the lines fit. Put them in pairs to discuss where they think the lines go and why. Ask them to identify the tenses.

Play the recording for students to check their answers. Check the tense together with the class (Past Continuous). You could outline the form of this tense on the board: *was/were* + verb + *-ing*.

Unit 3 • Good news, bad news! 45

Answers and audioscript

🔊 **3.2** **Penguin swims 5,000 miles every year to visit the man who saved his life!**

João says, 'I love the penguin like he's my own child and I believe the penguin loves me.'

João Pereira de Souza, 71, lives on an island near Rio de Janeiro, Brazil. He is a retired bricklayer but still works as a part-time fisherman. One day, about five years ago, **when he was fishing**, he found a tiny, sick penguin, on the beach near his home. The penguin's feathers were covered in oil – **the poor bird was dying**. João felt sorry for the sick, little bird, and so he took him back to his home. He cleaned him and fed him sardines, and he gave him the name Dindim. The penguin soon became strong and healthy again.

After a week or two, João went down to the seashore and tried to put Dindim back into the water. The penguin didn't want to go. He stayed with João, getting bigger and bigger – beautiful new feathers grew on his back. Eight months passed. João was very happy, **because he was enjoying the company of his new friend**. Then suddenly one day in February, Dindim disappeared. João was sad to lose him, but hoped that the bird just wanted to return to his penguin family.

Four more months passed. **João was walking sadly home from the beach**, when suddenly he heard a familiar 'honking' sound – Dindim was back.

So it was, and so it is! Every year since then, Dindim spends eight months with João and then disappears for four months. Where does he go? It is thought that he swims 2,500 miles to the coast of Argentina or Chile to start a penguin family and then swims 2,500 miles back to João. That's 5,000 miles a year to be with the man who saved his life.

The tense in bold is **Past Continuous**.

5 🔊 **3.3** This activity gets students asking and answering questions in the Past Simple and Past Continuous. At this point, don't worry too much about mistakes with the continuous – the *Grammar spot* will help clarify form. Focus attention on the example, highlighting the formation of the *wh*-question on the board if necessary: *question word + did + subject + infinitive*. Do question 2 together with a weaker group as a further example, especially as question 2 requires them to use Past Continuous.

Tell students to just work on the questions at this stage, not the answers. Give students time to work individually. Monitor and correct/assist as necessary. Then put students in pairs to compare their work.

Now in their pairs, ask them to take turns to ask each other a question and give the answer. Model this task with a confident pair if necessary.

Finally, play the recording for students to check their questions and answers. Answer any queries about the tenses. If a lot of students are still making mistakes with the formation of Past Simple questions, go over this aspect of grammar with the class together. You could also conduct a brief discussion to get their personal reaction to the article. Ask questions such as *What surprised you most when you read this article? What adjectives describe João? What adjectives describe the penguin?*

Answers and audioscript

🔊 **3.3 Questions and answers**

1 Q What **did** João find?
   A A tiny, sick penguin.
2 Q What **was** he doing when **he** found it?
   A He was fishing.
3 Q Where **did he** take the penguin?
   A He took it home.
4 Q What **did** he feed it?
   A Sardines.
5 Q How long **did** Dindim stay?
   A Eight months.
6 Q Why **was** João happy?
   A Because he was enjoying the penguin's company.
7 Q Which month **did** Dindim disappear?
   A February.
8 Q Which month **did** he return?
   A June.

GRAMMAR SPOT SB p31

1 Students read the note and focus on the sentences from the text. Ask them to circle the Past Simple verb forms. Elicit which are regular (*cleaned*) and which are irregular (*found, fed*), plus the infinitives of the irregular past forms.

2 Give students time to complete the question and negative forms. Check the answers.

Answers
did, didn't

3 Students now focus on Past Continuous. Ask them to circle the Past Continuous form in the example sentence. Check together. Elicit how the sentence would be different with third person plural pronoun at the start: **They** were …

Read through the notes with the whole class. Draw a timeline on the board to highlight the interrupted activity use of the two past tenses:

I was having a bath when the phone rang.

```
           I was having a bath
        ~~~~~~~~~~~~~~~~~~~~~~~~~
past ─────────────X─────────── present
              the phone rang
```

Elicit the formation of questions and negatives:
Question: *was/were* + subject + infinitive + *-ing*:
Was he fishing when he found the penguin?

Negative: subject + *wasn't/weren't* + infinitive + *-ing*:
He wasn't having a shower when he found the penguin.

EXTRA IDEA There is a lot of useful information in Grammar reference 3.1–3.3 on p144. Ask students to read it for homework after they have completed p31 of the Student's Book. In the next class, ask them if they have any questions. If they still have some problems forming the tenses, you could ask them some questions to see how much they remember:

- What is the negative, Y/N question and short answer for these sentences: *He finished yesterday. She wasn't working.*
- What is the past tense spelling of these verbs: *work, love, stop, plan, study, carry, play, enjoy*? What's the rule?
- What is the Past Continuous spelling of the verbs above?
- In stories, which tense describes the scene? Which tense tells the action?

Spelling

6 This exercise will help you to assess whether students know the spelling patterns for making regular Past Simple forms. Refer them to the spelling rules in Grammar reference 3.1 on p144 if needed. Ask them to write the words individually and then check their answers with a partner. Monitor carefully to check they have applied the rules correctly. Ask them to discuss the questions in their pairs.

Ask students who have the right spelling to write answers on the board. Discuss the rules as a class.

Answers
a) worked, stayed, wanted
b) tried, studied
c) arrived, lived, hoped
d) stopped, planned

1 by adding -ed
2 drop the y and add -ied
3 when there is a short vowel sound, followed by a single consonant, e.g. *stop, stopped*

Pronunciation

7 3.4 This exercise highlights the three possible ways of pronouncing the -ed endings.

Model the example verbs and the endings. Elicit the past of *look* and the correct spelling (looked – /lʊkt/). Do the same with the other examples. Ask students how many syllables there are in the present and the past forms, *look/looked* (1), *stay/stayed* (1), *visit* (2)/*visited* (3). In pairs, students continue the task. Monitor and help.

Play the recording so that students can listen and check the categories. Play the recording again so that students can listen and repeat. Do a quick drill round the room – you say the present tense of the verb, one of the students says the past tense. Put students in pairs to drill each other.

Answers and audioscript

3.4 Pronunciation – Past Simple /t/, /d/, /ɪd/
/t/ – looked, worked, passed, hoped
/d/ – stayed, cleaned, played, phoned, answered, enjoyed
/ɪd/ – visited, wanted

8 3.5 Focus attention on the weak form /ə/ in *was* /wəz/ and *were* /wə(r)/. The /r/ in *were* is silent unless it is followed by a vowel sound, e.g. *were eating* /wəriːtɪŋ/. Focus attention on the sentences. Make sure they understand that the underlining shows them the stressed syllables in the sentences. Play the recording, pausing after each sentence and getting students to repeat chorally and individually. Drill the sentences to help students with the different pronunciation of *was/were*, but don't make students feel self-conscious if they can't distinguish the forms fully.

Write the negative examples on the board and point out that *wasn't* and *weren't* are stressed in negatives and so have strong vowel sounds: /ɑ/ and /ɜː/.

/ˈwɒznt/
He wasn't listening.
/wɜːnt/
They weren't enjoying the party.

Also explain that the strong vowel sounds are used in short answers, e.g.:

/wɒz/   /ˈwɒznt/
Yes, I was./No, I wasn't.
/wɜː/   /wɜːnt/
Yes, they were./No, they weren't.

3.5 See SB p31.

Practice SB p32

Discussing grammar

1 This exercise helps students understand the differences between the Past Simple and Past Continuous. Read the pairs of sentences as a class. Give students time to discuss the differences in pairs.

Check the answers with the class. Write the following timelines on the board as a concept check:

1 When we arrived, she was making coffee.

When we arrived,
past ———————X——————— present
        ~~~~~~~~~~~
        she was making coffee.

2 When we arrived, she made coffee.

When we arrived,
past ———X—X——————————— present
        she made coffee.

Answers
1 In the first sentence she was in the process of making coffee when they arrived. In the second sentence they arrived first, and then she made coffee.
2 The first question asks what activity you were doing at the time when the accident happened. The second question asks what action you took after the accident happened.

2 Elicit the answer to number 1 as an example. Students work in pairs to decide which tense to use. Ask a range of students for their answers. If there is disagreement, write the relevant sentences on the board. Go back over these, referring back to the *Grammar spot* on p31 and/or the Grammar reference on p144 of the Student's Book if necessary, and getting students to self-correct as much as possible.

Answers
1 saw
2 was shopping, lost
3 stopped, was driving
4 did you break, was skiing, hit
5 cut, was cooking
6 Did you have

Talking about you – truth or lies?

3 The aim here is to practise the Past Continuous in a freer, personalized activity.

Read the instructions as a class and focus attention on the examples. Make sure they understand the rules for the game.

Give the class another example about you using a different time, with one true and one false sentence, e.g. *At 10.00 last Sunday morning, I was having a lie-in. At 10.00 last Sunday morning, I was shopping online.* Ask students to guess the true sentence and confirm whether they were right.

Unit 3 • Good news, bad news! 47

Give students time to write their sets of sentences for each of the times. Monitor carefully and check for correct formation of the Past Continuous.

Put students in pairs to play the game. Monitor and check for correct formation of the Past Continuous and pronunciation of the weak form in *was*. Note down any common errors to correct after the game. Elicit how many true sentences students guessed correctly and if any of them were surprising.

In your own words

4 Before you start, write *headline* on the board and make sure students understand this noun. Focus attention on the five headlines and check comprehension and pronunciation of *injured* /ˈɪndʒəd/, *texting*, *rat's tail*, *robbers*, *teenage*, *vase* /vɑːz/. Put students in small groups to discuss ideas of what the stories might be about. Elicit ideas from the class, but do not confirm or reject any suggestions. Encourage them to expand on ideas where they can.

5 🔊 **3.6** Students listen to two people discussing two of the five articles. Encourage them to take notes of key words or information if they wish. Play the recording.

Elicit which two stories the people talked about. Assist with the meaning and pronunciation of any unknown vocabulary as necessary, e.g. *stall*, *bite*, *chatting*, *splash*, *head first*, *fountain*, *YouTube*, *views*. Students may also like to know the meaning of some phrases: *not looking where she was going*, *caught on camera*, *I bet she feels silly*.

Put students in pairs to reconstruct the stories in their own words. This gives them a little time to prepare the stories before speaking in front of the class. Ask two students to recount the stories. If they have difficulty, allow other class members to contribute/help them.

Answers
Rat's tail found in sandwich – a man bought a sandwich from a food and drink stall on the High Street. He took a bite (presumably discovered the rat) and threw it in the rubbish bin. Woman injured while texting – she was walking in the town square texting and chatting to her friend, and she fell head first into a fountain. Someone was taking a video of the square and put the video on YouTube.

🔊 **3.6 Talking about the news**

A You get some really interesting stories on this Buzz News website.
B Let me see! … Oh … that's disgusting! How can you read about that? … ugh … does it say where the restaurant was?
A It wasn't a restaurant. He was shopping on the high street, and he bought it from a food and drink stall.
B So what did he do? He didn't actually eat it, did he?
A Well, he took a bite, and then he threw it in a rubbish bin.
B Ugh! Are there any nicer stories?
A Well, this one's quite funny.
B Why is it funny? The headline says she was injured!
A Yeah, but not badly – she was walking in the town square texting and chatting to her friend and …
B … and not looking where she was going!
A Exactly … when 'splash' – she fell head first into a fountain. But the funny thing is … someone was taking a video of the square at the time, so the whole thing is caught on camera, and now it's on YouTube with over a thousand views.
B Of course! I bet she feels silly. Who was she texting?
A I've got no idea, it doesn't say – but texting accidents are really common these days.

---

6 Students decide which headline interests them most. In their groups from exercise 4, ask them to spend time thinking of the details of the story. They can make up names and places and have fun with this creative task. With a weaker group, you could write prompts on the board to help them brainstorm different aspects of the story: *where, when, what, who, how long, how much, why, what next/final consequences*. For groups who have chosen the last headline, make sure they know how to say amounts of money, i.e. *five pounds, 50 million pounds*. Monitor and assist, eliciting self-correction of any tense mistakes as you go round. Encourage them to decide which of their group is going to say each part of the story when they tell it to the class. If you have time, they can practise it quietly and ask for help with any pronunciation queries.

Invite groups to stand up and recount their news story. Encourage the listening students to ask questions for clarification or to get further information. In large classes, students recount their stories to other groups.

You could ask students which story they think is the most interesting in a short feedback session.

Good news or bad news?

About the texts

There are two news articles which are exploited as a jigsaw reading activity.

Student A's text is about two brothers, Alistair /ˈælɪstə/ and Jonny Brownlee /ˈdʒɒni ˈbraʊnliː/, who both do triathlons (where competitors swim, cycle, and then run in the same event). The news story is about what happened in the Triathlon World Series – this competition began in 1989 and from it the world champion triathlete is named each year.

Student B's text is about a British mum, Tracey Williams /ˈtreɪsi ˈwɪliəmz/ and her son Nate /neɪt/ and their supermarket shopping trip. The story is set in Liverpool which is a city in the North of England. The shop mentioned is ASDA which is a supermarket chain in the UK.

The following vocabulary may be new to the students. You could pre-teach it or if you wish them to practise guessing vocabulary from context, let them read the article without pre-teaching, but be prepared to clarify some of the words.

Student A text: *compete, trouble, breathe, ground, proud*
Student B text: *payday, spot* (verb), *checkout, couldn't afford, hopeful, club together, post a message, staff*

7 Students read both articles for gist to find out whether they are good or bad news. Set a time limit for this task. Make sure they know not to worry about the missing words at this stage. Elicit answers from the class.

Answers
Good news

8 Divide the class in half, Student As and Student Bs. Focus each half of the class on the relevant box and highlight which article they are to concentrate on.

With a weaker group, you could elicit all the past forms orally before they start. Do this with books closed by saying the infinitives in random order to elicit the Past Simple forms (*see, run, write, go, begin, buy, fall, find, cost, feel, put, think, tell*) so they don't write them down.

Give students time to complete their article with the verbs in the Past Simple. They can check their answers with another student who has read the same article.

9 Make pairs of one Student A and one Student B and ask them to go through the texts together, checking the Past Simple verbs. If they have doubts, tell them to look at the Irregular Verbs list on pp158 of the Student's Book. Monitor their discussions to make sure the Past Simple verbs are correct. Elicit which regular past tense verbs they have found.

Answers
Student A
2 went   3 thought   4 saw   5 ran   6 put   7 fell   8 felt
Student B
2 fell   3 told   4 found   5 wrote   6 felt   7 bought
8 saw
Regular verbs:
Brotherly love – he did it for Mum!: started, pushed
'Sorry, Nate! Not until Payday!': spotted, picked, noticed, clubbed, posted, returned, turned

10 🔊 3.7 Students match each set of three sentences to the appropriate article. Check together then give them time to find where the sentences fit (using the symbol as they did in exercise 4 on p30).

Play the recording so students can check their answers. Elicit that all these sentences are in the Past Continuous. Remind students that sometimes this tense is used to set the scene and encourage them to identify this use: *The boys were doing well. Alistair was running behind … / Nate was shopping … .*

Answers and audioscript

🔊 **3.7 Good news or bad news?**
1 Brotherly love – he did it for Mum!
Brothers Alistair and Jonny Brownlee were just six and eight years old when they began doing triathlons. Two years ago, they went to London to compete in the Triathlon World Series. It was a hot day, but the boys were doing well – **they were nearing the finishing line**. Alistair was running behind his younger brother. He thought to himself, 'This is perfect – Jonny's going to win and I'm going to come second or third.'
Suddenly, with only 700 metres to go, Alistair saw that Jonny was in trouble. He wasn't running, **he was finding it difficult to walk** and he couldn't breathe. Alistair ran up to his brother. He put his arm round him and started to run with him to the finishing line. Their worried parents, Keith and Kathy, were at home in Yorkshire – **they were watching the race on TV** when Alistair finally pushed his brother over the line and Jonny fell to the ground. Fortunately, Jonny was soon well and running again. Their parents were very proud of both their sons.
2 'Sorry Nate! Not until Payday!'
Nate Williams, ten, was shopping with his mum, Tracey, in an ASDA supermarket in Liverpool when he spotted a huge toy panda – it cost £15. Nate immediately fell in love with it – he picked it up and carried it **while they were doing their shopping**. But at the checkout, **when she was paying**, his mum told her sad little boy that she couldn't afford the panda until her next payday.
Nate didn't want to say goodbye to his new friend 'Pandy'. So he found a cardboard box and wrote a message on it for other shoppers to read. It said:
'My mum didn't have enough money to buy me Pandy today, so she's buying me Pandy on 15th June – so please don't buy him as it will make me cry. Thank you so much, from hopeful future owner.'

Some shop workers noticed Nate's message. They felt sorry for the boy and so they clubbed together and bought the toy for him. They posted a message on Facebook to try and find him. Tracey saw the post, and they returned to the shop to get 'Pandy'. She couldn't believe how kind the staff were. She said: '**When we were leaving the shop**, Nate turned to me and said that it was the best day of his life.'

11 Focus students' attention on the example questions and the question word prompts. Give them plenty of time to write questions about their own story. They should do this individually. Monitor this question formation stage carefully and help students to self-correct errors. Encourage students to make Past Continuous questions if appropriate, e.g. *Where was Alistair running? What were Nate and Tracey doing when Nate saw the panda?*

In their pairs, tell students to ask and answer the questions. They aren't expected to answer instantly and can look in the article for the answers if they don't remember. Monitor and note any points for correction together at the end.

Project

This activity provides further speaking practice. You will need to build in time for students to do some research and make notes on their favourite news stories, probably for homework. Students then give a short presentation about their chosen news story to the class. In larger groups, you may need to stage the presentations across a series of lessons or get students to give their presentations in groups.

Read the task as a class and elicit a few examples of stories that have just been in the news. If you wish, you could give students the challenge of finding a good news story (local, national, or international). This will help to keep the atmosphere light and possibly avoid contentious political issues.

Ask students to use some of the following headings to help them do the research and organize their notes:
- Type of story
- Headline
- The people involved
- The place
- The background to the story
- What happened and why
- What people said about the story
- Why it's of interest

Remind students to bring some visuals or the original article to support their presentation. If you have Internet access at school/college, students could do their research and make notes during class time. If not, set the research for homework.

When students give their presentation in a later lesson, ask them to come to the front of the class (or stand up in front of their group in larger classes) and make sure the rest of the class is quiet and pays attention. Allow students to refer to their notes, but don't let them read the information from a script. Encourage the class/groups to ask questions to the presenter. Be generous with praise after students have presented their talk, as giving a presentation can be rather nerve-racking, especially for weaker students.

Encourage students to ask questions to each presenter about their news story when they have given their presentations. This helps practise question forms and is a natural stage which they would be likely to do in their own language. They can ask questions about the content of the story and about the presenter's opinion/reaction to it.

Additional material
For teachers
Photocopiable activity – Grammar: *The birthday present* pp179–80
For students
Online Practice – *Look again*
Workbook pp18–21, exercises 1–12
Online Practice – *Practice*

Reading and listening SB p34

A spy story

About the text

This is an extract from a novel by Ian Fleming /ˈiːən ˈflemɪŋ/ – an English author who used his background as a naval intelligence officer during the Second World War to inform his creative writing. Fleming is famous for his James Bond /dʒeɪmz bɒnd/ novels. This extract is from *The Man with the Golden Gun*. It was written in 1965 and made into a film in 1974 starring Roger Moore /ˈrɒdʒə mɔː(r)/ as James Bond.

In the extract, a woman called Mary Goodnight /ˈmæri ˈgʊdnaɪt/ comes to warn James Bond that a KGB agent is looking for him and James also talks about a gunman called Scaramanga /ˌskærəˈmæŋɡə/.

Ian Fleming's first James Bond book was *Casino Royale*, published in 1953. He wrote 14 Bond books in total. Many other authors have continued the James Bond series. There have been 26 James Bond films, from *Dr No* in 1962 to *Spectre* in 2015.

Useful vocabulary for students which you could pre-teach: *spy* (n), *creep* (past – *crept* /krept/), *urgently*, *gunshot*, *HQ* (*headquarters*), *gunman*.

1 Write *James Bond* on the board. Ask students what they know about him in a whole-class discussion. Help them with any vocabulary they may need (*secret agent, spy, secret service*).

2 Focus students' attention on the images of posters and ask them to discuss the questions. If they share the same L1, students may be able to help each other with translating titles of James Bond films. Elicit answers from the class. Encourage students to give their opinions about any Bond films they've seen. You could add information from the culture note if you wish.

3 🔊 **3.8** Elicit ideas about the story from students looking only at the pictures. Feed in any useful vocabulary they need (*switch on/off, pillow, urgently, curse, darkness*). Then play the recording for students to hear the whole extract and see if their predictions were correct. Encourage them *not* to read as they listen because you want them to practise their listening skills in these early exercises.

Talk about the recording and confirm the correct ideas they had. Make any corrections to the information together.

🔊 **3.8** See SB pp34–5.

4 Give students time to read the questions so they know what to listen out for. Play the recording again so they can answer the questions. Allow them to check in pairs before checking with the whole class.

Answers
1 James Bond, Mary Goodnight, Scaramanga – they are in a hotel room.
2 Through the window.
3 To give him an important message from headquarters – a top KGB man (Hendriks) is staying in the same hotel as James and is looking for him, and so is Hendriks' gunman, Scaramanga.
4 The bathroom.
5 'This is not your lucky day, Mr Bond. Come here both of you and put your hands up.' He turned on the lights and pointed his gun at James.

🔊 **3.8** See SB pp34–5.

5 Students can now read the text they've listened to. Give them time to find the lines in the text which match each picture. Do the first together as a demonstration if necessary. Check answers together.

Answers
Picture 1 = James Bond got back to his hotel room at midnight. The windows were closed and the air-conditioning was on. Bond switched it off and opened the windows.
Picture 2 = At 3.30 he was dreaming, not very peacefully, of three black-coated men with red eyes and angry white teeth. Suddenly he woke up. He listened. There was a noise. James Bond took his gun from under his pillow.
Picture 3 = James Bond got quietly out of bed, and crept slowly along the wall towards the window. Someone was breathing heavily behind the curtain.
Picture 4 = Bond pulled it back with one quick movement … golden hair shone in the moonlight.
Picture 5 = Bond put down his gun and tried to pull her through the open window.
Picture 6 = He quickly led her across the room to the bathroom. First he turned on the light then the shower. They sat down together on the side of the bath.
Picture 7 = Bond turned off the shower and opened the bathroom door. 'Now, come on!'
Picture 8 = Suddenly, a voice came from the darkness of the bedroom. Scaramanga walked to the door and turned on the lights. His golden gun was pointing straight at James Bond.

6 Give students time to read the statements 1–8. Deal with any vocabulary queries. Students work individually to do this true or false exercise. Encourage them to correct any incorrect information in the sentences.

Allow them to check their answers in pairs, then check together with the class.

Answers
1 ✓
2 ✗ He was dreaming of three black-coated men with red eyes and angry white teeth.
3 ✗ Mary Goodnight woke Bond at 3.30 a.m.
4 ✗ He was annoyed/irritated to see Mary Goodnight.

Unit 3 • Good news, bad news!

5 ✗ The window banged shut while he was pulling Mary through.
6 ✓
7 ✓
8 ✓

Language work

7 Focus students' attention on the example. Students work individually to complete the exercise. Check answers together. Check and drill pronunciation.

Answers
2 breathed
3 woke up
4 took
5 crept
6 shone
7 whispered
8 put
9 tried
10 led
11 gave
12 stood up

In your own words

8 The exercise aims to help students to recount a story they have read in their own words. Remind them to look at the pictures to guide their stories and ask them to cover the text. Put students in pairs to build up the story together and monitor to ensure they're using past tenses correctly.

As feedback, you could ask students to recount the story around the class, each student saying a small part of the story and building it up little by little.

Do any necessary error correction together.

What do you think?

This exercise involves students giving their opinions about the story they've heard/read and making predictions about how it continues and how it ends. Go through the questions with the class in order to deal with new vocabulary. You need to check words such as *assassin*, *terrorist*, *poker player*, *capture*, *escape*.

Put students in groups of three or four and encourage them to read and discuss the options for each question. Monitor carefully and make sure all students in each group are included in the discussions, and students make group decisions about the answers.

When they have had time to make their decisions, refer them to the story summary on p155 to compare their answers. Deal with any vocabulary queries from the summary, e.g. *hitman*, *bullets*, *engraved*, *capture*, *shoot*. Conduct a class feedback session about their discussions.

VIDEO In this unit students can watch a video about the *Titanic* – a tragic story that still fascinates people today. You can play the video clip on the Classroom Presentation Tool or download it from the Teacher's Resource Centre together with the video script, video worksheet, and accompanying teacher's notes. These notes give full guidance on how to use the worksheets and include a comprehensive answer key to the exercises and activities.

Additional material

For teachers
Photocopiable activity – Video worksheet: The *Titanic*

For students
Online Practice – *Look again*
Online Practice – *Practice*

Vocabulary and speaking SB p36

Adverbs

Possible problems

1 Most Pre-intermediate students will be aware of the difference between adjectives and adverbs, but will still make mistakes in their form and use. Some of these mistakes are related to the form of adverbs, particularly as there are a few confusing irregular ones. Most of the mistakes are to do with word order, and this is not a simple thing as there are many different possible positions for adverbs in a sentence.

2 Common patterns students need to know are that:
 – Adverbs do not usually go between a verb and its object, e.g. *He speaks German very well.* NOT **He speaks very well German.*
 – Adverbs usually go before a main verb, e.g. *He still lives there.*
 – Adverbs of manner (that say how something happens) go after main verbs, e.g. *I worked really hard.*
 – Adverbs usually go after *be* or an auxiliary/modal verb: *She's probably at work.*, *I can never remember her house number.*
 – If there is more than one adverb, the order is usually: manner + place + time, e.g. *We trained hard at the gym last night.*
 – Some adverbs can go before adjectives and other adverbs to modify them, e.g. *really happy, incredibly slowly.*
 – Adverbial time expressions commonly go at the beginning or end of sentences, e.g. *Last Thursday evening, I was sitting ... , I worked hard all last week.* Some adverbs commonly go at the start of sentences or clauses, e.g. *Suddenly, a large dog jumped ... , Unfortunately, I can't come.*
 – The adverbial phrase *very much* is usually used at the end of a sentence or clause, e.g *... that I want to see very much.*

1 As a lead-in, write *quiet* (adjective) and *quietly* (adverb) on the board and elicit the parts of speech. Ask students what they know about adverbs – but don't worry if they don't have much to say.

Read the instructions as a class and focus students' attention on the table. Elicit an adverb to go with *dream* (*peacefully*). Ask: *How can we dream?* to elicit *peacefully* and to show students that the adverbs in this exercise all describe how an action is done (adverbs of manner). Mime *dreaming peacefully* to get this idea across. Ask students to work in pairs to complete the task. Remind them that some verbs may match with more than one adverb. Weaker students may want to find the examples in the text on p34.

Go through the answers together.

Unit 3 • Good news, bad news! 51

> **Answers**
> dream peacefully
> wake up suddenly/slowly
> whisper quietly/slowly/urgently
> creep quietly/slowly
> get out of bed quietly/suddenly/slowly
> breathe slowly/heavily/quietly

2 This exercise consolidates how to form adverbs from adjectives. Elicit that the words in the box are adjectives and ask students to change the first from an adjective to an adverb (*clear – clearly*). Give them time to write the other adverbs, keeping in mind that one is irregular.

Put students in pairs to check their answers, then elicit answers from the class. Ask them to spell the adverbs aloud as this reinforces the -*ly* ending and you will also be able to check they have made the *y* to *i* spelling change for *noisily* and *easily*. Write them on the board.

> **Answers**
> clearly, noisily, carefully, easily, completely, well, badly, fluently
> well (good) is irregular

3 🔊 **3.9** Students use the adverbs from exercise 2 to complete the gaps. You could do the first one together as an example if necessary. When they have finished, play the recording so they can check their answers.

Put them in pairs to remember and practise the conversations. With a weaker group, you could refer them to the audioscript on p131. Monitor carefully and choose some confident pairs to act out their conversations for the class.

> **Answers**
> 1 badly
> 2 well
> 3 clearly
> 4 noisily
> 5 completely
> 6 carefully
> 7 fluently
> 8 easily

🔊 **3.9 Adverbs**
1 A My team played so badly. They lost five–nil.
  B No surprise there! They lose every time.
2 A Your team's rubbish. They never win!
  B Actually, they played their last game really well. They won easily.
3 A Now, do you understand the rules of cricket?
  B Well – you explained them really clearly, but I don't think I can remember them all.
4 A Can you try not to eat so noisily? It really does sound disgusting!
  B Sorry – I'm just really hungry. I'll try to eat more quietly.
5 A I'm so sorry. I completely forgot that it was your birthday today. Let me buy you a drink.
  B Never mind! I'm trying to forget how old I am!
6 A Thanks so much for having us. We've had a brilliant weekend.
  B Our pleasure – we'll have to do it again soon. Drive carefully and text us when you get home.
7 A Her Spanish is excellent!
  B Yes, I know, but she doesn't just speak Spanish fluently, she speaks French and German really well, too.
8 A My brother's very bright – he always passes his exams easily.
  B Lucky him! I'm always so nervous, I never do very well.

4 This exercise focuses on words that are both adjectives and adverbs – *fast*, *hard*, and *early*. Get students to read the pairs of sentences aloud. Then ask *adjective or adverb?* about each word in bold. If they have any difficulty, remind them that adjectives come before the noun in English and that adverbs give information about verbs.

The aim here is to help students understand that the adjective and adverb form of these words is the same. A common mistake is for students to apply the -*ly* ending and say or write *fastly* or *hardly*. (*Hardly* exists, but the meaning is different.)

> **Answers**
> Is this a **fast** train to London? (adjective)
> Slow down! You drive too **fast**! (adverb)
> I work **hard** and play **hard**. (adverb)
> She's a very **hard** worker. (adjective)
> I got up **early** this morning. (adverb)
> We caught the **early** train. (adjective)
> The adjectives and adverbs are spelled the same, but their position in the sentence is different.

Word order

5 Focus attention on sentence 1 and ask students to think about where they can put the two adverbs in brackets. Elicit ideas from the class and write them on the board, showing the different possible positions of the adverbs.

With a weaker group, go through the adverbs in brackets to check the meanings. The following may be new to all students: *regularly, continually, passionately*. Give students time to add the adverbs in the other sentences, working individually. Monitor and help where necessary. Let students check their answers in pairs. Remind them that there may be more than one possible answer. Check answers together with the class. Make sure the possible answers are clear and correct any mistakes.

> **Answers**
> 1 I was dreaming peacefully, when suddenly a loud noise woke me up./I was dreaming peacefully, when a loud noise suddenly woke me up.
> 2 I got up early in the morning and worked hard all day.
> 3 My grandma is nearly 80 and she still goes swimming regularly./My grandma is nearly 80 and she still regularly goes swimming.
> 4 I was just relaxing with a really good book when someone knocked loudly on the door./I was just relaxing with a really good book when someone knocked on the door loudly.
> 5 My sister is only three, but she can already read and write well.
> 6 Some of my friends are continually on Facebook. Even my dad's on Facebook./My dad's even on Facebook.
> 7 'Do you really love me?' 'Of course I do. I love you passionately.'/'Do you love me, really?'

A sad poem with adverbs!

6 🔊 **3.10** Check students understand the word *poem*. Ask them to read the questions and check comprehension of any tricky words, e.g. *to suit*. The adverbs *guiltily* and *gradually* in the poem may also be new.

Play the recording for students to listen to the poem and read it at the same time. Elicit answers from the class or put students in pairs to discuss the answers, and then conduct class feedback. Encourage students to give reasons for their choice of title.

> **Answers**
> A couple have split up – one of them has done something to feel guilty about.
> Best title = Love's a Cruel Game

52 Unit 3 • Good news, bad news!

EXTRA IDEA Ask students to read the poem without the adverbs. Does it make sense? (No – the adverbs add a lot of meaning in this poem).

🔊 **3.10** See SB p36.

7 Put students in pairs for this light-hearted activity. Students need to try to put feeling into their reading of the poem by varying their tone and stressing words which they feel are important. Different interpretations are possible. Encourage any confident students to give their rendition in front of the class.

In their pairs, they write a short poem. Tell them to use any adverbs they've studied in this lesson. They can refer back to exercises on the page for examples. The poem can be on any topic. Monitor carefully and feed in vocabulary students need to express themselves. Do error correction as you monitor so poems are ready to be read out. If you think students will be very self-conscious, you could group pairs together in small groups to read their poems in groups rather than the whole class. Monitor carefully. Praise examples of reading with feeling and highlight specifically how this was done (intonation, sentence stress, etc.).

Additional material
For teachers
Photocopiable activity – Vocabulary: *Think of …* pp181–2
For students
Online Practice – *Look again*
Workbook p22, exercises 1–3
Online Practice – *Practice*

Everyday English SB p37

Saying when

Possible problems

1 There are a number of difficulties relating to expressing times and dates accurately in English. The main problem students have is using the correct preposition with days, months, seasons, times, dates, and years:
- *on Monday, on New Year's Day*
- *in April, in summer*
- *at 7.00 a.m., at lunchtime, at the weekend*
- *on the fifth of June*
- *in 2020*

The situation is complicated by the fact that conventions vary between British and American English, e.g. *at the weekend* (BrE), but *on the weekend* (AmE).

2 Students forget to say the definite article *the* in dates (which is the convention in British English).
*I came here on second of June. (Correction: *I came here on the second of June.*)

3 Students might not remember all the ordinal numbers, especially *first, second, third,* and *twenty-first, twenty-second,* etc. Be prepared to drill these as a class if students have problems. The pronunciation of some ordinals is difficult because of consonant clusters, e.g. *fifth* /fɪfθ/, *sixth* /sɪksθ/, *twelfth* /twelfθ/, etc.

4 Students often get years wrong. You may need to remind them that we usually divide the numbers in years up to 1999 into two sets of two-digit numbers, e.g. 1980 – *nineteen eighty*; we use *oh* /əʊ/ not *zero* in dates, e.g. 1906 – *nineteen oh six*; years between 2001–2009 are read like ordinary numbers, e.g. 2009 – *two thousand and nine*; years from 2010 onwards can be read as numbers, e.g. 2013 – *two thousand and thirteen*, but are often read as *twenty thirteen*, etc.

5 Students often don't differentiate between the teens – 13–19 and tens 30–90 so that 13 and 30, for example, sound very similar. Draw attention to and drill the stress pattern difference to clarify: /ˌθɜːˈtiːn/ vs /ˈθɜːti/, etc.

This section brings together a number of ways of referring to time – a focus on dates, both British and American, a review and extension of the use of *in/at/on* or no preposition with time expressions, and a review of time expressions in reply to the question *When did you last … ?*

1 🔊 **3.11** Lead in to the lesson by checking students know the difference between *birthday* and *date of birth*.

Put students in pairs to answer the questions in exercise 1. Monitor and note any common mistakes with dates, but don't correct them at this stage. Play the recording and let students compare the answers with their own. If students had a lot of problems with ordinal numbers, get them to say 1st–20th quickly round the class and then write random ordinals up to 31st on the board and elicit the correct word. Drill any ordinals they find difficult to pronounce (see Possible problems above). Do error correction of the mistakes you noticed if necessary.

Answers and audioscript

🔊 **3.11 Saying dates**
A What's the date today?
B It's **April the twenty-third**.
A So tomorrow's **the twenty-fourth**.
B Yeah, and the day after tomorrow's **the twenty-fifth** – my birthday! When's your birthday?
A Oh mine's not until October. What year were you born?
B **1999**.
A We're the same age!
B But we're not twins! What's your exact date of birth?
A **17 – 10 – 99** (The seventeenth of the tenth, ninety-nine.)
B Sorry! What was that?
A I was born on **the seventeenth of the tenth, nineteen ninety-nine**.
B Ah! And do you know what time you were born?
A Yeah, just after midnight. What about you?
B I've got no idea what time I was born.

2 🔊 **3.12** Explain that there are two ways of saying dates in British English. Read the conversation as a class. Write another date on the board, e.g. *May 17*. Elicit the two ways of saying it, underlining the use of *the* each time: *the seventeenth of May/May the seventeenth*. Elicit the two ways of saying *3 February*. Put students in pairs to practise saying the rest of the dates in exercise 2. Monitor and help. Give students time to get the form right before playing the recording.

Play the recording, pausing after each pair of dates. Ask students to listen and check. Be prepared to drill the two ways of saying the dates if students have problems.

Unit 3 • Good news, bad news! 53

> **Answers and audioscript**
>
> 🔊 **3.12 Days and months**
> 1 the third of February
>   February the third
> 2 the sixth of July
>   July the sixth
> 3 the twelfth of June
>   June the twelfth
> 4 the twenty-fifth of December
>   December the twenty-fifth
> 5 the sixteenth of August
>   August the sixteenth
> 6 the first of May
>   May the first
> 7 the thirteenth of January
>   January the thirteenth
> 8 the thirty-first of October
>   October the thirty-first

3 🔊 **3.13** American English has a different convention for dates – the month, not the day, is usually given first, e.g. 8/21/12 – *August twenty-first two thousand twelve*. Note that it is normal in American English to omit *the* before the day and *and* in the year in dates like these. Explain to students that dates are said differently in American and British English. See if students know which of the dates from exercise 2 are British and which are American. Play the recording through once and elicit any differences students noticed. Play the recording again if necessary.

Go through the differences with the class, writing the examples from the script on the board if necessary.

> **Answers**
> Americans don't use 'the' before the date and they say the month first.

> 🔊 **3.13 American dates**
> February third
> July sixth
> June twelfth
> December twenty-fifth
> August sixteenth
> May first
> January thirteenth
> October thirty-first

4 Elicit the two ways of reading the first year (*twenty twelve* and *two thousand and twelve*). Put students in pairs to continue the task. Monitor and check carefully. Highlight any problems during the checking stage. Be prepared to drill the correct forms if necessary.

> **Answers**
> twenty twelve/two thousand and twelve
> two thousand and two
> twenty eighteen/two thousand and eighteen
> twenty twenty-five/two thousand and twenty-five
> nineteen eighty
> nineteen sixty-nine
> nineteen ninety-four
> eighteen forty-eight

5 🔊 **3.14** This listening task checks comprehension of dates and years in context. Tell students they are going to hear five short conversations, each containing a date.

Pre-teach *land on the moon, wedding anniversary,* and *expiry date* /ɪkˈspaɪəri/.

Play number 1 as an example and elicit the date. Play the rest of the recording, pausing after each exchange. Then check the answers with the class, correcting any mistakes. Highlight how the *expiry date* is said in the final conversation as this is different from the others, but the most common convention (and similar to the way we give a date of birth as the students heard in exercise 1). As an extension, put students in pairs to work out the two different ways of saying the dates in conversations 1–4.

> **Answers and audioscript**
>
> 🔊 **3.14 Important dates**
> 1 When did man first land on the moon?
>   On **July the twentieth, 1969**.
> 2 When's your wedding anniversary?
>   **November the eighth**.
> 3 When did the Berlin Wall come down?
>   **The ninth of November, 1989**.
> 4 When was your son born?
>   **December the nineteenth, 2014**.
> 5 What's the expiry date on your credit card?
>   **06 25**

Time expressions

6 Students now focus on the prepositions we use in time expressions. Elicit the answers to the first two expressions as examples. Students work individually to complete the time expressions. Monitor and check how well students do the exercise and find out how confident they feel about their choices, i.e. whether they know any rules or patterns to apply. You could let them check their answers in pairs before checking the answers with the whole class.

Tell students that we use *at* with times, e.g. *at six o'clock*. Put students in pairs and ask them to work out rules for the use of *in* and *on*, and when to use *no preposition*. Monitor and help.

When they have worked out most of the rules or if they have too much difficulty, ask students to turn to Grammar reference 3.4 on p144 where these are shown in a table.

> **Answers**
> 1 at six o'clock   9 in 2015
> 2 – last night   10 at the weekend
> 3 in the evening   11 on January 18
> 4 in the 1960s   12 – the other day
> 5 on Saturday   13 on Monday morning
> 6 in April   14 – yesterday evening
> 7 in summer   15 – two weeks ago
> 8 – this morning   16 at midnight

NB: in American English the weekend is often preceded by *on*, not *at* = *on the weekend*.

Talking about you

7 Give an example of a national holiday from your country, e.g. *Christmas Day is the 25th of December*. Put students in pairs, ideally with learners of different nationalities to tell each other the dates of national holidays. Note that some religious holidays do not have a fixed date – Easter and Ramadan, for example, are different every year.

Elicit examples from the class, building up a list on the board. As well as the date, encourage students to give further information about the origin of the holiday or what commonly happens on that day. If students are interested in the subject of national holidays, you could develop the topic into a mini-project in which students research the holidays of a country other than their own and present their findings to the class. Students could create posters with visuals and short texts, or presentations which could be uploaded onto the school website or VLE (Virtual Learning Environment).

8 Write on the board three dates that are important to you. Elicit from the class how to say them and see if they can guess their significance: e.g. *your birthday, your parents' wedding anniversary, the date you graduated*, etc. Give students time to write their own dates and then put them in pairs to guess each other's dates. Monitor and help as necessary. Elicit examples from the students in a whole-class feedback session. Students report on their partner's important dates.

9 Focus attention on the question *When did you last … ?* and the example answer and follow-up questions. Ask the same question to a few students and elicit a range of answers. Ask the follow-up questions to get more information.

Put students in small groups and get them to continue asking and answering the questions from the prompts in the list. Monitor and check for accurate use of the prepositions and time expressions. Remind them to use follow-up questions to continue their conversations.

Elicit what were the most popular activities and any interesting information they found out in their groups.

Additional material

For teachers

Photocopiable activity – Communication: *Guess when …* pp183–4

For students

Online Practice – *Look again*

Workbook p23, exercises 1–2

Online Practice – *Practice*

Writing   SB p38

Picture stories – narrative writing

Position of adverbs and adjectives

The aim of this writing section is to focus on the use and position of adverbs and adjectives in telling a story. It also provides recycling of the Past Simple and Past Continuous.

1 Students begin with an exercise similar to exercise 5 on p36 on the position of adverbs. This time they are also given adjectives to place in the sentences. Do sentence number 1 together with the class as an example. Students work individually to complete the task and then check their answers with a partner. Go through the answers with the class.

Answers

1 A large dog suddenly jumped up at me./Suddenly, a large dog jumped up at me.
2 Thank you for your kind invitation. Unfortunately I can't come./I can't come, unfortunately.
3 I got out of bed and went downstairs to make a nice cup of tea.
4 We had a lovely meal and then we went to the theatre.
5 I was sitting at home last Thursday evening when something very strange happened./Last Thursday evening, I was sitting at home when something very strange happened.
6 He's got three older sisters and I've got three older sisters, too.
7 There's an interesting programme on TV tonight that I very much want to see./There's an interesting programme on TV tonight that I want to see very much.
8 I worked really hard all last week./Last week, I worked really hard.

2 Pre-teach/Check the word *portrait*. Focus attention on the story title, *Aunt Camilla's* /kəˈmɪləz/ *Portrait* and the picture story. Put students in pairs to predict the story just from the pictures. Keep this stage fairly short.

Now, go through the story prompts which relate to each picture and pre-teach/check any new words used in the story, e.g. *hurry, refuse, order*. Elicit or point out that the story needs to be written in the past, using Past Simple and Past Continuous where necessary.

Give students in their pairs time to write the story. Monitor carefully and help them to self-correct errors.

When they are ready, invite students to read their stories to the class. If the class is large, make groups of three pairs and ask them to tell each other their stories and compare what is the same and what is different.

3 Finally, students turn to p154 and read the story there. Give them time in their pairs to discuss the differences between their own story and the one in the book. Elicit differences from pairs of students in whole-class feedback. Deal with any vocabulary from the story which may be new to the students, e.g. *furious, generously*. You could point out that *and they all lived happily ever after* is a common convention for ending fairy-tale stories.

4 Students have a second opportunity to write a picture story based upon the pictures on p155 *The burglar who fell asleep*. This time, the prompts to help them with their writing are much briefer. This allows students autonomy in choosing how to write the story.

Instruct them to use as many adjectives and adverbs as they can in their stories. Monitor and assist if students do the writing task in class, but if there isn't time in the lesson, you may need them to do this writing task as homework.

When the stories are finished, put students in pairs and ask them to read each other's stories. Give them time to discuss what is the same and what is different about their stories. Finally, students turn to p156 and read the news story there. Elicit what differences there are between this version and the ones they've written. Go through any vocabulary queries relating to this story e.g. *luxurious*.

If possible, take students' stories in for marking and encourage them to write a clean final draft, incorporating corrections, which can be displayed on the classroom wall so all the members of the class can read each others' work.

Additional material

For students

Online Practice – *Practice*

Workbook p23, *Review*, exercises 1–3

Online Practice – *Check your progress*

4 Food for thought

Introduction to the unit

The theme of this unit is food, with the engaging topics of supertasters and cultural differences in food names.

The first *Grammar* section aims to help students talk about food using correct expressions of quantity – *much/many/some/any*, etc. This is extended to include pronouns with *some/any/no/every*, e.g. *someone, anywhere, everything, nobody*, etc.

The focus of the second *Grammar* section is on the definite and indefinite articles: *the, a, an,* and zero article, and article use in common phrases such as *go home*.

The skills focus in the *Reading and speaking* section is on reading for specific information in a jigsaw reading activity and sharing information orally in groups. The topic is food-related and allows for the extension of the grammar in context.

The *Vocabulary and listening* focus also extends the grammar with work on how to say quantities of different types of food – *a bag of crisps, bottle of milk, can of Coke*, etc., and common non-food items: *a bunch of flowers, a box of matches*, etc. Students listen for gist and specific information – items bought and prices.

In the *Everyday English* section, students consolidate and extend their use of expressions of quantity and articles in the context of a dinner party. Here the main focus is on polite phrases, with an emphasis on making polite requests with *Can/Could I … ; Would you mind … + -ing*; and *Could I/you possibly … . Borrow* and *lend* are also recycled from Unit 1.

In the *Writing* section, students become aware of how adjectives can make a postcard more interesting. They write and 'send' each other postcards using interesting adjectives.

Language aims

Grammar

Expressions of quantity

Students review countable and uncountable nouns in the context of food in preparation to learn about expressions of quantity in positive and negative statements and questions, and also in offers and requests. They extend the use of *some/any/every/no* in an exercise, combining these with *thing, one/body* and *where*.

Articles

This section uses a discovery approach to identify the rules for articles *a/an/the* and zero article in a text. Students are asked to notice the exceptions to the rules in the common expressions *by bus, have lunch, go to bed*. This section also asks students to find and correct mistakes as an introduction to being able to edit their own work.

Vocabulary

A piece of cake

This section extends students' ability to talk about quantity. Students match amounts such as *a bag of, a piece of* to the things they collocate with (e.g. *crisps, cake*). The exercises focus on learning the collocations, personalizing them, and then practising in context.

Everyday English

Can you come for dinner?

This section brings the grammar and vocabulary strands together on the topic of eating and drinking. Students learn phrases for making and responding to polite requests first in relation to dining, then in a variety of contexts. The expressions *Can I/you …* and *Could I/you …* form the basis for the requests, with the even more polite forms *Could I/you possibly … ?* and *Would you mind + -ing* also being introduced and practised in a freer practice activity.

Additional material

Workbook

Students complete activities to help internalize the concept of countable and uncountable nouns in English, which may contrast with students' own languages. This is extended into using nouns that can be both countable and uncountable in English, before more focused work on more expressions of quantity. Then students continue working on pronouns with *some-/any-/no-* and *every-*. There is a set of exercises on the use of articles, and a text on an aspect of British culture to use them in context. Students also practise using common expressions like *a piece of … , a bottle of …* , etc. The unit finishes with further practice of invitations and offers, and a Grammar review.

After Unit 4 there is the first of the three *Stop and check* tests, which covers the Grammar and Vocabulary content in Units 1–4.

Photocopiable activities

There are photocopiable activities to review grammar (*Snakes and ladders*), vocabulary (*What do you need?*), and communication (*Can I get anyone a drink?*) at the back of the Teacher's Guide as well as on the Teacher's Resource Centre. There is also a worksheet to accompany the video on the Teacher's Resource Centre.

Notes on the unit

Unit opener page
Choose from these activities to engage your students with the topic and target language of this unit:
- Talk about the title
- Talk about the unit goals (*Grammar, Vocabulary, …*)
- Talk about the photo
- Watch the video
- Look at the bottom banner
- Do the activity

Refer students to the unit title, 'Food for thought'. Ask students what they think the title means (something that you think carefully/seriously about). Give an example: *That film about how plastic is killing fish in the ocean really gave me food for thought. I will try not to use so much plastic in future.* Ask students if they have any similar expressions in their language.

Refer students to the photo and elicit the food items. Students could also do this in pairs using a bilingual dictionary. Check and drill pronunciation: *chilli* /ˈtʃɪli/, *pecan* /pɪˈkæn; ˈpiːkən/, *fish/sardines, onions, lettuce* /ˈletɪs/, *spinach* /ˈspɪnɪtʃ/, *coffee, ginger* /ˈdʒɪndʒə(r)/, *saffron* /ˈsæfrən/, *almond* /ˈɑːmənd/, *egg, garlic, avocado* /ˌævəˈkɑːdəʊ/, *broccoli* /ˈbrɒkəli/, *star anise* /ˌstɑːr ˈænɪs/. Find out who thinks they could make a meal with some of the ingredients in the photo. Ask them what they would cook.

If you don't have time to watch the video introduction to the unit, go through the unit goals below the title: *Grammar, Vocabulary, Everyday English, Listening, Reading, Writing*. Give examples or use translation for unknown words.

Video (2 minutes approximately): The video gives a step-by-step overview of the unit. Play the video, pausing where necessary – especially for students to answer any questions, e.g. *What are your favourite foods?* This makes it a more interactive experience. Highlight the option of practising online.

As shown in the bottom banner, don't forget that there are many exercises to consolidate and practise the target language of the unit in the Workbook as well as online. There are links to these exercises on the relevant pages of the Student's Book and they can be done in class time or you can set them for homework.

Summary: If you're short of time, use the title and the photo to help students understand and engage with the topic, and then move straight on to the activity so that they can discuss the theme in more detail. If you have any more time, try to watch the video together. It is a clear and interesting introduction to the different parts of the unit.

Notes for activity:
Put students in pairs. Ask them to look at the photo and discuss their answers to the questions. Ask them to justify their choices where possible.

> **Suggested answers**
> 1 Healthy. They include egg, broccoli, avocado, onion, spinach, ginger, garlic, chillies, almonds.
> 2 Students' own answers.
> 3 The food types in the picture are all good for the brain.

Grammar SB p40
Expressions of quantity
Possible problems
Students at Pre-intermediate level will be familiar with a number of expressions of quantity, but they are still likely to make mistakes, especially in freer speaking. There are several issues related to correct use of expressions of quantity.

1 **Countable and uncountable nouns**
   Students may need help to understand that some nouns can be both countable and uncountable, depending on the context in which they are used:
   - *Two teas, please.* (countable and meaning 'two cups of tea')
   - *Tea is horrible.* (uncountable and meaning 'tea in general')

   Some uncountable nouns in English may be countable in other languages and cause mistakes such as:
   *I eat many bread. (Correction: *I eat a lot of bread.*)
   *We bought some furnitures. (Correction: *We bought some furniture.*)
   *I like a lot of city in my country. (Correction: *I like a lot of cities in my country.*)

2 **Expressions of quantity used with countable and uncountable nouns:**
   – *some/any*
   The rule that *some* is used in positive sentences and *any* in questions and negatives is useful as a guide.
   This unit extends the rule to cover the use of *something/anything*, etc., with practice exercises on p42.
   – *some* in requests and offers
   The use of *some* in questions that are requests, e.g. *Can I have some coffee?* and offers, e.g. *Would you like some wine?* might seem confusing, so the use of L1 might help to clarify this.
   – *much/many, a lot/lots of, a few/a little*
   The key areas that students might find confusing are:
   much + uncountable nouns in questions and negatives
   many + countable nouns in questions and negatives
   In positive sentences we usually use *a lot of/lots of* with both countable and uncountable nouns, e.g.
   *He has a lot of friends. NOT **many friends*
   *They have lots of money. NOT **much money*
   A lot of/Lots of is also used in questions and negatives.
   A few/A little could also cause confusion:
   a few + countable nouns, e.g. *a few friends*
   a little + uncountable nouns, e.g. *a little milk*

> **STARTER** SB p40
> This *Starter* introduces the topic of food by asking students to discuss their food choices and preferences. Introduce the unit by referring students to the photos of food. Elicit the names of the foods, but don't focus on them for too long at this point, as students will be doing more with them in exercise 2.
> 1 Ask students to work alone to make a list of what they ate and drank the day before. They can share their lists with a partner before sharing with the rest of the class. You could input some amount words at this point, e.g. *a cup of coffee, some toast,* but as this is a warmer, keep it light and quick.

Unit 4 • Food for thought   57

2 Refer students to the questions and check understanding of *healthiest, sweet, flavours,* and *spicy*. Elicit examples (e.g. healthy foods – fruit and vegetables; sweet things – candy, ice cream, sugar; strong flavours; spicy foods – chillies, curry). If there is time, ask some students follow-up questions: *What do you think makes a healthy diet? What sweet things do you like to eat?*, etc.

She's a supertaster

About the text

The text gives information about a real job in the food industry to help revise countable and uncountable nouns. Many companies employ supertasters to test their products. About a quarter of the population can be considered supertasters. The concept of special food for babies is relatively new. In the past, parents fed their babies soft foods or used a grinder to grind up whatever they were eating.

1 Refer students to the picture in the text to elicit *tongue* /tʌŋ/. Check pronunciation. Ask students if they know what the little bumps are called on the tongue (*taste buds*) and what they are there for.

Ask students to read the text and answer the questions. Check the answers. Ask if any of the students think they are supertasters. Find out if students think their tastes have changed as they have got older.

Answers
1 She eats baby food to test it for a company that makes it.
2 Because she is a supertaster – she has more taste buds on her tongue than most people.
3 Things with very strong flavours, including alcohol.

2 Ask students to match the nouns in the boxes to the pictures A–R. Drill the pronunciation of the foods. Check that *vegetables* has three syllables: /ˈvedʒtəblz/, and that *chocolate* has two: /ˈtʃɒklət/.

Ask them which set of words is countable and which is uncountable. Point out that all of the countable nouns in the box are plural. If possible, show students how to look in their dictionaries to find if a word is countable or not. Many dictionaries use a U for uncountable and a C for countable.

Answers
A	coffee	J	spices
B	sprouts	K	broccoli
C	milk	L	sugar
D	sweets	M	vegetables
E	a glass of white wine	N	peas
F	water	O	olives
G	chocolate	P	chillies
H	spinach	Q	taste buds
I	red wine	R	baby food

The box on the left is **Countable** and the box on the right is **Uncountable**.

EXTRA IDEA Give students three to five small slips of paper. Ask them to write down a food item on each. Collect these up into a 'hat'. Put students in teams of three. On a piece of paper each team draws a table with two columns labelled *countable* and *uncountable*. Take a slip out of the hat and read the food. Teams write the food in the correct column on their paper. Repeat as time allows. Check answers. The team with the most right 'wins'.

3 🔊 **4.1** As a lead-in to the activity, ask students if they have any questions they would ask Abbie /ˈæbi/. Put them in pairs to complete the interview. How many of their questions did they find? Play the recording so that students can check their answers. Put students in pairs to practise interviewing and answering the questions. Pairs swap roles so that each has a turn to be the interviewer and Abbie. Feedback on pronunciation issues, including intonation in asking the questions.

Answers and audioscript

🔊 **4.1 The baby food taster**

1 I How much **baby food** do you eat in a day?
A Quite a lot! About 500 spoonfuls. But they're small spoons!
2 I How many **taste buds** do you have?
A A lot! About 10–15,000 – the same as most babies.
3 I At home, do you eat a lot of **vegetables**?
A Yes, I love **peas**! But I only eat a little **broccoli** and **spinach**, and I can only eat a few **sprouts**.
4 I Do you drink any **coffee**?
A No, I drink tea, and lots of **water** to clean my taste buds.
5 I And do you drink much **milk?**
A I can only drink a little milk – it tastes like cream to me!
6 I Did you eat many **sweets** as a child?
A No, I don't like many sweet things, but I enjoy a little **chocolate**, if there isn't much sugar in it.
7 I Do you use any hot **spices** in your cooking?
A No, I don't and obviously, I don't eat any **chillies** – they're too hot for a lot of people!
8 I And do you drink any alcohol?
A Yes, I drink some. I don't drink any red **wine**, but I have a **glass** of **white** wine sometimes. But definitely no beer! Bleurgh!

GRAMMAR SPOT SB p41

1 Ask students why the interviewer asked *How much baby food …?*, but *How many taste buds …?* If students don't know, ask them which is countable and which is uncountable to see if they can figure it out. Refer them to the *Grammar spot* and go through exercise 1 together. First, students look at the groups A, B, and C. They write *plural countable, uncountable,* or *both* in the correct spaces at the top of the table. Ask students to find examples of each in the dialogue in exercise 3. They could highlight the examples in different colours, e.g. yellow for countable, green for uncountable, blue for both, or if they don't have highlighters, they could use the convention underline, double underline, circle.

Answers
Plural countable nouns = B
Uncountable nouns = A
Both = C

2 Read exercise 2 together. Give students one minute to correct the sentences. They should write one positive statement and one negative statement. Ask fast finishers to see if they can write a question for each. Write the correct sentences on the board.

Answers
There aren't many books in my bag. OR There are a lot of books in my bag.
There isn't much homework tonight. OR There's a lot of homework tonight.

Concept check with questions like: *Which can be plural: countable or uncountable nouns?* (countable)

Which do we use with uncountable nouns in questions and negatives? (much)

When do we use many? (with countable nouns in questions and negatives)

3 Give some examples of a request to ensure students understand what a request is (e.g. *Could I borrow your pen?*). Ask students why they think we use *any* in a question, but *some* in a request. Turn to the Grammar reference on p145, and ask students to read numbers 1, 2, and 3 under the section on *some* and *any*.

Answer
Can I have some orange juice? = a request

Tell students they can read about countable/uncountable nouns, *much/many*, *a few/a little*, and *a lot/lots of* in the Grammar reference on p145.

SUGGESTION On opposite sides of the board, write *some* and *any*. Students close their books. Read one of the sentences from the Grammar reference, but leave out *some/any*. Ask students to point to and say the word that goes into the sentence:

Teacher: *I'd like _____ eggs.*
Students: *some.*

Talking about you

4 Students work alone to write things they do and don't eat and drink.

5 Tell students to work in groups and ask each other questions. Model the question and answer activity: ask a student *Do you eat much … ?* Ensure the student gives a complete answer: *Yes, I eat a lot of … / No, I don't eat much …*, etc. Do this several times before putting students in groups of three to ask and answer questions. They shouldn't show each other their lists.

6 Students continue working in their groups to discuss the questions. Ask one student to be the group leader. The group leader reads the questions to the group and ensures everyone gets a chance to speak. Elicit a range of responses from groups in feedback.

Practice SB p42

Discussing grammar

1 This exercise gives students more controlled practice using expressions of quantity. This could be completed for homework if class time is short. When checking, ensure students understand why the answer is correct:

Teacher: *Why 'any'?*
Students: *Olives is a countable noun.*
Teacher: *Why 'some cake'?*
Students: *Because it's a request.*

This will help fix these rules in the students' mind and will also support students who are struggling with this grammar point.

Answers
1 1 any   4 any
   2 some   5 some
   3 some
2 1 much   4 many
   2 many   5 much
   3 much
3 1 a few   4 a few
   2 a lot of   5 a little
   3 a little

something/someone/somewhere

2 🔊 4.2 This section focuses on the compounds formed with *some, any, every,* and *no*. This is a logical extension, as the rules for *somebody/anybody*, etc. are the same for *some* and *any*. Before asking students to do this exercise, you could refer them to the Grammar reference on p145 to read rule number 4 under *some and any*, which deals with *someone, anything, anybody, somewhere,* etc.

Point out that *someone* and *somebody* mean the same. Do the first one together to ensure students understand what to do, then ask students to complete the exercise and compare answers in pairs.

Play the recording so that students can check their answers. Remind them that any of the *-one* answers can be replaced with *-body* and vice versa. Point out that *someone, everything*, etc. are all one word (not: *some one*). Play the recording again if needed. Put students in pairs to read and practise the conversations. Monitor and check for good pronunciation. Play the recording again if needed to draw attention to how the people sound, paying special attention to the intonation of the questions. Re-pair students if needed so they can practise both parts again. If allowed, ask students to record the conversations and listen back to check their own pronunciation and intonation.

Answers and audioscript

🔊 **4.2 *something, someone, somewhere***
1 A Did you meet **anyone** nice at the party?
  B Yes. I met **someone** who knows you!
2 A Ooh! I think I've got **something** in my eye!
  B Let me look. No, I can't see **anything**.
3 A Let's go **somewhere** hot for our holidays!
  B Fine. But we can't afford to go **anywhere** too expensive.
4 A Where are my glasses? I can't find them **anywhere**!
  B What are those on top of your head?
5 A What a wonderful party! **Everyone** had a great time.
  B I know. **No one** wanted to go home!
6 A Did you buy **anything** nice in the sales?
  B No, **nothing**. I couldn't find **anything** I liked.

🔊 4.3 This exercise gives students further contextualized practice. Read the instructions to the students and check they have understood what to do. Use the example dialogue to model the activity. Play the recording, pausing after each sentence so that students can say the complete sentence. Play the complete sentence so that students can repeat in chorus.

Unit 4 • Food for thought   59

Answers and audioscript

4.3 *something and nothing*
1 Do you know **anyone** famous?
2 The fridge is empty. There's **nothing** to eat!
3 There are no lights on. There's **nobody** at home.
4 Cintia's a lovely girl. **Everyone** likes her.
5 I don't like this café. Let's go **somewhere** else.
6 We're bored! There's **nothing** to do!
7 Hello? Is **anybody** at home?
8 You're quiet. Haven't you got **anything** to say?
9 Aaargh! I can't find my keys **anywhere**!
10 Help! Has **anyone** seen my keys?

Additional material
For students
Online Practice – *Look again*
Workbook pp24–6, exercises 1–9
Online Practice – *Practice*

The secret to a long life SB p42

Articles – *a/an, the*

Possible problems

1 By Pre-intermediate level, students are likely to have studied aspects of article usage, but will not be completely familiar with the main rules for *a/an, the*, or no article. They are likely to make mistakes in speaking and writing.
Articles will pose problems for students at this level, so they need a lot of practice. You might point out that we can make some words countable by adding the amount word, e.g. *two heads of broccoli; three bars of chocolate*. Students will learn some of these in the vocabulary section later in the unit.

2 Common mistakes students make are:
– *the* with uncountable nouns when talking in general:
*The water is important for the life. (Correction: *Water is important for life.*)
– Omission of articles:
*She lived in big house. (Correction: *She lived in a big house.*)
*She's teacher. (Correction: *She's a teacher.*)
– Wrong choice of article for first reference:
*We live in the small apartment. There is the park near my school. (Correction: *We live in a small apartment. There is a park near my school.*)
– Use of the article before some places and forms of transport:
*I go to the work at 9.00 a.m. (Correction: *I go to work at 9.00 a.m.*)
*Do you travel by the train? (Correction: *Do you travel by train?*)

This section continues the theme of food, but in relation to a long life with a profile of someone's grandfather.

1 Refer students to the photo of the grandfather on p43 of the Student's Book. Ask them how old they think he is. Read the questions in exercise 1 as a class and elicit a range of responses. You could find out if anyone knows who the oldest living person is.

2 **4.4** Ask students if they have ever tried traditional fish and chips and what they think of it. If necessary, give a brief description of the dish (white fish covered with batter – a mixture of flour, eggs, and milk – and then deep fried and served with chips). Although now not considered very healthy, fish and chips used to be seen as England's national dish.
Pre-teach/Check *shopkeeper, industrial, whole, contented,* and *to retire*. Give students time to read the questions. Play the recording and get students to follow the text in the Student's Book. Students check their answers in pairs before checking as a class. Ask students if they agree with the grandfather's secret to his long life.

Answers
1 He lived 101 years.
2 He lived in an old village near a big, industrial town in the North of England.
3 He had a fish and chip shop.
4 He had two children.
5 Because he was a happy and contented man.
6 He stopped work when was 78.
7 A glass of whisky before going to bed and lots of fish and chips.

4.4 See SB p42.

GRAMMAR SPOT SB p43

1 Read the first two sentences of the text again and elicit the first example (He was ⓐ shopkeeper). Ask students to read the rest of the text again and highlight or underline all the definite and indefinite articles, using different coloured highlighters if possible, or underline/circle.

Answers
My grandfather lived until he was 101 years old. He was ⓐ shopkeeper. He had ⓐ fish and chip shop in ⓐn old village near **a** big, industrial town in **the** North of England. He had ⓐ son and ⓐ daughter. **The** daughter is my mother. The family lived above **the** shop.
In those days, fish and chips was **the** most popular dish in **the** whole country. My grandfather made **the** best fish and chips in **the** area. People came to **the** village by bus especially to get them.
Everybody loved my grandfather because he was such ⓐ happy and contented man. He worked hard, but once ⓐ week he closed **the** shop and went to have lunch (not fish and chips!) with friends in **the** local pub. He didn't retire until he was 78 years old. He said that **the** secret to ⓐ long life was ⓐ glass of whisky before going to bed and lots of fish and chips.

2 Read the examples with the class. Elicit what is special about them (there is no article before the nouns).

3 Refer students to Grammar reference 4.2 on p145. Give them time to read the rules and then ask concept check questions to check understanding: *Which is used to refer to something for the first time?* (*a/an*); *When the speaker and listener know the thing or idea already, which do we use?* (*the*); etc. Ask students to find examples of rules for definite, indefinite, and no article in the text. Give an example: *He was a shopkeeper – use a with professions*. Elicit a range of examples.

Suggested answers

first reference:
a shopkeeper; a fish and chip shop; an old village; a big, industrial town; a son; a daughter; a happy and contented man; a long life; a glass of whisky

speaker and listener know the thing or idea already:
the daughter; the shop; the village; the shop; the local pub

only one of something:
the North; the whole country; the area; the secret

with superlative adjectives
the most popular dish; the best fish and chips

with expressions of quantity
once a week

before plural and uncountable nouns when talking about things in general
fish and chips

before some places and with some forms of transport
by bus; to bed

before meals
have lunch

Practice SB p43

Reading aloud

1 🔊 **4.5** Complete the first couple of sentences together, then ask students to complete the rest of the exercise in pairs. Monitor and refer students to the rules in the Grammar reference if needed. Play the recording for them to check answers. Play the recording again and ask students to repeat after each sentence. Put students in pairs to take it in turns to read the sentences as a way of consolidation.

Answers and audioscript

🔊 **4.5 My grandfather**
My grandfather was **a** shopkeeper.
He lived in **the** North of England.
He had a fish and chip shop in **an** old village.
His family lived above **the** shop.
He made **the** best fish and chips in the area.
Some people came by bus to the shop.
He closed the shop once **a** week.
He went to have lunch with friends.
He liked to have **a** little whisky before bed.

2 In this exercise, students need to think about the rules for articles. Elicit the answers to number 1 as an example and ask the students to give the rule. Students complete the exercise, looking back at the Grammar reference if needed. Pair up students who are struggling. Student A completes the even numbers and Student B completes the odd numbers. Ask fast finishers to find the rules. When checking as a class, ask students which rule they used to get the right answer.

Answers
1 a, a, The, the
2 a, an
3 –, –,
4 –, –
5 A, –, the
6 a, the
7 a, the, –,
8 the, a

Check it

This exercise helps students become better editors of their own and other students' work, which leads to more student autonomy. Do the first together as an example. Students work in pairs to find the mistakes. Discuss why they are wrong, and correct them. Again, students can refer to the Grammar reference if needed.

Answers
1 He's a postman, so he has breakfast at 5.00 a.m.
2 Love is more important than money.
3 I come to school by bike.
4 I'm reading a good book at the moment.
5 'Where are the children?' 'They're in the garden.'
6 I live in the centre of town, near the hospital.
7 My parents bought a lovely house in the country.
8 I don't eat cake because I don't like sweet things.

EXTRA IDEA If your students need more practice on the contrast between no article for talking about things in general, and the definite article for talking about specific things, write the following examples on the board and elicit why the article is or isn't used:

I think ice cream *is delicious.* (ice cream in general)
The ice cream *in this café is delicious.* (one specific type of ice cream)

Write these words on the board and ask students to write pairs of sentences to highlight the article use: *money, love, chocolate, cats, life*.

Additional material
For teachers
Photocopiable activity – Grammar: *Snakes and ladders* pp185–6
For students
Online Practice – *Look again*
Workbook pp26–7, exercises 10–15
Online Practice – *Practice*

Reading and speaking SB p44

Recipes for success

About the text

The three texts give information about the origin of food items that are very well-known today. Popsicles (ice lollies in the UK), chips (crisps in the UK), and chocolate chip cookies were all 'discovered' by accident. All of these foods were invented in different parts of the US, but were so popular that they are now sold all over the world. None of the inventors became rich from their inventions, though Mary Wakefield, the 'inventor' of the chocolate chip cookies, did get a lifetime supply of chocolate for giving her recipe to Nestlé.

Where possible, encourage students to use the context to guess new vocabulary. Some vocabulary you might want to check or pre-teach includes: *powder, stick, frozen, patent, fussy, fork, fried, baked, recipe, supply, cookie dough*.

1 Read the questions and elicit responses. Ask for a show of hands to see how many students prefer each food.
2 Tell students that all of these foods were invented by accident. Model the activity by asking a student to guess what the accident was, using one of the sentence frames on the page. Put students in pairs to make their guesses. Ask some students for their ideas in feedback.

Unit 4 • Food for thought

3 Put students into three groups: A, B, and C. With a larger class, you may have more than one A, B, C group. Each group reads the specified text and answers the questions. Make sure each person takes notes. Monitor to support the groups as they work.

4 Regroup the students into groups of three so that each new group has someone from group A, B, and C. They share their answers with each other. Ask students which of the stories is their favourite. Did any of the students guess the accident correctly (from exercise 2)? If students wish, they can read the other stories for homework.

Answers
Group A
1 Popsicles in the US, ice lollies in the UK.
2 Frank Epperson, in 1905 in San Francisco.
3 He left a drink made with water and flavoured powder outside, with a stick in it – it froze overnight.
4 Frank's friends.
5 They liked them.
6 No, because he sold the patent. The Popsicles company is now successful as a result.
7 2 billion per year are sold in the US.

Group B
1 Potato chips in the US, crisps in the UK.
2 George Crum, 1853, Saratoga Springs in New York State.
3 A customer in the restaurant where Crum was working as a chef, sent some fried potato chips back to the kitchen, complaining they were too thick. He made thinner ones – they were also sent back. He made them even thinner and they were then hard and crisp and impossible to eat with a fork.
4 The complaining customer.
5 He loved them.
6 No – he never got a patent for them and others saw an opportunity to make money. *Lays* is now a successful company as a result.
7 Over $1.5 billion worth of crisps every year.

Group C
1 Cookies in the US, biscuits in the UK.
2 Mary Wakefield, in the 1930s, in Massachusetts, US.
3 She was making some chocolate cookies, but she didn't have any baking chocolate, so she broke up some ordinary Nestlé's chocolate instead and put it into the mixture. The chocolate didn't melt enough and there were still pieces of it in the cookies.
4 Mary and her hotel guests.
5 Mary thought they were delicious and her guests agreed.
6 After Mary published the recipe in a local newspaper.
7 No – but she received a lifetime's supply of chocolate. Nestlé's started making bags of chocolate chips for people to bake with and they made a lot of money out of it.
8 3.5 billion are sold in the US every year.

5 This activity is a contextualized grammar practice. Seeing the grammar in context helps students understand when to use it. Students complete the sentences. If you have slower working students, put them into a group and ask each to complete either 1, 2, or 3. Check answers with students reading out their sentences.

Answers
1 –, a, the, the, the, an
2 –, some, the, –/some
3 some/–, any, The, the, –/some

Talking about you

6 The aim of this activity is fluency rather than accuracy. It provides an engaging way for students to share their stories. If they can't think of any times when something went wrong, ask them to invent a story, then the class can guess if the story is true or not. Give students time to think about their story and take notes. Less confident students can practise telling their story with a partner before sharing in a bigger group.

7 Regroup students so they can tell their story again to give them extra speaking practice. As a follow-up, ask them if they felt more confident telling their story the second (or third) time.

EXTRA IDEA Ask students to go online to find out if there are any more examples of foods (or other things) invented by accident. They share what they learned in the next lesson.

VIDEO In this unit students can watch a video about healthy and unhealthy foods, and how they are made. You can play the video clip on the Classroom Presentation Tool or download it from the Teacher's Resource Centre together with the video script, video worksheet, and accompanying teacher's notes. These notes give full guidance on how to use the worksheets and include a comprehensive answer key to the exercises and activities.

Additional material
For teachers
Photocopiable activity – Video worksheet: *What's good for you?*

For students
Online Practice – *Look again*
Online Practice – *Practice*

Vocabulary and listening SB p46

A piece of cake

Possible problems
Collocations
Sometimes amounts can be confusing due to different packaging in different countries. For example, we often say a *bottle or carton of milk*, though today milk generally comes in *jugs* in the US, or even *boxes* in the case of UHT milk. You may need to point out that, as with all collocations, some word combinations simply don't sound right in English (e.g. we wouldn't say *a slice of fresh tuna*), whereas others do (e.g. we would say *a slice of ham*).

Names and types of shop
Students may query the use of *'s* in words like *chemist's* and *newsagent's*. Explain that this means the *chemist's shop*, *newsagent's shop*, but we don't need to say the word *shop*.

This section focuses on collocations (amounts and packaging) to extend students' vocabulary. The vocabulary is contextualized in the conversations where people go into shops to buy different items.

1 🔊 4.6 Refer students to the heading, *A piece of cake,* and elicit a description, e.g. *Is it square or triangular or either? Do you prefer a big piece of cake or a small one? What's another way to say 'piece of cake'?* (*slice*). Tell students that the expression, *It's a piece of cake* means *It's easy*. At the

62 Unit 4 • Food for thought

end of the exercise, find out if students thought it was a piece of cake.

Refer students to the photo of a shopping trolley. How many of the items in the trolley can they identify?

Put students in small groups to match the amounts in A with the things in B. Some amounts in A will be used more than once.

Play the recording so that students can check their answers. Point out that *a* and *of* are not stressed and are hard to hear, but the other words are stressed and sound clearer: *a bag of crisps* /əˈbægəvˈkrɪsps/. Tell students that small words such as *a* and *of* are usually unstressed and sound like /ə/. Write the symbol on the board and tell students that this sound is called the *schwa*. Tell students to try to imitate this pronunciation. Play the recording again so that students can repeat the phrases using the schwa sound.

Answers
a bag of crisps/sweets
a bottle of beer/Coke/milk/wine
a box of matches/tissues
a bunch of bananas/flowers
a can of beer/Coke/tuna
a loaf of bread
a packet of chewing gum/crisps/ham/tissues/sweets
a pair of jeans/socks
a piece of bread/cake/paper
a slice of bread/ham/cake

4.6 A piece of cake
a bag of crisps
a bag of sweets
a bottle of beer
a bottle of Coke
a bottle of milk
a bottle of wine
a box of matches
a box of tissues
a bunch of bananas
a bunch of flowers
a can of beer
a can of Coke
a can of tuna
a loaf of bread
a packet of chewing gum
a packet of crisps
a packet of sweets
a packet of tissues
a pair of jeans
a pair of socks
a piece of bread
a piece of cake
a piece of paper
a slice of bread
a slice of cake
a slice of ham

2 This exercise could be done in class if you think your students know prices, or students could find out the prices of things for homework. If possible, ask students to find out the exchange rate between the British Pound, the American Dollar, and their currency. They could also visit an online shop such as Tesco or Waitrose (in the UK) or Kroger or Walmart (in the US) to find out how much things cost in those countries and compare them to the cost in their country. Are things cheaper or more expensive in each country? Give each student a 'shopping list' or allow them to write their own from the list in exercise 1. Put students in small groups to compare their lists and prices. Monitor to check and support students as needed. Check and correct pronunciation.

3 This activity provides a nice change of pace. Put students in teams of three or four. Allow each team to give themselves a team name. Write the team names on the board. Students should have their books closed. Call out one of the words in A. The first team to shout out a good collocation gets 1 point if the word is on the list in exercise 1, and 2 points if it isn't. If you are worried about noise, ask students to raise their hand – the first hand up with a right answer gets the point, with no points for a shout out.

At the shops
4 4.7 This exercise is a listening for gist. Refer students to the chart and make sure they know what each shop is: in the UK a newsagent's sells magazines, newspapers, sweets, an off-licence sells alcohol, a delicatessen (deli for short) sells cooked meats and cheeses, and special or unusual foods that come from other countries, and a chemist's sells medicines, make-up and toiletries. Pre-teach/Check vocabulary from the conversations: *The Times* (newspaper), *latte, sparkling, to take away, paracetamol, ID* (short for identification).

Ensure students understand just to listen for the name of the shop at this point.

Answers
1 a newsagent's
2 a clothes shop
3 a café
4 a chemist's
5 an off-licence
6 a delicatessen

4.7 At the shops
1 C Can I have a copy of *The Times*, please.
  S That's £1.60, please.
  C And … can I have a box of matches, too, please. And I'll take a packet of this chewing gum.
  S Sure. That's £2.90 altogether, then.
2 C Excuse me, how much are these shorts?
  S Those are £19.99 a pair.
  C Have you got any in blue?
  S No, sorry, they only come in black and brown.
  C OK. I'll try the brown pair on, then.
3 C Can I get two lattes and a bottle of sparkling water, please.
  S To have here, or take away?
  C To have here.
  S What size lattes?
  C Regular. And three slices of that chocolate cake, too, please. It looks good.
  S It is! So, that's £16.10, please.
4 C Could I have some paracetamol, please?
  S Do you want a bottle or a packet?
  C Er, two packets, please. And a box of tissues.
  S OK, that's £2.98, then.
5 C Four cans of beer and three packets of crisps, please.
  S How old are you?
  C 18.
  S You don't look 18. Have you got any ID?
  C Not on me, no.
  S Then I can't sell you the beer.

        C OK, I'll take the crisps then and four cans of Coke.
        S Right. £5.30, please.
    6   C Four slices of ham, please.
        S Certainly, madam. There you go. Anything else?
        C Er, a piece of that blue cheese, please? Is it Roquefort?
        S No, it's Stilton. Very nice though. It'll go well with this lovely white loaf.
        C OK, I'll take one.
        S Lovely. That'll be £14.20 altogether.

5 **4.7** Students now listen for specific information so that they can fill in the chart. Play the recording. Pause after each conversation so students can compare answers. Play the entire recording again so that students can check before checking as a class. Review and drill some different prices, especially the difference between the stressed syllables in *19* (nineteen) and *90* (ninety), *18* and *80*, etc.

> **Answers**
> 1 Newsagent's: a copy of *The Times*, a box of matches, a packet of chewing gum = £2.90
> 2 Clothes shop: a pair of shorts = £19.99
> 3 Café: two lattes, a bottle of sparkling water, three slices of chocolate cake = £16.10
> 4 Chemist's: two packets of paracetamol, a box of tissues = £2.98
> 5 an off-licence: three packets of crisps, four cans of Coke = £5.30
> 6 a delicatessen: four slices of ham, a piece of blue cheese, a loaf of white bread = £14.20

6 Do the first question together as an example. Students say where the people said the lines and what they are talking about. If they can't remember, ask them to look at the audioscript on p132.

> **Answers**
> 1 clothes shop - shorts
> 2 clothes shop - shorts
> 3 café - latte
> 4 café - chocolate cake
> 5 chemist's - paracetamol
> 6 off-licence - beer
> 7 delicatessen - blue cheese

7 Allow students to choose the conversation they want to memorize. If allowed, ask them to record themselves using their mobile phones, and listen to self-assess their pronunciation and fluency. If you have very strong students, you could allow them to extend the conversation so that they buy more things. In a small class, students can act their scene out in front of the class. In a large class, students can act out their conversations in groups.

EXTRA IDEA Students practise asking and answering questions in this milling activity. Write the following questionnaire on the board for students to copy, or put it in a handout:

ONLINE SHOPPING QUESTIONNAIRE
What shops are there near you? What can you buy there?
Where do you like to shop? Why?
What is your least favourite shop? Why?

Tell students they are going to find out about shopping habits in the classroom. They should interview three or four people. Allow them to move around and ask the questions. They write the answers on their sheet or handout. Monitor and help as needed.

Discuss the responses with the whole class.

Additional material
For teachers
Photocopiable activity – Vocabulary: *What do you need?* pp187–8
For students
Online Practice – *Look again*
Workbook p28, exercises 1–3
Online Practice – *Practice*

Everyday English SB p47

Can you come for dinner?

This section practises making and responding to polite requests firstly in the context of a meal, then in a wider, personalized context.

CULTURAL NOTE English can seem overly polite to students who come from a language background where requests are more direct: *Give me the salt* is a perfectly acceptable request in some cultures. You may need to explain this difference and emphasize that English speakers may think they are rude if they don't follow the rules of politeness. English speakers in the US tend to use *Can I/you … , please?* rather than the more British, *Could I/you … , please?* or the more formal, *Could I/you possibly … ?*

Possible problems
would like
Pre-intermediate students will be familiar with *would like*, but may confuse it with *like*, especially in the use of the two auxiliary verbs *do* and *would*:
*Do you like a coffee? (Correction: *Would you like a coffee?*)
*I like a cup of tea, please. (Correction: *I'd like a cup of tea, please.*)

would you mind + *-ing*
This way of making polite requests may be new, and students may need help with the concept and how to reply to questions with *Would you mind … ?*
In this context, *mind* = 'object to'. If the person agrees to the request, the answer is negative, e.g.
*Would you mind opening the window?
*No, not at all. (= I'm happy to open the window.)
To answer negatively, it's common to say sorry and explain why you can't accept the request, e.g.
Would you mind lending me your mobile?
I'm sorry, I can't. I'm low on credit.

Intonation
Students can often sound 'flat' or even rude if they don't use appropriate intonation. Requests often have a falling – rising intonation at the end:

*Would you like some tea?

*Would you mind giving me some water?

1 Refer students to the photo to answer the questions. Ask different students to name some of the foods and drinks they see. Ask students if they think this is a typical dinner party.

2 **4.8** Pre-teach/Check *would you like* and *would you mind* + *-ing*. Put an example of each on the board:

Would you like some tea?
Would you mind giving me some water?

Ask students which is an offer, and which is a request. Point out that *would you like* is a fixed phrase. Do a quick substitution drill to practise:

Teacher: *tea*
Students: *Would you like some tea?*
Teacher: *orange juice*
Students: *Would you like some orange juice?*

Draw students' attention to the difference between:

Do you like tea?
Would you like some tea?

The first is a question about likes; the second is an offer. Ask students what their response to each would be, e.g. *No, I don't like tea*; *No thank you, I'm not thirsty*.

For the request, *Would you mind giving me the recipe?* draw students' attention to the use of the *-ing* form. Do a quick substitution drill to practise this form:

Teacher: *help me wash the dishes.*
Students: *Would you mind helping me wash the dishes?*

Point out that if you are happy to help, your response is negative:

A *Would you mind helping me?*
B *No, not at all.* (= No, I don't mind. I'm happy to help.)

Point out that in English, if you can't accept the request, to be polite you should say sorry and explain why:

A *Would you mind helping me with the dishes?*
B *Sorry, I can't. I'm late for class.*

Go through the questions on the left and the replies on the right, checking students understand *pass the salt*; *Anyone for seconds?* (meaning a second helping of food); *to have room for* (literally to have room in your stomach for more food); *Mm!*; *Just a drop* (just a little); *still or sparkling* (water without or with bubbles); *decaf* (decaffeinated).

Students work in pairs to match the questions on the left with the replies on the right.

Answers
1 a 2 f 3 h 4 e 5 a 6 c 7 g 8 d

SUGGESTION Ask students to say whether each of the questions is an offer or a request. Questions 1, 2, & 4 are requests; questions 3, 5, 6, & 8 are offers.

Play the recording so that students can check their answers. Play the recording again so students can focus on the next line. If needed, play the recording a third time, pausing so that the class can say the next line as a group. Put students in pairs to practise saying the conversations.

🔊 4.8 Can you come for dinner?

1 A **Mm! This soup's lovely! Would you mind giving me the recipe?**
  B **Not at all. I found it online – I'll email you a link to it.**
  A **Oh, great. I think my kids will love it!**
2 A **Could you pass the salt, please?**
  B **Yes, of course. Do you want the pepper, too?**
  A **No, thanks, just the salt.**
3 A **Anyone for seconds?**
  B **No, thanks. It's delicious, but I couldn't eat another thing!**
  A **Well, there's dessert to come, you know!**
4 A **Can I have some water, please?**
  B **Sure. Do you want still or sparkling?**
  A **Just tap water is fine, actually.**
5 A **Has everyone got room for dessert?**
  B **Well, I have! It looks fantastic! Did you make it yourself?**
  A **I did. It's my grandmother's recipe.**
6 A **Would anyone like some more ice cream?**
  B **Yes, please! I'd love another spoonful of the strawberry.**
  A **Here you are. Help yourself!**
7 A **How would you like your coffee?**
  B **Black with no sugar, please. Do you have any decaf?**
  A **Yes, I do. Would anyone else like decaf?**
8 A **Can I get you some more wine?**
  B **Er ... Just a drop, please. I'm driving.**
  A **Ah, I'll let you pour it!**

3 🔊 **4.9** This exercise practises making requests. Do the first two together as a class, ensuring students understand why sentence 1 is *Can/could I ... ?* and sentence 2 is *Can/could you ... ?*, then ask students to complete the exercise. They compare answers in pairs before checking as a class.

Students practise the requests with a partner. To add an element of chance to the dialogues, ask the student who is replying to flip a coin – heads is a *Yes* and tails is a *No*.

Student A: *Can I have some apple juice, please?*
Student B: (flips the coin; it's tails) *No, sorry, we don't have any apple juice.*

Do a couple together as an example.

Answers and audioscript

🔊 4.9 Can I? / Could you?

(note that *Can* and *Could* are interchangeable)
1 A Can I have some apple juice, please?
  B Sorry, we haven't got any apple juice. Will orange juice do?
2 A Could you tell me where the toilets are?
  B Yes, the gents are over there, first on the left.
3 A Can I see the menu?
  B Here you are. Today's specials are on the board over there.
4 A Could I use your phone to make a call, please?
  B Sure. Have you not got any signal again?
5 A Could you lend me an umbrella, please?
  B Yes, of course. Keep it if you like – I've got lots of them!
6 A Can you take me to the station?
  B Oh, yes, is that the time? Let's go or you'll be late.
7 A Could you help me with this homework, please?
  B Well, I can try, but I'm not very good at maths!
8 A Can you give me a lift to the airport?
  B Of course. What time's your flight?
9 A Could you explain that again, please?
  B Of course. I know it isn't easy to understand.

4 🔊 **4.10** Explain that *Can ... please?* and *Could ... please?* are already polite, but sometimes it's necessary to be especially polite, for example, when your request is a difficult one, or when you are asking someone to do something for you. Illustrate this on the board:

Could I have an apple juice please? (simple request)
Could you tell me where the toilets are? (simple request)
Could you give me a lift to the station? (more difficult request.)

This last request involves someone driving you somewhere. This might not be convenient for them, so we make the request even more polite by adding *possibly* or using *Would you mind + -ing*:

Could you possibly give me a lift to the station?
Would you mind giving me a lift to the station?

Unit 4 • Food for thought 65

This more polite form shows that you understand your request is difficult or that it may cause the person some inconvenience.

Students make requests 4–9 even more polite using one of the two forms. Note that either form can be used in the sentences.

Play the recording so that students can compare their answers. Play the recording again, stopping after each request so that students can repeat. Put students in pairs to practise making requests and giving replies. If time is short, organize it so that Student A makes the even-numbered requests, and Student B makes the odd-numbered requests.

Answers and audioscript

🔊 **4.10 Polite requests**
4 Could I possibly use your phone to make a call? (Would you mind if I used your phone …)
5 Could you possibly lend me an umbrella? (Would you mind lending me …)
6 Would you mind taking me to the station? (Could you possibly take me to …)
7 Would you mind helping me with this homework? (Could you possibly help me …)
8 Could you possibly give me a lift to the airport? (Would you mind giving me …)
9 Would you mind explaining that again, please? (Could you possibly explain that to me again, please?)

5 Give students a bit of time to think of some things to request from other people in the class, then let them mill around making requests. If your classroom is small, you could devise a game: Give three or four slips of paper to each student. They write down one request on each, e.g. *borrow a book*; *help with homework*; *explain the grammar*; etc. Write a few examples on the board to get them started. Put students into groups of three. They put their slips in the middle of the table. Student A takes a slip and makes a request to student B who responds. Student C gives a point to A for a correct request and a point to B for a correct reply. The turn passes to B who takes a slip and makes the request to student C with A rewarding points. The game continues in this way until all the slips are used up.

Additional material

For teachers
Photocopiable activity – Communication: *Can I get anyone a drink?* pp189–90

For students
Online Practice – *Look again*
Workbook p29, exercises 1–2
Online Practice – *Practice*

Writing SB p48

Writing a postcard

Style and synonyms

1 If you have some postcards, bring them in to show the students as a lead-in. Pass them around and ask students to identify where they came from. Invite students to ask you questions about your travels.

Look at the photo in the postcard in exercise 1. Ask students where they think it is.

Read the questions in the instructions, then ask students to read the postcard. Allow them to discuss the answers in pairs before checking as a class.

Answers
They're in France, in the Alps, near Mont Blanc. They're having a hiking holiday. They like the picture on the postcard as it shows the view from the restaurant they're in. The problem with the postcard is that they overuse the word *nice*.

SUGGESTION If you find that students have never sent a postcard, ask them how they keep in touch with friends and family when they go on holiday. A lot of people nowadays send text messages, upload photos to social media, use video calls, and some gap-year students (students who take a year out of their studies to travel) write a blog to keep their loved ones informed. Whatever the form of communication, the kinds of information people share is probably the same.

2 Ask students if they think using *nice* 11 times in a postcard makes the writing interesting – probably not! Ask students what words describe things to elicit *adjectives*.

Read the instructions in exercise 2. Read each adjective in the box, pausing to allow students to repeat. Ask students to find all the one-word adjectives that have three syllables (*excellent, fabulous, amazing, wonderful, delicious, beautiful*), two syllables (*lovely*) and one syllable (*good*). Students complete the exercise, then compare answers in pairs. Go through answers as a whole class, asking students to read the entire sentence to check pronunciation. Note that there are multiple possibilities for each sentence.

SUGGESTION Help students notice where the adjective comes in each sentence. Ask them to underline the adjective and the noun that it describes, then ask: *Does the adjective come before or after the noun? What's different in the sentences*: *We're having a nice time.* and *The mountains are nice*?

Answers
1 We're having a wonderful/fabulous/lovely/good time in the Alps, near Mont Blanc.
2 The mountains are lovely/amazing/wonderful/beautiful at this time of year.
3 There are lots of beautiful/amazing/wonderful/lovely wild flowers.
4 We had lunch in this fabulous/excellent/amazing/ wonderful/beautiful/lovely restaurant today.
5 We wanted to send this postcard because the picture on it is so amazing/fabulous/wonderful/beautiful/good.
6 The weather was clear and sunny/excellent/fabulous/ wonderful/beautiful/out of this world/lovely/good, so the view really was spectacular/amazing/beautiful!
7 The food was really good/delicious, too.
8 Lucas said the French fries were excellent/fabulous/ amazing/wonderful/delicious/out of this world/lovely/good.
9 My 'Grandmothers's roast chicken', was delicious/excellent/ fabulous/amazing/wonderful/out of this world/lovely/good.
10 The chocolate 'Dôme' with spiced caramel sauce was truly out of this world/excellent/fabulous/wonderful/delicious/ spectacular.

66 Unit 4 • Food for thought

3 Put students in pairs to read the postcard aloud using the adjectives they chose in exercise 2. To contextualize this activity, tell students they are sending an audio postcard home, so they need to make it sound like they are having a great time. As an alternative activity, Student A begins reading the postcard. When s/he gets to a word that is different from what Student B has, Student B says, 'Stop!', says the word s/he has, and then continues reading from that point. When s/he gets to a word that is different from what Student A has, s/he says, 'Stop!', says the word s/he has, and continues reading from that point. This makes the activity more engaging because students have to listen carefully to each other to hear when a different word is said.

4 In preparation for this activity, ask students to bring in a photo from a holiday they took. The photo can be an actual photograph or a printout on paper. In class, ask them to think about what they want to say about the holiday. They can use the postcard as a model. Refer them to the list of adjectives in exercise 2, and the list of ideas in exercise 4. Give them time in class to write their postcards. Give support as needed.

If possible, ask students to tape, glue, or staple their photo to their writing, or they could affix it with a paperclip. They swap their 'postcards'. Read one of the postcards as an example, using the sentence frame from the exercise. Ask the students to read the postcard aloud to a group or to the class.

SUGGESTION If your class is struggling to think of adjectives, do a brainstorming session on the board. Write the categories on the board and brainstorm other adjectives they could use for each, e.g. journey – *long, hot, boring, exciting*; weather – *hot, cold, rainy, cloudy*; accommodation – *clean, dirty*; food – *delicious, horrible/terrible*.

ALTERNATIVE ACTIVITY Ask students to create actual postcards from their photos. Download and print a postcard template from the Internet and give one to each student. They affix their photo to the front and write their postcard on the left-hand side and 'address' the card to a student in class. This would be a good follow-up activity if you plan to ask students to edit and perfect their postcards. Once they have been 'sent', they could be displayed on a bulletin board.

Additional material
For students
Online Practice – *Practice*
Workbook p29, *Review*, exercises 1–3; *Stop and check* Units 1–4, pp30–1
Online Practice – *Check your progress*

5 The future's in your hands

Introduction to the unit

In this unit, the themes of hopes, ambitions, and plans provide the context for the presentation and practice of verb patterns and ways of talking about the future.

The first *Grammar* section introduces verbs followed by infinitives and/or *-ing* forms, and prepositions followed by *-ing*.

In the second *Grammar* section, students are introduced to *will, going to*, and Present Continuous for ways of expressing the future. They learn to distinguish when to use each. There is also a focus on the difference in pronunciation between *want* and *won't* as these are commonly misheard and mispronounced by students.

The skills practice includes a *Listening and speaking* section on a family's hopes and dreams for the future in which students listen for specific information. This contextualizes and extends the future forms covered previously.

The *Reading and speaking* skills practice features success stories about two young men. The focus here is on reading for specific information, sharing information about the text orally, and using the critical thinking skills of analysis, evaluation and creativity. One of the activities extends the use of future forms to make suppositions, and there is a roleplay in which students show their understanding of the texts.

The *Vocabulary and speaking* section introduces literal and idiomatic phrasal verbs. The focus is on form – which words go together – and meaning. There is the option to bring in dictionary work here to teach students how to find phrasal verbs.

Everyday English practises the language for expressing doubt and uncertainty. Students learn how to use words and expressions to agree 100%, be uncertain, and to disagree 100%.

The *Writing* section links the theme of the unit, grammar, and vocabulary with a writing task to prepare a talk on 'My dreams for the future'.

Language aims

Grammar

Verb patterns

Students are introduced to verb patterns in the context of people commenting about their current life and hopes for the future. They are asked to find examples of verb patterns in a noticing activity before studying and applying the rules. The verb patterns in this section are:

Verb + *to* + infinitive
Verb + *-ing*
Verb + *-ing* or *to* + infinitive with no meaning change
Verb + preposition + *-ing*
like doing vs *would like to do*

going to, will, and Present Continuous for future

Ways of discussing the future are introduced in the context of friends making plans. Students learn about which future forms they should use in different contexts. There is also focus on pronunciation – using short forms – *I'll, you'll*, etc. – and the contrast between *want* /wɒnt/ and *won't* /wəʊnt/.

Vocabulary

Phrasal verbs – literal and idiomatic

Students learn common literal and idiomatic phrasal verbs in this section and use them to talk about themselves as a way of contextualizing and personalizing the meaning.

Everyday English

Expressing doubt and certainty

Students learn words and phrases for expressing certainty and doubt. They have the opportunity to hear the expressions used in conversations and to use them in a group speaking activity.

Additional material

Workbook

Students practise using verb patterns, infinitives, and *-ing* forms, in texts about a climatologist and someone close to retirement. There is discrete practice of *like* vs *would like*. There are several tasks focusing on future forms. There is an exercise on uses of *will* in offers and decisions, and a section where *will, going to* and Present Continuous forms are used to express the future. There is further practice of phrasal verbs and on the different meanings of *get*. There is more practice on expressing doubt and certainty. A Grammar and Vocabulary review closes the unit.

Photocopiable activities

There are photocopiable activities to review grammar (*Verb patterns quiz*), vocabulary (*Phrasal verbs pair-up*), and communication (*Anything's possible!*) at the back of the Teacher's Guide as well as on the Teacher's Resource Centre. There is also a worksheet to accompany the video on the Teacher's Resource Centre.

Notes on the unit

Unit opener page

Choose from these activities to engage your students with the topic and target language of this unit:
- Talk about the title
- Talk about the unit goals (*Grammar, Vocabulary, …*)
- Talk about the photo
- Watch the video
- Look at the bottom banner
- Do the activity

Refer students to the unit title, 'The future's in your hands'. Ensure they know that *future's* is a contraction for *future is*.

Ask students if they know what this expression means (we can change our future if we want to).

Ask students to look at the photo and think about how it relates to the topic of the unit. Ask *Is there anything surprising about the girl?* (she looks very young but perfectly at home in a chemistry laboratory!).

If you don't have time to watch the video introduction to the unit, go through the unit goals below the title: *Grammar, Vocabulary, Everyday English, Reading, Listening, Writing*. Give examples or use translation for unknown words.

Video (2 minutes approximately): The video gives a step-by-step overview of the unit. Play the video, pausing where necessary – especially for students to answer any questions, e.g. *What are your hopes and plans for the future?* This makes it a more interactive experience. Highlight the option of practising online.

As shown in the bottom banner, don't forget that there are many exercises to consolidate and practise the target language of the unit in the Workbook as well as online. There are links to these exercises on the relevant pages of the Student's Book and they can be done in class time or you can set them for homework.

Summary: If you're short of time, use the title and the photo to help students understand and engage with the topic, and then move straight on to the activity so that they can discuss the theme in more detail. If you have any more time, try to watch the video together. It is a clear and interesting introduction to the different parts of the unit.

Notes for activity:
Put students in pairs. Ask them to look at the photo and discuss their answers to the questions. Ask them to justify their choices where possible.

> **Suggested answers**
> 1 She is doing a science experiment. She looks a little shocked and is covered in dirt, and she is probably enjoying herself.
> 2 A scientist.
> 3 Students' own answers.

Grammar SB p50

Verb patterns

> **Possible problems**
> 1 This unit focuses on verb patterns, covering verbs followed by the infinitive form (with *to* or without *to*), verbs followed by the *-ing* form, and the prepositions *of*, *with*, and *to + -ing*. Mistakes of form are common with verb patterns.
> * *I'm thinking of work as a designer.* (Correction: *I'm thinking of working as a designer.*)
> **She hopes finding a job soon.* (Correction: *She hopes to find a job soon.*)
> **He want have a restaurant.* (Correction: *He wants to have a restaurant.*)
> 2 Two possible patterns with *like* are also presented, and these cause problems of form and use.
> Common mistakes:
> **I like play football.* (Correction: *I like playing football.*)
> **I'd like having a drink.* (Correction: *I'd like to have a drink.*)
> **I'm thirsty. I like a Coke.* (Correction: *I'm thirsty. I'd like a Coke.*)
> **Do you like to come to the cinema tonight?* (Correction: *Would you like to come to the cinema tonight?*)
> 3 In this unit, we suggest that for a general preference, *like* + *-ing* is used. Students might come across *like* + *infinitive* – this use of *like* has more of an idea of '*this is how I prefer to do things*' rather than '*I enjoy*'.
> **I like to keep my desk tidy.*
> 4 The verb patterns presented in this unit are such high-frequency items, that once you have presented them, they will automatically be revised and practised in many classroom activities. Students may still make mistakes in subsequent lessons, but you can refer them to the list of Verb patterns on p158 of the Student's Book.

> **STARTER** SB p50
>
> This *Starter* section introduces verb patterns in the context of hopes and plans.
>
> Start by telling students about your own hopes and plans, using the sentence frames in the *Starter* box. Refer students to the *Starter* box to complete the sentences with their own ideas.
>
> Ask students to share their sentences with the class. The focus at this point is on expressing their ideas, not on grammar, so avoid over-correcting at this point. If you feel you must correct, you might simply repeat the sentence correctly, but with your focus very much on the meaning of what the student said. In a large class, put students in groups to share their sentences and ask several students to read one to the class.
>
> You could add a game-like element to this activity by asking students to complete three sentences truthfully, and one with a lie. The other students guess which one is false.

Hopes and plans

1 Refer students to the photos and quotes. Check that students understand *fed up with, paramedic* /ˌpærəˈmedɪk/ (the person who works in an ambulance), *ads* (advertisements), *debts, retired*. Discuss the questions with the class. Ask follow-up questions to help students engage with the people: *Do you feel the same as Damian? Why do you think Marek wants to change?*, etc.

Possible answers
Damien is a student. He hates school. He wants to stop doing exams.
Paula is a paramedic. It's a stressful job. She needs a break.
Marek works in advertising. He wants to change his job.
Claire has three children. She is very tired. She wants to go back to work.
Grace is a student. She is worried. She has a lot of debts and she hates owing money.
Angus is retired. He is happy. He wants to do his hobbies.

2 🔊 **5.1** Pre-teach/Check: *looking forward to, earn, well-paid, regret, award, owe* /əʊ/, *exhausted* /ɪɡˈzɔːstɪd/. Ask students to work in pairs to match the sentences to the people.

Play the recording so that students can listen and check their answers. Play it again so that students can focus on what else each person says. Ask them to take notes and discuss in groups. Alternatively, give each student a different person to take notes on, then put them in groups to share.

Answers
1 Marek   4 Angus
2 Claire   5 Paula
3 Damian   6 Grace
Additional information:
Damien's mum and dad say he can't leave school.
Paula's going to read and sunbathe on her holiday.
Marek wants to work in New York for a couple of years.
Grace is going to have a job interview next Friday.
Claire is fed up with staying at home all day.
Angus's wife wants them to go travelling, but he just wants to go fishing.

3 🔊 **5.1** Ask students to read the gapped sentences, then play the recording so that they can complete them. Play the recording again if needed so that students can write who said each line. Ask students which person they are most like – if any!

Answers
1 to work (Marek)
2 to do (Paula)
3 hate (Grace)
4 staying (Claire)
5 wants, spending (Angus)
6 can't (Damian)

🔊 **5.1 Hopes and plans**
Damian
I'm so fed up with taking exams. I hate school. I'd like to leave now and get a job, any job. I want to earn some money, but my mum and dad say that I can't leave school. They think I'll regret it later, but I don't think I will.
Paula
I'm a paramedic. I love my job, but it's very stressful, and I need a break. Fortunately, I'm going on holiday next month. We love going to Spain – we go every year. I'm planning to do nothing but read and sunbathe on the beach for two whole weeks!
Marek
I work in advertising. I won an award for one of my ads. But now I need a change. I'm thinking of applying for a job with a big company in New York. I saw it advertised online, and it looks like the job for me. I'd love to work there for a couple of years.
Grace
I'm a student in my last year at university. I've got debts of over £35,000. I'm going to study really hard for my exams because I hope to get a well-paid job and pay my debts. I hate owing so much money. I'm going for an interview next Friday. Wish me luck!

Claire
I've got three kids under five. I love them dearly, but I'm so tired – and I miss my work at the hospital. I'm looking forward to returning to my job when the baby's older. I get fed up with staying at home all day, especially in winter. My husband's great when he's at home, but he often works late.
Angus
I'm retired at last, and I can now enjoy doing my favourite things. I try to go fishing every day, but my wife sometimes asks me to help in the house. She wants to us to go travelling now I'm retired, but I'm just happy spending all day by the river.

GRAMMAR SPOT SB p51
This *Grammar spot* focuses on several verb patterns. An infinitive is the base form of the verb, with or without *to*. Some verbs are followed by *to* + infinitive and some are followed by *-ing* forms, with or without meaning change. Only those without meaning change are covered here. Prepositions are followed by the *-ing* form.

1 Use the board to highlight the three different verb forms with examples:
- verb + *to* (infinitive)   I *want to work* in a school.
- verb + *-ing*   I *like* study*ing*.
- preposition + *-ing*   I'm *thinking of* study*ing* today.

Pre-teach/Check the meaning of *verb, infinitive, preposition*. Draw students' attention to these in the examples on the board. Ask students to highlight or underline an example of each in exercises 1–3. Students compare answers before checking as a class.

Answers
- verb + *to* = I try to go fishing every day
- verb + *-ing* = We love going to Spain.
- prepositions *of, with* and *to* + *-ing*: I'm looking forward to returning to my job when the baby's older.

2 Read exercise 2 to the students and elicit the difference between the two sentences. Ask concept check questions to ensure they understand the difference:
1 I like working in New York.
   Do I work in New York now? (yes); *Do I enjoy my work in New York?* (yes).
2 I'd like to work in New York.
   Do I work in New York now? (no); *Is this something I want to do in the future?* (yes).

Answers
The first sentence refers to now. The second sentence is hypothetical and refers to the future.

3 Tell students to complete the sentences from the prompts. Correct in whole-class feedback, highlighting the different patterns.

Answers
I hope to work in New York.
I'd love to work in New York.
I'm thinking of working in New York.
I enjoy working in New York.
I'm looking forward to working in New York.
I'm fed up with working in New York.
I can't work in New York.

SUGGESTION There are several ways to organize this exercise, depending on the students. Here are some suggestions:

70 Unit 5 • The future's in your hands

- **Guided discovery approach for stronger students**: Ask students to complete the sentences as directed in the *Grammar spot*, then refer them to Grammar reference 5.1 on p146 to read the rules and correct their sentences.
- **If students need more support**: Use the board to categorize the verbs before students start. Draw a four-column table on the board with the headings: *verb + to + infinitive*; *verb + -ing*; *preposition + -ing*; *infinitive without to*. Ask students to categorize the verbs in the exercise under each heading before writing their sentences.
- **Deductive approach**: Refer students to the Grammar reference on p146 to read the rules before writing their sentences.

SUGGESTION Ask students to look at the list of verb patterns on p158. In pairs, they write five to ten gapped sentences using the verbs, but leaving out the infinitive or -ing form. They swap papers with another pair who completes the sentences correctly.

Practice SB p51

Discussing grammar

1 **5.2** Read the instructions and question 1 with the students, and make sure they understand that there may be one or two correct verbs. Students work in pairs to tick the correct verbs. Play the recording so they can check their answers. Refer students to the rules in the Grammar reference if needed.

Answers

2	a, b	6	b, c
3	c	7	c
4	a, b	8	c
5	c		

5.2 Verb patterns 1
1 I want to work in Paris.
   I'd like to work in Paris.
2 I'm fed up with doing housework.
   I hate doing housework.
3 She can't leave work early tonight.
4 I hope to see you again soon.
   I'd like to see you again soon.
5 He often enjoys playing computer games with his friends.
6 We're thinking of going to Italy for our holidays.
   We like going to Italy for our holidays.
7 We're looking forward to having a few days off soon.
8 Are you good at learning foreign languages?

2 **5.3** Students work in pairs to make the sentences in exercise 1 grammatically correct with the words that were not used. Do number one together as an example of how they will have to change the sentence to make it grammatical. Monitor and support as needed. Ask confident students to read their sentences aloud to the class to check answers.

EXTRA IDEA Make cards with the verbs from the *Grammar spot*. Students work in groups of four. Each group has a set of cards with three of the verbs. Each student writes three sentences about themselves, one of which is false. They read out their sentences, and the rest of the group has to decide which one is false. Students who guess correctly win a point. The winner is the student with the most points.

Answers and audioscript

5.3 Verb patterns 2
1 I enjoy **working** in Paris.
2 I don't want **to do** housework.
3 She wants **to leave** work early tonight.
   She'd like **to leave** work early tonight.
4 I'm looking forward to **seeing** you again soon.
5 He often wants **to play** computer games with his friends.
   He often asks **to play** computer games with his friends.
6 We're hoping **to go** to Italy for our holidays.
7 We're going **to have** a few days off soon.
   We'd love **to have** a few days off soon.
8 Do you want **to learn** foreign languages?
   Do you like **learning** foreign languages?

Asking for more information

3 **5.4** Ask students to complete the questions in the conversations, using number 1 as an example. Check as a class before asking students to read the conversations with a partner. Ask them to take turns so that they each get the chance to ask the question. Play the recording so that students can hear the rest of the conversation. Put students in pairs to practise them. Weaker students can use the audioscript at the back of the book if needed. Ask fast finishers to make up their own endings to the conversations.

Answers and audioscript

5.4 Asking for more information
1 A I hope to go to university.
   B **What do you want to study?**
   A I'm going to study philosophy and politics. I'd like to be prime minister.
   B Really? I think that's the worst job in the world!
2 A My favourite hobby is cooking.
   B **What do you like making?**
   A Well, I love baking cakes, all kinds of cakes.
   B OK, can you make me a huge chocolate one for my birthday?
3 A I'm bored.
   B **What would you like to do?**
   A Nothing. I'm happy being bored.
   B Well, that's OK then!
4 A I'm looking forward to the party.
   B **Who are you hoping to see there?**
   A No one special. I just like parties.
   B Me too!
5 A We're planning our summer holidays.
   B **Where are you thinking of going?**
   A We want to go camping this year.
   B Ugh! Camping! I hate sleeping in tents.

Talking about you

4 Give students a few minutes to read the questions and think of suitable answers, then put them in pairs to have the conversations. As an alternative, write the four questions on the board and ask students to stand up. They find at least three people to put the questions to in a milling activity. Elicit a few responses in whole-class feedback. Ask students to report what another person said to practise third person singular forms.

Unit 5 • The future's in your hands   71

> **Additional material**
> **For teachers**
> Photocopiable activity – Grammar: *Verb patterns quiz* pp191–2
> **For students**
> Online Practice – *Look again*
> Workbook pp32–3, exercises 1–5
> Online Practice – *Practice*

Have you got any plans? SB p52

going to, *will*, and Present Continuous for future

> **Possible problems**
> 1 In this unit, *will* to express a future intention decided as you speak is contrasted with *going to*, which expresses a pre-planned intention. Students might well perceive this conceptual difference quite easily, but will often forget to apply it. Knowing which future form to use can cause ongoing problems for many students.
> Common mistakes:
> *'Have you booked a holiday yet?' *'Yes. We'll go to Spain.'* (Correction: *We're going to Spain.*)
> **What will you do tonight?* (Correction: *What are you doing tonight?*)
> **What do you do tonight?* (Correction: *What are you doing tonight?*)
> 2 Students often use the base form of the verb to express a spontaneous offer or intention, rather than *will*.
> *'The phone's ringing.' *'OK. I answer it.'* (Correction: *OK. I'll answer it.*)
> **I open the door for you.* (Correction: *I'll open the door for you.*)
> 3 Present Continuous is introduced here to express:
> - a planned future arrangement: *I'm meeting my cousin for lunch*.
> - arrangements with *go* and *come*: *She's coming on Friday. I'm going home early tonight.*
> Note that although it's possible to use *going to* with *come* and *go*, it is less common. Sometimes there is little difference between *going to* and Present Continuous for future arrangements, so students need to be aware of this: *We're seeing a film this evening./We're going to see a film this evening.*
> 4 The unit also draws attention to the difference in pronunciation between *want* /wɒnt/ and *won't* /wəʊnt/ – a difficult difference to hear and say.
> 5 Students may also have problems in hearing and saying the short form, *I'll*, *you'll*, etc. The /l/ sound in the contractions is called the dark /l/ and is produced far back in the throat, unlike the clear /l/ in words such as *love* or *like*.

1 Refer students to the photos of Pete and Daisy. Ask them which one looks happier and why that might be. Check that they understand *positive* and *doubtful*. Ask: *What are positive people like? What are doubtful people like?* Put students in pairs to complete the exercise. When checking, ensure students understand the contrast: Positive Pete has a lot of plans for the future. Doubtful Daisy, in contrast, is not very positive. She doesn't know what she is going to do. She doesn't have plans. Ask students if they are more like Positive Pete or Doubtful Daisy.

2 🔊 **5.5** Play the recording so that students can check their answers. Check that students understand *to catch up with her news* (to find out about what she's been doing).

Answers
1 d, h   2 c, g   3 a, e   4 b, f

🔊 5.5 Have you got any plans?

1 Pete and Ben
B = Ben   P = Pete
B Hi Pete! I'm just calling to catch up with your news! How are you? How's work?
P Hi Ben! I'm fine. Work's fine, but there's a lot happening as always. It's good to hear from you.
B Pete, isn't it your birthday soon?
P It is.
B Are you going to have a party?
P Of course I am. I'm going to invite all my friends as usual.
B Great! I'll look forward to that. So, what are you doing this evening?
P This evening? I'm meeting Tom for a drink after work. Do you remember Tom? He's an old school friend.
B Of course I remember Tom. Great guy!
P Yeah! Would you like to join us?
B Oh, sorry I can't. I'm working late this evening, but give him my best!
P I'll do that.
B But what about the weekend? Are you doing anything interesting this weekend?
P Yes, I am. I'm going to my cousin's wedding in the country. You know, my cousin Karen?
B Karen's getting married! That's great! I didn't know that. We're busy people, you and I.
P I know. I need a break.
B We all do. Where are you going on holiday this year?
P I'm going to have a winter holiday this year. I'm going skiing for ten days in the Swiss Alps. I'm really excited.
B Wow, that sounds fantastic. Oh I love skiing. Let's meet before you go. I'll call or text you.

2 Daisy and Ella
E = Ella   D = Daisy
E Hey Daisy! Where are you?
D Ella! I'm at home. I was thinking of calling *you* for a chat!
E Great! How are you? Are you doing anything interesting this weekend?
D No, I'm not. Perhaps we can do something together. I'll call or text you on Friday and we can …
E Sorry Daisy, I can't see you this weekend – I'm going on holiday on Saturday.
D Oh, lucky you! Where are you going to?
E Greece, for a week. I can't wait! What about you? Where are you going on holiday this year?
D Well, I'd like to go to Spain with friends … but I'll probably just go to Scotland with my family as usual. Hey, are you back from Greece for my birthday on the 25th?
E Yes, I am. Are you going to have a party?
D I don't think so. Maybe I will, but maybe I won't. I had a big one last year for my eighteenth.
E Oh, of course! That was an amazing party – we all had the best time! Maybe we'll just meet for a drink this year. Anyway, I'd like to see you before I go away. What are you doing this evening?
D Not much! I just wanted to chat to you and catch up. Why don't you come over to my place?
E OK, I'll come now, but I won't stay late. I'm going to start packing.

72   Unit 5 • The future's in your hands

3 🔊 **5.5** Read the questions in exercise 3 together, then play the recording. If your students struggle with this type of exercise, put them in pairs. Student A listens for and answers the odd numbered questions and Student B does the even numbered ones. If needed, play the recording again. When checking as a class, ask the questions and elicit full sentence responses from students.

Answers
1 To catch up.
2 Tom is Pete's old school friend. Karen is Pete's cousin.
3 He's working late.
4 He wants to meet up with Pete before he goes skiing.
5 She's going on holiday.
6 Greece
7 Spain
8 She says that she'll come over now, but she won't stay long.

Talking about you

4 Refer students back to exercise 1. Ask them to underline or highlight the way Pete and Daisy talk about the future. What do they notice that is different about their answers? Put them in pairs to ask and answer the four questions. You could ask them to be a Positive Pete or a Doubtful Daisy in their responses to add a bit of dramatic roleplay to the exercise.

GRAMMAR SPOT SB p52

Read through the rules as a class. Ask students who uses *going to* and Present Continuous more – Positive Pete or Doubtful Daisy. Why does Doubtful Daisy use *will*? (She doesn't have plans. She decides at the time of speaking.) Other things to note:

1 Demonstrate the pronunciation of *I'll* /aɪl/. Elicit and check the pronunciation of the negative *won't* /wəʊnt/.

2 Point out that there is sometimes very little difference between *going to* and Present Continuous for future, e.g.:
- *What are you going to do in the summer?*
- *What are you doing in the summer?*

It's also a good idea to remind students that the verbs *go* and *come* are not generally used with *going to*, but with the Present Continuous, e.g.:
- *I'm going to go shopping. – I'm going shopping.*
- *I'm going to come to France. – I'm coming to France.*

Refer students to the Grammar reference on pp146. They could read this for homework and ask questions in the next lesson.

Practice SB p52

Discussing grammar

1 🔊 **5.6** Students work in pairs. For each of the conversations in exercise 1, ask them to say whether the speakers are referring to planned events or something they have just decided at the moment of speaking. This will help them decide which future form to choose. Play the recording so they can check their answers.

Answers and audioscript

🔊 **5.6 Discussing grammar**
1 A Have you decided which university to apply for?
  B Oh yes, **I'm going to** apply for Oxford.
2 A I haven't got your mobile number.
  B Really? **I'll** text it to you right now.
3 A We don't have any fruit in the house.
  B **I'm going** shopping soon. **I'll** get some apples.
4 A My bag is really heavy.
  B Give it to me. **I'll** carry it for you.
5 A Tony's back from holiday.
  B Is he? **I'll** give him a call.
6 A What **are we having** for supper?
  B **I'm going to** make Spaghetti Bolognese and salad.
7 A I promised not to tell anyone.
  B You can tell me, **I won't** tell a soul.

SUGGESTION Focus students' attention on the pronunciation of the dark /l/ sound in sentences in the audioscript. Play the recording and ask them to repeat. Help them discriminate between *I* and *I'll* – give each student a different coloured slip of paper. Read the following sentences. Students hold up one colour if they hear *I'll* and another if they don't. Repeat the activity using different subjects: *you'll/they'll*, etc.

I'll go to Oxford.
I cook dinner.
I travel to Turkey.
I'll see who is at the door.

What can you say?

2 🔊 **5.7** Read the instructions to the students, pointing out the example given for the first conversation. Choose students at random to elicit other responses to the first line. Play the recording, pausing after each line, and eliciting responses. As an alternative, pause and ask students to write down a possible response to each one. Ask them to compare answers in pairs, and elicit a few responses for each question.

🔊 **5.7 What can you say?**
1 Why are you looking forward to the weekend?
2 I haven't got your brother's phone number.
3 Tim can't come out with us on Saturday.
4 I can't find my phone!
5 Congratulations! I hear you've got a new job.
6 Are you going to come for a coffee with us after class?

3 🔊 **5.8** Play the recording. How close were students' responses to the ones in the recording? Be prepared to explain the use of the echo tag in conversation 2. Echo tags are used to show interest or surprise, and echo/repeat the auxiliary verb in the main statement (answer 2).

Unit 5 • The future's in your hands 73

🔊 5.8 What can you say?

1. **A** Why are you looking forward to the weekend?
   B Because I'm going to stay with an old school friend.
2. **A** I haven't got your brother's phone number.
   B Haven't you? I'll text it to you now.
3. **A** Tim can't come out with us on Saturday.
   B That's a shame! What's he doing?
   A He didn't say.
4. **A** I can't find my phone!
   B Not again! I'll check in the kitchen for you. You check in your pockets!
5. **A** Congratulations! I hear you've got a new job.
   B Yes, in Canada. I'm going to work in Toronto.
6. **A** Are you going to come for a coffee with us after class?
   B I'd love to. Where are you going?

Will you, won't you?

4 🔊 **5.9** Read the heading aloud to the students. Ask what sound they can hear between the words *won't* and *you* when you say *won't you* /wəʊntʃuː/. Point out that this /tʃ/ sound happens when a /t/ sound is followed by a /j/ sound. It's important to be aware of this when listening, as this can cause misunderstanding in understanding natural speech. Read the instructions to the students and show them the example to ensure they know to first write the sentence in A and then match it to the sentence in B. Play the recording so students can check their answers. Play the recording again, pausing so that students can focus on the final line which gives the reason for the speaker's decision. If there is class time, put students in pairs to read the sentences using the audioscript on p133.

Answers and audioscript

🔊 **5.9** *will you, won't you?*

1 f **2** d **3** a **4** h **5** c **6** b **7** g **8** e

1. I think you'll enjoy this film. You won't be disappointed. It's really exciting.
2. I think I'll call Laura. I won't text her. I have too much to tell her.
3. I think you'll pass your driving test. You won't fail again. It's your fourth time!
4. I think my team will win. They won't lose this time. They've got a new manager.
5. I think it'll be warm today. You won't need your jumper, just take a T-shirt.
6. I think I'll join a gym. I won't go on a diet. Diets never work for me.
7. I think they'll get divorced. They won't stay together. They argue all the time.
8. I think I'll go by train. I won't fly. I hate flying.

Pronunciation – *want* or *won't*?

5 🔊 **5.10** Focus on the sounds /ɒ/ and /əʊ/. Get students to notice the shape of the mouth for the /ɒ/ sound – it's quite open with slightly rounded lips. Contrast this to the mouth shape for /əʊ/ – the mouth moves from the /ə/ to the /ʊ/ sound, from a more open lips to rounded ones. The /əʊ/ sound is actually two sounds (a diphthong) which is why the mouth moves. Play the recording so students can listen and repeat the sounds. Ask them to focus on their mouth as they do. Play the recording as many times as needed for the students to feel comfortable hearing and saying the sounds.

🔊 **5.10** See SB p53.

🔊 **5.11** Read the instructions with the students. If possible, give them each two different coloured cards – one for *want* and the other for *won't*. After each sentence, they hold up the card for the word they hear. This will allow you to see clearly what word students are hearing and which students need more support in differentiating the two sounds. Play the recording again so that students can repeat.

Answers and audioscript

🔊 **5.11** *want* or *won't*?

a	We **want** to leave now.	/ɒ/ /wɒnt/
b	I **won't** be late.	/əʊ/ /wəʊnt/
c	She **won't** marry him.	/əʊ/ /wəʊnt/
d	They **want** to have a party.	/ɒ/ /wɒnt/
e	I **won't** know until tomorrow.	/əʊ/ /wəʊnt/
f	Tell me what you **want**.	/ɒ/ /wɒnt/

EXTRA IDEA For extra practice saying *won't* /wəʊnt/ and *want* /wɒnt/, you could try the following activity. Write these sentences on the board and get students to listen and repeat. Note that the *to* in the first set of sentences is very short and sounds like /tə/.

/ɒ/ **want**	/əʊ/ **won't**
I want to fly.	I won't fly.
We want to go.	We won't go.
We want to leave now.	We won't leave now.
I want to be late.	I won't be late.
She wants to marry him.	She won't marry him.
They want to have a party.	They won't have a party.

Additional material
For students
Online Practice – *Look again*
Workbook pp34–5, exercises 6–12
Online Practice – *Practice*

Listening and speaking SB p53

Different generations – what can we look forward to?

1. Refer students to the photo on p53. Ask them to describe it. What do they think is the relationship of the people in the photo? Put students in groups of three or four to brainstorm family vocabulary, and complete exercise 1. Ask students to draw a family tree of the family in the photo. Ask questions to elicit other family vocabulary: *What is the sister of my mother or father called?* (aunt /ɑːnt/); *Brother of my mother or father?* (uncle /ˈʌŋkl/); *Daughter/Son of my sister or brother?* (niece /niːs/, nephew /ˈnefjuː/); *Child of my aunt or uncle?* (cousin /ˈkʌzn/), etc. Note that *in-laws* are family through marriage, *half-brothers* and *half-sisters* are the children of one parent but not the other, *stepsister* and *stepbrother* are the children of *stepmother* or *stepfather* (not blood-related), and *great-grandparents* are the parents of the grandparents. Introduce the concept of extended family (*aunts, uncles, cousins, in-laws*) and nuclear family (*grandparents*, *parents* and *children*). Definitions of extended and nuclear family will vary according to culture, and in some cultures there are different words for *aunt* and *uncle* depending on whether they are the father's or mother's side. Some cultures do

Unit 5 • The future's in your hands

not distinguish between half- and step-siblings. Find out which family members students consider close family and which they consider extended family. Be sensitive to the fact that some students may have lost family members. Ask students to share what they call grandparents in their country with the rest of the class.

2 Model this activity with the students by drawing a small family tree on the board to include yourself and at least three family members. For three of the family members, write some information about them using the prompts in exercise 2. Use the prompts to tell the students about them, and include information about their hopes and plans for the future. Ask students to work alone to think about the family members they want to discuss, then put them back in groups to share the information. If your students are confident, ask them to ask each other questions to elicit the information from each other. You could put the questions on the board to support lower-level students: *What's her/his name? How old is she/he? What is her/his relationship to you? What's her/his job? What is she/he interested in? What are her/his hopes and plans for the future?*

3 🔊 **5.12** Ask students to read the exercise and explain to you what they will have to do. Play the recording so they can complete it. This is a challenging exercise, so you may have to scaffold it. Play the recording through once, and allow students to discuss their ideas. Ask them how old each person is – write the ages on the board. Ask students to do some deductive reasoning: to try to work out a rough family tree. Play the recording again, and allow students to discuss their answers in pairs. Check as a group.

Answers
1 aunt, daughter, 29
2 nephew, grandson, 9
3 grandad, dad, 59

🔊 **5.12 Different generations –** *what can we look forward to?*

H = Harry E = Emma R = Richard

H Auntie Emma, are you having a party for your birthday?
E Oh, I don't know Harry – I really don't want to think about my birthday.
R Come on, Emma, it's a special birthday. We've all got special birthdays this year – Harry's going to be ten, I'm going to be 60, and you're going to be 30!
H Yeah – Grandad, that's really special! I can't wait to be ten. I'll be in double figures!
R Huh, you're growing up much too fast for my liking! Slow down!
H Grandad, I've got a really good idea … let's have a party for all three of us! We'll invite all our friends – it'll be huge! I love parties.
R OK, Harry, but careful … it's a nice idea but big parties are expensive – we'll have to talk to your Grandma.
E I'm not sure I want to have a party at all. It's all right for you two – you're looking forward to your birthdays – I'm not! I'm going to be 30! I can't believe it. It seems so old. Some people say 30 is the new 20 – but not for me. What have I got to look forward to now? A nine-to-five job in the city!
R Just a minute – do you think I want to be 60? You've got the rest of your life to look forward to.
E Yeah, but Dad, you're happy with your life – you have your two children and your grandchildren … and you love your job and Mum loves her job, too.
R OK, we like our jobs, but being a doctor isn't easy – it's very stressful and teaching teenagers is not easy for your mum either … we'd like to retire soon, but that's not possible for another few years.
E Well, I'd love to go travelling again … like I did when I was 23.
H I want to do that! Me and my friend, Zac, are going to travel the world together. We're planning it now. Where did you go, Auntie Emma?
E I went with a friend from university and we went all over the world – Australia, New Zealand, South America. We even spent three weeks on the Galapagos Islands – that was amazing. We had a fantastic time. We were away for a whole year.
H Oh wow! The Galapagos Islands! Did you see the tortoises?
E Of course we did.
H Fantastic! I'll tell Zac. He won't believe it!
R Ah yes – wonderful … but then it was difficult when you came back.
E Yeah, it was difficult to start studying again. And Dad, you know I'm still not sure I want to be a lawyer.
R Come on, you've nearly finished your studies. You're sure to get a good job, and then you and John can get married and …
E … and have babies and on and on … like you and Mum. Dad, I'm not sure I'm ready for all this. I know both you and David were married at my age, but …
R Yes, and your brother's very happy with his life.
H Of course he is … Daddy's got me and Rosie … er … actually, Rosie's a bit of a pain sometimes – she cries a lot.
E Harry – she's only five! Oh, I don't know … maybe John and I will go travelling together before we finally grow up and settle down!
H Yeah! Can I come?
R Well, Emma, the future's in your hands! At your age your mum and I had two kids, two full-time jobs, and not a lot of money.
E Oh Dad! I know – bring out the violins. I'm sorry – I know how lucky I am, it's just …
R … that's OK Emma. I understand more than you think. Now, what about this party?!
H Yeah!

---

4 Read the questions with the students so they know what information to listen for. Ensure students understand *to settle down* (to get married and possibly have children). If you have less confident students, put them in pairs so that Student A answers the odd-numbered questions and Student B answers the even-numbered ones. Allow them to discuss the answers before checking as a class.

Answers
1 They are all important birthdays.
2 Harry is looking forward to his birthday because he'll be in double figures (10), Emma is not looking forward to her birthday because she's going to be 30 and she thinks that's old.
3 Harry's good idea is to have a party – Richard and Emma aren't sure about it.
4 Doctor and teacher.
5 Zac is Harry's friend and they're planning to travel the world together.
6 Emma went to the Galapagos Islands. Harry would like to go.
7 David is Richard's son and Emma's brother. Rosie is Richard's granddaughter and Emma's niece.
8 Being a lawyer and having children.
9 John is Emma's boyfriend. She'd like to go travelling again before she settles down.

What do you think?

Put students in groups of three or four to discuss the questions. Assign a group leader whose job it is to make sure everyone contributes to the discussion. In feedback, ask a member from each group to share some of the information they discussed.

This would be a good opportunity to revise past tenses and consolidate future forms by asking students to think about what life was like for Richard when he was 30, and what life will be like for Harry when he is 30. Ask students *What was life like when your parents or grandparents were 30?/What will life be like when today's children are 30?*

Give students time to think about areas of life, writing notes under the following headings:

Unit 5 • The future's in your hands 75

- Family size and location
- Domestic life
- The role of women
- Education
- Employment
- Free time

Students can compare their ideas in small groups, or you could set it up as a project, with students presenting their ideas to the class with supporting visuals.

Additional material
For students
Online Practice – *Practice*

Reading and speaking SB p55

He was only 16 …

About the text

Both reading texts are true stories. The first story is about a boy with a lot of determination, but this got him into trouble. He is a hacker – a person who illegally gains access to other people's computers. Keeping computer systems safe from hackers, or cyber criminals, costs billions of pounds a year. Ironically, hackers, though they do face criminal prosecution for their crimes, often do get good IT jobs – their ability to create viruses and hack into systems helps build better computer security.

The second story is about a boy from a slum in Kenya who has become one of Kenya's most promising ballet dancers. He trained in the United States, and also won a place at a top ballet school in London. He has performed in the *Nutcracker* in Nairobi, and his career is promising. His story shows that passion and determination can take you far.

1 Ask students to look at the photos and headings, and check they understand *slum, ballet, cyber hacker*. Ask students which boy they think is most likely to succeed in their future career and why. Pre-teach/Check: *scholarship, virus, chaos, to crash the network, bullied, status, court, trial, IT*.

2 Divide the class into two groups, A and B. Group A reads about Adam Mudd and Group B reads about Joel Kioko. Students work with others in their group to discuss and answer the statements 1–7. Each student should take notes.

Answers
Group A – Adam Mudd
1 ✓
2 ✓
3 ✓
4 ✗
5 ✗
6 ✓
7 ✓ – he'll be in prison

Group B – Joel Kioko
1 ✗
2 ✓
3 ✗
4 ✓
5 ✓
6 ✗
7 ✓ – he'll be training at the English National Ballet School in London

3 Regroup the students in pairs so that each pair has a student from Group A and one from Group B. Tell them to first briefly summarize the story they read, then read the true statements. If students wish, they can read the text they didn't read as homework.

4 This critical thinking exercise gets students to apply what they know about each story to new information in the form of quotations. Students stay in their AB pairs to read the sentences and decide who they think said each one. Write sentence frames on the board to help lower-level students: *I think … said this because …* Encourage them to find evidence in the text to support their decision. In feedback, encourage students to give you reasons for their choices.

Answers
1 I didn't do it for the money. = Adam, because it was all about status for him.
2 This court does not believe that you didn't know what you were doing. – The judge at Adam's trial (it mentions the court, so is clearly a court case).
3 Thank you! We love coming to your lessons. – Joel's students – he's teaching ballet to kids now.
4 We had no idea what he was doing. We'll help him all we can now. – Adam's parents – they're claiming they didn't know what he was doing.
5 I'm a bit worried about being so far from home. – Joel – he'll be in London, which is far from his home in Kenya.
6 You're going to be a big star one day! Joel's teacher – he could be a world-famous ballet dancer.
7 We tried to make friends with him. We didn't bully him. – Kids at Adam's college – he accused them of bullying.
8 I'm going to use my experience to help others. – Could be either boy – Joel could help other poor children in his home town; Adam could help other kids who have been bullied and/or who are good with computers.

Roleplay

This is an entertaining free practice speaking activity which requires students to use a little creativity. Demonstrate the task to students by eliciting one question they would like to ask Joel and Adam. Divide the class into A and B groups. Group A students work together to create a list of questions to ask Joel. Group B thinks of questions for Adam. Every student writes the questions. Monitor the groups to support the question writing. Regroup the students in pairs so that each pair has a student from Group A and one from Group B. Student A asks the questions first, with Student B roleplaying the part of Joel. Students swap roles with Student A being Adam and Student B asking questions. Choose two to three pairs of students to act out their interviews in front of the class.

What do you think?

This speaking section encourages students to synthesize the information learned from the reading. Pre-teach/Check *perhaps*. Put students in groups of three to five and assign roles: the leader reads the questions and ensures everyone has the opportunity to speak. The reporter is in charge of sharing the group opinions with the class. The controller supports the others in their use of *will*.

Language work

This activity revises verb patterns in a fun and competitive way. Set a timer. Give students three to five minutes to find and highlight/underline verb patterns in the articles. Students count how many they found – the highest number 'wins'. Ask the winner to read out his/her verb patterns to check, then ask other students what verbs they found.

Answers
Adam Mudd: Adam started selling; he explained these attacks by saying; he denied doing anything wrong; he wanted to make friends; Adam found it difficult to make friends; the judge refused to free him.
Joel Kioko: Joel took up dancing; this is what I wanted to do; she invited him to train with her; he started teaching children; his dream is to become a principal dancer; he'd like to run a dance school; he wants to show them; he would like to move his family out of Kuwinda.

VIDEO In this unit students can watch a video about young people who have turned their lives around and have become an inspiration to others. You can play the video clip on the Classroom Presentation Tool or download it from the Teacher's Resource Centre together with the video script, video worksheet, and accompanying teacher's notes. These notes give full guidance on how to use the worksheets and include a comprehensive answer key to the exercises and activities.

Additional material
For teachers
Photocopiable activity – Video worksheet: *Inspirational young people*
For students
Online Practice – *Look again*
Online Practice – *Practice*

Vocabulary and speaking   SB p56

Phrasal verbs – literal

Possible problems

1 Literal phrasal verbs are verbs followed by prepositions or adverbs, where the meaning of the phrase is very close to that of its constituents, e.g. *put on* (a coat), *take off* (your shoes).
Although literal phrasal verbs shouldn't pose too many problems in <u>meaning</u>, students may make mistakes in <u>form</u>, for example, by leaving out the adverb or preposition, or misplacing it:
*She looked her coat but couldn't find it. (Correction: *She looked for her coat but couldn't find it.*)
*Pay back me the money you borrowed. (Correction: *Pay me back the money you borrowed.*)
2 Idiomatic phrasal verbs have a meaning that can't be guessed from the words that make up the phrasal verb, e.g. *pick up* (some Spanish), *look up* (a word).
Idiomatic phrasal verbs can pose problems in <u>meaning</u>, so it's important that students learn synonymous expressions for each.

Phrasal verbs – literal

1 Mime picking something up off the floor and elicit the phrasal verb. Write on the board: *pick up*. Underline the verb. Ask students what the second word is (a preposition). Tell them this is a *literal* phrasal verb because you are actually doing the action. Use the same phrasal verb to demonstrate idiomatic meaning: Teacher: *I picked up Spanish when I lived in Spain*. Ask students if you literally picked it up to elicit that you *learned* it. Explain that this is an *idiomatic* phrasal verb. Idiomatic phrasal verbs have a non-idiomatic synonym.
Give students a few minutes to decide which is literal and which is idiomatic. Mime carrying out the rubbish and taking the baby up to the room. Ask students for another way to say the idiomatic phrasal verbs (He *did/completed* 600 virus attacks; He *started* dancing).

Answers
a = idiomatic   b = literal

2 Students work in pairs to complete the sentences. Ask volunteers to read the sentences to the class. Point out that both words are stressed in a phrasal verb. Drill as needed.

Answers
1 off   2 on   3 up   4 down   5 at   6 back

3 Ask students to match the phrasal verbs to the pictures. Check answers. Put students in pairs. Student A has book closed. Student B mimes an action for Student A to guess. After three actions, they swap roles, with Student B guessing and Student A miming.

4 Ask students to complete the sentences with phrasal verbs from exercise 3. Ensure students know they may have to change the form of the verb. Do the first sentence together as an example.

Answers
1 looking for   4 Pick, up
2 try, on   5 throw, away
3 Turn around   6 Turn, off

Phrasal verbs – idiomatic

5 Students work in pairs to match the phrasal verbs with the synonymous phrases. When checking, ask one student to read the sentence with the phrasal verb and another to read it with the phrase. Check pronunciation.

Answers
He will stop dancing if he is homesick.
She learnt Spanish bit by bit when she worked in Madrid.
Their new business became successful very quickly.
I'm just calling to get up-to-date with your news.

6 Refer students to the pictures and ask them to match them to the phrasal verbs. Check as a class and ask questions to check understanding of each: *Who looks after a baby? Where can you look up a word? What do you do if you run out of petrol? Have you ever fallen out with your friend? Who do you get on well with?*

Answers
1 look after a baby
2 get on well with someone
3 run out of petrol
4 look up a word
5 fall out with someone

7 Students use the phrasal verbs from exercise 6 to complete the exercise. Check they have the right verb tense in feedback.

Answers
1 look, up   4 ran out of
2 get on, with   5 fell out with
3 look, after

Unit 5 • The future's in your hands   77

Talking about you

8 🔊 **5.13** Students complete the exercise, changing the verbs as needed. They compare answers with a partner. Play the recording so they can check answers. Students then ask and answer the questions in pairs. Alternatively, ask students to stand up and find someone they don't usually work with to ask questions to.

Answers and audioscript

🔊 **5.13 Talking about you**
1 Do you use a dictionary to **look up** new words?
2 How do you usually **catch up** with your friends' news? Do you text or call?
3 Do you always **get on well** with your parents or do you sometimes argue?
4 Do you ever **fall out** with friends and stop speaking to them?
5 Are you good at **picking up** foreign languages?
6 Where did you **grow up**? Do you still live there?

Additional material

For teachers
Photocopiable activity – Vocabulary: *Phrasal verbs pair-up* pp193–4

For students
Online Practice – *Look again*
Workbook p36, exercises 1–4
Online Practice – *Practice*

Everyday English   SB p57

Expressing doubt and certainty

Ask students if they think it will rain tomorrow. How sure are they? Are they 100% certain it will/won't rain, or is there some doubt? Write on the board: *100% certain it will rain/not sure/doubt it will rain/100% certain it won't rain*. Take a poll to see where students stand on each of the propositions. Refer students to the title of the section and the photo to see what they will be learning about.

1 Do the first question together as an example, then put students in pairs to discuss the others. In feedback, ask students to tell you the expressions for *I agree 100%*, *disagree 100%*, and *not sure*.

Answers
Agree 100% = Of course he will. Yes, absolutely. Definitely!
Disagree 100% = No chance. Definitely not. Not a chance.
Not certain = He might do. Mmm … maybe. I doubt it. I think so. Mmm … I'm not sure. I don't think so. Perhaps. They might do. Anything's possible.

2 🔊 **5.14** Read the instructions to the students, then play the recording.

Answers and audioscript

🔊 **5.14 Expressing doubt and certainty**
1 A Do you think Damian will pass his exams?
  B **I doubt it**. He's fed up with school.
  C I know. He has **no chance** at all. He wants to leave and get a job.
2 A Does Marek earn a lot of money?
  B **Yes, absolutely**. He earns a fortune.
  C **Mmm … I'm not sure**. I've heard he wants to change his job.
3 A Is England going to win the World Cup?
  B **Not a chance.** They're not good enough.
  C They might do. **Anything's possible**, but I think it's very unlikely.

3 🔊 **5.14** Play the recording again so that students can listen to the stress and intonation. Play it again, but pause after each sentence so that students can repeat. Put students in groups of three to practise the conversations. They take it in turns to ask the questions and give answers. If you have stronger students, ask them to write their own questions to ask their group members.

4 🔊 **5.15** Students work in pairs to complete the conversations. Fast finishers can roleplay them. Play the recording so that students can compare their answers. Ensure students have answers that are similar in meaning to the audioscript.

Answers and audioscript

🔊 **5.15 Are you sure?**
1 A Paula's job is really stressful, isn't it?
  B **Absolutely**. She's a paramedic.
  A Is she having a holiday soon?
  B I **think** so. She says she **might** go to Spain.
2 A Isn't it Emma's birthday next week?
  B Yes, **definitely**. It's on the 21st.
  A So she's a Capricorn.
  B No, I **don't think so.** I think she's an Aquarius.
3 A Do you think Anita and Paul are in love?
  B **Definitely**. They're going to get married next June in Hawaii.
  A Hawaii! Are you going to the wedding?
  B **Not a chance**. I can't afford it.

5 🔊 **5.16** Put students in groups. They take it in turns to ask the questions, and everyone gives their opinion using the phrases from exercise 1. When they have finished, play the recording. Ask students to tell you if there is any information that is surprising or that they didn't know.

🔊 **5.16 What's your opinion?**
1 A Did Mark Zuckerberg invent Facebook?
  B Definitely. It was in 2003, when he was at Harvard University – but three other students helped him do it.
2 A Was David Bowie American?
  B No, I don't think so. He died in America, in New York, in 2016, but I'm pretty sure he was English. I think he was born in London.
3 A Was Sherlock Holmes a real person?
  B Absolutely not. He's from a book by a writer called Conan Doyle.
4 A Is the population of China more than two billion?
  B It might be. I don't know. It's definitely more than one billion.
5 A Do some vegetarians eat fish?
  B I'm not sure you can be vegetarian if you eat fish. But I have a friend who says she's vegetarian, and she eats fish.
6 A Is the weather going to be nice this weekend?
  B I doubt it. It's cold and wet today.
7 A Are you going to be rich and famous one day?
  B Not a chance. I'd like to be a bit richer than now, but I wouldn't like to be famous.
8 A Is your school the best in town?
  B I'm not sure if it's *the* best, but it's definitely *one* of the best!

Additional material
For teachers
Photocopiable activity – Communication: *Anything's possible!* pp195–6
For students
Online Practice – *Look again*
Workbook p37
Online Practice – *Practice*

Writing SB p58

Writing for talking

In this *Writing* section, students write a talk which they then give to the class. If you have a very large class or little class time, you can split the class into several groups. In that way, several presentations can be held at the same time. An alternative would be for students to audio or video record themselves giving the speech. The recordings could be posted on a class blog or Facebook page or shared in a closed WhatsApp group.

1 Introduce the topic by reading the question. Give students some time to think about their answers and write some notes. Ask some students for feedback.

2 🔊 5.17 Students listen while they read Susannah's talk. Put students in pairs to answer the questions about her future. After checking, play the first part of the recording again, and ask students to draw a forward slash (/) where Susie pauses and circle words she stresses. Do the first paragraph together as a class. Point out that a full stop generally indicates a pause and a fall in intonation to let the listener know you have finished a thought. Longer sentences have pauses, too – after a complete thought or where there is a comma. Play the second paragraph for students to mark. They compare answers in pairs, then practise reading the paragraph with attention to pauses and stressed words.

🔊 **5.17** See SB p58.

Answers
• **Definite plans:** to visit and spend Christmas with her brother in Australia
• **Not sure about:** which course to study – fashion or landscape design
• **Hopes, ambitions:** to have own business and work for herself; to marry and have children
• **Dreams:** to run a successful gardening company with about 20 employees; to design beautiful gardens; to have a beautiful house, two beautiful children, and a successful husband

3 Give one or two examples of the kinds of phrases students should be looking for in Susannah's text. They work alone to underline words or phrases that would be useful for them, then compare with a partner. In feedback, ask students which words and phrases they chose and write ones on the board that you think will be useful.

Possible answers
At the moment I'm … I often dream about … I have big plans and I'd like to … My most immediate plans are … I'm going to … I need to make a final decision about … I'm thinking of … It's difficult because … In five or ten years' time I would like to … Perhaps I'll … One day I hope to … In my dreams I see myself … I'll …

4 Students rewrite the first paragraph about themselves. Monitor to give support as needed. Students read their paragraphs to each other in pairs.

5 Ask students to write the talk in class. Support the process by referring students to the questions from exercise 2, and remind them to use phrases from exercise 3. Ask them to mark with a '/' where they will pause, and circle words they want to stress.

Put students in pairs to practise their speech. They should comment on each other's use of phrases, pausing, and stress. You can re-pair them for a second practice prior to their whole-class (or group) presentation, but this time they should stand up as if they were in front of the class so that their partner can comment on their body language and eye contact as well. If possible, ask students to record themselves for homework, and give a copy of their presentation – without the pauses and stressed words marked – to another student. They listen to each other's recordings and mark where they heard the pauses and stresses. They can then compare what they think they did with what the other person heard. You might also ask them to video themselves giving the presentation so that they can notice their body language (are they fidgeting or moving in a distracting way?) and eye contact. (Tell them it's OK to use notes, but they shouldn't read – it's much more interesting to the audience if they have good eye contact at times.)

Before the presentation to the class, it's worth agreeing some rules of polite behaviour. Agree on a list with the class, for example: *Listen with respect*; *Keep eye contact with the presenter*; etc. Ask students to think of a question to ask the presenter afterwards. Call on one or two students to ask their question.

Additional material
For students
Online Practice – *Practice*
Workbook p37, *Review*, exercises 1–2
Online Practice – *Check your progress*

Unit 5 • The future's in your hands   79

6 History repeats itself

Introduction to the unit

In this unit, the theme of history repeating itself provides the perfect context for contrasting the Present Perfect and the Past Simple.

The *Grammar* section contrasts these tenses by looking at famous people who followed in their parents' footsteps. Present Perfect for experiences along with the adverbs *always, never,* and *ever* are introduced in the context of an interview with an archaeologist.

The *Vocabulary* section covers word endings and stress patterns of multi-syllable words. Knowledge of the function of word endings allows students to use language more flexibly, and awareness of word stress patterns helps them not just speak with better pronunciation, but also aids listening comprehension.

In the *Reading and speaking* section, students learn how Present Perfect is used in newspaper headlines to introduce recent events. The skills practised here are reading to correct false information, understanding vocabulary from context, and using information to form opinions. Students also conduct research for a presentation.

Family history is the focus of the *Listening and speaking* section. Students listen for specific information, and also focus on anaphoric pronoun referencing in the text. They use ideas from the listening to give their opinion in a discussion.

Everyday English focuses on question tags to show agreement, including the cultural convention of saying more than just *yes* and *no* in reply to question tags.

In the *Writing* section, students use textual cues (grammar, phrases, and dates) to order paragraphs in a biography about Princess Diana, then apply this knowledge in writing a biography of Prince Harry.

Language aims

Grammar

Present Perfect, *for* and *since*, *ever* and *never*

This unit introduces students to and practises two uses of the Present Perfect:

- an action or state which began in the past and continues to the present
- experiences in life before now

Present Perfect for past actions with results in the present and adverbs common with this use are introduced in the Grammar reference to support teachers and students if needed.

Past Simple and Present Perfect are also contrasted and practised.

The unit also covers issues related to Present Perfect such as the use of the full form in short answers (*Yes, I have.* rather than **Yes, I've.*), the time expressions *for* and *since*, and use of *ever* and *never* for experiences in life before now.

A guided discovery approach is used so that students focus first on the context in which the Present Perfect and Past Simple are used. Students are asked to notice the grammar before seeing the rules. This context-first approach helps students internalize the contexts in which each is used so that they develop a deeper understanding of when each tense is used.

Vocabulary

Word endings and stress

This section supports students' word building skills, which will give students more flexibility in their reading and writing, and will also lay the foundation for paraphrasing – a necessary skill in academic writing. The section covers common noun, verb, and adjective endings, and students also learn how the stress pattern changes with the word form.

Everyday English

Agree with me!

The aim of this section is to give students exposure to question tags with falling intonation that ask for agreement. Question tags are used in spoken English, but not in formal written English. The aim is practice and awareness rather than perfection and use in this section.

Additional material

Workbook

Students complete a text using Present Perfect with regular and irregular verbs. Questions and short answers using the Present Perfect are practised, as are the adverbs of frequency and time. The Past Simple is contrasted with the Present Perfect in several tasks. A reading text contrasts the use of Past Simple, Past Continuous, and Present Perfect. Students focus on word endings which denote word function, and then on word stress in nouns and adjectives. Question tags used to invite agreement are focused on in the final tasks, and the unit ends with a Grammar review.

Photocopiable activities

There are photocopiable activities to review grammar (*How long have you … ?*), vocabulary (*I'd love to be famous!*), and communication (*Question tags*) at the back of the Teacher's Guide as well as on the Teacher's Resource Centre. There is also a worksheet to accompany the video on the Teacher's Resource Centre.

Notes on the unit

Unit opener page

Choose from these activities to engage your students with the topic and target language of this unit.

- Talk about the title
- Talk about the unit goals (*Grammar, Vocabulary,* …)
- Talk about the photo
- Watch the video
- Look at the bottom banner
- Do the activity

Refer students to the photo on p59. What do they think it shows? Elicit/Pre–teach some vocabulary: *shield* /ʃiːld/, *banner/flag, soldiers*. Ask students what time period they think the soldiers are from. Explain that this is a re-enactment – people dressing up like soldiers from the past to re-enact a battle. In England, groups get together to re-enact the battles from the Wars of the Roses (between the House of Lancaster and House of York in the 15th century), and the English Civil War (between King Charles I and Parliament in the 17th century). Find out if this kind of event happens in the students' cultures.

Refer students to the unit title, 'History repeats itself'. *Do we learn from mistakes/disasters in history?* (often it appears we don't).

If you don't have time to watch the video introduction to the unit, go through the unit goals below the title: *Grammar, Vocabulary, Everyday English, Reading, Listening, Writing*. Give examples or use translation for unknown words.

Video (2 minutes approximately): The video gives a step-by-step overview of the unit. Play the video, pausing where necessary – especially for students to answer any questions, e.g. *Are you interested in history?* This makes it a more interactive experience. Highlight the option of practising online.

As shown in the bottom banner, don't forget that there are many exercises to consolidate and practise the target language of the unit in the Workbook as well as online. There are links to these exercises on the relevant pages of the Student's Book and they can be done in class time or you can set them for homework.

Summary: If you're short of time, use the title and the photo to help students understand and engage with the topic, and then move straight on to the activity so that they can discuss the theme in more detail. If you have any more time, try to watch the video together. It is a clear and interesting introduction to the different parts of the unit.

Notes for activity:
Put students in pairs. Ask them to look at the photo and discuss their answers to the questions. Ask them to justify their choices where possible.

Suggested answers
1 Roman.
2 To entertain people, because they enjoy it, because they are interested in history and want other people to be.
3 Students' own answers.

Grammar SB p60

Present Perfect, *for/since*

Possible problems

1 Students will be familiar with the form of the Present Perfect, but are still likely to make mistakes. The key area of confusion is likely to be in the use of the Present Perfect, particularly when contrasted with the Past Simple.

2 The Present Perfect is used to refer to actions 'completed some time before now, but with some present relevance', and so joins past and present. In English, we can say *I have seen the Queen.* (at some indefinite time in my life), but not **I have seen the Queen yesterday*. In many other European languages, the same form of *have* + the past participle can be used to express both indefinite time (Present Perfect) and finished past time (Past Simple). Many languages use a present tense to express unfinished past.
   Common mistakes include:
   **I have watched TV last night.*
   (Correction: *I watched TV last night.*)
   **When have you been to Russia?*
   (Correction: *When did you go to Russia?*)
   * *I live here for five years.*
   (Correction: *I have lived here for five years.*)

3 *For* and *since*
   Students can be confused about when to use *for* and *since* with Present Perfect:
   For is used with periods of time – *for* three years/two months/ages/a long time/a fortnight.
   Since refers to a specific point in time – *since* last week/yesterday/1999/Monday/July 7th.
   Common mistakes:
   **She's lived in Oxford since three months.*
   (Correction: *She's lived in Oxford for 3 months.*)
   **I've worked here for January 1st.*
   (Correction: *I've worked here since January 1st.*)
   **She's known him for week.*
   (Correction: *She's known him for weeks.*)

STARTER SB p60

1 Start by reviewing the Past Simple and past participle forms of common verbs (sometimes referred to as the *second* and *third forms of the verb*) on p158.

2 Most verbs are regular, but most common ones are irregular and the forms have to be memorized. A fun way to revise the forms is through 'verb tennis'. Put students into pairs. Student A 'serves' by saying the first form (infinitive); student B 'returns' with the second form (past tense); student A 'hits it back' with the third form (past participle). Student B then serves. Points are won by the server, or when one student misses. Score as in tennis – *love, 15, 30,* etc.

Unit 6 • History repeats itself 81

Answers

Base form	Past Simple	Past participle
live	lived	lived
have	had	had
be	was/were	been
sing	sang	sung
go	went	gone/been
eat	ate	eaten
know	knew	known
wear	wore	worn
move	moved	moved
work	worked	worked
write	wrote	written

Live, move, work are regular. The others are irregular.

In famous footsteps

About the text

The three texts highlight three situations in which the children of famous parents have followed in their parents' footsteps to also become famous for similar things their parents did. The first text is about Steve Irwin /stiːv ˈɜːwɪn/ and his daughter, Bindi /ˈbɪndi/. Students might remember Steve's TV series, *Crocodile Hunter* – a documentary aimed at teaching the world more about wildlife. Steve was killed by a stingray barb during the filming of *Ocean's Deadliest*. The second text is about Princess Diana /daɪˈænə/ and her son Prince Harry /ˈhæri/. Princess Diana was the wife of Charles /tʃɑːlz/, the Prince of Wales, son and heir of Queen Elizabeth /əˈlɪzəbəθ/ II of England. Harry is their younger son. Diana was known for her charitable work, and was patron of over 100 charities. She was killed in a car accident in Paris in 1997. The third text is about musician John Lennon /dʒɒn ˈlenən/ and his son, Julian /ˈdʒuːliən/. John is best known in connection with The Beatles, though his musical career and political activism (e.g. bed-ins in support of the peace movement) continued up to his death in 1980. He was shot dead outside his apartment in New York City by Mark Chapman /mɑːk ˈtʃæpmən/.

1 Ask students what they think the title 'In famous footsteps' means. Give examples to demonstrate meaning: *Her father was a famous doctor, and she became a famous doctor – she followed in his footsteps*. Refer students to the photos and elicit information about the people. Check pronunciation and spelling of *daughter* /ˈdɔːtə(r)/.

Answers
1 father and daughter
2 mother and son
3 father and son
Pair 1 is connected with wildlife.
Pair 2 is connected with charity work.
Pair 3 is connected with music.

2 ◉ 6.1 Students work in pairs to discuss the sentences and write the names. When checking, help students notice the verb tenses used: *Which ones are in the past? Why?* (the people are no longer alive). *Which ones are in the Present Perfect? Why?* (the people are still alive and working). Play the recording so students can check their answers.

Answers and audioscript

◉ 6.1 **Famous people**
1 **John Lennon** wrote the famous song *Imagine*.
2 **Prince Harry** has been Patron of the *HALO* Trust since 2013.
3 **Steve Irwin** always wore a khaki shirt and shorts.
4 **Bindi Irwin** has sung with The Crocmen and The Jungle Girls.
5 **Princess Diana** married Prince Charles in 1981.
6 **Julian Lennon** has written a children's book.

3 ◉ 6.2 If needed, do a quick review of the form of Present Perfect on the board before setting this exercise. Allow students to discuss answers in pairs. Monitor and support as needed. Play the recording for students to check their answers. At this point, students may be making mistakes with the choice of tense, but reassure them that the next sections will help them learn which tense to use.

Answers and audioscript

◉ 6.2 **In famous footsteps**

Steve and Bindi Irwin
1 Steve **grew** up on his parents' wildlife park in Australia and became a popular TV personality with his TV series *The Crocodile Hunter*. He **died** in 2006 while filming a programme about stingrays. Bindi **has been** a TV personality since she was two! Since her father died, she **has made** many wildlife TV programmes of her own. She **starred** in the film *Free Willy 4* in 2010 and also *Return to Nim's Island* in 2013. Bindi sings too, and **has made** five albums with Bindi and the Jungle Girls.

Princess Diana and Prince Harry
2 Diana **did** a lot of work with charities in Africa, and she once **walked** through a minefield in Angola to bring attention to the work of *HALO*. Since 1988, this organization **has found** and destroyed over 1.6 million landmines around the world. Harry **has done** charity work for many years and **has continued** his mother's work with *HALO* in Africa. He **has visited** minefields in Mozambique and Angola, and in 2017 he **asked** all governments to stop using landmines by the year 2025.

John and Julian Lennon
3 John **wrote** most of The Beatles' songs with Paul McCartney. After The Beatles, John **became** a solo artist and also **did** a lot of work for the Peace Movement with his wife Yoko Ono. Julian **began** playing guitar and drums when he was ten, and **has made** six solo albums. In 2006, he **produced** a film about the environment, called *Whale Dreamers* and he **has** recently **written** a children's book called *Touch the Earth*.

4 ◉ 6.3 Students write the questions using the prompts. You can add a bit of challenge to this activity by asking pairs to write the questions on slips of paper which they put into the middle of the table. They close their books. One student takes a slip and reads the question. The other student has to answer from memory. Play the recording so that students can check their questions. After checking, ask students to find the rule in the Grammar reference for each question.

Answers and audioscript

◉ 6.3 **Questions and answers**
1 Where **did** Steve Irwin **grow up**? (finished action)
  He grew up on his parents' wildlife park in Australia.
2 When **did** he **die**?
  He died in 2006.

82 Unit 6 • History repeats itself

3 How many films **has** Bindi Irwin **starred** in? (experiences in life before now)
   She's starred in two films.
4 How many albums **has** she **made** with The Jungle Girls? (experiences in life before now)
   She's made five albums.
5 Where **did** Princess Diana **walk** through a minefield? (finished action)
   She walked through a minefield in Angola.
6 Where **has** Prince Harry **visited** minefields? (experiences in life before now)
   He's visited minefields in Mozambique and Angola.
7 What **did** Harry **ask** governments to do in 2017? (finished action)
   He asked them to stop using landmines.
8 Who **did** John Lennon **write** songs with? (finished action)
   He wrote songs with Paul McCartney, for The Beatles.
9 When **did** Julian Lennon **begin** playing the guitar? (finished action – although he still plays, he *began* at a point in time. He is no longer *beginning* to play)
   He began playing the guitar when he was ten.
10 How many solo albums **has** Julian **made**? (experiences in life before now, or began in the past and continues to the present if he is still making solo albums)
   He's made six solo albums.

GRAMMAR SPOT SB p61

This *Grammar spot* uses a guided discovery approach to:
- help students notice the form and meaning differences in Past Simple and Present Perfect
- help students learn when to use *for* or *since*

1 Refer students to exercise 2 to find three examples of each tense. Students can use different coloured highlighters or underline one tense and circle the other. Write the verbs on the board in two columns headed *Past Simple* and *Present Perfect* to further draw attention to the difference in form of each.

Answers
Past Simple = 1, 3, 5
Present Perfect = 2, 4, 6
We form the Present Perfect with *have/has* + past participle.

2 Ask students to try to explain the use of different tenses in the two sentences. Ask questions, if needed, to lead students to the meaning: *Is Steve Irwin alive or dead? Is he still making TV programmes? What about Bindi? Is she still alive and making TV programmes?* Note that in the sentence about John Lennon, the form of the verb isn't wrong, but the sentence is grammatically wrong because John Lennon is no longer alive.

Answers
Past Simple is used in the first sentence because Steve Irwin is dead.
Present Perfect is used in the second sentence because Bindi Irwin is still alive.
The sentence about John Lennon is wrong because he is dead – the sentence implies that he is still alive.

3 Elicit when each is used. It may be helpful to draw a table on the board with the headings: *Period of time – for*; *Point in time – since*. Brainstorm expressions that will go in each category. Do a quick check:

students close their books. Call out a time expression (*a long time, 2018, 8:00, three hours; a month*, etc.). Students say whether each is preceded by *since* or *for*. Ask students to read Grammar reference 6.1 on p147.

Answers
We use *for* a time period. We use *since* for a point in time

Practice SB p61

How long … ?

1 Students fill in the gaps with *for* or *since*. After checking, students test each other in pairs. Student A says the expression and Student B (without looking) says *for* or *since*. They swap roles and repeat. Ask students to think of two more examples to add to the list.

Answers
1 for half an hour
2 since 2001
3 since I was 14
4 for a long time
5 since ten o'clock
6 for three months
7 since October
8 since last Tuesday
9 for two weeks

2 **6.4** Read the instructions to the students. Ensure they understand there is more than one possible answer. Do the first one together as an example. Students read their combinations aloud in pairs before listening to the recording. Check that students' A–B combinations are correct and that they make sense with C. Ask students to make sentences like the ones in the exercise. Ideally, they would speak them rather than write them, though weaker students may need to write before speaking. In feedback, ask three or four confident students for their sentences.

Answers and audioscript
6.4 for or since
1 I've known John for many years. We met at university.
2 I last went to the cinema a month ago. The film was really boring.
3 I've had this watch since I was a child. My grandad gave it to me.
4 I lived in New York from 2017 to 2019. I had a great time there.
5 I've lived in this house since 2015. It's got a beautiful garden.
6 We last had a holiday two years ago. We went to Spain.
7 I haven't seen you for ages. What have you been up to?
8 We haven't had a break for over an hour. I really need a coffee.

3 **6.5** Lead in to this section by asking students what kinds of questions we ask when we want to get to know someone better. Brainstorm some ideas. Refer students to exercise 3 to complete the interview. Play the recording so students can check. Play it again so that students can repeat, paying attention to using falling intonation for the questions. They practise the interview in pairs.

Unit 6 • History repeats itself 83

> **Answers and audioscript**
>
> 🔊 **6.5 Questions and answers**
> A Where do you live, Vicki?
> B In a flat near the town centre. It's nice because it's got a balcony.
> A How long **have you lived** there?
> B **For** three years, but it feels like I've been there longer.
> A So why **did you** move there?
> B Because I wanted to walk to work. I hated the commute from my last place!
> A And what **do** you **do**?
> B I work for a pharmaceutical firm. I'm in the marketing department.
> A Ah. How long **have you worked** there?
> B **Since** 2015. It's a really good company to work for.
> A Hmm. So what **did you** do before that?
> B Um, I was a student in Edinburgh. I studied Chemistry and Biology.

Talking about you

4 Pair up students who don't usually work together or who don't know each other well for this activity.

As a follow-up, try the following activity to add a bit of fun and challenge to asking questions. Ask each student to think of a famous person – alive or dead – without telling anyone. Their partner has to guess who it is by asking questions: *Has this person been on TV?*, etc. As a longer alternative, ask pairs to research a famous person – alive or dead. They write a set of 'quiz' questions. These can be a mixture of T/F (e.g. *X has won three gold medals. – T or F?*), short answer (e.g. *Where did X grow up?*), and multiple choice (e.g. *Which film was X's first? A, B, or C?*). They could do research about the person for homework if needed. Monitor to check they are using the correct tenses in their questions. Put pairs together to 'quiz' each other.

Digging up the past SB p62

Present Perfect – *always*, *ever* and *never*

Possible problems

> **1** This second presentation covers the use of the Present Perfect to talk about an experience some time before now. It also consolidates the use of the Past Simple to refer to finished actions at a definite time in the past.
>
> **2** The adverbs *ever* and *never* are frequently used with the 'experience' meaning of the Present Perfect. These are both 'indefinite' time references – *ever* (= at any time up to now), *never* (= at no time up to now). *Ever* is often used with the Present Perfect and a superlative to talk about the best/biggest/most exciting, etc. thing experienced up to now.
> Common mistakes include:
> *Did you ever try Japanese food? (Correction: Have you ever tried Japanese food?)
> *We didn't ever seen a play in English. (Correction: We've never seen a play in English.)
> *I never went to the US in my life. (Correction: I've never been to the US in my life.)
> *He hasn't never won a competition. (Correction: He's never won a competition.)
> *It's the best film I ever see in my life. (Correction: It's the best film I've ever seen in my life.)
> *I haven't never worked in a restaurant. (Correction: I've never worked in a restaurant.)
>
> **3** It's worth noting that Present Perfect is not as widely used in American English. Students may have heard American English, so you may need to clarify. Examples include:
> *Are you going to the film? No, I already saw it.* (AmE)/*No, I've already seen it.* (BrE)
> *Did you try the food yet?* (AmE)/*Have you tried the food yet?* (BrE)
> *I can't find my phone. Did you see it anywhere?* (AmE)/*Have you seen it anywhere?* (BrE)

About the text

Although the main character in the interview is fictitious, the artefacts from the tomb of Tutankhamun /tuːtənˈkɑːmən/ are some of the most travelled in the world. Probably the best-known exhibition tour was *The Treasures of Tutankhamun* tour, which ran from 1972 to 1981. This exhibition was first shown in London at the British Museum from March 30 until September 30, 1972 and finished in Hamburg in July 1981.

The Great Wall of China was mostly built by the Ming Dynasty, though it was started by the Qin Dynasty (221–227 BC) when glutinous rice flour was used to bind the bricks! It took more than 1,800 years to build the wall we know today. It is actually a collection of walls rather than one long structure. Contrary to urban myth, it can only be seen from space with the aid of a telescope.

The Sahara is the third largest desert in the world; it covers much of North Africa and extends to an area of 9,200,000 square kilometres (3,600,000 square miles).

The Nile flows through at least nine nations – from its origins at Lake Tana in Ethiopia (Blue Nile) and Lake Victoria (White Nile) or even further upstream to Burundi to its eventual meeting with the Mediterranean Sea in Egypt. The Guinness Book of World Records lists the Nile as the longest river in the world – 6,695 kilometres.

A Land Rover is a powerful, four-wheel-drive vehicle designed for travelling over rough or steep ground.

1 Refer students to the photos of Frieda, and ask, *What kind of person do you think Frieda is? What countries has she been to?* Pre-teach/Check *to live abroad*, *to have a passion for*, and *ancient history*. Ask students to read the introduction to find out what her job, nationality, and passions are. Briefly drill the pronunciation of *archaeologist*: /ˌɑːkiˈɒlədʒɪst/. Elicit what an archaeologist does. Find out if any students have a passion for history and ancient civilizations. Has anyone lived abroad?

> **Answers**
> Frieda Hoffmann is German. She's been to South Africa, China, Algeria, Kenya, and Egypt. Her passions are ancient history and writing.

2 🔊 **6.6** Read the questions with the students, then ask them to read the interview and put the questions on the right line. Play the recording so that students can check their answers. Ask students to guess from context what *pharaoh*, *tomb*, *to look after myself* mean. What do they think about her life? Would they like to see the things she's seen? If you have time, put students in pairs to conduct the interview – Student A is the interviewer and Student B is Frieda. Encourage good intonation – both in the questions and the answers.

Answers and audioscript

🔊 **6.6 Frieda Hoffmann, archaeologist and writer – Part 1**
I = Interviewer   F = Frieda

I Frieda Hoffmann grew up in Germany, but has lived most of her life abroad. Her passion is ancient history, and she has written several books about ancient Egypt.
Frieda, you've travelled a lot in your lifetime. **Which countries have you been to?**
F Well, I've been to a lot of countries in Africa, and I've been to China and Nepal. I've never been to South America, but I'm planning a trip there soon.
I **When did you first travel abroad?**
F When I was six. My family moved to England.
I **Why did you move there?**
F Because my father got a job as Professor of History at Cambridge University.
I **Have you always been interested** in archaeology?
F Yes, I have. When I was ten, there was an exhibition about Tutankhamun, the Egyptian king, in London. My father took me to see it, and I was fascinated! After that, I knew I wanted to be an archaeologist and work in Egypt.
I **How many times have you been to Egypt?**
F Oh, … I've been there 30 times at least! I go as often as I can.
I **Have you ever made an important discovery?**
F Yes, I've made some very important discoveries, including some important ancient tombs near Cairo.
I And you've written books about Egypt, too, haven't you? **How many books have you written?**
F I've written three about the pharaohs. And I've written a book about a journey I made from Cairo to Cape Town.
I **How did you travel?** By train? Or by car?
F By Land Rover, of course!
I Ah, yes. And in all your travels, **have you ever been in any dangerous situations?**
F Oh my goodness, yes! I've often been in danger. But I've learnt to look after myself!

3 This exercise gives students the opportunity to practise questions and answers in the third person. Students write out the questions, then take turns to ask and answer them – preferably from memory! When checking as a class, ask one student to ask the question, and another to answer it.

Answers

Has she ever been to South America? No, she hasn't.
When did she move to England? When she was six.
Where did her father get a job? He got a job at Cambridge University.
When did she see the Tutankhamun Exhibition? She saw the Tutankhamun Exhibition when she was ten.
How many times has she been to Egypt? She's been there 30 times at least.
How many books has she written? She's written four books.

GRAMMAR SPOT   SB p62

1 Read the instructions as a class. Give students time to think about the answers to the questions. Let students check in pairs before checking with the class.

Answers

- You've travelled a lot in your lifetime. (Present Perfect – refers to an experience some time in your life.)
- Which countries have you been to? (Present Perfect – refers to an experience some time in your life.)
- When I was six, my family moved to England. (Past Simple – refers to a definite time in the past.)

2 Read the examples as a class. Point out that the verb form with *never* is positive although the meaning is negative, and that you can't say
I haven't never been to South America.

If appropriate, get students to translate *ever* and *never* into their own language.

Note that the response to *Have you ever been in danger?* is: *No, **I've never** been / I **haven't ever** been in danger.* or *Yes, I've been in danger before.*

Ask students to read Grammar reference 6.2 on p147 for homework and ask questions as needed in the next lesson.

Practice   SB p63

Present Perfect or Past Simple?

About the text

Frieda refers to the revolution in Cairo in 2011 in the interview. The anti-poverty, corruption and political repression uprising, inspired by a similar successful uprising in Tunisia in 2010, led to the then President Mubārak to step down after several weeks of mass protests.

In this section, students listen to more of the interview with Frieda to focus on the different use of Past Simple and Present Perfect.

1 🔊 **6.7** Ask students to read the gapped sentences, then play the recording. Allow them to compare answers and play the recording again if needed. When checking, ask students to say why each tense is used.

Answers and audioscript

🔊 **6.7 Frieda Hoffmann – Part 2**

1 I Do you go back to Germany much?
   F No, I don't. **I've been** back a few times to visit relatives, but **I've never lived** there again. I feel more English than German now, and I've forgotten a lot of my German.
2 I What **did** you **study** at university?
   F I **studied** Ancient History at Cambridge.
   I Did you enjoy it?
   F Oh, yes, I had a wonderful time! The course was amazing, and Cambridge is a great place to live.
3 I **Have** you ever **had** any other jobs, apart from being an archaeologist?
   F Yes, I **have.** I've **done** all sorts of jobs – I even **worked** as a waitress when I was at university.
   I Really! What was that like?
   F I loved it! I was a tour guide, too, in the holidays. I met some really interesting people!
4 I You said you've often been in danger. What's the most dangerous situation you've **ever been** in?
   F Well, I **had** a very difficult time in Cairo during the revolution in 2011. I **spent** two weeks inside my friend's house – it was too dangerous to go out! Of course, I'm fortunate – I can leave a country when things get really dangerous. It was the local people I felt sorry for.

Unit 6 • History repeats itself   85

2 🔊 **6.7** Play the recording again and ask students to take notes on any extra information they hear. Elicit ideas as a class.

3 Put students in pairs to ask and answer questions using the prompts. Choose a confident student and do the first together as an example. Encourage students to do this orally instead of writing the questions first.

> **Answers**
> Has she ever worked in a restaurant? Yes, she has.
> When did she do that? When she was at university.
> Has she ever crossed the Sahara? Yes she has.
> When did she do that? When she was in her early thirties.
> Has she ever travelled up the Nile? Yes she has.
> When did she do that? In 2002.
> Has she ever walked the Great Wall of China? Yes she has.
> When did she do that? In 2010.

Talking about you

4 This exercise combines the use of Present Perfect to ask about experiences with Past Simple to give more information about what happened. This is what people would naturally do in communication, and students need to see this exercise as communication and not just grammar practice. Start by demonstrating the activity. Ask students a *Have you ever … ?* question until someone says yes, then ask a follow-up question for more information. Students could work in pairs to do this exercise, or you could do it as a *Find someone who …* milling activity: they move around the room asking the questions in order to find someone who says yes and can tell about what happened. Encourage students to come up with two more *Have you ever … ?* questions to ask each other. To allow extra practice with third person, ask students to tell the class about one of the people they spoke to, e.g. *X has been to America. He went there in …*

Additional material
For teachers
Photocopiable activity – Grammar: *How long have you … ?* pp197–8
For students
Online Practice – *Look again*
Workbook pp38–41, exercises 1–14
Online Practice – *Practice*

Vocabulary and pronunciation SB p63

Word endings and word stress

1 Misplaced word stress is the main reason many learners of English are misunderstood when speaking. This exercise focuses students' attention on stressed syllables and how they can change according to word form. Lead in by writing the noun endings *-er*, *-ian*, and *-ist* on the board, and asking students to tell you any jobs they can think of that finish with the endings, e.g. *teacher*. Focus attention on the examples in the Student's Book. Draw students' attention to how words can change: *What does an archaeologist study?* (archaeology); *What does a writer do?* (writes); *What does a historian study?* (history).

Answers
-ist, -er, -ian

2 🔊 **6.8** Students could use dictionaries to complete this exercise. Elicit the job from *photograph* and note the change in word stress: ′photograph → pho′tographer. Put students in pairs to make the names of jobs from the words. Monitor and help as necessary. Play the recording so that students can check their answers. Then play the recording again and get students to repeat chorally and individually.

Answers and audioscript

🔊 **6.8 Word endings for jobs**

<u>ar</u>tist	<u>far</u>mer
ac<u>coun</u>tant	poli<u>ti</u>cian
in<u>ven</u>tor	in<u>ter</u>preter
pho<u>tog</u>rapher	as<u>sis</u>tant
e<u>con</u>omist	<u>buil</u>der
elec<u>tri</u>cian	trans<u>la</u>tor
<u>ac</u>tor	re<u>cep</u>tionist
mu<u>si</u>cian	

3 🔊 **6.9** Check that students understand *parts of speech*. Write *Parts of speech* on the board and draw a circle around it. Draw lines radiating out from the circle and elicit parts of speech (*noun*, *verb*, *adjective*, *adverb*, *pronoun*, etc.) Ask students for examples of each. Refer them to the chart in exercise 3, and read the instructions together. Draw attention to dropped *e* from *reserve → reservation* and explain that some words will change spelling when the ending is added. Allow dictionary use to check spelling if possible. Write answers on the board to ensure students have the right spelling, and play the recording so students can repeat the words and underline the main stress in each word.

Answers and audioscript

🔊 **6.9 Word endings**

reser<u>va</u>tion	re<u>serve</u>
expla<u>na</u>tion	ex<u>plain</u>
be<u>ha</u>viour	be<u>have</u>
invi<u>ta</u>tion	in<u>vite</u>
de<u>ci</u>sion	de<u>cide</u>
<u>stu</u>dent	<u>stu</u>dy
col<u>lec</u>tion	col<u>lect</u>
<u>ar</u>gument	<u>ar</u>gue
dis<u>cus</u>sion	dis<u>cuss</u>
<u>fame</u>	<u>fa</u>mous
<u>dif</u>ference	<u>dif</u>ferent
ex<u>pense</u>	ex<u>pen</u>sive
<u>dan</u>ger	<u>dan</u>gerous
suc<u>cess</u>	suc<u>cess</u>ful
<u>mu</u>sic	<u>mu</u>sical
<u>kind</u>ness	<u>kind</u>
pos<u>si</u>bility	<u>pos</u>sible
<u>health</u>	<u>heal</u>thy

4 🔊 **6.10** This exercise demonstrates how knowing word forms creates flexibility in using English. Refer students to the example and play the first pair. Play the next sentence and pause the recording to elicit a sentence with *famous*. Continue playing the first sentence and eliciting the second to the end. If you find students are struggling with this activity, write the first sentences on the board with the word form for the changed sentence in brackets. Allow

86   Unit 6 • History repeats itself

students some time to think about how to change them, then play the recording for them to listen and check.

Answers and audioscript

🔊 **6.10 Different word forms**
1 I collect postcards.
   I have a collection of postcards.
2 I've never wanted fame.
   I've never wanted to be famous.
3 Can we discuss your work?
   Can we have a discussion about your work?
4 Is he behaving OK?
   Is his behaviour OK?
5 Health is very important.
   It's important to be healthy.
6 It's time for a decision.
   It's time to decide.
7 I'm not very good at music.
   I'm not very musical.
8 We often argue.
   We often have arguments.

5 🔊 **6.11** This exercise shows typical stress patterns of two-syllable nouns, adjectives, and verbs, and some three-syllable nouns. Not all two-syllable words follow this pattern (e.g. *success* and *expense* in exercise 3). Note that although *difference* looks like three-syllable words, in British English it has two syllables /ˈdɪfrəns/. Ask students to look at the words in the chart and think about which syllable is stressed. Play the recording so that students underline the stressed syllable. Some students will have trouble hearing the difference. Demonstrate stress patterns kinaesthetically: an upward hand gesture = stressed syllable, downward gesture = unstressed syllable. You could also clap the syllables: loud clap = stressed, soft clap = unstressed. Students do the motions with you. Elicit other examples for each group of words.

Answers and audioscript

🔊 **6.11 Word stress**
Two-syllable nouns: <u>dan</u>ger, <u>kind</u>ness, <u>cri</u>tic, <u>ar</u>tist, <u>di</u>fference
Two-syllable adjectives: <u>heal</u>thy, <u>friend</u>ly, <u>fa</u>mous, <u>di</u>fferent
Two-syllable verbs: in<u>vite</u>, ex<u>plain</u>, dis<u>cuss</u>, em<u>ploy</u>, de<u>cide</u>, com<u>pete</u>
Nouns ending in -*tion* and -*sion*: invi<u>ta</u>tion, expla<u>na</u>tion, compe<u>ti</u>tion, am<u>bi</u>tion, de<u>ci</u>sion

SUGGESTION Ask students to keep a word forms chart similar to the one on p63 of the Student's Book in a separate section of their notebook. They could also add a column for adverbs. Students use the chart to note down and keep a record of word forms. They should underline the stressed syllable in each word. Periodically, quiz the class on the forms, e.g.
   Teacher: *Reservation is the noun. What's the verb?*
   Students: *Reserve.*
You could also ask them to change sentences by using a different form, e.g. *Have you made the reservation? Have you reserved the room?* In addition to the flexibility in language use this helps foster, this also helps with the skill of paraphrasing – an important skill to have if doing academic work where paraphrasing is needed to avoid plagiarism caused by direct copying.

Additional material

For teachers
Photocopiable activity – Vocabulary: *I'd love to be famous!* pp199–200

For students
Online Practice – *Look again*
Workbook p42, exercises 1–3
Online Practice – *Practice*

Reading and speaking SB p64

The not so distant past

About the text
The reading starts with news headlines that appear to be very current, but which turn out to be ancient. Headlines using Present Perfect follow the third use outlined in the Grammar reference on p147 – *a past action with results in the present*. The first headline is an allusion to the Iraq war which began with the invasion of Iraq by the United States in 2003. The second could be referring to Syrian refugees trying to enter Turkey where walls have been built to try to keep them out or separated, or it might be alluding to President Trump's promised wall along the US-Mexican border. The third headline could refer to a recent protest against big companies avoiding tax by moving their money to offshore bank accounts. It's an interesting concept that history repeats itself and that the same problems we have today were faced by our ancestors. In the past, the Roman Empire spanned Europe, parts of Africa, and much of Asia. The Goths were Eastern Germanic tribes who fought the Romans, but who were invaded by the Huns – warrior bands from the East who also fought the Romans and whose greatest leader, Attila, lives on in legend. Parts of Hadrian's Wall still stand in the North of England as a reminder of the threat of Scottish 'barbarians' invading Emperor Hadrian's Roman Britain. In the section, *The Romans in Britain*, the reading takes an optimistic turn in looking at the positive influences of the Romans on Britain, even though they were foreign invaders. The line, *What good have the Romans done for us?* is taken from a Monty Python comedy film, the *Life of Brian* – a film many students may be familiar with.

1 As a lead-in, write *History repeats itself* on the board and ask students what they think it means. Can they think of any examples? See if they have a similar expression in their own language.

Answer
It means when similar events happen again and again.

2 🔊 **6.12** Pre-teach/Check *headlines, captured, executed, refugee, foreigners, protest, tax*. Play the recording as students read along. Discuss each headline in turn, using the questions as prompts. Find out if students have any of these problems in their country. Be sensitive to the subjects in the headlines as some students may have been affected by events. Keep the discussion factual and steer students away from voicing strong opinions which might upset others.

Unit 6 • History repeats itself   87

🔊 **6.12** See SB p64.

> **Answer**
> fighting in Iraq; refugees and leaders building walls to keep people out; protests about rich people avoiding tax

3 Ask students to read the headings, *Same old problems* and *The Romans in Britain*, and predict what these sections will be about. Did they know there were Romans in Britain? Give students a moment to read the questions, then ask them to read the section to find the answers. Ask them if they were surprised by what they read. Check as a class.

> **Answers**
> 1 Mesopotamia.
> 2 To escape the Huns, who were invading their land.
> 3 Hadrian.
> 4 To pay for wars and unemployment. Rich people knew where to move their money so that the government couldn't tax it.
> 5 Because the Romans ruled Britain for nearly 400 years.

4 Pre-teach/Check *aqueduct* /ˈækwɪdʌkt/, *luxury* /ˈlʌkʃəri/, *flushing, sewage* /ˈsuːɪdʒ/, *currency, leap year, minced meat*. Avoid teaching the vocabulary in exercise 5 at this point, and deter students from using dictionaries. Ask students to read the last two sections quickly. Note that *foreign peoples* refers to many groups of people – this is an example of an uncountable noun used as a countable noun in certain contexts (see Unit 4). Students work in pairs to correct the statements. Check as a class and ask students what new information they learned from the article.

> **Answers**
> 1 There are 9,600 km of **old Roman** roads in Britain.
> 2 The British **used a global currency before – Roman coins**.
> 3 There were **copies** of the first Roman newspapers **in public places**.
> 4 The Romans **didn't need** to wear lots of pairs of socks in their villas.
> 5 Roman aqueducts in the cities were **completely new in Britain**.
> 6 The British used **new recipes the Romans brought with them** to make food for the Romans.
> 7 We have **continued to use** the Roman year.

SUGGESTION Ask students to add new words to their vocabulary notebooks. *Luxury* could be added to their word forms chart: *luxury* (n); *luxurious* (adj); to *luxuriate* /lʌɡˈʒʊərieɪt/ (v); *luxuriously* (adv). You could use this opportunity to teach the phonemic symbols in some of the new words: /æ/, /ʌ/, /ʃ/, /uː/, /dʒ/.

Vocabulary

5 The aim in this exercise is to work out the meaning of these words from context. This section could be done prior to exercise 4, or as a review of new vocabulary learned from the reading. Students work in pairs to match the words and definitions and find them in the text. Go through the answers as a class and check/drill pronunciation. Identify stressed syllables and teach any new phonemic symbols. Students could look in the dictionary to find out how to write the words using the phonemic script, or they could just identify difficult sounds in the words that they have problems pronouncing, e.g. the /ptʃ/ combination in capture /ˈkæptʃə(r)/ or the /ksɪz/ combination in taxes /ˈtæksɪz/. Ask students to make revision cards to learn the words: they write the word on one side with the stressed syllable underlined, and the phonemic transcription below the word if possible. On the other side, they write the definition. They can use these cards to test each other in pairs. These can be collected and distributed again in another lesson as a revision of the vocabulary.

> **Answers**
> 1 e 2 c 3 g 4 i 5 f 6 h 7 a 8 j 9 b 10 d

What do you think?

Give students a few minutes to read and think about the questions before putting them in small groups to discuss. Follow up with a whole-class discussion.

Project

The project question is an important one. Migration of peoples has occurred throughout human history, and all cultures have been influenced by others at some point – arguably, cultures are constantly being influenced by others today! Looking at cultural change over time helps us realize that culture is not static, and that today's culture was created out of change. For the project, put students in groups of three or four to research the question. If possible, allow class time for them to do research on the Internet. If allowed, you could take them on a field trip to a local museum where they could find out more. Each student should find at least one foreign cultural influence on their country and prepare an interesting PowerPoint slide which gives information about this. Each group presents their PowerPoint presentation to the class.

VIDEO In this unit students can watch a video about the impact the Romans had on life in Britain. You can play the video clip on the Classroom Presentation Tool or download it from the Teacher's Resource Centre together with the video script, video worksheet, and accompanying teacher's notes. These notes give full guidance on how to use the worksheets and include a comprehensive answer key to the exercises and activities.

Additional material
For teachers
Photocopiable activity – Video worksheet: *The Romans in Britain*
For students
Online Practice – *Look again*
Online Practice – *Practice*

Listening and speaking   SB p66

Family history

About the listening

This section gives the opportunity to focus on the idea of living history in a more personalized way, with a focus on researching family history. Genealogy has become very popular in recent years and the researching of family trees has become much easier thanks to the Internet and access to online records, and TV programmes such as *The Secret*

Unit 6 • History repeats itself

History of My Family, and *Who Do You Think You Are?* have also had an influence. Students listen to David talking about researching his family history and then to a conversation between David and his grandmother. The conversation takes place on 'Skype' – an Internet network that you can use to make telephone calls. The tasks are listening for specific information and understanding referencing in the conversation. Key places mentioned in the script are: Newcastle /ˈnjuːkɑːsl/ is a large city and port on the River Tyne in north-east England. The city used to have large coal-mining and shipbuilding industries, but most of these have now closed down. Perth /pɜːθ/ is the capital and largest city of the Australian state of Western Australia. The Orkney /ˈɔːkni/ Islands are a group of islands off the north coast of Scotland. They comprise approximately 70 islands, of which 20 are inhabited. Farming and fishing are the traditional industries. Some of the vocabulary may be new, so be prepared to pre-teach/check the following items, especially with less confident classes: *great-grandmother/children, ancestors, Norwegian, to make a living, dressmaker, shipyard, to keep in touch*. Also check the pronunciation and silent *s* in island /ˈaɪlənd/.

1 Lead in to the topic by telling the students a bit about your family history. Put students in small groups to discuss the questions. Encourage them to ask each other questions to find out more. Elicit a range of answers in the class feedback session.

2 **6.13** Focus attention on the map of Australia and the photo of David. Read the instructions to exercise 2 as a class. Ask *Where is he from?* (England, but he lives in Perth), *How old is he?* (33), *What is he interested in?* (researching his family history). Focus attention on the other maps and give students a few minutes to read the questions. Play the recording without stopping. Put students in pairs to compare their answers. Play the recording again if needed and let students check/complete their answers. Check the answers with the class. Find out what other information the students remember or found interesting. Ask prompt questions if needed, e.g. *What nationality is David's wife?* (Australian) *How old is his grandmother?* (89), etc.

6.13 David Taylor Bews
I come from Newcastle in England, but I live in Perth, Australia, now. I've been here nearly ten years. My wife, Jodie, is Australian, and our children, Russell and Alice, were born here. Alice is named after her great-grandmother – that's my grandmother – Alice Bews. She's 89 now and still lives in Newcastle, and she's in great shape for her age. Now, there's a programme on TV, called *Who Do You Think You Are?*, where famous people find out all about their family histories, going right back. I love it, and it's made me want to know more about my own family history. You can do a lot of research online, but even better, I've started finding out more from my grandmother – and she loves talking about it all! I knew that she was one of nine children, which is amazing, but I didn't know she was the youngest, and the only one born in England. Her brothers and sisters were all born in Scotland, and that's where we all come from originally, from the Orkney Islands, which are in the very north of Scotland. My great-grandfather was a farmer there over a hundred years ago. And, I love this, my grandmother told me that our family's ancestors were actually Norwegian – they came over to Scotland in the 9th century. She says that's why we all have blonde hair in our family – isn't that amazing?

Anyway, it became more and more difficult for my great-grandparents to make a living there as farmers, so they travelled south, and finally arrived in the north of England, in Newcastle, with their eight children. Alice was born not long after they arrived.

Answers
1 He's lived in Perth for nearly ten years.
2 The two 'Alices' in his life are his daughter and his grandmother.
3 She lives in Newcastle.
4 They were all born on the Orkney Islands.
5 He was a farmer.
6 The family's ancestors came over to Scotland from Norway.
7 There are a lot of people with blonde hair in the family.
8 It became difficult for Alice's great-grandparents to make a living in farming.

3 **6.14** Ask students if they ever use Skype to talk to friends or family. Do they think this is a good way to keep in touch? Give students a few minutes to read the questions, then play the recording. Put students in pairs to compare answers and play the recording again if needed for them to check/complete their answers. Discuss the answers as a class.

6.14 Talking to Grandma
D = David   A = Alice
D So, Grandma, your parents came from the Orkney Islands – is that right?
A Yes. My mother was called Jane. She grew up there, and she got married when she was only 17.
D And you were her ninth child, weren't you?
A Yes, and I was the only one born in England. Life was really hard for my mother – you see, my father died when I was only three.
D Oh, I didn't know you were that young when it happened! That's awful!
A Well, it means I can't really remember him at all.
D So what did your mother do?
A She worked as a cleaner, and a dressmaker.
D Wow, her life wasn't easy then, was it? She had two jobs, and all those children! That's …
A Oh, yes, she was an amazing lady. My two eldest brothers, Peter and William, they got work in the shipyards, so that helped a lot. Ah, … it's not easy being the youngest – all my brothers and sisters have died now – I'm the only one left.
D I know. So, did you marry young, Grandma?
A No, I didn't marry till I was 22.
D But that's young! Really young!
A Oh, that wasn't unusual in those days. And I only had three children.
D Only! Two's enough work for us! And, you've got lots of grandchildren and great-grandchildren, haven't you?
A Yes, I have. They live all over the world – it's not just you that's gone to live abroad.
D I know. I have cousins in New Zealand and America. But cousin Peter still lives near you, doesn't he?
A Oh yes, he does. And he's helped me to keep in touch with you all with this Skype thing.
D It's great, isn't it?
A Oh yes, I love it. I can talk to all my grandchildren, and I've seen all my great-grandchildren as soon as they were born. And I get emails and texts all the time – it's all really wonderful, isn't it?
D It is, Grandma. Anyway, it's been great talking to you. I've got more questions, but I'll save them till next time.
A OK. You will stay in touch, won't you?
D Of course, I will, Grandma. Bye for now!

Answers
1 *She* got married when she was only 17. – Alice's mother
2 I can't really remember *him* at all. – Alice's father
3 She had *two jobs* and all *those children*. – She was a cleaner and a dressmaker. She had nine children.
4 *They* got work in the shipyards. – Alice's two eldest brothers
5 *That* wasn't unusual in those days. – getting married young
6 *They* live all over the world. – Alice's grandchildren and great-grandchildren. They live in Australia, New Zealand, and America.
7 *He*'s helped me to keep in touch with you all. – David's cousin Peter
8 *It's all* really wonderful, isn't it? – using technology like email, Skype, and texting to keep in touch.

4 Put students in groups. Each student takes it in turn to tell a part of David's story – just one sentence, then it's the next person's turn. The groups see how long they can keep going with each person telling a different part of the story.

Sample answer
David's ancestors came over to Scotland from Norway in the 9th century. They moved to the Orkney Islands and worked there as farmers over a hundred years ago. David's great-grandparents were both born in the Orkney Islands. They had nine children and eight of them were born in Scotland.

It became more and more difficult for the family to make a living in farming, so they travelled south to Newcastle. Their youngest child, David's grandmother Alice, was born soon after they arrived.

Alice's father died when she was only three. Life was very hard for her mother. She worked as a cleaner and a dressmaker, and she had a big family. Alice's two eldest brothers got work in the shipyards so that helped the family.

Alice married when she was 22 and she had three children. Alice is now 89 and she still lives in Newcastle. She has lots of grandchildren and great-grandchildren, living in all over the world. David's cousin Peter still lives near Alice and he helps her keep in touch with the rest of the family.

David also comes from Newcastle, but he's lived in Perth for nearly ten years. His wife, Jodie, and their children, Russell and Alice, were born in Australia. Alice is named after David's grandmother, Alice Bews.

What do you think?
Give students a few minutes to think about the questions, then put them in groups to discuss. Elicit ideas from a number of students in a whole-class discussion. Be aware that the topic of family history can be a sensitive one, so discuss these questions only as far as you feel students are comfortable.

Additional material
For students
Online Practice – *Practice*

Everyday English   SB p67
Agree with me!

Possible problems
1 The idea of a follow-up question or tag is a feature of many languages. However, the way this is formed is often simpler in other languages than in English with the use of a single word or fixed phrase to express the idea of 'Is that right?'/'Do you agree with me?' The rules for forming tags are fairly simple and students should have few problems recognizing how the system of tags works. The basic rules are:
– The question tag uses the same verb as the main part of the sentence. If this is an auxiliary verb, e.g. *have*, or a modal verb, e.g. *can*, then the question tag is made with the auxiliary verb. We use *do/does* in Present Simple tags, and *did* in Past Simple tags.
– If the main part of the sentence is positive, the question tag is negative; if the main part of the sentence is negative, the question tag is positive.
  • He's a teacher, **isn't he**?
  • You don't work in advertising, **do you**?
  • They've bought a new house, **haven't they**?
  • She can't swim, **can she**?
2 The other factor with question tags is intonation. The two main patterns are as follows:
– If the question tag is a real question where you want to know the answer, you use rising intonation.
– If you already know the answer or you are simply asking for agreement, you use falling intonation.
The Student's Book limits the practice to just the pattern with falling intonation – those question tags that ask for agreement, so avoid mentioning the difference in tag type at this stage. Exercise 4 also covers the need to add more information after answering a question with a tag to keep the conversation going.

1 🔊 6.15 Introduce the idea of intonation going up or down. Give an example of each: *Do you like history?* (rising). *I like history.* (falling). Use your hand to signal the rise or fall. Read the instructions to the students, then play the recording so they can listen to the intonation. Play it again, pausing so that they can repeat, using the same falling hand gesture. Students may feel awkward using intonation, so keep the tone light and playful. You could ask students to over-exaggerate the intonation in a stereotypical British voice; this can help overcome any stigma. Ask students what the purpose of the questions at the end is to elicit that the speaker wants the listener to agree with them.

🔊 6.15 See SB p67.

Answer
The intonation goes down in all sentences.

2 🔊 6.16 Students read the conversations in pairs and discuss how the question tag is formed. If needed, ask prompting questions to lead students to understand the rules: *What's the main verb? What verb does the question tag use? If the main verb is **is/will/have/can**, what verb is in the question tag?* (same) *If the main verb is in the past, what auxiliary do we use in the question tag?* (past) *Is the question tag always negative if the sentence is positive and positive if the sentence is negative?* (yes). Use the board to illustrate the rules. Play the recording, pausing so that pairs can repeat the conversations.

> **Answers**
> We form question tags as follows:
> - The question tag uses the same verb as the main part of the sentence. If this is an auxiliary verb, e.g. *have*, or a modal verb, e.g. *can*, then the question tag is made with the auxiliary or modal verb.
> - We use *do/does* in Present Simple tags, and *did* in Past Simple tags.
> - If the main part of the sentence is positive, the question tag is negative; if the main part of the sentence is negative, the question tag is positive.

🔊 **6.16** See SB p67.

3 Students complete the sentences with a question tag. Do the first two together if students are struggling. Ask more confident students to read their sentences to the class with falling intonation on the question tag.

> **Answers**
> 1 wasn't it
> 2 doesn't she
> 3 didn't you
> 4 is it
> 5 hasn't it
> 6 will you

4 🔊 **6.17** Read the instructions with the students and ask them why it's important to say more than just *Yes* or *No* in reply to a question tag. Elicit that it keeps the conversation going and is considered polite. Find out if the issue is the same in students' language. Play the recording for students to check their answers, and play it again if needed for them to practise the intonation. Refer students to the audioscript on p135 to read and practise the conversations.

> **Answers and audioscript**
>
> 🔊 **6.17 Replying to tags**
> 1 A Dominic's party was brilliant, wasn't it?
>   B **Yes, it was. I had a great time on the dance floor! (b)**
> 2 A Karen knows a lot about gardens, doesn't she?
>   B **Yes, she does. She's helped me a lot with mine. (e)**
> 3 A You went to school with my brother, didn't you?
>   B **Yes, I did. We've been good friends ever since. (a)**
> 4 A Learning a language isn't easy, is it?
>   B **No, it isn't. It takes time, and lots of practice. (d)**
> 5 A My English has improved a lot, hasn't it?
>   B **Yes, it has. You sound much more natural now. (f)**
> 6 A You won't forget to call me, will you?
>   B **No, of course not. I'll call as soon as I get home. (c)**

5 Students turn to p156 in the Student's Book. There they will find six conversations which are quite basic. They choose two conversations to develop by adding question tags and more information. They practise the conversations in pairs. As a follow-up, students can either act one of their conversations out in front of the class, or in front of a smaller group if the class is large. Encourage theatricality! You might also ask them to audio record themselves using the record function on their phone. In this way, they can listen to what they sound like and decide if they need to work on intonation more. They can also play their recording to a group of students instead of performing it.

SUGGESTION You could do a forum theatre type activity here. In forum theatre, actors act out a scene in which there is controversy, and spectators can stop the action and take over a role when they feel they can make a difference. In this case, ask two students to act out one of the basic conversations. Ask a volunteer to come up and take the place of Speaker B. They then do the conversation again, but the new person uses question tags to try to keep the conversation going for longer. If one of the speakers gets into difficulty, stop the conversation, and ask if any volunteers can step in to help out. They continue from the point the other speakers left off. This kind of activity not only illustrates how conversations can succeed or fail, but also gives students a chance to try out some ideas in a non-threatening environment.

Additional material
For teachers
Photocopiable activity – Communication: *Question tags* pp201–2
For students
Online Practice – *Look again*
Workbook p43, exercises 1–2
Online Practice – *Practice*

Writing SB p68

A biography

Ordering paragraphs

The aim of this *Writing* section is to write a biography, organized into appropriate paragraphs. The text and task type provide an opportunity to review linking words and relative pronouns.

About the text

The text is a short biography which briefly covers Princess Diana's charitable work, and what happened to these charities after her death. Students use the information about Harry to write a similar piece.

1 Remind students that they read about Princess Diana and Prince Harry at the start of the unit. Refer them to the photos on p68. See how much they can remember about their charity work.

2 Check that students understand what a *biography* is. Read the instructions with the students and check that they understand that the paragraphs are in the wrong order. They work in pairs to discuss the right order of the paragraphs. In feedback, ask them what clues (dates, phrases, etc.) they used to help them decide the right order. Point out that the text is organized chronologically. Draw students' attention to some of the features of the text:

dates: *the 80s; the 90s; in the 1980s* – this is a way of referring to decades – the years 1980–1989, for example. Check students understand this way of talking about time periods.

Unit 6 • History repeats itself 91

referencing: *Diana did the same for leprosy* (paragraph 3) here the text refers back to the previous paragraph – she 'completely changed people's ideas about [AIDS]' … *changed people's idea about the illness* – refers back to the mention of AIDS earlier in the sentence. *Two other hospitals …* (paragraph 4) – refers back to hospitals mentioned in paragraphs two and three. *Both are in London* (paragraph 4) – refers to Great Ormond Street Hospital and the Royal Marsden. Point out these phrases and ask students to say what they refer to. Refer students to the last sentence in paragraph 6. Ask them to find the reference for 'the one (the photograph) with the AIDS victim.' (in paragraph 2)

Ask students which tense – Past Simple or Present Perfect was used in the biography and why. (Past Simple because Diana is no longer alive/these are completed past actions.)

Answers
1 When Diana Spencer married Prince Charles and became Princess Diana, she also became one of the biggest celebrities of the 80s and 90s. She wasn't a typical British royal, however. She had an informal style and a special ability to connect with ordinary people.
2 In the 1980s, people lived in fear of the newly-discovered AIDS virus, and were afraid of contact with people suffering from it. In 1987, Diana opened Britain's first AIDS hospital ward. The photograph of her shaking hands with AIDS patients, without wearing gloves, completely changed people's ideas about the illness.
3 Diana did the same for leprosy. The fear of catching it from sufferers is centuries old, and when Diana visited a leprosy hospital in Indonesia, her advisers suggested she didn't touch them. Diana sat on their beds and held their hands, showing that you can't catch leprosy through physical contact.
4 Two other hospitals that Diana often visited were the Great Ormond Street Hospital for Children and The Royal Marsden. Both are in London, and have many child cancer patients. Diana spent many hours with them, saying, 'Some of them will live and some will die, but they all need to be loved while they are here.'
5 After her divorce from Prince Charles in 1996, Diana appeared less in public, and did less charity work. However, she continued to be patron of some charities, including Centrepoint, for homeless people. She visited the charity's shelters regularly up until she died.
6 In the same year as her death, 1997, she visited Angola to bring attention to the problem of landmines. The photograph of her walking through a recently cleared minefield is as famous as the one with the AIDS victim.
7 It was after her death that Diana became known as 'the People's Princess'. Many people wanted to give money to the charities which she supported, and the Princess Diana Memorial Fund managed the £34m that was collected.

3 Ask students to tell you the charitable activities that Diana supported. Were they surprised to learn about the range of charities she was involved in? Ask them to think of some adjectives to describe her.

Answers
Raising awareness about AIDS and leprosy – they aren't contagious through touch;
Raising awareness about the dangers of landmines;
Visiting hospitals to be with child cancer patients (Great Ormond Street Hospital for Children/The Royal Marsden);
Supporting homeless people (Centrepoint)

4 Refer students to the notes about the life of Prince Harry. Ask them to tell you what similarities they found with Diana's life. Can they use the same or similar adjectives to describe Harry? Ask students what tense is used in the notes and why (Past Simple for completed past actions). Point out that, although Harry is still alive, the events in the notes are completed past actions. Write this on the board to compare:
From 2009–2012, Harry trained as an Apache helicopter pilot.
He has flown helicopters since 2009.

Ask concept check questions: *Is the training finished?* (yes) *Does he still fly helicopters today?* (yes)

Answers
Harry has also worked for a lot of charities; he has a similar personality to his mother and is good at connecting with people, and he's not a typical royal.

5 Put students in pairs to discuss which information should go in each paragraph. Is there any information they would like to add? Ask them to number the points according to the paragraph they will go into. Give students class time to do the writing. Monitor and give support where needed. Students share their paragraphs with another student.

SUGGESTION A number of high-profile people are involved in charitable works. If students are interested in finding out more, ask them to do Internet research to find celebrities and wealthy patrons who support charitable causes. Famous examples include Angelina Jolie (UNHCR Goodwill Ambassador), Bob Geldof (Band Aid/Live Aid), etc. Ask students to prepare a short piece with photos outlining the work the person did or has done. Students can share in a poster presentation.

Additional material
For students
Online Practice – *Practice*
Workbook p43, *Review*, exercises 1–2
Online Practice – *Check your progress*

7 Simply the best

Introduction to the unit

The theme of this unit is describing people and places. This provides a useful context to practise the question, *What's it like?*, and to review adjectives which show opinion in the first *Grammar* section.

In the second *Grammar* section, comparatives and superlatives are introduced and practised in a general knowledge quiz, and their use is extended in the context of employing the best candidate for a job.

In the *Vocabulary* section, students work on using synonyms to make their descriptions more interesting and antonyms as a way of expressing agreement.

In the *Listening and speaking* section, people talk about the best things in their lives that are free, and the skill here is ordering photos in the order heard and completing a chart with information from the listening. Students are then challenged to speak about their favourite free things in a short speech.

In the *Reading and speaking* section, three people describe their favourite picture, and discuss why they like it and how it makes them feel. Students read for specific information, then use their notes to summarize what they have read orally. They read again to find descriptive language and find synonyms for adjectives in the text.

The *Everyday English* section continues with language for talking about what's on in a city and the language for suggesting places to go. This provides a great opportunity to find out about places to see in London.

The *Writing* section introduces and practises relative pronouns in the context of describing your hometown. Students see how joining sentences with relative pronouns *which, that, who,* and *where* to make defining relative clauses can add interest to their writing.

Language aims

Grammar

What's it like?, comparatives and superlatives

This section introduces the question, *What's … like?* as a way of eliciting a description. In this question, *like* is a preposition. This is contrasted with the question *Do you like … ?* Students read and listen to an interviewer ask about what Berlin is like.

Students are next introduced to comparative and superlative forms of adjectives, focusing on the formation of regular and irregular forms as well as short and longer adjectives, and the use of *as … as* and *… than …* They practise the /ə/ sound in the pronunciation section.

Vocabulary

Synonyms and antonyms

The theme of describing is continued in this section where students focus on using synonyms to add variety to descriptions. Antonyms are introduced as a way of agreeing with people by using *not very* + antonym. This section also revises question tags.

Everyday English

What's on?

The aim of this section is to discuss things to do. Students learn to read and interpret a listing of *What's on* in London. They then read and listen to a typical conversation between two people discussing what they might go and see. The language for suggesting places and listing what's on is practised in a conversation.

Additional material

Workbook

Students ask and answer questions contrasting *What's it like?/ What do you like?/What does he look like?* in present and past forms. They compare two people, and describe what they look like and what they are like. Comparisons are extended with students doing tasks on comparatives, superlatives, *than, like,* and *as … as.* To contextualize these, students read a text about the youngest person to climb Mount Everest. Students also practise synonyms and antonyms. The unit ends with a Grammar and Vocabulary review.

Photocopiable activities

There are photocopiable activities to review grammar (*What's it like?*), vocabulary (*I think …*), and communication (*I don't want to do that!*) at the back of the Teacher's Guide as well as on the Teacher's Resource Centre. There is also a worksheet to accompany the video on the Teacher's Resource Centre.

Notes on the unit

Unit opener page

Choose from these activities to engage your students with the topic and target language of this unit:
- Talk about the title
- Talk about the unit goals (*Grammar, Vocabulary, …*)
- Talk about the photo
- Watch the video
- Look at the bottom banner
- Do the activity

Start by eliciting people and things – sports people, teams, musicians, actors, cars – who students think are the 'best'. Do they agree on all of them? Suggest that the 'best' for one person may be different from the 'best' for another. Refer students to the unit title. Do they recognize this expression? (Some students might recognize it as a song title from the 1980s by Tina Turner.) Note that 'simply' in this expression is there to add emphasis.

Refer students to the photo on p69. Ask students if they know the name for the bird in the photo. Then ask why the image of the peacock is a good one to illustrate the unit title. Elicit possible reasons.

If you don't have time to watch the video introduction to the unit, go through the unit goals below the title:
Grammar, Vocabulary, Everyday English, Reading, Listening, Writing. Give examples or use translation for unknown words.

Video (2 minutes approximately): The video gives a step-by-step overview of the unit. Play the video, pausing where necessary – especially for students to answer any questions, e.g. *What's your hometown like?* This makes it a more interactive experience. Highlight the option of practising online.

As shown in the bottom banner, don't forget that there are many exercises to consolidate and practise the target language of the unit in the Workbook as well as online. There are links to these exercises on the relevant pages of the Student's Book and they can be done in class time or you can set them for homework.

Summary: If you're short of time, use the title and the photo to help students understand and engage with the topic, and then move straight on to the activity so that they can discuss the theme in more detail. If you have any more time, try to watch the video together. It is a clear and interesting introduction to the different parts of the unit.

Notes for activity:
Put students in pairs. Ask them to look at the photo and discuss their answers to the questions. Ask them to justify their choices where possible.

> **Suggested answers**
> 1 Peacock. It is displaying its coat to attract a mate.
> 2 Yes, by wearing beautiful clothes and make-up.
> 3 Students' own answers.

Grammar SB p70

What's it like?

Possible problems

1 The question *What … like?* asks for a description. In this context *like* is used as a preposition, but students may only have experience of *like* as a verb, e.g. *I like dancing./Do you like her?*
The answer to the question *What … like?* does not contain *like* with the adjective:
*What's John like? *He's like nice.* (Correction: *He's nice.*)

2 Students may find *What … like?* a strange construction to ask for a description which would be translated as *How is … ?* in some languages such as Italian or Spanish. In English, *How is she?* is an inquiry only about her health, not about her character and/or looks, e.g. *How is she? She's very well/ fine.*

> **STARTER** SB p70
>
> Lead in to the topic by telling students about some of your favourite things. Use the phrases listed in exercise 1: *I just love … , I really like …* . Elicit a few favourite things from the class using the list in exercise 1. Model and drill the stress in the phrases: *I really like … , I just love …* . Refer students to the *Starter* box and put them in pairs to compare favourite things. If you have time, do a milling activity: ask students to find others in the class who share favourite things.

My favourite things

1 Refer students to the photos and caption. Can they recognize who or what is depicted? Give them a few minutes to discuss the photos and speculate about the man's favourite things. Discuss ideas as a class. Use this as an opportunity to practise using third person: *He just loves … , He really likes …* , etc.

> **Possible answers**
> A favourite music/composer – Johann Sebastian Bach
> B favourite actor – Daniel Day Lewis
> C favourite food – Nuremburg sausages
> D favourite TV programme – *The Americans*
> E favourite football team/sport – Bayern Munich/football
> F favourite book – *Border Trilogy* by Cormac McCarthy
> G favourite musician – Hélène Grimaud

2 **7.1** Refer students to the list of adjectives. Pre-teach/ Check meaning or ask students to find the definitions or synonyms in a dictionary. Read the list of adjectives to the students. Drill the pronunciation and clap out the number of syllables for each word. Write the following stress patterns on the board and ask students to put the words under the stress pattern.

O	cool, sad
Oo	spicy, shocking, brilliant, funny
oO	unique
Ooo	talented
oOo	amazing, fantastic, exciting, delicious
Oooo	fascinating
oOoo	reliable

94 Unit 7 • Simply the best

Ask students to find adjectives from previous units to add to the list. Possible adjectives:

O	cold
Oo	noisy
oO	asleep
Ooo	interesting
oOo	expensive
Oooo	necessary
oOoo	identical

This would also be a good opportunity to teach any new phonetic symbols for sounds. Tricky words to pronounce include *spicy* /ˈspaɪsi/, *delicious* /dɪˈlɪʃəs/, *unique* /juːˈniːk/, *fascinating* /ˈfæsɪneɪtɪŋ/, *brilliant* /ˈbrɪliənt/. Students can add words to the phonetic charts in their Student's Book on p159 or in their notebooks.

Play the recording. Ask students to tick the adjectives the speaker uses in his description.

CULTURE NOTE: *Sauerkraut* is cabbage that has been preserved in salt water.

Answers
talented, spicy, shocking, amazing, exciting, cool, delicious, unique, brilliant, funny, fantastic, sad

7.1 My favourite things
I = Interviewer M = Mat
I Hello, and welcome to *My Favourite Things*. Today I'm talking to the German photographer, Mat Hennek. Welcome, Mat.
M Hi.
I So, let's start with your favourite actor. You've chosen Daniel Day Lewis. Why do you like him so much?
M He's such a brilliant actor – I just love him in all his films. He's so talented, but he only does what he wants to do, and believes in, which I think is great.
I Yes, he certainly deserves his three Oscars. And what about the world of sport?
M Well, I'm a football fan, and Bayern Munich is my team – I'm crazy about them. I always find them exciting to watch, and for me, they're simply the best – even when they aren't!
I Ah, you're a real fan! Now, your choice in music is interesting.
M Yes, Bach. I think his music is very special, unique in fact, and it's never ever boring. And of course my favourite musician is my partner, the pianist Hélène Grimaud. She's the coolest. You're always in the best hands when she's playing for you.
I That's lovely. OK, now to food.
M Well, I really like simple, country food. And I'm German, so my favourite meal is probably Nuremberg sausages and sauerkraut.
I Nuremberg sausages? I've never heard of those. What are they like?
M They're quite small, … a little bit spicy, and … so delicious!
I Mmm, I must try them! And your favourite book?
M I'm a great fan of the American writer, Cormac McCarthy, and I've chosen his *Border Trilogy*.
I Ah, I've never read his writing. What's it like?
M It's amazing – it's almost like poetry. His books are sad in some ways, but always full of hope.
I Well, I'll put him on my reading list. So, finally, your favourite TV programme?
M Oh, I thought *The Americans* was fantastic! It's a series about Russian spies living in America in the 1980s. It's quite shocking sometimes, but it can also be very funny.

3 **7.1** Refer students back to the photos. Ask them to match the adjectives Mat uses to describe each. Play the recording again so they can check. Check answers as a class and correct pronunciation of the adjectives as needed.

Answers
talented = Daniel Day Lewis
spicy = sausages
shocking = TV programme, *The Americans*
exciting = Bayern Munich
cool = Hélène Grimaud
delicious = sausages
unique = Bach
brilliant = Daniel Day Lewis
funny = TV programme, *The Americans*
fantastic = TV programme, *The Americans*
sad = the books he likes by Cormac McCarthy

GRAMMAR SPOT SB p70

Read the question and elicit the answer. Check that students understand the difference: *Which question is asking for a description/needs adjectives in the response?* (What are his books like?) Do a drill around the room using the topics from the *Starter* section, e.g.: Teacher: *Do you like football?* Students: *Yes, I do./ No, I don't.* Teacher: *What's it like?* Students: *It's exciting/boring*. Refer students to the Grammar reference section 7.1 on p148 to read about the form and use of *What … like?* Check understanding: *Can we say 'it's like exciting'?* (No, though in spoken AmE sometimes *like* is used in this way. It's very informal and not encouraged as standard English). *Is 'like' a preposition or a verb in the sentence: What's it like?* (preposition). *What's the verb in that sentence?* (is). Ask each student to write two questions with *What … like?* They ask and answer the questions in pairs.

Answers
Do you like Cormac McCarthy's book?
Yes, I do./No, I don't.

What are his books like?
They're sad in some ways./They're full of hope.

Practice SB p71

What's Berlin like?

1 **7.2** This exercise focuses on the use of *is* or *are*, depending on whether the noun in the question is singular or plural. Read the instructions, and refer students to the box. Ask them which nouns are singular and which are plural to raise awareness of which verb should be used. Students complete the sentences, then play the recording for them to check their answers. Find out if any of the students have ever been to Berlin. Do they agree with Mat?

Unit 7 · Simply the best   95

Answers and audioscript

🔊 **7.2 What's Berlin like?**
I = Interviewer   M = Mat

1 I What's Berlin like?
   M It's a really exciting city. There's so much going on all the time.
2 I What's **the weather** like there?
   M It's OK. It gets hot in summer and very cold in winter, and we do get quite a lot of rain, but people don't go there for the sunshine!
3 I What **are the people** like?
   M Berliners are great – they're a very interesting mix. It's a very cosmopolitan city, and it attracts unusual people!
4 I And what **are the buildings** like?
   M Amazing! Lots of them are famous and historical, but there are some fantastic modern ones, too.
5 I What **are the restaurants** like?
   M They're brilliant! You can find food from every country in the world, and some great traditional German food, too!
6 I What**'s the nightlife** like?
   M It's fantastic! There are lots of really good bars and clubs, and some wonderful theatres and concert halls. It's the best thing about Berlin!

2 If you think your students need some controlled practice, put them in pairs to read the dialogue, taking turns to read the part of the interviewer and Mat. In feedback, draw students' attention to the extra information Mat gives in order to explain his opinions. Ask: *Why does Mat think Berlin is exciting?* (because there is so much going on all the time).

Give students some time to think about their own answers to the questions about the town/city they live in now. They should think about an adjective and a reason. Monitor to support students in adjective choice and pronunciation as needed. Put students in pairs to ask and answer the questions. Student A is the interviewer. Regroup students so that they are with a different partner. This time Student B is the interviewer. In whole-class feedback, elicit a few answers from the students.

Additional material
For teachers
Photocopiable activity – Grammar: *What's it like?* pp203–4
For students
Online Practice – *Look again*
Workbook pp44–5, exercises 1–5
Online Practice – *Practice*

Good, better, best!

Comparatives and superlatives

Possible problems

1 Although students will have practised comparatives and superlatives before, they are still likely to make mistakes.
   - Students often mix up the basic rules of *-er/-est* with short adjectives, and *more/most* with longer adjectives:
   She's more tall than me. (Correction: *She's taller than me.*)
   He's the most rich man in the world. (Correction: *He's the richest man in the world.*)
   - They may form 'double' comparisons:
   I'm more fitter than her. (Correction: *I'm fitter than her.*)
   - Students often omit *the* before superlatives, use *of* instead of *in* with superlatives, and *that* instead of *than* in comparatives:
   She's tallest of the class. (Correction: *She's the tallest in the class.*)
   It's more expensive that I thought. (Correction: *It's more expensive than I thought.*)

2 Irregular forms *good/better/best* and *bad/worse/worst* often need reviewing, as do the spelling changes – *-ier/-iest* with adjectives that end in *-y* and doubling of the consonant in short adjectives with one vowel and one consonant:
   He's the better player in the team. (Correction: *He's the best player in the team.*)
   It's dryer here than in the north. (Correction: *It's drier here than in the north.*)
   This flat is biger than mine. (Correction: *This flat is bigger than mine.*)

3 Students may also make mistakes with *as … as* to show that two things are the same or equal, and *not as … as* to show that two things aren't the same or equal can sometimes cause confusion:
   He's as clever than his brother. (Correction: *He's as clever as his brother.*)

4 As well as difficulty in producing the correct form, students often need help with pronunciation, especially of weak forms. The Student's Book provides practice of the weak forms used in comparisons:
   /ə/   /ə/
   I'm older than Jane.

1 🔊 **7.3** Read the instructions to the students and refer them to the photos. Ask if they know any of these cities. Ask students to first read the interview. Play the recording for students to read, listen, and complete the sentences. They compare answers in pairs. Play the recording again if needed. Check as a class. Ask students which city they think is Mat's favourite. They should give a reason for their opinion. Ask students if anyone has ever been to these cities – what are they like?

Answers and audioscript

🔊 **7.3 Mat's favourite city**
I = Interviewer   M = Mat

I Do you travel a lot, Mat?
M Oh, yes! I often go with Hélène on tour – we've been to Tokyo, Munich, and Santa Barbara recently.
I And what are they **like**?
M Well, they're very different cities! Tokyo is obviously the biggest, and the **busiest**. It's **much** bigger **than** Munich, and much **more** modern.
I And is it more interesting?
M Er, in some ways, yes, but I think they're all interesting cities. And, in fact, for me the best and **most** interesting is Santa Barbara.
I Really? Why?
M Well, it's much smaller **than** the other two cities, and it isn't **as** exciting – it doesn't have Tokyo's skyscrapers or Munich's history. But it's unusual to find a city that's so beautiful and calm, and so green.

I Santa Barbara sounds like the **best** city for relaxing. And what about food – which is the **best** city for food?
M Oh, for me, Tokyo has the **most** delicious food – simple and fresh – I just love Japanese food!
I So is it better **than** sausages and sauerkraut?
M Mmm, I don't know about that!

GRAMMAR SPOT   SB p71

1 Ensure students understand the terms, *comparative* and *superlative*. Ask them to find examples in the interview with Mat. Elicit the comparative and superlative forms of the adjectives and write them on the board in a table. Elicit the rules for forming the comparative and superlative forms. Point out the spelling changes for *big, busy, wet, noisy*. Elicit the spelling rules. Drill the pronunciation, with particular attention to the /ə/ at the end of comparatives.

Answers
Rule: add *-er/-est* to one-syllable adjectives.
(a) older, oldest;   (e) smaller, smallest
Rule: short adjectives ending in one vowel + one consonant, double the consonant and add *-er/-est*.
(b) bigger, biggest;   (f) wetter, wettest
Rule: adjectives ending in *-y*, change *-y* to *-i* and add *-er/-est*.
(c) busier, busiest;   (g) noisier, noisiest
Rule: adjectives of 3+ syllables are preceded by *more* and *the most*, and do not have *-er/-est* added.
(d) more interesting,   (h) more delicious, most
    most interesting;   delicious

2 Elicit the irregular forms and add them to the table on the board. Drill the pronunciation. Before moving on to exercise 3, ask students to help each other learn the forms in pairs. Student A says an adjective, Student B says the comparative, Student A says the superlative (with *the*, e.g. *the oldest*). Student B then says an adjective, and they continue in this way. Encourage them to think of adjectives from earlier in the unit and from other units. Monitor and support if they get stuck.

Answers
good, better, the best
bad, worse, the worst

3 Ask students, *Which is bigger, Berlin or Tokyo?* Elicit a positive and negative sentence: *Tokyo is bigger than Berlin. Berlin isn't as big as Tokyo.* Write these on the board. Write: *Is Berlin as big as Tokyo?* Underline *as … as …* in the question and negative sentences, and *than* in the positive one. Point out that we can also use *as … as …* in a positive sentence to mean they are the same: *My friend is **as** old **as** I am.* (we are the same age). Students read and answer question 3 to check they understand the meaning of the sentences.

Answer
Munich

In your own words

2 Put students in pairs. Ask them to brainstorm some cities or towns in their country, or some places that they have been to or would like to visit. They compare the places using the adjectives in the *Grammar spot* and from the listening texts. Ask them to write 5–6 comparison questions about their places, e.g. *Which is bigger, ___ or ___? Is ___ more modern than ___?* They work with another pair to ask and answer the questions. In feedback, ask them to name the oldest, busiest, wettest, etc.

As an alternative, if possible, ask them to research two cities on the Internet. They should agree on which two cities they want to find out about, then each research one. Give them some ideas for information to find out: size, age, things to do, number of people who live there, tourists, festivals, history, weather, etc. Once they have done their research, they come back together to make their comparisons. Put some sentence frames on the board to support lower-level students: *Which is bigger, ___ or ___? I think ___ is bigger because it has more people. Is ___ as noisy as ___? I don't think so. ___ has a lot of parks and bicycles. It hasn't got as many cars.* They can write their comparison questions for another pair as above.

SUGGESTION When there is a spare five minutes of class time, do some activities to help students remember the spelling of the new words they are learning. Here are a few ideas:

1 Write words on the board, but leave out the vowels. Students write the complete word. e.g. *mzng* → *amazing*. In checking, ask students to spell the word to practise saying the letter names as well.

2 Play a game of 'snowman' – draw a series of lines on the board – one line per letter of the word (e.g. __ __ __ __ __ __ __ __). Students call out a letter. If the letter is in the word, write it in the correct space. If not, begin to draw a snowman. Students try to guess all the letters in the word before you have completed the snowman (draw: head, body, eye, eye, nose, mouth, arm, arm, hat = nine guesses).

3 Ask students to look through their books or notebooks and find words with patterns, e.g. double letters: *brilliant, funny, cool, small, tall, difficult*; silent letters: *shocking, fascinating*; words with *ea*: *team, meat, read, weather, health, great* (with *ea* words, students can categorize them into sounds – /iː/ *meat, team, read* [base verb]; /eɪ/ *great, break*; /e/ *weather, health, read* [past tense]).

Practice SB p72

Pronunciation

This section practises the /ə/ (schwa) sound at the end of comparisons in British English, and the schwa sound in *than*. It's more important at this stage that students learn to hear rather than produce the schwa sound as it will help with their listening skills. Students may notice that in American English, the *-er* is pronounced /ər/.

1 **7.4** Play the recording so that students can hear the /ə/ sound. Play it again so they can listen and repeat. Ask students which words are stressed and which are unstressed. (*than, as … as* are all unstressed). Point out that this sound is only used in unstressed words and syllables.

7.4 See SB p72.

Unit 7 • Simply the best   97

2 🔊 **7.5** This drill helps students practise the schwa sound in conversation. Ask students why some of the words are in capitals (they are emphasized, so they are stressed more than the other words). At this point you might draw students' attention to the fact that some words are stressed, and others are not in English, and this is what gives English its rhythm. On the board, write: *Tokyo's bigger than Berlin*. Say the sentence and ask students which words they think are stressed (*Tokyo, bigger, Berlin*). Underline these. Ask students what parts of speech these are (nouns and adjectives). Explain that words that give the main information such as nouns, adjectives, adverbs and verbs (except for *is*, *have*, etc., as these are often auxiliary verbs) are usually stressed. Others are not stressed and that is what makes them harder to hear.

Refer students back to the conversation in exercise 2 and remind students that the words in CAPITALS are emphasized, so they are even more stressed than usual. Play the first conversation in the recording – students just listen. Play it again, pausing for students to repeat. Look at the three other adjectives and elicit the comparative forms. Play all three conversations. Put students in pairs to practise the conversation. Monitor for good pronunciation. If possible, allow them to record themselves and listen back – are they producing the /ə/ sound?

🔊 **7.5** See SB p72.

3 🔊 **7.6** The poem is a nice way to wrap up the pronunciation section. Ask students to read the poem and underline the places they think they will hear the /ə/ sound. Note that the *the* before *best* has been dropped to keep the rhythm of the poem. Play the recording. Were they right? Play it again, clapping out the rhythm as a class. Put students in pairs to recite and memorize the poem – clapping the rhythm at first until they feel they have got it right. Ask a confident student to recite the poem from memory.

🔊 **7.6** See SB p72.

General knowledge quiz

4 🔊 **7.7** This activity focuses on general knowledge to get students to practise comparative and superlative forms. Set this up as a team competition. Firstly, refer students to the photos to identify what each shows. Teach the English pronunciation of some of the trickier places and words: Burj Kalifa /ˈbɜːʒ kəˈliːfə/, Eiffel /ˈaɪfəl/ Tower, Shanghai Maglev /ˈʃæŋhaɪ ˈmæɡlev/, hippopotamus /ˌhɪpəˈpɒtəməs/ ('hippo' for short). Read the instructions and example to the students. Give students a few minutes to write their sentences. Monitor and support as needed. Ask fast finishers to write their own example on the board. Ask each group to read out one or two of their sentences. Play the recording. How many did they get right? Ask the students what other information they heard. If they are interested, play the recording again so they can listen for the extra information. Was any of the information surprising?

Answers and audioscript

🔊 **7.7 General knowledge quiz**
1 Monaco is **much smaller than** Malta, but Vatican City is **the smallest** country – less than half a square kilometre.
2 The Eiffel Tower is **nearly as tall as** the Empire State Building, but the Burj Kahlifa in Dubai is **the tallest** by far – 828 m.
3 The Atlantic Ocean is **bigger than** the Arctic Ocean, but the Pacific Ocean is **the biggest** – it's twice as big as the Atlantic.
4 The Japanese Bullet Train **isn't as fast as** the Italian AGV Italo. The Shanghai Maglev is **the fastest** train, at 431 kph.
5 The lion is **more dangerous** than the shark, killing about 100 people every year compared to the shark's ten. The hippopotamus is **the most dangerous** – it kills about 500 people a year.

SUGGESTION You could extend superlatives by asking students to visit the Guinness Book of World Records page on the Internet to find interesting records in the hall of fame. Ask students to tell the class which records they thought were the most amazing and why. Have they ever thought of trying to set a world record?

Best for the job?

About the text

Many companies have a Human Resources (HR) department (or Personnel department) which recruits new employees. The department wishing to employ a new member of staff sends the information about the job and type of person they want to employ to the HR department. HR advertises the job, reviews the job applications, and interviews the candidates. They may create a shortlist of candidates for the hiring department to interview further. In this text, the Information Technology (IT) department is looking for a marketing assistant. The profiles are what HR have put together to help make a final decision.

5 If you have students who have jobs, lead in to the discussion by finding out what process they went through to get the job. Did they see the job advertised somewhere? Did they fill in an application? What kinds of things do employers usually look for? If you have pre-work students, get them to think about jobs family members have. See if they know the process for finding a job and explain what companies do when they look for people to hire.

Pre-teach/Check *marketing assistant, qualified, confident, salary, Human Resources, shortlist, profile*. Read the exercise with the students. Make sure they understand the context and explain the process for recruiting new employees if needed. Ask students which of the items in the list is more important in a job – experience, confidence, friendliness, etc. Is that a good salary for a marketing assistant?

6 🔊 **7.8** Read the instructions with the students. Refer them to the shortlist of candidates on p73. Students read the information, then complete the summary in pairs. Ensure they know to put one word in each space. This is a challenging exercise as it requires students to understand the information given in symbols, apply it to the gap fill, and also choose the right words and grammatical structure. If you find students are struggling to get started, play the first part of the recording as a model of the kind

of information needed. Give students time to discuss and complete the exercise, monitoring and supporting as needed. Play the recording for students to check their answers.

Answers and audioscript

🔊 7.8 Best for the job?

Age
Adam Bates is the **oldest**. He's 32. Jasmine Wyland is the **youngest** – she's only 26. Rachel Slater is a bit **younger than** Adam. She's 30.

Present salary
Adam earns **the most** – he has the **highest** salary by far, £32,000. Jasmine doesn't earn nearly **as much as** Adam, only £25,000, and Rachel earns quite a lot **more than** Jasmine, £28,000.

Experience
Adam has **the most** experience, but he doesn't have **much more than** Rachel. They both have a lot **more** experience **than** Jasmine.

Qualifications
Rachel is **the most** qualified. She isn't much **more** qualified than Adam, but she's **a lot more** qualified than Jasmine.

Happy to travel
Adam is **happiest** to travel, and Rachel is a lot **happier** to travel than Jasmine.

Who gets the job?

7 Read the instructions with the students. To support this activity, write *friendly, confident, good at teamwork* on the board. Ask a confident student to compare Jasmine and Adam using *friendly*. Ask another student to compare them using *confident*. Put students in pairs to make similar comparisons.

8 Tell students they are going to work in a group to decide which person to employ. They must all agree, and they must be able to give reasons for their decision. Draw their attention to the sentence frames to help support the conversation. Give them a few minutes to reach a consensus, then ask for each group's decision. You could make the final hiring decision based on how good the reasons given by each group are.

SUGGESTION If you have students who work, ask them what some of the qualifications and characteristics are for their job. If they aren't working yet, they could find out about jobs they would like to do or ask their parents what qualifications and characteristics are needed for their job.

Additional material
For students
Online Practice – *Look again*
Workbook pp45–7, exercises 6–13
Online Practice – *Practice*

Listening and speaking SB p73

The best things in life are free

About the listening

The listening section extends the theme of descriptions. Five people talk about the things they love in life that are free. Students hear adjectives, comparatives, and superlatives used in context to help them internalize the structures. The focus is on the content and listening for specific information and personalized speaking rather than the grammar in this section.

1 Refer students to the title of the section. Ask them if they agree that the best things in life are free. Give them a minute to think about three things they love that don't cost any money before sharing their list with a partner. Collate a list of ideas on the board.

2 🔊 7.9 Ask students to look at the photos and say what they show. Use this as an opportunity to pre-teach/check the following vocabulary from the listening text: *energetic, vet's* (short for 'veterinarian's surgery'), *sunset, hug, sweets, chatting*. Play the recording so that the students can number the photos in order. Were any of the things the speakers talked about the same as the students' lists from exercise 1?

Answers
1 A   2 B   3 E   4 F   5 D   6 C

🔊 7.9 The best things in life are free

Jane
Oooh, I think there are lots of things I like that don't cost anything. Let me think … sunsets. There's nothing more beautiful. My house is on a hill opposite some fields, and in the evening when I look out of the living room window, I see some amazing sunsets. And … well friends and family are the most important thing in my life. I've just become a grandmother to the most gorgeous baby boy. And hugs are free! I love hugs with all my grandchildren – they're something that money can't buy! But my youngest son still lives at home, he certainly isn't free. He costs me a lot of money!

Robin
Well, I work in an office in the city, and for me, the best thing is being in the countryside. I don't mind what the weather is like – even if it's rainy and windy, it's great to be outside, in nature. I like to be on my own when I go walking – it's a great time to think. But I suppose I do spend money driving to the countryside, so … if you really want something that's free, then the park is the next best thing. There's a lovely park near my flat. It's got a small lake, and some wonderful trees, and I often go there for a quick walk after work – it's the easiest way to put the day's work behind me.

Charlotte
Erm, well, I don't have to pay for much in my life, just sweets, because I'm only eight, but … I think the best thing for me is playing with my little sister, Ava. She's only four, so I'm a lot older than her. I've also got a brother, Dominic. He's six, but he doesn't like the games I like, so he isn't as much fun to play with as Ava. She's always waiting for me when I come home from school. She thinks I'm the best person in the whole world! We usually play hospitals, or schools. I'm the doctor or teacher, of course, because I'm the biggest.

Ella
Definitely the best thing in my life is being with my boyfriend, Alex. Of course, we sometimes do things together that cost money, like going to the cinema, but we don't need to spend anything to have a good time – we often just go out for walks or sit around chatting. He makes me laugh so much – he's the funniest person I know – and he's also the nicest friend anyone could have. We've been together nearly a year now, so it feels like our relationship just gets better and better. I think I'm really lucky.

Oliver
The best thing that's free in my life is my dog, Fudge. My uncle gave him to me for my thirteenth birthday. He was a puppy, and he's 11 now, so we've grown up together. He was SO cute as a puppy, but I think he's even more beautiful now. What's he like? Well, he's very loving, and … he's also a bit crazy, and he's great fun to play with. He may be getting older, but he's still far more energetic than I am – I'm

always more tired than him after a walk! And, I know it's very lucky that I haven't had to take him to the vet's very often – because that definitely isn't free!

3 Refer students to the chart. Ensure they understand that they need to listen and complete the chart. If you have lower-level students, put them in pairs and ask each student to complete part of the chart. They then share answers to complete the entire chart. Play the recording without stopping. Give students time to compare. Play it again if needed for students to complete their charts. Go through the chart eliciting the answers from various students.

Answers
Jane loves sunsets, and her family and friends (including her baby grandson). She loves sunsets because she thinks there's nothing more beautiful. She loves her family and friends because she thinks they're the most important things in life and she loves hugs with her grandchildren. Her youngest boy isn't free – he still lives at home and seems to need a lot of money.
Robin loves going to parks. He thinks it's great to be outside in nature and he likes to be on his own and go walking as it gives him time to think. He spends money driving to the countryside, so that isn't free.
Charlotte loves her little sister. She likes her because she's fun to play with, she's always waiting for her to come home from school, and she thinks that Charlotte is the best person in the world. Sweets aren't free.
Ella loves her boyfriend. She loves him because he makes her laugh so much and he's the nicest friend anyone could have. Going to the cinema isn't free.
Oliver loves his dog – he loves playing with him. He loves him because he's beautiful, loving, crazy, and fun, and they grew up together. Taking him to the vet's isn't free.

4 Set this up as a 'two-minute challenge'. Read the instructions with the students. Give them a few minutes to think about what to say. Put them in pairs. Student A will speak first. Set a timer for two minutes and challenge the students to speak for the two minutes. When the timer sounds, praise the students for their efforts. Repeat for Student B. Put students in groups of four so that they can tell others about what their partner said so they can get practice with third person, and get to know each other better.

Additional material
For students
Online Practice – *Practice*

Reading and speaking SB p74

Favourite pictures

About the text
In this section, three people talk about their favourite picture. *Tiger in a Tropical Storm,* also known as *Surprised!* was painted in 1891 by French artist Henri Rousseau (1844–1910). Rousseau is most famous for his jungle-themed paintings. His artistic style has been labelled *naïve, primitive,* and sometimes *surrealist.* Mat Hennek (born 1969) is a prolific photographic artist. He started as a portrait artist in Berlin, then switched his focus to natural landscapes. *Kliffküste* is part of his *Woodlands* series which depicts portraits of trees in various forests and seasons. Auguste Macke (1887–1914) was the leader of the German Expressionist group *Der Blaue Reiter* (The Blue Rider), and is an important Rhenish Expressionism artist. His painting, *Girls under Trees* shows a group of girls in pinafores protecting themselves from the sun under some trees. Macke is known for his use of colour in his paintings, and this colourful painting is typical of his work. Text B refers to the Grimm Brothers' fairy tale, *Hansel and Gretel* in which a brother and sister get lost in the woods and kidnapped by a witch when they nibble on her house made of cake and sweets.

1 Direct students to the introduction to the article and the pictures. Ask students which is their favourite and why. If they are interested, tell them a bit more about the artists and time periods they work(ed) in. Ask students to choose a picture to work in pairs to describe. Write prompts on the board: *In this picture I can see … . It's … . It makes me think about … . When I look at it I feel … .*

2 This activity is a jigsaw reading which students should be familiar with by now. Divide the class into three groups. Group A reads about *Tiger in a Storm*, Group B reads about *Kliffküste*, and Group C reads about *Girls under Trees*. All students should take notes. Possible vocabulary to pre-teach/check includes: *bolt of lightning, thunder, storm, shadow, fairy tales, screensaver*. Avoid pre-teaching the highlighted words in the text at this point.

3 Regroup students so that there is one person from each ABC group in each new group. Students share information with the others. Monitor to ensure use of third person. Do they agree with what is said about the pictures? In class feedback, ask students if they have a favourite picture in their house. Where did they get it? Where is it? You could ask them to take a photo of it with their phone to share with the rest of the class. Students could answer the four questions from exercise 2 when discussing their favourite picture.

Example answers
A She bought it from the National Gallery in London.
  It is in her bedroom on the wall opposite her bed.
  She loves the colours in *Tiger in a Tropical Storm* and also the shapes of the leaves and plants. She says that she feels as if she is in the jungle. She loves the tiger with its wonderful face, and that it shows her that it's OK to be scared.
  The negative feelings she talks about are worrying about things, being afraid of life, and finding it difficult to sleep – the painting helps her to cope with these feelings.
B He bought it at an art gallery in Berlin.
  It is on the wall above the fireplace in his living room.
  Greg loves the Matt Hennek's photo, *Kliffküste*, because it's amazing and it looks like a painting. He loves the light and the fascinating shapes and he never gets tired of it.
  The negative feelings he talks about are related to the back of the woods – which looks dark, mysterious and scary – like the woods where Hansel and Gretel got lost. He uses the photograph to analyse what mood he is in – whether he connects with the light part or the dark part of the wood at that moment.
C A friend gave it to her as a present.
  It is in her kitchen, and she also has it as a screensaver on her computer.

Sandra loves *Girls under Trees* because of the colours. She thinks it's gorgeous. She also loves the fact that it's a bit out of focus – but she thinks it makes it more beautiful. She thinks the girls in it are having a good time without any boys there and it's full of life and happiness – it makes her feel good when she looks at it.

The negative feelings she talks about are related to the artist. She is sad and upset that he died very young in the First World War, and what a waste of a life that was.

4 Ask students to read the texts that they didn't read before. Still working in their ABC groups, they answer the questions about who talks about what in their text. Ask them to circle or highlight where they found the information in each text. In class feedback, ask students to say where they found the information.

> **Answers**
> 2 Greg and Sandra
> 3 Lucy and Sandra
> 4 Lucy and Sandra
> 5 Lucy and Greg
> 6 Lucy
> 7 Lucy and Sandra
> 8 Sandra

Vocabulary

5 This exercise foreshadows the synonym work coming up in the next section and also starts them thinking about word choice in writing. For words that are not familiar to the students, they have to use the context in order to make a guess about the meaning. Students work in pairs to compare answers before checking as a class. Ask students if they know the word that means *a word with a similar meaning* (synonym). Go over the pronunciation of the words and teach new phonemic symbols as needed, using the phonemic chart on p159. Give students time to add the words to their vocabulary notebook, noting down the stress patterns and main phonemic symbol as appropriate.

> **Answers**
> like (v) = adore, enjoy, love
> light (adj) = bright
> difficult (adj) = hard
> wonderful (adj) = lovely, great, amazing, beautiful
> afraid (adj) = terrified, scared, frightened
> see (v) = notice
> terrible (adj) = awful
> interesting (adj) = fascinating
> not very clear = out of focus

What do you think?

Give students a few minutes to think about the questions, then put them into groups to discuss. Tell students to bring in a photo of their favourite picture, or tell them to find a copy of it on the Internet. Elicit feedback from a number of students in a whole-class discussion.

VIDEO In this unit students can watch a video about Scotland to find out more about this beautiful country and the people who live there. You can play the video clip on the Classroom Presentation Tool or download it from the Teacher's Resource Centre together with the video script, video worksheet, and accompanying teacher's notes. These notes give full guidance on how to use the worksheets and include a comprehensive answer key to the exercises and activities.

> **Additional material**
> **For teachers**
> Photocopiable activity – Video worksheet: *Scotland*
> **For students**
> Online Practice – *Look again*
> Online Practice – *Practice*

Vocabulary SB p76

Synonyms and antonyms

1 Refer students to the examples to elicit *synonym* /ˈsɪnənɪm/ and *antonym* /ˈæntənɪm/. Elicit some more examples of synonyms and antonyms.

> **Answers**
> *bright* and *light* are synonyms, *beautiful* and *lovely* are synonyms, *dark* and *light* or *dark* and *bright* are antonyms.

2 🔊 **7.10** Remind students about the exercise in Unit 4 in which the word *nice* was repeated over and over again. What was wrong with that? (boring to read, not very interesting). Find out if, in their first language, it's also the case that you shouldn't repeat words. Refer them to the picture and ask what they think the people are talking about. Play the recording as students read the conversation. What's wrong with it? Ask if it is common in their culture to talk about the weather. (Explain that this is very common in the UK, and that this kind of conversation is called *small talk*.)

> **Answers**
> They use the same adjective throughout (*nice*).

🔊 **7.10** See SB p76.

🔊 **7.11** Put students in pairs to change the conversation using the words *beautiful*, *nice*, and *horrible*. Play the recording for checking. Ask students to redo the conversations with the same intonation/stress pattern as in the recording. Encourage them to have a bit of fun with this by exaggerating the stress and intonation.

🔊 **7.11 A lovely day!**
A It's a lovely day, isn't it?
B Yes, it's beautiful.
A But it wasn't very nice yesterday, was it?
B No, it was horrible!

Synonyms

3 🔊 **7.12** Read through and drill the pronunciation of the words in the box. Ask students to underline the stressed syllable (*difficult, frightened, intelligent, unusual, correct*). Allow them to compare their answers in pairs before playing the recording to check. Play the recording again so that students can focus on the extra line in each conversation. Find out if anyone in the class is scared of spiders, and if anyone has ever been to a country where they drive on the opposite side of the road. Students test each other in pairs. Student A says an adjective, and Student B says the synonym. As an extension, ask pairs to write one conversation using each of the words in the box. They read their conversation to another pair.

Unit 7 • Simply the best 101

Tell students to add these words to their vocabulary notebooks. A useful way to record these is in pairs – *scared = frightened*; *right = correct*, etc. If they are keeping track of words with double letters, they can add *correct*, *difficult*, and *intelligent* to the list, and *pleased* to the list of *ea* words.

Answers and audioscript

🔊 **7.12 Synonyms**
1. A I'm scared of spiders.
   B Well, a lot of people are **frightened** of big ones!
   A Yeah, but even the small ones are a problem for me.
2. A Let's check the answer key to see if it's right.
   B Yes, it's **correct**!
   A Oh good – I really wasn't sure about that one.
3. A It's strange that Dave left without saying goodbye.
   B Yes, that is **unusual**.
   A Maybe he was in a hurry today.
4. A I think I'll find it hard to drive on the left when I'm in the UK!
   B It'll be **difficult** at first, but after a while you'll be fine.
   A I can't imagine it – it's the wrong side of the road!
5. A Are you happy with your new phone?
   B Yes, I'm very **pleased** with it. The camera's fantastic!
   A I think I might get one of those myself then.
6. A Tommy's a clever boy, isn't he?
   B Yes, he's very **intelligent** for a ten-year-old.
   A I've had some very adult conversations with him.

4 Drill the pronunciation and mark the stressed syllables of the words in the box (good-looking, amazing, crazy, awful, well-known, normal). Point out that the hyphenated adjectives have stress in both the first and second part of the word. Put them in pairs to think of a synonym, using a dictionary if needed. They should underline the stressed syllable. Elicit a range of synonyms from students and check pronunciation and stress before asking students to write their sentences. When writing the sentences in pairs, each student must write the sentences down so they can use them in the next exercise.

Possible synonyms
good-looking: attractive, handsome, pretty, beautiful
amazing: fantastic, wonderful, brilliant, great
crazy: mad, bonkers
glad: happy, pleased
large: big, huge, enormous, gigantic, massive
awful: terrible, really bad, horrible
well-known: famous
normal: usual, regular

5 Put students in new pairs. Each student reads a sentence, and the other student must think of a reply using a synonym as in the example. In feedback, ask a few confident pairs to enact their conversations. Ask students to add the words to their vocabulary notebooks.

Antonyms

6 This section revises question tags while practising antonyms. Ask students to read the cartoon. Does the man/woman agree or disagree with the woman/man? How does s/he do it? Point out that *It's not very …* and *It isn't very …* , mean the same thing.

7 Put students in pairs to think of opposites, using a dictionary if needed. There is more than one possible answer, so in feedback, write their ideas on the board for others to copy. Be sure to underline the stressed syllables. With weaker classes, conduct a quick substitution drill with each word: Teacher: *It's boring*. Students: *It's not very interesting*., etc.

Possible answers
boring = interesting
noisy = quiet
rude = polite
stupid = clever
dirty = clean
miserable = happy, cheerful
slow = quick, fast
cold = hot

8 🔊 **7.13** Draw students' attention to the question in the cartoon dialogue in exercise 6 and in the example. Remind them that the tag is positive because the question is negative. Put students in pairs. Student A reads lines 1–4 with Student B responding, and Student B reads lines 5–8 with Student A responding. Encourage good intonation and use of question tags with falling intonation. Play the recording. If there is time, pair up students again to practise the conversations with a new person.

🔊 **7.13 Antonyms**
1. A This film is so boring!
   B Mmm, it isn't very interesting, is it?
2. A It's so noisy in this restaurant!
   B Yes, it isn't very quiet, is it?
3. A That man was really rude!
   B Yes, he wasn't very polite, was he?
4. A That was so stupid of you!
   B Yes, it wasn't very clever of me, was it?
5. A These plates are dirty.
   B Mmm, they're not very clean, are they?
6. A Pat always seems so miserable.
   B Yes, she never seems very happy, does she?
7. A This computer is so slow!
   B Mmm, it's not very fast, is it?
8. A It's really cold in here!
   B Yes, it's not very warm, is it?

SUGGESTION Try this vocabulary revision activity whenever you have time. Ask each student to look through their books or notebooks and find five to ten vocabulary words. They write them on slips of paper without showing anyone. Put students in pairs – they put their vocabulary words face down on the table. Student A starts by picking up a word and trying to explain the word so that Student B can guess. Give them some prompts to support this: *It's the same as … . It's the opposite of … . It's a noun, and it is something that you … .*

Additional material
For teachers
Photocopiable activity – Vocabulary: *I think …* pp205–6
For students
Online Practice – *Look again*
Workbook p48, exercises 1–4
Online Practice – *Practice*

Everyday English SB p77

What's on?
This section focuses on the language used when talking about the entertainment you can enjoy in a city. This includes the language of making suggestions and also key question forms for finding out about times, venues, prices, etc.

About the text
The listings are for a range of places in London (see Notes below), but the language used is typical of the entertainment information available about any city from a range of sources.

The places referred to in this section are:

British Museum – The famous museum of human history and culture, located in central London. Established in 1753, its collections, which number more than 13 million objects, are amongst the largest and most comprehensive in the world and originate from all continents.

Tate Modern – The highly recognizable Tate Modern building is located in the former Bankside Power Station in London. The gallery space retains many of the features of the former power station including a huge 35-metre high, 152-metre long hall known as *The Turbine Hall*, the Chimney, the new Switch House, and the Tanks. The space allows for very large exhibitions, and visitors can see films, performances, attend tours, talks, and workshops as well.

Royal Academy of Arts – More than a gallery, the RA is primarily an academy run by artists and architects who are elected by their peers in recognition of their work. It hosts exhibitions and events including an annual summer exhibition – the world's largest open submission exhibition – and is home to the Royal Academy Schools. It recently celebrated its 250-year anniversary.

Royal Albert Hall – A large concert hall located in South Kensington, in London. It seats 2,500 people and is used as a venue for music, dance, and talks. The London Philharmonic Orchestra performs the majority of its London concerts there. Every summer it holds the Proms (Promenade Concerts), where a large number of the audience can buy cheaper tickets and stand to hear the concerts.

New London Theatre – Although the building is modern, the site on which it is built has been used for entertainment since Elizabethan times (= during the reign of Queen Elizabeth I, 1558–1603). The theatre is known for showing big musicals such as *Cats* and *Joseph and the Amazing Technicolor Dreamcoat* as well as big productions such as *War Horse*.

Odeon Cinema – A British chain of cinemas, which is one of the largest in Europe. The flagship cinema, the Odeon Leicester Square, is one of the largest cinemas in Britain and host to many of London's film premières.

Sea Life London Aquarium – The aquarium hosts a range of sea life, from tiny seahorses to huge sharks. Visitors can explore the rock pools and look for the elusive octopuses. The aquarium also educates about the sea life in British waters around the coast, the creatures living in the River Thames, and the creatures living in the rainforest.

Symbols used
Film – The current cinema film classifications in Britain are given below. U, 12A, 15, and 18 are referred to in the cinema listing on SB p77:

U – Universal, suitable for all ages.

PG – Parental Guidance, certain scenes may be unsuitable for children under 8.

12A – generally not recommended for children under 12; children under 12 only admitted if accompanied by an adult, aged at least 18 years.

15 – only those over 15 are admitted.

18 – only those over 18 are admitted.

R18 – only those over 18 are admitted and only at licensed cinemas due to adult nature of the content.

Transport – the symbol that indicates the nearest Underground station is: ⊖

1 Lead in to the topic by asking students how they find out about things to do in their town/city (local newspaper/magazine, the Internet, mailings direct from a cinema/theatre, friends/family/colleagues, etc.). Check comprehension of *What's on?* (= What's happening at local places of entertainment?). Remind students that this question can be used to talk about TV and radio, e.g. *What's on Channel 5?* Refer them to the listings text and ask them how many different places are listed (six). Ask them to look at the pictures and say what kinds of things they can do at each place (e.g. learn about history, look at art, attend musicals, see fish, hear music, watch a film).

Focus attention on one of the listings and elicit the type of information given (place, address, nearest Tube station, opening times, what's on, description, prices). Cinema listings also give the age classification – see Notes above. Put students in pairs to complete the exercise. In feedback, have a class discussion about *What's on*: Which of the events they would like to see and why? Do they have a similar rating system for films? Are similar events more or less expensive where they come from? Have they seen any of the shows or exhibitions?

> **Answers**
> 1 Members and under 12s.
> 2 It's free.
> 3 Sunday and Tuesday.
> 4 1
> 5 Headphones.
> 6 *Mary Poppins Returns*.

2 🔊 **7.14** Ask students to read the conversation first, then play the recording so they can listen and fill in the gaps. They compare answers in pairs. Play the recording again if needed. Ask them to practise the conversation in pairs, swap roles, and practise again.

Unit 7 • Simply the best   103

Answers and audioscript

🔊 7.14 What's on?

A What shall we do today?
B I'm not sure. Let's have a look. How about **going to the cinema**?
A Er, no, I don't **feel like** seeing a film.
B OK … What about an exhibition?
A Maybe. **What's on**?
B There's Modigliani at the Tate Modern.
A Mmm … not my **kind of thing**. What else?
B There's an exhibition called *Living with gods* about beliefs in different cultures.
A That sounds interesting! **Where's it on**?
B The British Museum.
A Oh good, the British Museum's free.
B Yeah, but this is a special exhibition, and it's £15.
A Oh, OK. **We can get the Tube** to Russell Square. What time is it open?
B They're open ten till six. And, **we could go to** a Silent Disco at the London Aquarium afterwards.
A Oh, I'd love to! Come on, **let's go**!

3 Draw students' attention to the language the speakers use to make suggestions about where to go. Write these on the board: *How about/What about* (+ *-ing*?); *How about/What about* … (a film/show, etc)?; *There's* … . *We could see* … (a film/an exhibition). Do a quick drill to practise this language: Ask a student *What shall we do today?* The student uses one of the expressions on the board to make a suggestion. Do this several times so that students get the idea. Put students in pairs to have a similar conversation. Lower-level students may wish to write out their conversations before practising them.

4 If possible, bring in some flyers, leaflets, or newspapers which advertise what's on. You could also display a website of what's on in the city, or ask students to research what's on and make a list. As an alternative, put students into groups and assign each group a different type of venue – cinema, theatre, etc. Some groups may have the same venue type depending on class size. Ask each group to create a 'What's on' poster for their venue, remembering to include the times, days, location, and prices. Post these around the room. In pairs, students look to see what's on and discuss what they want to do.

Additional material
For teachers
Photocopiable activity – Communication: *I don't want to do that!* pp207–8
For students
Online Practice – *Look again*
Workbook p49
Online Practice – *Practice*

Writing SB p78

Describing my hometown

Relative pronouns *which, that, who, where*

The overall theme of describing people and places is continued in this *Writing* section with a description of the students' hometown. Language support is provided with a *Grammar spot* and practice on relative pronouns.

Possible problems

1 This section focuses on defining (restrictive) relative clauses. This type of clause does not require a comma, but students often make the mistake of adding one:
   *We bought a house, which cost £300,000.
2 The most common mistake students make is to leave the pronoun in:
   We bought a house which it cost £300,000. (Correction: *We bought a house which cost £300,000.*)
3 Students don't generally have a problem knowing which pronoun to use for people, places, or things. In some languages, there is not a distinction made between *who* and *which*, so make sure students understand that *who* is used for people and *which* for animals and things:
   My teacher is a professor which works hard. (Correction: *My teacher is a professor who works hard.*)
   I have a dog who always begs for food at the table. (Correction: *I have a dog that always begs for food at the table.*)

1 Focus attention on the sentence opener and complete it about yourself as an example. Give students one or two minutes to complete the sentence. Ask a few individuals to share their information with the class. Write a complete example on the board and point out that *where* is a relative pronoun, and *I was born* starts a relative clause. Put brackets around (*where I was born*). Ask students what the subject is (*The town*) and draw a line under it. Ask them what the verb is (*is* or *has*). Draw two lines under the verb. Point out that the subject is singular, so the verb is singular.

GRAMMAR SPOT SB p78

1 Read the notes and sentences as a class. Point out that the relative pronouns in **bold** are used to give more information about the noun that goes before them. Also highlight that *who*, *which*, and *that* replace the pronoun *he*, *it*, etc.
   I met a man who is from my town. (NOT *I met a man who he is from my town.*)

2 Give students time to complete the rules. Let them check in pairs before checking with the class.

Answers
- *who* is for people.
- *where* is for places.
- *which* or *that* is for things.

2 Elicit the answer to number 1 as an example. Give students time to complete the exercise. Let them check their answers in pairs before checking with the class.

Answers
1 That's the man **who** helped me start my car.
2 That's the restaurant **where** we had dinner last night.
3 These are the children **who** need a lift home.
4 We found a wallet **that** had a lot of money in it.
5 This is the parcel **which** arrived this morning.
6 That's the hospital **where** I was born.

About the text

Pittsburgh /ˈpɪtsbɜːg/ is in the state of Pennsylvania /ˌpensəlˈveɪnɪə/ in the north-east of the US. It has an industrial heritage and historically it was known for the production of iron, steel, and coal. Its modern economy is

104 Unit 7 • Simply the best

largely based on healthcare, education, technology, and financial services.

Linda Barnicott is a Pittsburgh artist who has painted many places and scenes of life in the city. She uses rich pastel colours and is popular with the local population and a wider international audience.

Andy Warhol /ˈwɔːhəʊl/ was an American artist of immigrant parents from Slovakia who had an important influence on modern art and music, particularly the Pop Art style. He is particularly known for his images of ordinary objects like the *Campbell's Soup Can* and screen prints of famous people like Marilyn Monroe.

There are a number of new words to help make the description vivid. Encourage students to use the context to help them with new vocabulary and to pool knowledge with other students, or use a dictionary when necessary. With lower-level classes or if you are short of time, you could pre-teach/check some of following vocabulary: *bank* (of a river), *to cross, thriving, dozen, iron* /ˈaɪən/, *steel, steel mill, to suffer, to hurry to work, deserted, surrounded by, to inspire, to display, to raise* (a child), *liveable* (= good for living in), *tough* /tʌf/.

3 Check pronunciation of the name of the city /ˈpɪtsbɜːɡ/. Ask them what they know about Pittsburgh. If possible, show it on a map of the US. Elicit any information students may know. Focus attention on the pictures of the city. Elicit further information about the city from the images (it has an industrial past, a river runs through it, etc.).

4 Draw students' attention to the gapped text and ask them to read it through quickly. Focus attention on the example. Then give students time to complete the text, working in pairs. Monitor and help as necessary. Check the answers with the class. Students then answer questions 1–7, working in their pairs. Check the answers.

Answers
Text:
2 which/that   5 which   8 where
3 which/that   6 which/that   9 who
4 where   7 who

Questions:
1 In Pennsylvania, in the US.
2 There are over 400.
3 It's named after William Pitt, the Prime Minister of Britain in the 1700s.
4 It was a thriving, industrial town. It had dozens of factories that produced iron and steel.
5 It is thriving again with theatres, shops, and restaurants.
6 Linda Barnicott and Andy Warhol.
7 They're tough but friendly. They have lived through good and bad times. They make the writer proud to be from Pittsburgh.

5 Write the questions on the board and get students to brainstorm possible words and phrases for each section. Give students time to write notes about their hometown. Many students may not know much about their hometown, so if possible, give them some time to research information about it on the Internet. You may ask them to do the research prior to the lesson.

As students do their writing, monitor and help as necessary. Ideally, students should write their description in class. If appropriate, ask students to find a few visuals to support their description, e.g. a map, historical and contemporary images, photo of famous people/products from the town/city, etc.

6 Ask a few students to read out their descriptions for the class. When students give their talk, ask them to come to the front of the class (or stand up in front of their group in larger classes) and make sure the rest of the class is quiet and pays attention. Allow students to refer to their notes, but don't let them read the whole talk directly from the script. Encourage the class/groups to ask questions to the presenter. Get students to compare some of the towns and cities during a short feedback session. This gives the opportunity to recycle comparatives and superlatives from earlier in the unit. If possible, display the descriptions on the classroom wall or noticeboard to allow students to read each other's work. If appropriate, you could get students to vote for the description they think is the most interesting. If you check the students' work, point out errors but allow students to correct them themselves. Try to limit correction to major problems to avoid demoralizing the students.

Additional material
For students
Online Practice – *Practice*
Workbook p49, *Review*, exercises 1–2
Online Practice – *Check your progress*

8 Living dangerously

Introduction to the unit

The theme of this unit is danger and it includes sports, careers, and lifestyles that could be considered 'dangerous living'.

The *Grammar* section uses the theme of dangerous activities to introduce the modal auxiliary verbs *have to/don't have to* for obligation, and *can/can't* for possibility. Students practise using these modal auxiliary verbs in the context of talking about sports.

The second grammar point, *should/must* for giving advice, is introduced in the context of an advice column on the theme of fitness. This reading activity also practises the skill of understanding headings and using information to form opinions. Students practise giving advice in a number of contexts. There is also the opportunity for a longer project at the end of the section.

In the *Listening and speaking* section, students continue the theme of *should* for advice by taking a health and fitness quiz. Students then discuss whether they agree with the advice given and talk about their own ideas for what makes a healthy lifestyle.

In the *Reading and speaking* section, they learn about the dangerous work of two stuntwomen and a stuntman. The skills here are connecting new information to what is known, reading and listening for specific information. The *What do you think?* section gives students the opportunity to voice their opinions.

The *Vocabulary and speaking* section introduces students to parts of the body and clothes. The body vocabulary helps prepare them for the topic, *At the doctor's* in the *Everyday English* section. Students roleplay a scene at the doctor's to practise the language and vocabulary presented.

In the *Writing* section, students learn about formal and informal language for use in emails, standard beginnings and endings, and standard formal structure. They then write a formal and informal email.

Language aims

Grammar

have to/don't have to, should/must

This section introduces *have to* for strong obligation and *don't have to* for absence of obligation. The pronunciation section focuses on the difference in pronunciation between *have to/has to/had to* and *have a/has a/had a* in sentences. *Should/shouldn't* for advice and *must/mustn't* for strong advice are introduced in the context of an advice column with a health and fitness doctor.

Vocabulary

Parts of the body, things to wear

Some of the parts of the body in this section may be known, but others will be new. Clothes vocabulary is introduced and the two categories are tied together as students talk about where each item of clothing is worn. Students practise the clothing vocabulary in two separate speaking activities.

Everyday English

At the doctor's

The aim of this section is to roleplay going to the doctor. First students learn terms for talking about symptoms and diagnosis. They then listen to a conversation between a patient and a doctor. They use this conversation as a model for their own freer roleplay. The scenario brings in the cultural element of payment for medical treatment in the UK which students can contrast to what happens in their own country.

Additional material

Workbook

Students complete two texts using *have to/don't have to* to express obligation or lack of it in past and present forms. There is an exercise on *have* vs *have to* to distinguish between possession and obligation. Students then work on *must*, contrasting *mustn't* and *don't have to*. Students then do tasks contrasting *should, must,* and *have to* to express advice or obligation. The Vocabulary revises and extends clothes and parts of the body, which leads into a section on illnesses and injuries. There is a Grammar review to close the unit.

After Unit 8 there is the second of the three *Stop and check* tests, which covers the Grammar and Vocabulary content in Units 5–8.

Photocopiable activities

There are photocopiable activities to review grammar (*Do you agree?*), vocabulary (*What shall I wear?*), and communication (*What seems to be the matter?*) at the back of the Teacher's Guide as well as on the Teacher's Resource Centre. There is also a worksheet to accompany the video on the Teacher's Resource Centre.

Notes on the unit

Unit opener page

Choose from these activities to engage your students with the topic and target language of this unit.

- Talk about the title
- Talk about the unit goals (*Grammar, Vocabulary, …*)
- Talk about the photo
- Watch the video
- Look at the bottom banner
- Do the activity

Elicit reactions from students to the photo on p79. Does it make them scared when they look at it? Ask *What sport is he doing?* (rock climbing, perhaps extreme rock climbing as he isn't wearing a helmet and has minimal equipment); *What equipment do you need for this sport?* (ropes, harness /ˈhɑːnɪs/, rock-climbing shoes/boots, helmet, karabiner /ˌkærəˈbiːnə(r)/, pins); *Have you ever done any rock climbing?* If there is a student in the class who does rock climbing, ask them to tell the class more about it and why they enjoy doing it (if appropriate). Refer students to the unit title, 'Living dangerously'. Check/Drill pronunciation: /ˈdeɪndʒərəsli/. Elicit and put the word forms on the board: *danger* (n); *dangerous* (adj); *to endanger* (v); *dangerously* (adv).

Ask students why they think some people like living dangerously (e.g. for the thrill/excitement, to test themselves/ see how far they can go, etc.) Brainstorm some other examples of 'living dangerously'. Ask students what else they might do dangerously (e.g. driving at very high speed, canyoning /ˈkænjənɪŋ/, open water swimming, cliff diving). If you don't have time to watch the video introduction to the unit, go through the unit goals below the title: *Grammar, Vocabulary, Everyday English, Reading, Listening, Writing*. Give examples or use translation for unknown words.

Video (2 minutes approximately): The video gives a step-by-step overview of the unit. Play the video, pausing where necessary – especially for students to answer any questions, e.g. *Do you have a healthy lifestyle?* This makes it a more interactive experience. Highlight the option of practising online.

As shown in the bottom banner, don't forget that there are many exercises to consolidate and practise the target language of the unit in the Workbook as well as online. There are links to these exercises on the relevant pages of the Student's Book and they can be done in class time or you can set them for homework.

Summary: If you're short of time, use the title and the photo to help students understand and engage with the topic, and then move straight on to the activity so that they can discuss the theme in more detail. If you have any more time, try to watch the video together. It is a clear and interesting introduction to the different parts of the unit.

Notes for activity:

1 Put students into pairs. Ask them to look at the photo and discuss their answers to the questions. Ask them to justify their choices where possible.

Suggested answers

1 The man is rock climbing. Students' own answers.
2 because they like to take risks, they enjoy the adrenalin rush
3 sky diving, riding white water rapids, bungee jumping

Grammar SB p80

have to/don't have to

Possible problems

1 This section introduces *have to*, which expresses obligation. This may be new to some of your students. Students also get the opportunity to review *can/can't* for possibility.
2 The *Grammar spot* gives an overview of the question, negative, and past forms of *have to*. Although you can expect form mistakes, the main area of confusion is often with *must*. Students often don't realize that *must* with second and third person sounds very authoritarian, and so is not an appropriate form to use, for example, between two adults. Students may use *must* to refer to a general obligation, when *have to* would sound more natural, more personal, and less like an order, for example:
   *My parents must work six days a week. (Correction: My parents have to work six days a week.)
3 *Should* is more appropriate for mild obligation or advice, especially when speaking with someone of equal status or authority. In this unit *must* is taught to express strong advice and strong obligation.
   Common mistakes:
   *You've got hiccups. You must drink a glass of water.
   (Correction: *You should drink a glass of water.*)
4 Student's Book p81 has an exercise to highlight the different pronunciations of *have, has,* and *had*. The forms are presented in context in pairs of sentences – one with *have* for possession followed by *a*, and the other with *have to*. In the examples with *have/has/had* followed by *a*, the final sound of the verb is voiced before a /ə/:
   I have /hæv/ a good job.
   He has /hæz/ a nice camera.
   We had /hæd/ a good time.
   In the examples with *have to*, the final sound of the verb is unvoiced before /tə/:
   I have /hæf/ to work hard.
   She has /hæs/ to train a lot.
   We had /hæt/ to get up early.
   Note that Unit 8 does not cover the difference in meaning between *mustn't* (= it isn't allowed) and *don't have to* (= it isn't necessary), although there is an exercise in the Workbook to cover this point.

STARTER SB p80

Lead in to the section by referring students to the photo on p80. Ask *What sport does he do?* Find out if anyone in the class is a surfer. Ask *How dangerous do you think surfing is? Why?* Refer students to the list of activities in the box. Check they understand the meaning of each. Use mime to demonstrate unknown sports. Check students' pronunciation of each. *Cycling* /ˈsaɪklɪŋ/, *gymnastics* /dʒɪmˈnæstɪks/, *skiing* /ˈskiːɪŋ/, may be tricky because of the way they are spelled. Ask students to underline the stressed syllables in each activity and categorize them under the following stress patterns:

Unit 8 • Living dangerously 107

Oo	boxing, cycling, football, skiing, surfing, yoga
oOo	gymnastics, karate
OOo	horse-riding, skateboarding, skydiving
OoOo	motor racing, mountaineering, scuba diving

As a class, add any other sports students do, and discuss which activities are the most and least dangerous and why. Focus on generating ideas and interest in the topic instead of correct grammar here, but gently correct pronunciation of the sports.

Find out if any students do the dangerous activities or if they know anyone who does. An alternative is to do this as a *Find someone who …* activity. Ask each student to write the activities in a column down the left-hand side of a sheet of paper. They mill around asking: *Have you ever … ?* (to revise Present Perfect from Unit 6) or *Do you … ?* (to revise Yes/No questions) If they find someone who has done the activity, they write their name down and ask a follow-up question to find out more, e.g. *How long have you been … ? Where do you … ?* The aim is to find someone for each activity, and practise asking follow-up questions. Be sure to model the activity and also check that students know to change the noun to a verb: *Have you ever boxed? Do you box?* Use the board to write the verb forms of each activity. Alternatively, they could use *do* or *play*: *Have you ever done boxing?/Do you do boxing? Have you ever played football?/Do you play football?*

The big wave surfer!

About the text
The listening takes the form of an interview with big wave surfer, Kurt Weiner. Although Kurt is fictional, what he discusses is not. Big wave surfers need good fitness, and physical training is important. Yoga helps them not just hold their breath for long periods of time, but also helps to strengthen their diaphragm. The Banzai Pipeline is a famous surf reef break on the North shore of O'ahu /əʊˈɑːhuː/ in Hawaii. It produces huge barrel-shaped waves popular with advanced surfers. It's a highly dangerous wave which has killed or hospitalized a number of surfers. Three Tables Cave is also in O'ahu. It's called 'three tables' because of the flat sections of reef that are visible at low tide. The ledges, arches, and lava tubes near the tables create caves that are popular with swimmers and snorkellers.

1 **8.1** Ask students to read the instructions and questions so that they know what to listen for. See if they can predict any of the answers, or if they have ever watched big wave surfing competitions. Play the recording. Allow students to compare answers and play the recording again if needed.

Answers
1 He does yoga because it helps with learning to hold your breath and it also helps keep him calm when things get difficult.
2 He can hold his breath for over four minutes.
3 His dad took him surfing before he was two years old.
4 He goes swimming underwater at Three Tables Cave – it's great for breath-holding practice.
5 Yes, he has. He's travelled all over the world from Mexico to China.
6 It's one of the most famous waves in the world.

8.1 Kurt Weiner – big wave surfer
I = Interviewer   K = Kurt
I Kurt, do you have to be very fit and strong to be a big wave surfer?
K Yeah, you do. You have to be strong in mind and body. It's a fantastic sport but a dangerous one. I find doing yoga helps me a lot.
I Yoga!?
K Yeah, a lot of surfers do yoga. You have to learn to hold your breath – and yoga helps with that and … of course it helps you keep calm when things get difficult.
I I can understand that.
K I've learned to hold my breath for over four minutes. That was one of the first things I had to learn – the bigger the wave the longer you have to do it.
I Four minutes! Wow! Kurt, did you have to start surfing when you were very young to be as good as you are today?
K I can't remember when I didn't surf – my dad took me before I was two years old.
I So, do you have to start young if you want to be a good surfer?
K Well, you don't have to, but it helps and living here it's the natural thing to do – it's just part of life on O'ahu.
I You say have to keep fit, so how often do you train?
K Well, I don't have to train every day, but I do most days – I go swimming underwater. I go to Three Tables Caves near my home – it's great for breath-holding practice.
I And do you travel to surf?
K I do, a lot. I've been to surf spots all over the world, from Mexico to China … but right on my doorstep is one of the most famous waves in the world – the Banzai Pipeline. It's a fantastic ride!
I Kurt, you're a lucky guy. I hear you have a surf school, too. Can you teach me to surf?

2 **8.2** Students first read the instructions and sentences, then play the recording for them to fill in the gaps. They compare answers in pairs before checking as a class. Do a quick meaning check without going into the grammar at this point: *Is it necessary for him to be fit and strong? Is it necessary for him to learn to hold his breath?*

Answers and audioscript
8.2 You don't have to, but it helps!
1 Kurt, **do you have to** be very fit and strong to be a big-wave surfer?
2 You **have to** be strong in mind and body.
3 You **have to** learn to hold your breath.
4 That was one of the first things I **had to** learn.
5 Kurt, **did you have to** start surfing when you were very young to be as good as you are today?
6 I **can't** remember when I didn't surf.
7 So, **do you have to** start young if you want to be a good surfer?
8 You **don't have to**, but it helps!
9 I **don't have to** train every day, but I do most days.

3 **8.3** Put students in pairs to complete the questions. Then play the recording for students to check. Put them in pairs to read the dialogue so that they can begin to internalize the *have to* forms.

Answers and audioscript

8.3 Questions and answers
1 **Does** Kurt **have to** train hard?
  Yes, he **does**. He **has to** train very hard.
2 Why does Kurt do yoga?
  Because surfers **have to** hold their breath for a long time.
3 **Do** all surfers **have to** start young?
  No, they **don't have to**, but it helps.

GRAMMAR SPOT SB p81

1 Pre-teach/Check *obligation*, then read the first exercise in the *Grammar spot* with the students. Ask students which of the activities in the *Starter* require training: *Do you have to train to be a boxer?* (etc.). Elicit, *Yes, you do./Yes, you have to (train)./No you don't./No you don't have to (train).*

2 Give students a minute to complete the exercise, then check as a class. Ask students why the verb changes to *had* in the third sentence (past tense).

Answers
Do you **have to** work at the weekends?
No, I **don't have to** work at the weekends.
But I **had to** work last weekend.

3 This question checks that students understand the meaning difference between *can/can't*, *have to/don't have to*. After checking the answers, ask questions to illustrate the difference: *Can you cycle? Do you have to cycle to class every day?*

Answers
It's not possible = can't
It's necessary = have to
It's not necessary = don't have to

Practice SB p81

Pronunciation

1 **8.4** See Possible problems on p107 of the Teacher's Guide for notes on the pronunciation of the forms of *have*. Focus attention on the sentences. Ask *Is the word* **have** *pronounced the same or differently in each sentence? What is it that changes?* (the last sound). Play the recording and let students listen to the different pronunciations. Ask students to focus on the word that follows the forms of *have/has/had* and explain that this affects how each is pronounced. Play the recording again, pausing after each sentence and ask students to repeat. Drill the sentences round the class.

8.4 See SB p81.

have to – forms and tenses

2 Put students in pairs to complete the exercise. Be sure they know that they might have to use the affirmative *have to*, the negative *don't have to*, the question form, or the past tense. Check as a class with students reading the entire sentence with good pronunciation of the forms.

Ask pairs to write two sentences and a question with *have to*, but leave a gap as in exercise 2. They swap papers with another pair and complete each other's gapped sentences.

Answers
2 has to
3 doesn't have to
4 don't have to
5 did, have to
6 had to
7 Do, have to

Talking about sports

3 This activity adds an element of fun and challenge, as students have to guess the activity by asking questions. This is also a good review of *Yes/No* questions in general and helps reinforce the meaning of *have to/don't have to* for necessity/obligation and *can/can't* for possibility. Ask students to choose an activity from the *Starter* on p80, but to keep it secret. Put students in groups. Students use the sentence frames to ask each other *Yes/No* questions and guess the activity. Do one together as a class as an example. You could extend this activity further by giving each student five slips of paper. They write an activity (any activity – swimming, ironing, cooking, etc.) on each slip of paper, then put the slips in the middle of the table. One student takes a slip and the others ask questions to guess the activity.

4 Model the exercise by telling the students about an activity that you do. For example: *I play tennis. I don't play in a team. I don't have to wear special clothes, but I have to wear tennis shoes. I can't do it anywhere – I have to go to a tennis court.* If possible, set this up so that students create a personal profile type video of themselves talking about their sport or activity. This will give them the opportunity to really show others more about their activity in an engaging way. Videos can be shared on the class or school VLE or blog.

SUGGESTION You could practise the past of *have to* by asking students to discuss rules at home when they were younger. Write the following questions on the board or on a worksheet:

1 *What did you have to do to help around the house?*
2 *Did you have to be home by a certain time?*
3 *Did you always have to tell your parents where you were going?*
4 *What rules did you have to follow?*

Put students in small groups of three or four to discuss the questions. In the feedback, ask one student from each group to summarize the comments made.

What should I do? SB p82

should/must

Possible problems

1 See p107 of the Teacher's Guide for notes on possible confusion between *must* and *have to*. The *Grammar spot* in this section reviews the question, negative, and *he/she/it* forms of modals. There is an introduction to modal auxiliary verbs on p149 in the Grammar reference. You could ask students to read this before you begin

Unit 8 • Living dangerously 109

this section. *Must* (strong obligation) and *should* (mild obligation) present few problems of meaning in the context of advice, but learners often want to use an infinitive with *to* after them:
*You should to do your homework. (Correction: *You should do your homework.*)
*You must to see the doctor. (Correction: *You must see a doctor.*)
Should expresses an opinion and is often introduced with *I think …* : *I think you should ask for a pay rise.*

2 Note that we usually introduce a negative opinion with *I don't think + should*, rather than with *I think + shouldn't*: *I don't think you should leave your car there.*

3 It is possible to form questions with *must*, but *have to* is more common. *What time do we have to leave?* (rather than *What time must we leave?*)

1 Lead in to the topic of a healthy lifestyle. Brainstorm some ideas about what it means to have a healthy lifestyle. Elicit *keep fit* and check students understand this term. Refer students to the questions in exercise 1. They ask and answer the questions in pairs. Elicit ideas in whole-class feedback.

2 The text takes the form of an advice column that could be found in a magazine, newspaper, or online. Ask students to look at the text and say where they think they might find a text like this and what kind of text it is (an advice column in a magazine or blog). Find out if students have ever read an advice column like this before. Where do they go to get advice? How do they know that the advice is good advice? Ask them what kind of doctor Dr Drew /druː/ is. See if students can guess the meaning of *queries* /ˈkwɪəriːz/ from the context. Other words they may need support with include: *sprained, ankle* /ˈæŋkl/, *advice, gentle* /ˈdʒentl/, *injury*. Ask students to read just the headings and predict what the problems are as a whole class. Tell students to read the rest of the problems section to see if they were right. In pairs, students discuss what the problems are. Ask if they are more like James, Cheryl, Adam, or Millie. As a class, brainstorm some advice for each person.

GRAMMAR SPOT SB p82

1 Read the sentences together. Point out that *must* is for <u>strong</u> advice whereas *should* is much softer and expresses what the speaker thinks is the best thing to do.

Answer
'You must see a doctor.' expresses stronger advice.

2 Elicit other modal verbs (*can, could, shall, will, would*) and ask students what modal verbs have in common. Tell them to turn to Grammar reference 8.2 on p149 to find five things they have in common:
- They go with another verb.
- They don't have a third person singular *-s*.
- They don't have a *do/does* in the question.
- They don't have a *don't/doesn't* in the negative.
- Most refer to the present and future. Only *can* has a past tense form: *could*.

Elicit the question and negative for *should* and *must* and write these on the board. Point out that questions with *must* are unusual when talking about advice. We generally change the question to use *have to*:

Must I see a doctor? (unusual/archaic)
Do I have to see a doctor? (more common)
Ask students if we ever say, *He musts …* or *She shoulds … ?* (no). Do we ever say, *She must to … / He should to … ?* (no).

Answers
Questions with *should* = *Should I see a doctor? What do you think I should do?*
Negative with *should* = *shouldn't* (should+not) *He shouldn't sit at his desk all day.*
Questions with *must* are unusual when talking about advice. We more often transfer the question and negative to *have to*, which uses *do/don't*. *Do I have to see a doctor? You don't have to see a doctor.*
Negative with *must* = *mustn't* (must+not) *He mustn't run before his ankle has healed.*
We don't add *-s* with *he/she/it* when we use *must*.

3 Tell students to read the advice from Dr Drew and match the advice to the problems. They write the person's name in the space provided. Do they think Dr Drew's advice is good? Is there any additional advice they would give?

Answers
a Dear Adam
b Dear Millie
c Dear James
d Dear Cheryl

4 ◉ 8.5 Tell students Dr Drew has some more advice that they need to help her with. Refer them to the exercise. Allow them to check in pairs before listening to check as a class. Tell them to match the new advice with each person. Ask students why Dr Drew uses stronger advice with Adam than with the others. (Possible answer – She feels that Adam's injury could get worse if he doesn't go to see a doctor and keeps on running.)

Answers
1 should, shouldn't (James)
2 don't think you should (Millie)
3 don't have to, should (Cheryl)
4 must, mustn't (Adam)

◉ 8.5 See SB p82.

Practice SB p83

Giving advice

1 ◉ 8.6 In this section students practise giving advice. Give them a moment to think of some advice they would give in each situation. Ask them to work in pairs. Student A tells Student B one of the problems and Student B gives advice. They swap roles so that each has the opportunity to ask for and give advice. Monitor and check students are using *should/shouldn't, must/mustn't*. Play the recording. Ask students if their advice was similar. Did they have any good advice they would like to share?

110 Unit 8 • Living dangerously

8.6 Giving advice

1. **A** I'm hopeless at all sports.
   B You shouldn't worry about it. Lots of people aren't sporty, but you should make some exercise part of you daily routine – walking more quickly can help.
2. **A** I can't sleep at night.
   B You must do more exercise during the day. Why don't you walk to work? And you shouldn't drink so much coffee just before bedtime.
3. **A** I don't like my brother's new girlfriend.
   B I don't think you should tell your brother. I think you should try to find some good things about her.
4. **A** I've got an important exam tomorrow, and I'm really nervous.
   B I don't think you should study any more today. You must get a good night's sleep tonight. Don't worry. I'm sure you'll pass, and if you don't it's not the end of the world.
5. **A** A boy in my class is bullying me.
   B You must tell your teacher or ask your mum to talk to the teacher.
6. **A** I fell off my bike and banged my head – now I've got a bad headache.
   B Oooh that looks bad! You must go to A and E immediately and get an X-ray. I'll drive you, I don't think you should go alone.
7. **A** My computer's behaving very strangely.
   B Mine does that all the time. You should do what I do – turn it off, wait a while, then turn it on again. It's the only thing that ever works for me.
8. **A** My car's making a funny noise.
   B It sounds bad – you mustn't drive it. You should call the garage.

What do you think?

2. Students work in pairs to make sentences orally using the cues in the chart. Do one together as an example. Ask several confident students to tell the class one of their sentences in feedback. Elicit one more idea for each.

A trip to your country

3. An engaging way to do this activity would be to ask students to imagine they work for the tourist agency and they have been asked by their boss to prepare some advice for the website for tourists coming to their country. Read the list of things they might include in their advice together. Students can work in pairs if they are from the same country. Ask them to prepare their advice in writing. You could extend the activity by asking students to design the tourist information 'webpage'. This could be done on paper or on the computer and could include pictures as illustrations. Display the 'webpages' around the room. If you have a school website or VLE, you could upload them there as an example of student work.

SUGGESTION Review the grammar of modals with a team competition. Put students in teams of three or four. Write the following sentences on the board or give them as a handout. Books are closed. Teams have three minutes to find and correct the incorrect sentences. They swap papers for marking.

1. Do you have be fit to be a big wave surfer?
2. You didn't had to start young, but it helps.
3. I can hold my breath for a long time.
4. Do you have to a special surfboard?
5. Do you must train hard every day?
6. Do you think I should to stop running?
7. Can she sings?
8. It's dangerous. He musts be careful!
9. They shouldn't train when they are injured.
10. I must see a doctor last week.

(Answers: 1 – Do you have to; 2 – didn't have to; 3 – correct; 4 – Do you have; 5 – Do you have to; 6 – should stop; 7 – sing; 8. must; 9 – correct; 10 – had to).

Additional material

For teachers

Photocopiable activity – Grammar: *Do you agree?* pp209–10

For students

Online Practice – *Look again*

Workbook pp50–3, exercises 1–12

Online Practice – *Practice*

Listening and speaking SB p83

A health and fitness quiz

1. Ask students if they think they know a lot about health and fitness. Pre-teach/Check *skip breakfast* (not eat breakfast), *weigh* /weɪ/, *hurt* /hɜːt/, *rehydrate* /riːˈhaɪdreɪt/ (replace water lost from sweating), *No pain, no gain* (if it doesn't hurt, it isn't doing any good). This is a good opportunity to teach the phoneme /ɜː/, and students can also add *weigh* to their list of words with silent letters in their notebooks. Refer them to the quiz to decide if the statements are true or false. Discuss students' answers in feedback without saying if the statements are true or false. Encourage students to say why they think the statements are true or false.

2. **8.7** Play the recording. How many did they get right? Be sensitive here, because different cultures will have different ideas about fitness and health. Find out if anyone disagrees with the advice and why. Find out how many people know what they should do to keep healthy and fit, but who don't do it, e.g. how many people in the class skip breakfast? If you think students might be interested, explain that the word *breakfast* actually means 'to break the fast' – it's the first meal of the day after fasting all night

Answers

1 ✗   2 ✓   3 ✓   4 ✓   5 ✗   6 ✗   7 ✗   8 ✓   9 ✗   10 ✗

8.7 A health quiz – answers

1. You shouldn't skip breakfast.
   This is not true. Skipping breakfast does not necessarily make you unhealthy. However, the fact is, that people who do have breakfast are more likely to look after their health generally – they eat healthily and exercise regularly, so they're more healthy anyway.
2. You should weigh yourself regularly.
   This is true. Weighing yourself regularly helps you to keep a healthy weight. But you shouldn't do it too often – not every day, once a week is enough.
3. You must always warm up before hard exercise and cool down after.
   Yes, this is a good idea. Some fast walking to start and perhaps some yoga or Tai Chi afterwards.
4. Swimming is one of the best forms of exercise you can do.
   This is true. Some people say that swimming is the perfect exercise for the body. Tai Chi is also very good because it is both movement and relaxation. And don't forget walking! It's a simple but powerful way to keep healthy, as long as you do it in comfortable shoes!
5. You should do 30 minutes continuous activity rather than 10 minutes 3 times a day.

Unit 8 • Living dangerously 111

This is not true. Best is short periods of 10 minutes, but it's fine to do both. You should try to do at least 150 minutes a week.

6 You should always exercise until it hurts – no pain, no gain!
This is not true. You don't have to feel pain when you exercise to keep fit. Do it slowly at first. Little and often is better, and then build up to harder, longer exercises.

7 If you want to lose weight you should drink water after a meal.
No, you should drink water before a meal. It helps you feel full, and you won't eat too much.

8 If you don't feel full after a meal, you should wait 15 minutes and see how you feel then.
This is a good idea. Sometimes you want to eat more just after a meal, but if you wait 15 to 20 minutes, your food fills your stomach and you start to feel full.

9 You should always choose water over other drinks to rehydrate after exercising.
Not true. It doesn't have to be water. Any non-alcoholic drink will rehydrate you.

10 It's better to exercise in the morning rather than the afternoon or night.
Not true. There is no best time. The important thing is just to exercise – you can do morning, afternoon, or night!

Talking about you

3 Pre-teach/Check *screen time* and explain that this can include looking at anything with a screen – TV, phone, laptop, etc. Put students in groups of three or four to discuss the quiz. Appoint a group leader whose job it is to ensure everyone speaks and who keeps the conversation going. In feedback, ask one student from each group to comment on what the group said about each of the questions.

EXTENSION Ask the groups to make a plan for a healthy lifestyle to follow for a 15-year-old boy/girl at school, for an office worker, and for a busy housewife with small children. They should work out what each should eat, how much and what sort of exercise they should take, how much sleep etc. When they have done that, they can present their ideas to another group.

SUGGESTION If you have older students, ask them to create their own health quiz for parents of small children. What questions would they ask to give advice to parents about keeping their children healthy? If you have teen students, it might be more fun to have an anti-health quiz. Ask them to write a quiz to advise people on how they can be really unhealthy. See how many really unhealthy things they can come up with!

Additional material

For students
Online Practice – *Practice*

Reading and speaking SB p84

Two stuntwomen and a stuntman

About the text

The reading text gives information about two real-life female stunt doubles. Stunt doubles stand in for actors when there are dangerous scenes in films – fight scenes, falls, or crashes, for example. In the UK, stunt doubles join the National Stunt Register which shows potential employers that they have the skills needed to perform dangerous stunt work. Stunt doubles should be physically fit and good at things such as sport, martial arts or boxing, high diving, riding, driving, gymnastics, swimming, trampolining, etc. In the UK, people can train to be stunt doubles at the British Action Academy. Some well-known actors do their own stunts: Tom Cruise broke his ankle doing a stunt for *Mission Impossible 6*. Christian Bale, Daniel Craig, and Cameron Diaz have also done their own stunts in films. Stunt doubles' salary varies according to experience and the risk of the stunt. You might ask students to look at job comparison sites to find out about salaries. In general, a stunt double's salary is anywhere between $5,000–$70,000 a year, but the best doubles can earn up to $250,000 a year. A very dangerous stunt can pay a lot of money – the stunt double who jumped off the CN Tower in Toronto was paid $150,000 – the highest paid stunt ever.

1 Refer students to the photo. Find out what students know about the job of stuntman or stuntwoman. Students discuss the questions in pairs and then discuss in open class. Ask them what sort of films use stunt doubles most. Find out if students know of any stunt doubles or actors that use them from films other than Hollywood.

> **Answers**
> A stuntman or stuntwoman has to do dangerous things in the place of actors, such as fall out of windows or cars, fall off horses, jump over obstacles, etc.

2 Students discuss the questions in pairs and then discuss in open class. Ask them what sort of films use stunt doubles most.

3 Pre-teach/Check the definitions of the adjectives in the box. Drill the pronunciation and ask students to underline the stressed syllable, or categorize them as below:

oOo	ath<u>le</u>tic
oOoo	com<u>pe</u>titive
Oo	<u>cra</u>zy, <u>heal</u>thy, <u>spor</u>ty
OoOo	<u>ea</u>sy-<u>go</u>ing
Ooo	<u>sen</u>sitive
O	brave, fit, strong, slim, thin

Check the pronunciation of the /θ/ sound in *athletic* /æθˈletɪk/ and *healthy*. Point out that *slim* has a positive meaning whereas *thin* has a negative one. Show students an example: *He's very slim and athletic. He's very thin and unhealthy-looking. Sensitive* may be a false friend depending on the students' first language. Here it means 'aware of and able to understand other people and their feelings' or, alternatively, 'easily upset'. Elicit a list of the qualities students think are necessary to be a stunt double. Encourage students to give reasons for their choices.

4 Read the instructions and questions with the students. Check they know to read just the Fact Files and introduction to answer the questions. They compare answers in pairs before checking as a class. Did they find any of the information surprising? Have they seen any of the films Dayna and Amanda have been in? How many students like action films like these?

> **Answers**
> Amanda Foster /əˈmændə ˈfɒstə/ is from England – she isn't married. Dayna Grant /ˈdeɪnə ɡrɑːnt/ is from New Zealand – she is married.
> Stuntwomen earn more money than stuntmen in New Zealand, because they recognize that stuntwomen can't wear as much protective clothing as men, so it is even more dangerous for them.
> Amanda has worked in *James Bond 007: Die Another Day*, *A Knight in Camelot*, *World War Z*, The *Harry Potter* series, *Ninja Assassin*
> Dayna has worked in *Mad Max: Fury Road*, *The Chronicles of Narnia*, and *Xena: Warrior Princess*.

5 Read the questions together and check understanding of *suitable* /ˈsuːtəbl/, *star*, *crash diet* (a short-term weight-loss diet with the aim of rapid results). Divide the class into two groups. Group A reads about Amanda Foster. Group B reads about Dayna Grant. Allow students from each group to work together to answer the questions. Monitor and support as needed.

> **Answers**
> **Group A**
> 1 She was sporty and was a PE teacher and a film extra.
> 2 On a film set she heard someone say that there were no British black stunt actresses, so she decided to be the first.
> 3 Whoopi Goldberg, Halle Berry, Tom Cruise, Brad Pitt (and Naomie Harris)
> 4 Sword fighting, jumping over tables, jumping on top of Brad Pitt and biting his face.
> 5 Gymnastics, trampolining, motorcycle racing, martial arts.
> 6 Because she wants to see how they move because the viewer has to believe that she actually is the star.
> 7 Many times. She doesn't want to talk about her worst injury. She says: 'All I can say is that as long as I leave a day's work in my own car and I don't have to leave in an ambulance, it's been a good day.'
> 8 Her children are grown up now and are proud of their mum.
> **Group B**
> 1 She was a gymnast and a horse rider.
> 2 Two friends, who were stuntmen, asked her to audition to be a stuntwoman on *Xena: Warrior Princess*.
> 3 Charlize Theron, Gwyneth Paltrow, Tilda Swinton (and Lucy Lawless)
> 4 Shave her head, spend nine months in the Namibian desert, run alongside a truck and fall under its wheels.
> 5 Martial arts (judo, karate), archery, chariot driving.
> 6 Because they have to spend a lot of time together.
> 7 Yes – she slipped, and her head fell on a dagger. She says: 'I was a bit of a mess.'
> 8 Her son thinks she's not a normal mum.

6 Pair up students in AB pairs to compare information. Student A asks the questions to Student B first, then they swap roles with Student B asking the questions and Student A giving the information. Discuss information from the texts further as a class. Do any of the students fancy becoming a stunt double?

Listening – a stuntman's story

7 **8.8** Students now listen to the story of a stuntman. Refer students to the questions/heading in bold in the articles. Tell them to write them down and leave some space to take notes as they listen. Point out that Andy might not ask the questions in the same way. Play the recording. Students compare answers. Monitor to check they are using third person. If students are struggling, put them in pairs and divide up the questions. Play the recording again if needed. In feedback, ask students if they saw the film, *Captain Corelli's Mandolin*, and if they are familiar with the actors Andy has worked with.

> **Answers**
> **How did he become a stuntman?**
> He loved all sports at school and he loved climbing trees, so he thought then that he wanted to become a stuntman – but he didn't have the courage to do it until he was 29.
> **Which celebrities has he worked with?**
> Ralph Fiennes, Toby Stephens, Pierce Brosnan, Nicholas Cage
> **How do stunt doubles prepare for a film?**
> He worked at skills, such as horse riding, high diving, and martial arts. He talks through stunts with the director.
> **Has he been injured much?**
> Not too much – just a few bumps and bruises. He also sprained his ankle, but that was in the park and not after doing a stunt.
> **Final word**
> He doesn't do much stunt work now and his wife is happy about that, but his sons love to hear about his work as a stuntman.

8.8 Andy Lambert – a stuntman's story
J = Justin   A = Andy Lambert

J Andy, I've often wondered … and never asked – how did you become a stuntman?
A Well … I first thought about it when I was at school. I always loved sports – all sports – athletics, swimming, even pole vaulting – anything and everything – and I loved climbing trees, too, so I thought … hmmm … I'd like to be a stuntman.
J Really? You actually had the idea at school? It's not a job many people think of.
A Well, I did … but then I thought that the people doing it had to be very special in some way – so it couldn't be me. But eventually when I was 29, I had the courage and got started. Twenty-nine is quite late for a stuntman.
J So what were the first jobs you did?
A Well, I worked as a film extra at first on some TV dramas – I was the person sat at the bar or just one of the crowd. But at the same time I worked at other skills – you have to do that – horse riding, high diving, and martial arts, of course. I did judo competitions, and I built a portfolio of photographs of myself.
J You really planned it carefully then.
A Yeah, I was keen … and finally I got my first job. It was on a film called *Onegin* – a Russian romantic drama with Ralph Fiennes – I was doubling for Toby Stephens, Maggie Smith's son.
J Oh yeah – then what?
A Well, after that I got work on a Bond film, one with Pierce Brosnan, when he comes crashing through a restaurant window in a speedboat. That was me!
J I saw the film – I didn't recognize you!
A That's good – you're not meant to!
J I know! So … how do you prepare for a film like that?
A First, you have to talk through the stunts with the director – so, for example, if you're going to fall out of a window you have to talk about how he, or she, wants you to move in the air and land – hit the ground, you know.
J Whoah, Andy! It sounds so dangerous. Have you ever been injured?
A Not too much. I'm lucky. Just a few bumps and bruises, but a lot of stuntmen and women do get injured – sprained ankles, broken arms and legs, and the like. If you think about it, if you have to fall off a horse say 10 or 12 times in one day, you're not going to feel great.
J I'm laughing, but …
A Actually, there was another injury.
J What was that?
A Well, I was going to do a really big film, in Greece – it was *Captain Corelli's Mandolin* with Nicolas Cage, and then just before I had to leave I sprained my ankle.
J What a shame! How did you do that?
A Well, I was running in my local park and I fell – can you believe it?

J You're kidding! You don't do much stunt work now do you?
A No, I don't. I haven't done much since I married and had kids – my wife was pleased when I stopped, but my sons love to hear about when Dad was a stuntman. I still love a bit of danger in my life.
J OK – how about a game of squash with me now. That's enough danger for me!

What do you think?

Put students in small groups with a group leader to discuss the questions. If possible, allow them to find the names of actors who do their own stunts and find out how much stuntmen and women typically earn. Ask for feedback from each group during a whole-class discussion. As an extension, if you have students from countries with a film industry, ask them to research to find out who the stunt people are and which stars have used them.

EXTRA IDEA Tell students to work in small groups and to think of two other dangerous jobs, for example, fire officer, construction worker, miner. Ask them to think about what is involved in the job, and what qualities someone needs to do the job.

VIDEO In this unit students can watch a video about an underwater photographer and find out more about his job. You can play the video clip on the Classroom Presentation Tool or download it from the Teacher's Resource Centre together with the video script, video worksheet, and accompanying teacher's notes. These notes give full guidance on how to use the worksheets and include a comprehensive answer key to the exercises and activities.

Additional material
For teachers
Photocopiable activity – Video worksheet: *Under water*
For students
Online Practice – *Look again*
Online Practice – *Practice*

Vocabulary and speaking SB p86

Not a thing to wear!

Possible problems

Students may get confused between *dress* and *wear*:
*I don't have anything to dress. (Correction: *I don't have anything to wear.*)
*I dress my jacket and tie. (Correction: *I'm wearing my jacket and tie.*)
– *To dress* is to put clothes on:
I get dressed in the morning.
– *To wear* is to have clothes on your body:
I'm wearing my best jacket.
A *dress* is a particular item of clothing mostly worn by women.

1 **8.9** As a lead-in, ask students if they ever feel they have nothing to wear. How many clothes do they think they have? More than what they can see in the pictures on p86 or less? Do a quick poll to find out who has the most pairs of shoes. Ask students on what part of the body they wear their shoes as a segue into the listening. Explain that they are going to hear a children's song – any parents in the class might like to teach it to their children. The song uses actions – ask students to stand up so they can do them! As the song is sung, they should touch the part of the body they hear with both hands. Talk them through the song slowly the first time and do the actions with them. Then play the song which will get them moving much faster!

Answers
head, shoulders, knees, toes, eyes, ears, mouth, nose

8.9 A children's song
Head and shoulders, knees and toes, knees and toes!
Head and shoulders, knees and toes, knees and toes!
And eyes and ears and mouth and nose!
Head and shoulders, knees and toes, knees and toes!
Arms and legs and feet and hands, feet and hands!
Arms and legs and feet and hands, feet and hands!
And eyes and ears and mouth and nose!
Head and shoulders, knees and toes, knees and toes!

2 Refer students to the list. They label Person X with the parts. Check and drill pronunciation. Tricky words include *wrist* (silent w) /rɪst/, *waist* /weɪst/, *fingers* /ˈfɪŋɡə(r)z/, *knees* (silent k) /niːz/, *head* (ea word with /e/ sound) /hed/ and *ankle* /ˈæŋkl/ which you might want to distinguish from *uncle* /ˈʌŋkl/. Note that in some languages, the word for *fingers* and *toes* is the same – *fingers* in Spanish, for example is *dedos*, and *toes* is *dedos de los pies* (fingers of the feet). If students are interested, you could teach them the names of the fingers starting with the thumb: *thumb* (silent b) /θʌm/, *index finger* (*pointer finger* in the US), *middle finger*, *ring finger* (so-called because that is the finger the wedding ring is worn on because it is closer to the heart), *little finger* (*pinky* /ˈpɪŋki/ in the US). Interestingly, toes don't have names like the fingers do. Ask fast finishers to find words for other body parts.

EXTRA IDEA If appropriate, you could play a game of *Simon Says* to practise the body parts. Everyone stands up. The rule is, when Simon Says do something, you do it. If Simon doesn't say to do it, you don't. Do an example so that students understand: Say, *Simon says put your hands on your head. Simon says touch your fingers. Touch your knees. Oh! Simon didn't say!*

Once students understand, play the game. If a student moves when Simon didn't say, or if the student touches the wrong body part, that student sits down. The 'winner' is the last one standing. Go faster and faster to try to get students 'out' as you progress.

3 Lead in to the next section by talking about what you are wearing. You could bring in a box of clothes and say to the students that you have been invited to a party, but have nothing to wear! Pull out various items (from the list in exercise 3) and name them, put some on, but reject them all. Keep involving the students by saying, *Should I wear this (jacket)?*, etc. The aim is to introduce the vocabulary in an amusing and engaging way.

Ask students to look at the list of clothing and check they know the words. Check/Drill the pronunciation of *wear* /weə/. Allow them to use a dictionary to look up any words that are unknown. If you have a projector connected to the Internet, you could pull up examples of clothing to clarify any tricky ones. A low-tech idea is to bring in pictures from clothing magazines. Students find clothing items, cut them out and stick them onto the board with a label for each item.

114 Unit 8 • Living dangerously

Check and drill the pronunciation, using phonetic symbols as needed. Check that students are saying a /dʒ/ sound (not /j/) for *jacket* /ˈdʒækɪt/, *jeans* /dʒiːnz/, *jumper* /ˈdʒʌmpə(r)/; a /v/ sound (not /w/) for *vest* /vest/; /suːt/ not /swiːt/ for *suit*, *tracksuit*, and *swimsuit*, and that they are pronouncing the /h/ in *helmet*. Differentiate between *skirt* /skɜːt/ and *shirt* /ʃɜːt/. Ask them to work in pairs to say where each item of clothing goes as in the examples to review prepositions and body parts while learning the new vocabulary.

As a follow-up revision in a later class, you say where the item goes, and students say what it is. See how many they can get in one minute. Students can also do this in pairs. Student A: *It's something that goes around the waist.* Student B: *Belt?*

Students can also add these words and the body words to their vocabulary notebook in separate sections headed, 'body' and 'clothes'. They should include phrases such as *What are you wearing? I'm wearing a …* as well.

Answers
a a dress – on the body
b a shirt – on the top half of the body, and tie – round the neck
c a skirt – on the bottom half of the body
d a hoodie – on the top half of the body
e jeans – on the bottom half of the body
f sunglasses – on the face/eyes
g sandals – on the feet
h a sports vest – on the top half of the body
i gloves – on the hands
j a watch – round the wrist
k a cap – on the head
l a tracksuit – on the body
m a jacket – on the top half of the body
n a scarf – round the neck
o shorts – on the bottom half of the body
p a jumper – on the top half of the body
q boots – on the feet
r socks – on the feet
s goggles – on the eyes
t a suit – on the body
u a belt – round the waist
v a helmet – on the head
w a T-shirt – on the top half of the body
x trainers – on the feet
y swimsuit – on the middle part of the body
z leggings – on the bottom half of the body

Dress Person X

4 Read the instructions with the students. Students work in pairs. They decide the situation they want to dress Person X for, then decide what she or he should wear. Write this sentence frame on the board: *… is wearing …*. Students pair up with another pair and tell them the clothes Person X is wearing so that the other pair can guess the situation she or he is dressed for.

Talking about you

5 Put students in pairs to ask and answer the questions. Check pronunciation of *bought* /bɔːt/. Ask students to think of one more question to include in their discussion. You could do this as a milling activity so that students can ask and answer the questions several times.

SUGGESTION Play a guessing game with the students. A student describes what someone in the class is wearing and the others guess the person. e.g. *This person is wearing a green hoodie …* . Another alternative is to do this as a fashion show. Bring in a bunch of old newspapers, wrapping paper, plastic bags, etc., plenty of tape or duct tape, and several sets of scissors. Students work in small groups to make clothes for a fashion show. Students model the clothes with one group member describing the outfits for the class, e.g. *Miranda is wearing the perfect clothes for a skiing holiday. She is wearing a …* .

Additional material
For teachers
Photocopiable activity – Vocabulary: *What shall I wear?* pp211–2
For students
Online Practice – *Look again*
Workbook p54, exercises 1–3
Online Practice – *Practice*

Everyday English SB p87

At the doctor's

This section deals with vocabulary and functional language of going to the doctor's. Lead in to the section by asking students about their own experiences, without getting too personal, e.g. *When did you last go to the doctor's? What's your doctor like?* Alternatively, lead in by writing a few of the symptoms of a cold on the board, e.g. *a sore throat* /sɔː(r) θrəʊt/, *a runny nose*, *a high temperature* /ˈtemprətʃə(r)/, *a terrible headache* /ˈhedeɪk/. Say *I've got a terrible cold. What should I do?* and elicit advice from different students to revise *should/must*. Point out the difference between *to have a cold* (= to have an illness) and *to be cold* (related to temperature; If you are cold, you should put on a sweater).

1 Focus attention on the pictures and get students to read out the words and phrases in the box. Check pronunciation of *diarrhoea* /ˌdaɪəˈrɪə/. The word is notoriously tricky to spell. Elicit the correct word for picture A. Then get students to work in pairs to match the rest. Check answers and drill pronunciation. Deal with any questions about the conditions. Note that with the flu, people generally have a fever and sometimes vomiting and diarrhoea.

Answers
A a sprained ankle
B diarrhoea
C food poisoning
D flu
E an allergy
F a sore throat
G a cold

2 🔊 **8.10** This exercise focuses on symptoms and diagnoses. *Symptoms* are signs that the body is not well, whereas *diagnosis* is identifying the cause of the problem. Pre-teach/Check *symptoms*, /ˈsɪmptəm/, *diagnosis* /ˌdaɪəɡˈnəʊsɪs/, *glands*, *aches* /eɪks/, *swallow*, /ˈswɒləʊ/, *sneezing*, *swollen* /ˈswəʊlən/, *coughing* /ˈkɒfɪŋ/. To help remember these terms, mime them where possible. For *swollen*, you can put your hand on your throat and mime *swallowing* with a pained look on your face, for example.

Unit 8 • Living dangerously 115

Check students understand that *have got* = *have*. Do the first one together as an example. Students compare answers before listening to the recording to check. Play the recording again so students can focus on what else the doctor says. Put students in pairs to roleplay the patient and doctor conversation, using the chart in exercise 2 or the audioscript on p137.

Answers and audioscript

◉ 8.10 The doctor's diagnosis

P = Patient   D = Doctor

1   P I can't stop coughing and blowing my nose.
     D You've got **a cold**. It's just a bad cold.
2   P I've got a fever, my whole body aches, and I feel awful.
     D You've got **flu** – just go home and go to bed.
3   P It hurts when I walk on it.
     D You've got **a sprained ankle**. It looks quite bad. You should go for an X-ray.
4   P I keep going to the toilet.
     D You've got **diarrhoea**. It's probably something you've eaten. You can get some pills from the pharmacist.
5   P My glands are swollen, and it hurts when I swallow.
     D You've got **a sore throat** – let me see! … Ah yes … it's tonsillitis.
6   P I keep being sick, and I've got terrible diarrhoea.
     D You've got **food poisoning**. It will pass in a few hours – oh dear … the toilet's just over there!
7   P I start sneezing when I'm near a cat.
     D You've got **an allergy**. Lots of people are allergic to cats. You can take antihistamine pills – you can get a packet from the chemist.

3 **◉ 8.11** This exercise focuses on listening for specific information, so students should cover the conversation in the book to avoid reading it during the first listening. Read the questions together so that students know what to listen for. Pre-teach/Check *prescribe/prescription, allergy* /ˈælədʒi/, *penicillin, to take things easy, sickness* (In this context, *sickness* means *vomiting*), *fever* (fever is a synonym for a very high temperature), *swollen, to pop this in your mouth* (to put this – the thermometer – in his mouth), *to take things easy*. Ask students to cover the conversation in the book. Play the recording. Students compare answers in pairs. Play the recording again if needed for students to complete their answers. Weaker students can listen and read the second time round if needed. Elicit answers in feedback, ensuring students switch from first to third person when talking about Edsom's /ˈedsəmz/ symptoms.

Answers

1 He's had a bad headache for a few days and he's got a sore throat. He feels hot, especially at night. He can't sleep because he feels hot and he starts coughing when he lies down.
2 What seems to be the problem? Any sickness or diarrhoea? Do you feel hot? Does this hurt? Are you allergic to penicillin?
3 She thinks he has an infection.
4 She prescribes antibiotics/penicillin.
5 She tells him not to go to work for a couple of days, to drink plenty of liquids, and to take things easy.
6 He has to pay £8.80 for the prescription.

4 **◉ 8.11** Put students in pairs to complete the conversation. Play the recording so that students can check their answers. Put them in pairs to practise the conversation. They should each take turns being the doctor and the patient. If possible, move the chairs around so that the students are facing each other across a desk. Give the doctors some simple props, e.g. a pad and pen for writing the prescription. Remind the doctors to mime taking Edsom's temperature. Encourage students to act out the symptoms. With lower-level classes, you could drill the doctor's questions first, focusing on the intonation. Give students time to act out the scene in their pairs. Monitor and check for good pronunciation. If students have a lot of problems or sound 'flat', drill key lines chorally and individually. Students then continue practising in their pairs.

Answers and audioscript

◉ 8.11 Seeing the doctor

D = Doctor   E = Edsom

D Hello. Come and sit down. What seems to be the **problem**?
E Well, I haven't felt **well** for a few days. I've had a bad **headache**, and now I've got a **sore throat**.
D Any sickness or diarrhoea?
E No, I haven't been **sick** or had any diarrhoea.
D Do you feel hot?
E Yes, especially at night. I can't sleep because I feel hot, and I start **coughing** when I lie down.
D OK, I'll just **take** your temperature. Can I just pop this in your mouth?
E Aaargh!
D Ah, yes. You do have a bit of a **fever**. Now, let me see your throat. Open your **mouth** wide, please.
E 'ot can u see?
D Pardon?
E Can you see anything?
D Yes, your throat looks very red. Does this **hurt**?
E Ouch!
D And your glands are **swollen**.
E Is it serious?
D No, not at all. You just have a bit of a **throat** infection. You should have antibiotics. Are you allergic to penicillin?
E No, I'm not.
D Good. Now, you **shouldn't** go to work for a couple of days, and you **must** drink plenty of liquids. Just take things easy for a while. I'll write you a prescription.
E Thank you. Do I have to pay you?
D No, no. Seeing me is free, but you'll have to pay for the **prescription**. It's £8.80.
E Right. Thanks very much. Goodbye.

Roleplay

5 Before starting this free roleplay stage, ask students to imagine they don't feel very well and to write down a list of symptoms. Get students to change roles and act out a new conversation with a different set of symptoms. Students continue changing roles and repeating the scene with different information each time. Monitor and help as necessary. Check for accurate use of the key language and for good pronunciation. Note any common errors, but don't highlight and correct these until after the pairwork. When they are done, point out one or two of the good and not so good things you heard (without saying names) and write them on the board. See if students can correct the errors.

Additional material
For teachers
Photocopiable activity – Communication: *What seems to be the matter?* pp213–14
For students
Online Practice – *Look again*
Workbook p55
Online Practice – *Practice*

Writing SB p88

Writing emails

Comparing formal and informal

The aim of this section is to write a formal and an informal email using the new language learned.

1 Start by asking students how many emails they write/ receive a day. Are the emails mostly work-related, social, marketing emails from companies, emails from things they've subscribed to, or other? Ask *How does an email from a friend differ from a work-related email?* to elicit that one tends to be informal and the other formal. Ask students how formal emails usually begin and end. What about informal ones? Read the instructions with the students to ensure they understand that there is more than one match possible. Match the first beginning to all possible endings as a whole class as an example. Put students in pairs to match the beginnings and endings of emails, and to decide which are informal/formal. Check answers as a class. Point out that we use *Dear Sir or Madam* when we don't know the name of the person we are writing to. The standard convention for *Dear … + Mr/Mrs/Ms* + family name is to end with *Yours sincerely*, while *Dear Sir or Madam* uses *Yours faithfully*. Note that it's also possible to write, *Hi Mum* instead of *Dear Mum*. At this point you might also like to review titles:

- Mr – man, married or unmarried
- Miss – unmarried woman
- Mrs – married woman
- Ms – can be married or unmarried; used when you don't know, and is also becoming more standard as a title for women in general
- Dr – for men or women who have completed their PhD or medical degree

Answers
1 a, b, c, d, g (informal)
2 f (formal)
3 a, b, c, d, g (informal)
4 e (formal)
5 a, b, c, d, (g) (informal)
6 a, b, c, d, g (informal)

2 Refer students to the online advertisement /əd'vɜːtɪsmənt/ for an English school, and give them a few minutes to read it. Check comprehension of *principal* /'prɪnsəpl/. Answer the questions as a class.

Answers
It's in York in the UK.
You can study English.
You can contact Harriet Lombard.

A formal email

3 Ask students to look at the formal email. Ask *Who is it from? Who is it to? Can you predict what it will be about?* Students complete the email with words and phrases from the box. Check answers as a class. Check students have understood the email: *Where did Concetta see the advertisement? Why is she writing the email?* (for information about the courses, and accommodation). Ask students why Concetta wrote the email using formal language. Point out that the phrase, *I look forward to + -ing* is a common ending. In this case, it is a polite way of saying that you await/expect a reply.

Answers
1 advertisement
2 interested in
3 frequently
4 However
5 to improve
6 application form
7 some information
8 to hearing
9 sincerely

4 Draw students' attention to the labels on the parts of the email. This is a standard structure for any formal email. Ask students if emails in their language follow a similar pattern. Give students time to discuss different greetings and endings for letters and emails in their language. Elicit these in a class discussion about formality expectations. You may point out that in formal emails we do not generally use contractions (*I am writing* not *I'm writing*), phrasal verbs or informal expressions (*improve* not *get better*), full words (*advertisement* not *ad/advert*), and use standard phrases like *Yours sincerely,/Yours faithfully*.
We use formal emails in the following situations:

- business emails when we do not know the person we are corresponding with
- corresponding with people at a higher professional level in business, or academia
- asking for information from organizations like colleges, universities, or official departments

An informal email

5 This exercise focuses on the use of formal or informal language to express the same ideas in the context of a formal and informal email. Students read the informal email, then compare it to the formal one, identifying the synonymous phrases. Put students into pairs to find the phrases. Ask them to put them into two columns – informal and formal. You could also ask them to identify and label the parts – *greeting, introduction, main part, conclusion, ending* – in the informal email. Although informal emails don't have to follow a set structure like formal ones do, there is nonetheless a logical structure.

Unit 8 • Living dangerously   117

> **Answers**
> I'm thinking of coming = I am interested in coming
> use English a lot = I have to use English frequently
> I want = I would like
> especially for my pronunciation = I would especially like to improve my pronunciation
> an interesting ad = your advertisement
> I'd love to = I would like
> Can't wait to = I look forward to hearing from you as soon as possible

6 Writing is always more realistic when there is a context, purpose, and audience in mind. Before getting started on writing, ask students to think about: *Where did you see the advertisement?* (e.g. online, in a newspaper, etc.) *When do you want to go to the school?* (in the summer holidays, next year, etc.) *Why do you want to go to the school?* (I need English to speak with my English son-in-law., I want to have a holiday and learn some English at the same time.; I want to visit my friend., etc.) *What do you want Harriet Lombard to do?* (send information about prices, enrol me for a … week course, etc.). Once they have this context and purpose clear in their minds, ask students to write the email. If possible, give students an email template to write on, or allow them to use a computer and print out the email. Put students in pairs for peer review. Ask *Does the email have all five parts? Is the language formal?* Students then write an informal email to an English friend telling them about their upcoming trip to the UK. Before writing they should think about who they are writing to and why. You could ask them to 'send' the email to another student in the class. Brainstorm some ideas with the class on what the friend might say in reply, then ask them to reply to their friend's email.

EXTRA IDEA Make a photocopy of the email below for students to work on. Tell students to read the email, find ten mistakes, and correct them. The mistakes may be grammar, vocabulary, or using the wrong level of formality/informality. Then either have whole-class feedback, or get them to work in groups to correct the mistakes. Then you can give each group a copy of the answer to check their answers.

TO: Marion Harrison

SUBLECT: Trip to London

Dear Marion,

Just let you know I'm hope to do my English course in August. My English exam on September 5 to get into the Engineering Department in Madrid University. I know it'll be very difficult and I like improve my grammar, which I know is awesome. I know I should to work on my pronunciation too.

Last summer when you were here in Madrid, you say I could stay with you while I'm doing my course. Is that still OK with you? My course starts on August 4 and lasts three weeks. I will arriving on August 2 and have go back to Madrid on August 27 for my cousin's wedding on August 28. I'm really looking forward to see all the family together again.

Can't wait to hear all your news. I hope we can be together in August.

Love

Isabella

> **Answers**
> Hi Marion
> Just 1) **to** let you know I'm 2) **hoping** to do my English course in August. My English exam 3) **is** on September 5 to get into the Engineering Department in Madrid University. I know it'll be very difficult and 4) **I'd like to** improve my grammar, which I know is 5) **awful**. I know I should 6) **work** on my pronunciation too. Last summer when you were here in Madrid, you 7) **said** I could stay with you while I'm doing my course. Is that still OK with you? My course starts on August 4 and lasts three weeks. I 8) **arrive / 'm arriving** on August 2 and I have 9) **to** go back to Madrid on August 27 for my cousin's wedding on August 28. I'm really looking forward to 10) **seeing** all the family together again. Can't wait to hear all your news. I hope we can be together in August.
> Love
> Isabella

Additional material
For students
Online Practice – *Practice*
Workbook p55, *Review*, exercises 1–2; *Stop and check* Units 5–8, pp56–7
Online Practice – *Check your progress*

118 Unit 8 • Living dangerously

9 What a story!

Introduction to the unit

This unit looks at the theme of storytelling and the conventions of traditional storytelling. A folk tale from the Middle East, *The Story of Mula and the Miserable Man*, provides the perfect context for the introduction of Past Perfect to express an action in the past which happened before the main action in the past, and review of narrative tenses in the first *Grammar* section. There is also a focus on the pronunciation to improve listening comprehension of the contraction *'d* in Past Perfect.

Conjunctions (joining words) of reason, result, contrast, and time, e. g. *so, because, although, when, as soon as,* are introduced and practised in connection with a humorous story about a professor and his driver in the second *Grammar* section.

The *Listening and speaking* section has an interview with a book publisher about young adult literature. The skill here is on close listening for specific information, and giving opinions with reasons during speaking.

The story theme continues in the *Reading and speaking* section with a story by the British short story writer, Saki.

In the *Vocabulary and speaking* section, students learn positive and negative adjectives to talk about feelings, e.g. *homesick, jealous, upset, amazed,* and the situations where you feel these emotions.

Exclamations with *so* and *such* is the topic for the *Everyday English* section, and students practise using these in conversations that also recycle adjectives.

In the *Writing* section, students read a review of the classic book *Frankenstein*, and use it as a model to write their own film or book review.

Language aims

Grammar

Past Perfect and narrative tenses

Students read a story and write and answer questions in the Past Continuous and Past Simple to revise these two narrative tenses. Still focusing on the story, they put lines from the story containing Past Perfect into the correct places so that they can internalize the concept of things happening before the main events in the story. A guided discovery approach is used to introduce Past Perfect so that the students can use their understanding of the story to inform their learning of the grammar. Because the contraction *'d* in Past Perfect is hard to hear, students listen to and identify sentences with the contracted form. They discuss the difference in meaning between sentences in the Past Simple, Past Continuous, and Past Perfect.

Joining words

Conjunctions of time, result, reason, and contrast are introduced. These will help students make sense of narratives and make their writing more cohesive. Students first practise by choosing the right word or phrase. They then combine sentences with a conjunction. Finally, they create their own sentences with the conjunctions.

Vocabulary

Feelings

The idea of positive and negative connotation is introduced in this section with adjectives to describe feelings. Students practise a conversation in which they talk about their feelings.

Everyday English

Exclamations with *so* and *such*

Students learn how to use *so, such, such a/an, so many,* and *so much* in exclamations. Again, a guided discovery approach is used in which students hear the exclamations in context first, then look at sentences to work out the rules of use. They work on using correct stress and intonation in exclamations in preparation for reading a conversation and then writing and performing their own.

Additional material

Workbook

Students complete a folk tale using Past Simple and Past Perfect. There is an exercise on making sentences using these tenses to give reasons for actions and events. There are several tasks on conjunctions, including sentence completion, and sentence transformations. There is a vocabulary exercise on adjectives of emotion. There is also a task on homonyms, such as *flat, bear,* and *match*. Finally students practise exclamations with *so* and *such*, and the unit ends with a Grammar review.

Photocopiable activities

There are photocopiable activities to review grammar (*Two news stories*), vocabulary (*Feelings*), and communication (*Guess what I did!*) at the back of the Teacher's Guide as well as on the Teacher's Resource Centre. There is also a worksheet to accompany the video on the Teacher's Resource Centre.

Notes on the unit

Unit opener page

Choose from these activities to engage your students with the topic and target language of this unit.

- Talk about the title
- Talk about the unit goals (*Grammar, Vocabulary, …*)
- Talk about the photo
- Watch the video
- Look at the bottom banner
- Do the activity

Refer students to the unit title *What a story!* Point out that we use *what* in this way for emphasis. In this case it means that the story was especially good. Give other examples: *What awful weather! What a beautiful flower! What a day I've had!*, etc. Ask students if they have heard any good stories lately. Put them in small groups to discuss.

If you don't have time to watch the video introduction to the unit, go through the unit goals below the title: *Grammar, Vocabulary, Everyday English, Reading, Listening, Writing*. Give examples or use translation for unknown words.

Video (2 minutes approximately): The video gives a step-by-step overview of the unit. Play the video, pausing where necessary – especially for students to answer any questions, e.g. *What was your favourite story when you were a child?* This makes it a more interactive experience. Highlight the option of practising online.

As shown in the bottom banner, don't forget that there are many exercises to consolidate and practise the target language of the unit in the Workbook as well as online. There are links to these exercises on the relevant pages of the Student's Book and they can be done in class time or you can set them for homework.

Summary: If you're short of time, use the title and the photo to help students understand and engage with the topic, and then move straight on to the activity so that they can discuss the theme in more detail. If you have any more time, try to watch the video together. It is a clear and interesting introduction to the different parts of the unit.

Notes for activity:

Put students in pairs. Ask them to look at the photo and discuss their answers to the questions. Ask them to justify their choices where possible.

> **Suggested answers**
> 1 Telling a story to her friends.
> 2 Yes, she seems very animated and expressive. Her facial expression shows that she is telling the story with passion and she is using her hands, too. Her friends are laughing and leaning in to listen carefully.
> 3 Students' own answers.

Grammar SB p90

Past Perfect and narrative tenses

> **Possible problems**
> 1 Unit 3 covered the difference between Past Simple and Past Continuous. (See p44 of the Teacher's Guide for Possible problems associated with these tenses.)
> This unit extends the coverage of narrative tenses with a review of Past Simple and Continuous and the introduction of the Past Perfect, which expresses an action completed before another action in the past.
> 2 This is probably the first time your students will have met the Past Perfect. Students will be familiar with the components that make up the form of the tense (*had* + past participle), and the concept doesn't usually present students with many problems, though some students may put the Past Perfect in the wrong part of the sentence:
> **After she finished cleaning, the children had made a mess.* (Correction: *After she had finished cleaning, the children made a mess.*)
> Students need to understand the relationship between the Past Simple and Past Perfect, and using stories provides a natural context for this.
> 3 One problem that may occur is that students confuse the contracted form of the Past Perfect *'d* (*had*) with the contracted form of *would*.
> *She said she'd bought the tickets.* (= had)
> *She said she'd buy the tickets.* (= would)

STARTER SB p90

The stories presented in the *Starter* box will probably be familiar to students. *Peter Pan* is the story of a boy who never grew up and who lives on an island with a fairy named Tinkerbell and a group of lost boys who are forever battling the terrible Captain Hook. *Peter Pan* has been turned into a number of films. *The Adventures of Pinocchio* is a tale of a wooden string puppet lovingly carved by Geppetto. Although initially prone to mischief, Pinocchio eventually proves himself worthy and becomes a real boy. The Disney film *Pinocchio* is perhaps the best-known adaptation of the original book. *Mary Poppins* is a story about a nanny who is hired to look after the children of the Banks family. The children soon discover that although she is very strict, she is also magical. The three original books were turned into the well-known Disney films of the same name.

Lead in to the topic by finding out about students' favourite book or story. This could be from their childhood or it might be something they have read recently. See if they can give a short summary using the sentence frame: *It's about … .* Ask them who the characters are. This could be done in small groups in a larger class. Tell them about your favourite story or a good book you've read. With books closed, read the excerpts to the students from the books in the *Starter* section. Ask students if they think they know the book the extracts come from. Ask them to open their books and work in groups to match the characters in the pictures with the books. Find out if students have read any of these stories.

Answers
A *Mary Poppins*
B *Pinocchio*
C *Peter Pan*
Line 1 = *Peter Pan*
Line 2 = *Pinocchio*
Line 3 = *Mary Poppins*

A folk tale

About the text

The Story of Mula and the Miserable Man is a traditional folk tale from the Middle East. It follows typical folk tale conventions: the setting and characters are simple and stereotypical, and there is a moral or lesson to be learned from the story. Folk tales generally follow a formulaic structure with repetitious patterns (things happening in threes or the use of wishes, etc.) and themes (dark woods, meeting people on travels, etc.). Folk tales originated as oral tales passed from one generation to the next. They served the purpose of passing on wisdom, creating a sense of group identity, and providing entertainment.

1 Refer students to the picture and title. Ask *What kind of story is a folk tale? What kinds of things do we usually find in folk tales?* (e.g. magic, meeting strangers, trickery, wise old men or women, etc.) Elicit that they often have a *moral* or lesson. Find out what folk tales students know about. Note that each culture will have their own folk tales, so this section provides a good opportunity for students to share folk tales from their culture. Pre-teach some of the key vocabulary through guided questioning: Ask *What kind of man do you think Mula is?* to elicit *wise*. *Why do you think he is wise?* (because we often meet wise old men in folk tales/because he will teach the other man a lesson). *How do you think the man feels?* (unhappy → miserable) *What is he carrying?* (a sack) *Is he rich?* (no, poor and dirty) *What's he wearing?* (traditional Middle Eastern clothes) *Where are they?* (on a road/near some woods) *What has the man got in his hand?* (a stick) Put students in pairs to say what they see in the picture and to identify Mula.

Answers
Mula is the old man with the stick.

2 Refer students to the three morals. Pre-teach *strangers* (people you don't know), *possessions* (things you own), *appreciate* (to be thankful for what you have). Ask them to predict what they think the moral will be. Tell students to read the story and decide which of the three sentences is the moral. Find out if anyone has heard this tale before or if they have a similar tale in their culture.

Answer
Appreciate what you have, however little!

3 🔊 9.1 Before learning about Past Perfect, this exercise revises questions in the Past Continuous for ongoing actions in the past, and the Past Simple for completed past actions. Look at the first question together. Draw students' attention to the answer to the question which gives the clue about what verb goes in the gap. Ask students why they think the question is in the Past Continuous (it was an ongoing action in the past). Look at number 3 together. Ask students what tense they think the question is in. (Past Simple) Allow students to work together to complete the rest of the exercise, then listen to check. Clear up any questions about the use of Past Simple and Past Continuous, and refer students to Grammar reference 3.1–3.3 on p144 if needed. Ask each pair to write one more question about the story. They ask another pair their question.

Answers and audioscript

🔊 **9.1 Questions about Mula**
1 Where **was** Mula **walking** when he saw the man?
  Along the road through the woods.
2 What **was** the man **carrying**?
  A dirty, old sack.
3 What **did** the man **do** when Mula took his sack?
  He sat down and cried.
4 Where **did** Mula **put** the man's sack?
  In the middle of the road.
5 How **did** the man **feel** when he got his sack back?
  Very happy.

4 🔊 9.2 Give students some time to read the sentences and put them in the correct places in the story. Ask them not to focus on the verbs in red yet. Play the recording so that students can check their answers. Do they agree that Mula is wise? How true do they think the moral is?

Answers and audioscript

🔊 **9.2 The story of Mula and the miserable man**
A wise old man called Mula was walking along the road through the woods, when he saw a man walking towards him.
The man was carrying a dirty, old sack. He looked very unhappy, and when Mula asked him why, the man told him his story.
He was all alone, **because his wife had left him**, and he was also poor and homeless **because he had lost his job and his house**.
'Everything I own is in this old sack', he said. 'My life is miserable.' And he walked off.
After the man had gone a few yards, Mula ran past him, took his sack, and ran into the woods. The man was afraid to follow – **he had heard it was easy to get lost in these woods**.
'Now my life is even more miserable!' he said. And he sat down and cried.
Meanwhile, further down the road, Mula came out of the woods and put the man's sack in the middle of the road. Finally, when **he had stopped crying**, the man set off again, walking slowly and sadly. Suddenly, he saw his sack. 'My sack!' he shouted. He picked it up – everything was still inside it! He was overjoyed, and walked happily on towards the city, singing as he went.
'Well', said Mula. 'That's one way to make someone happy.'
The moral of the story is … Appreciate what you have, however little.

ALTERNATIVE ACTIVITY Ask students to share a folk tale from their culture. If possible, ask them to bring in the story book, or they could download and print out an illustration from the tale to bring in. Put them in small groups. Each person tells their story to the group. Note that not all students will necessarily know any folk tales, so you might make it optional to share a story for those who are knowledgeable/interested.

Unit 9 • What a story! 121

GRAMMAR SPOT SB p91

1 Students should recognize the Past Simple and Past Continuous. Ask them what they notice about the Past Perfect – how is it formed? Look at the verbs in red in exercise 4.

Answers
The man *was carrying* a sack. = Past Continuous
He *told* Mula his story. = Past Simple
He *had lost* his job. = Past Perfect

2 Read the question with the students. They look back in the story to find the answer. Check comprehension: *Which happened first – he was alone, or his wife left him?* Draw a timeline on the board to illustrate the difference between the tenses:

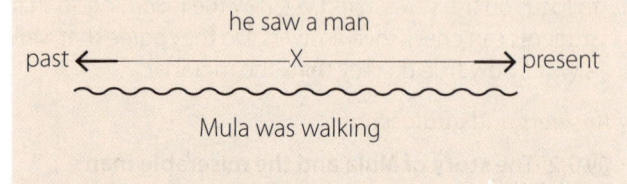

```
                he saw a man
past  ←————————X————————→ present
              ~~~~~~~~~
              Mula was walking

past  ←————X—————————X————→ present
        his wife        he met Mula
       had left him
```

In narratives, we can also use a series of Past Simple tenses to show actions that follow each other:
Mula ran past him, took his sack and ran into the woods.

```
         Mula ran  / took  / ran (into)
past  ←——————X———————X———————X———→ present
```

Answers
He was all alone because his wife had left him.

3 Students complete the rule. After checking, show students the contraction
 • after pronouns:
 He had lost his job → *He'd lost his job.*
 • the negative:
 He had not taken his things → *He hadn't taken his things.*
 • and the question:
 When had his wife left him? (no contraction)

Answer
past participle

5 🔊 **9.3** Put students in pairs to ask and answer the questions. Lower-level students can look at exercise 4 for support. Play the recording for them to check.

Answers and audioscript

🔊 **9.3 Questions about the story**
1 A Why was the man all alone?
  B Because his wife **had left** him.
2 A Why was he poor and homeless?
  B Because he**'d lost** his job, and his house.
3 A Why was he afraid to follow Mula into the woods?
  B Because he**'d heard** it was easy to get lost in them.
4 A Why was his sack in the middle of the road?
  B Because Mula **had put** it there.
5 A Why was he so happy?
  B Because he**'d found** his sack again, with everything still inside it.

SUGGESTION This unit provides the perfect opportunity to introduce students to reading for pleasure, or *extensive* reading. The key components of extensive reading are that students choose what to read and that they read at a level that is easy or comfortable for them. This means that they are not having to look up a lot of new words (maximum two new words per page). The key benefits are many, but include improved grammar and vocabulary, increased motivation, and enjoyment. To set up extensive reading in the classroom, provide students with a range of graded readers for them to choose from. Graded readers allow students to read at the right level, and there are many genres of graded reader, so students can find something that interests them. Set a time limit for finishing the books and ask students to write a short summary or book review which they share with others in the class or they could post the reviews on a class blog. You could set a three-book challenge – each student must read three books by the end of term.

Practice SB p91

Pronunciation

1 🔊 **9.4** This section helps students to hear the contraction *'d*. This contraction is more likely after a pronoun – *I/you/he/she/it/we/they* – than after a name or noun: e.g. *His wife had left him.* But: *She'd left him.*

Read the instructions with the students and play the first pair of sentences as an example of what to listen for. Play the recording again for another practice at hearing the contraction. Pause after each so that students can repeat. You could also ask students to practise the contraction in pairs. Refer students to the audioscript on p137. They take it in turns to read one of the pairs of sentences. The other student says if it's the first or second sentence. Don't worry too much if students have problems pronouncing the contraction. At this level, it's more important that they learn to hear it.

Answers
2 = 1   3 = 1   4 = 2   5 = 1   6 = 1

🔊 **9.4 Pronunciation**
1 He lost his job.
  He'd lost his job.
2 We'd missed the bus.
  We missed the bus.
3 They'd all left.
  They all left.
4 But you met him before!
  But you'd met him before!
5 I'd checked the doors.
  I checked the doors.
6 She'd asked everybody.
  She asked everybody.

2 🔊 **9.5** Give students a few minutes to match the lines and compare answers in pairs. Play the recording so that students can check. To check understanding, divide the class into six groups. Assign each group a sentence. They draw a timeline which illustrates their sentence. Collate one timeline for each sentence on the board.

Answers
1 d   2 e   3 f   4 c   5 a   6 b

122 Unit 9 • What a story!

9.5
1 I got a fabulous view of the Alps as we were flying over them.
2 I felt tired all day yesterday because I hadn't slept much the night before.
3 Just as I was falling asleep, the neighbour's dog started barking.
4 Tom's new girlfriend seemed familiar. I was sure I'd seen her somewhere before.
5 I was nervous before the flight because I'd never flown before.
6 My brother rang me while I was out shopping.

Discussing grammar
3 This exercise focuses on the meaning change caused by the verb tense. Go through the first set of sentences as a class. Ask students which happened first – arriving or cooking – in each. Ask two confident students to act out each sentence. You could also ask students to draw a timeline for each sentence. Monitor and ask three students with correct timelines to add them to the board. Put students in pairs to discuss the rest of the sentences. When checking as a class, use timelines to illustrate the differences if needed. As an extension, ask pairs to finish three of the sentence beginnings in exercise 3 with their own endings. Allow them to change the sentence beginnings if they wish. They share sentences with another pair who then draw a timeline to illustrate it. As an alternative, instead of reading each other's sentences, ask students to act them out for another pair who then try to guess the sentence.

Answers
1 When I arrived she cooked dinner. = I arrived first, then she cooked.
When I arrived she was cooking dinner. = She was in the process of cooking dinner when I arrived.
When I arrived she had cooked dinner. = When I arrived the cooking had already finished and dinner was ready.
2 He spoke good French because he was living in France. = He lived in France for a time and so he spoke French all the time and his French got better.
He spoke good French because he had lived in France. = He lived in France in the past (not now, probably) and so he spoke good French. / His French got better while he lived in France in the past.
3 I listened to music while I did my homework. = I did my homework at the same time as listening to music.
I listened to music when I'd done my homework. = I did my homework first, and then after that, I listened to music.
4 She gave me a book, and I read it. = She gave me the book first and then once I had the book from her, I read it.
She gave me a book, but I'd read it. = She gave me a book, but I had read it before she gave it to me.
5 When I got home, the children were going to bed. = I arrived home, the children were in their bedrooms, in their pyjamas.
When I got home, the children had gone to bed. = I arrived home, the children were in bed, and perhaps asleep.

SUGGESTION The form *'d* is the contraction of both *had* and *would*. If you think students would benefit from further discrimination and pronunciation practice of *'d*, you can read out the following sentences and get them to write *had* or *would* for each one. Check the answers (see brackets) and then dictate the sentences. Get students to practise the sentences in pairs.

1 I called at Jack's house, but he'd gone out. (had)
2 We'd like to go to the zoo today. (would)
3 When I got to the shop, it'd already closed. (had)
4 I'd love to visit your country one day. (would)
5 I was so tired last night! I'd had such a busy day! (had)
6 I think she'd like to go for a meal. (would)

The role-swap SB p92

Joining words

Possible problems
This is the first time that a number of conjunctions have been brought together in a grammar presentation. Students may have problems with choosing the correct conjunction in context and also with word order.
Time
The conjunctions of time covered in this section are: *when, while, as soon as, after, before, as,* and *until*. They can go at the start of the sentence or in the middle when used to join two clauses.
We use *when, as soon as, before,* and *after* to say that things happen one after another or in a sequence.
We use *when, while,* and *(just) as* to say that things happen at the same time. These are often used with a continuous form, especially for longer actions.
We use *until* to mean 'up to the time when'.
Result and reason
So introduces a result or consequence; *because* introduces a reason.
- *He was bored, so he went for a walk.* (cause result)
- *He went for a walk because he was bored.* (result cause)

Common student mistakes include:
Misplacing *so*: **So he was bored he went for a walk.*
Comma mistake: **He went for a walk, because he was bored.*
Sentence fragment: **Because he was bored. He went for a walk.*
Contrast
But and *although* both express contrast. *Although* is more formal than *but*, and is often used in more formal writing. *Although* joins two clauses. It can go at the start of the sentence, in which case a comma separates the clauses. (It can also go in the middle of the sentence, in which case it is preceded by a comma.) *But* joins two clauses. It must go before the second clause.

About the text
This story is a humorous story about a professor and his driver who swap roles. It is a type of anecdote /ˈænɪkdəʊt/ – a short, amusing story about a real person or event. Anecdotes are often personal accounts of events and are the kind of story people often tell in social situations in order to be amusing or make people laugh. Professor Higgs is an *astrophysicist* /ˌæstrəʊˈfɪzɪsɪst/ – someone who studies the physical and chemical structure of the stars and planets.

In this section, students focus first on the story, then on the conjunctions. This guided discovery approach helps students internalize the meaning before focusing on form. If your students have questions about the conjunctions in exercise 2, you could explain the meaning of some of the conjunctions (see Possible problems, above) before moving on to exercise 3. Reassure students that they will learn about the conjunctions in the *Grammar spot* that follows.

Unit 9 • What a story! 123

1 Refer students to the title and pictures in the story. Ask them to tell each other what they think the story is from the pictures. Look at the title of the section – *role-swap*. What do they think this means? How does it relate to the professor and his driver? Ask students what kind of professor they think Higgs is, then ask them to read the first two lines of the story to find out. Elicit what they think an astrophysicist does and see if anyone would like to try to pronounce it!

2 🔊 9.6 Ask students to read the story and choose the correct joining words. They compare answers in pairs. How close was the story to their own version from exercise 1? How do they think it will end? Play the recording so students can check their answers. Had they guessed the ending? Find out if they think Harry knew the answer to the question.

Answers and audioscript
🔊 **9.6 The professor and his driver**
Professor Higgs, one of the world's top astrophysicists, was giving a six-month lecture tour of universities around Europe. He only had one more lecture to give **before** the tour ended. Higgs didn't like flying, **so** he travelled by car. He had his own driver **because** he was too tired to drive **after** he'd finished his lectures.
One morning, **as** they were driving to the last lecture, his driver, Harry said, 'You know, Professor, I always sit in the hall **when** you give your lecture, and I know it so well by now, I think I could give it myself!' Of course, Harry was only joking, **but** Professor Higgs knew Harry was a clever man, and he wanted to test the idea.
As soon as they arrived at the university, the professor and Harry swapped clothes. The professor then sat quietly at the back of the hall **while** Harry gave the lecture.
Harry had a fantastic memory and gave the lecture perfectly! He waited **until** the audience had finished clapping and started to leave the stage. Suddenly, someone stood up and said they wanted to ask a question. Harry listened to the long, complicated question, and then he spoke: 'Mmm, that's a very good question. And **although** it seems a difficult one, the answer is actually very simple. In fact, it's so simple that I'm going to ask my driver to answer it for you.'

3 Refer students to the questions. Check that they understand that they need to answer the question starting with the conjunction. Point out that sentences do not normally start with conjunctions in writing – this is spoken English. For number 2, ensure students understand that *as* in this sentence means the same as *while*. Students work in pairs to ask and answer the questions. Check as a class.

Answers
1 Because he didn't like flying.
2 As they were driving to the last lecture.
3 As soon as they arrived at the university.
4 Until the audience had finished clapping.

GRAMMAR SPOT SB p92
1 Read number 1 as a class. Point out that *so* in the first sentence means 'as a result' – *Higgs didn't like flying. As a result he travelled by car*. In the second sentence, *because* gives a reason – *Why did he have his own driver? The reason was because he was too tired to drive*. *Although* in the third sentence is a contrast. Ask students to notice where the commas are. Point out that conjunctions connect two sentences. Ask students to identify the two sentences in each joined sentence. We know these are sentences because they have a subject and a verb in each. Show students how the sentences beginning with *although* and *because* can change position:
Because he was too tired to drive, he had his own driver. (comma needed when *because* comes at the beginning)
It seems a difficult question, although the answer is simple.

2 Read number 2 as a class. Point out that *when, as,* and *while* can be used to talk about things happening at the same time:
• Don't text *when/while/as* you are driving.
When, as soon as, before, and *after* are used in sequencing events:
• *When* I had drunk the milk, I went to bed.
• *As soon as/After* I drank the milk, I went to bed.
• I drank the milk *before* I went to bed.
Until is used to mean 'up to the time when':
• I watched TV *until* it was time for bed.
Ask students to read Grammar reference 9.2 on p150. For the two example sentences, check students understand the sequence of events (they arrived at the university and then they swapped clothes/the lecture and the sitting at the back happened at the same time). Show students how it's possible to rewrite the sentences:
• *They swapped clothes as soon as they arrived at the university.*
• *While Harry gave his lecture, he (the professor) sat at the back of the hall.*

4 Students complete the exercise, then compare answers in pairs. Check as a class.

Answers
1 so
2 Although
3 while

In your own words
5 Ask students to cover up the story and just use the prompts to tell the story. They can do this in pairs with one student telling one part, then the other telling the next. Once they've had a go at telling the story, give them another challenge to try to tell the story from memory with their books closed. They can do this again in pairs with each student telling a different part of the story, or they can try to tell the entire story by themselves. You could ask students to create a recording of the story using a storytelling app – there are apps available where students use avatars to create an animated video and then record their voice, or they could use the photos from

the book as the backdrop to their telling. These could be shared on the class blog or VLE. As an alternative, ask students to think of a short story that they know. Ask them to share their story in pairs or small groups.

Practice SB p93

Discussing grammar

This section gives students more practice with joining words and using Past Perfect.

1 Give students a few minutes to complete the exercise and compare answers in pairs. When checking answers as a class, get students to say why the sentence makes sense with one word and not the other.

> **Answers**
> 1 When   5 as
> 2 while   6 Before
> 3 until   7 After
> 4 as soon as   8 although

2 ◉ 9.7 In this exercise, students use the word in capitals on the right to join the two sentences on the left. In each pair of sentences, one should have the Past Perfect in it. Look at the example sentence together. Which action came first? (Note that we can also say, *I'd done my homework when I went to bed.*, *When I went to bed, I'd done my homework*, and *When I'd done my homework, I went to bed*). Monitor to support students who are struggling with this exercise. Help them to decide what kind of conjunction it is (time, result/reason, or contrast). Play the recording so students can check their answers. Play it again so that students can listen and repeat. In feedback, go over both possible answers. Note that in sentence 7 and 8, there is only one possible sentence construction. (*so* and *but* are coordinating conjunctions. They join two independent clauses and are always preceded by a comma. The other coordinating conjunctions are *for, and, nor, or, yet*.) Check students' use of commas.

> **Answers and audioscript**
> ◉ **9.7 Discussing grammar**
> 1 I went to bed when I'd done my homework.
> 2 After I'd driven two hundred miles, I stopped for coffee.
>   (I stopped for coffee after I had driven two hundred miles.)
> 3 She bought a car as soon as she'd passed her driving test.
>   (As soon as she had passed her driving test, she bought at car.)
> 4 I didn't go to live in Italy until I'd learnt Italian.
>   (Until I had learnt Italian, I didn't go to Italy.)
> 5 Although I'd enjoyed reading the book, I didn't like the film.
>   (Although I didn't like the film of it, I had enjoyed reading the book.)
> 6 His mother sent him to bed because he'd been naughty.
>   (Because he'd been naughty, his mother sent him to bed.)
> 7 I'd burned the chicken, so we went out to eat.
> 8 Jill invited me to stay for lunch, but I'd arranged to have lunch with Jo.

Talking about you

3 This exercise offers students the chance to practise using the joining words in a range of contexts and with a range of tenses. To support weaker students, first read the sentences and discuss what tenses could be used in the second part. Below is a list of possible tenses:

> **Answers**
> Can use the following tenses:
> 1 Past Perfect/Past Continuous/Past Simple
> 2 Present/Present Perfect
> 3 Present Simple
> 4 Past Simple (note the use of Past Simple in the first half – Past Perfect could also have been used.)
> 5 will/going to/Present Continuous
> 6 Past Simple/Past Continuous
> 7 Past Simple
> 8 Past Continuous

Give students a few minutes to write their sentences in class or set it for homework. They read their sentences to each other in pairs. Higher-level students can ask a question about each sentence. Encourage weaker students to ask at least four questions. Collect students' sentences for checking.

Additional material
For teachers
Photocopiable activity – Grammar: *Two news stories* pp215–7
For students
Online Practice – *Look again*
Workbook pp58–61, exercises 1–10
Online Practice – *Practice*

Listening and speaking SB p93

Young adult literature

About the text

The listening takes the form of an interview with Liz Davis who works for a book publisher. The books she mentions include *Peter Pan* by J.M. Barrie (mentioned in the Student's Book on p90), *The Storyteller* by Saki (told on pp94–5 of the Student's Book), *The Lord of the Rings* by J.R.R. Tolkien, *The Lion, the Witch and the Wardrobe* by C.S. Lewis (the second book is *The Chronicles of Narnia*), the *Harry Potter* series by J.K. Rowling, and *The Hunger Games* by Suzanne Collins. All of these books have been turned into films except for the short story, *The Storyteller*. Liz talks about the evolution of children's literature, and how it reflects what is going on in the wider world.

1 Refer students to the pictures of the book covers and the questions. Pre-teach/Check *literature* /ˈlɪtrətʃə(r)/. Find out if anyone has read any of the books. Ask students to say what they think the stories are about and if any of them look interesting to read. Some students may have seen the film versions of these stories. Read the questions in exercise 1 and elicit answers.

> **Answers**
> The difference is that young adult literature is aimed at teenagers.
> The children's books are *Oliver and the Seawigs* and *The Lion, the Witch and the Wardrobe*, and *Wolf*; the young adults' book is *Tightrope*.

2 ◉ 9.8 Pre-teach/Check *golden age* (a period during which something is very successful), *fantasy, Cold War, evil, drugs* (here, it means illegal drugs taken for recreational use). Give students a minute to read the questions, then

Unit 9 • What a story! 125

play the recording. Allow students to compare answers in pairs before checking as a class. Play the recording again if needed.

Answers
1 The 19th century and the 1950s.
2 *Alice in Wonderland*, *Peter Pan*, *The Storyteller*, *The Lord of the Rings*, *The Lion, the Witch and the Wardrobe*, The *Harry Potter* series, *The Hunger Games*

🔊 9.8 An interview with Liz Davis
I = Interviewer   L = Liz Davis

I Hello, and welcome to Bookworld. This week in the studio we have Liz Davis from YAP, Young Adult Publishers. Liz, many people get confused about the difference between children's literature and young adult literature. Are they sometimes the same thing?
L Yes, they can be. Some of our books are for children as young as 12 and they aren't very different from other children's books. But many of the novels we publish are for 15- to 18-year-olds, and the stories and subjects in those are not what you usually find in children's literature. They're, well, more adult.
I Now, children's literature is very big business at the moment – is that because of the recent popularity of young adult fiction?
L No, not really. We're in a golden age of children's literature for all ages right now. And it isn't the first golden age – there have been three. The first came in the 19th century, with the earliest fantasy books for children. *Alice in Wonderland* and *Peter Pan* were the first novels where ordinary children had adventures in a magical world.
I And until then, children's books had been quite serious and educational, hadn't they?
L Oh, yes! People thought children's stories should teach them morals. They were about children getting into dangerous situations in life because they'd behaved badly, and only the well-behaved children managed to escape! There's a lovely story called *The Storyteller,* by a writer called Saki, which makes fun of this idea.
I And when was the second golden age?
L In the 1950s. There'd been the Second World War, and the atomic bomb, and a lot of children's stories were now more serious, about saving the world from evil. Tolkien's *Lord of the Rings* is a good example, and C.S. Lewis's *The Lion, the Witch and the Wardrobe*. It's not just the children in the story that are in danger; it's everything.
I And isn't that true of a more recent example of young adult fiction, the *Harry Potter* series?
L Yes, although I'm not sure it's correct to call the *Harry Potter* books young adult fiction. They were the first children's books that people of all ages read – from the very young to the very old! It's only the later *Harry Potters*, when the children become teenagers, that are more like young adult literature, but they're still not typical examples because they're all about the problems of using magic. Modern young adult novels are usually about the ordinary everyday problems that teenagers experience.
I So the stories aren't set in fantasy worlds anymore?
L No, not so much. Some are, the *Hunger Games* books, for example. But most young adult literature is set in the very real world that teenagers live in.
I Too real for some parents!
L Yes, that's true. In the past, people often complained that young people's literature had never shown the reality of teenage life. Now, many parents aren't happy to find their children reading books that go into so much detail about relationships with the opposite sex, and about alcohol and drugs.
I And how do you feel about that?
L Well, these problems are part of life for teenagers today, and I think it helps if they see people learning to get through them. What I don't like is when young adult novels end miserably – I know most teenagers like to be miserable sometimes, but I think they're looking for a happy ending really!

3 Give students a couple of minutes to read the questions. Play the recording. In pairs, students compare answers. In whole-class feedback, elicit the answers.

Answers
1 For 15- to 18-year-olds. The stories and subjects in them aren't what you usually find in children's literature – they're more adult.
2 They were the earliest fantasy books for children. Before that, children's books were serious and educational.
3 There had been the Second World War and the atomic bomb.
4 They were the first children's books that people of all ages read.
5 The later *Harry Potter* books. They are not typical of modern young adult novels because they are not about the ordinary everyday problems that teenagers experience.
6 People complained that young people's literature had never shown the reality of teenage life.
7 Many parents worry about children reading about all the problems of relationships, and of alcohol and drugs.
No, Liz thinks it helps if teenagers see people learning to get through modern problems.
8 She doesn't like the fact so many young adult novels end miserably. She thinks teenagers like happy endings, really.

What do you think?

The focus in this activity is discussion and fluency. Students should give their opinions and also give reasons for them. Put students in small groups for the discussion. Assign a group leader to lead the discussion and ensure everyone gets a chance to speak. Monitor and support groups as needed. Ask for someone from each group to share their group's ideas with the class. Elicit names of stories students know from their culture which teach children to behave and books that had a big effect on them when they were young.

Additional material
For students
Online Practice – *Practice*

Reading and speaking   SB p94

The train journey

About the text

The story was written by Hector Hugh Munro, pen named Saki /ˈsɑːki/, a Scottish writer who was known for his satirical stories about social life in upper class Edwardian England. (King Edward VII was King of Britain 1901–1910. He became king after Queen Victoria died. The British Empire was still in place, and this era was characterized as a kind of golden age of the upper classes in Britain.) The version in the Student's Book is an adaptation of the original story. In *The Storyteller*, three children are travelling with their aunt on a train. The aunt has a hard time keeping her curious and chatty nieces and nephew entertained. She tells a story intended to teach children to always be good. The children find the story extremely uninteresting. A young man travelling in the carriage offers to tell them another story. His story at first seems like it will be another story about being good, but when he says the girl in the story was *horribly* good, the children become very interested. This negative connotation to the idea of being good made the man's story more realistic – after all, who can be perfectly good all the time? In the man's story, the little girl gets eaten up by a wolf who could hear her medals (which she got for being good) clinking together where she hid shivering in fear. The children on the train love the story, but the aunt feels it was inappropriate and undid years of moral guidance.

1 Read the question and see if students remember Liz's mention of Saki in the interview. (She said he liked to poke fun at children's stories aimed at teaching morals.) Ask them to read the fact file about him and answer the questions.

Answers
He wrote in the early 1900s.
His short stories often made fun of the self-important upper classes.

2 Refer students to the picture. Ask them the questions in a class discussion. Ask them where the people in the picture are to elicit *carriage* /ˈkærɪdʒ/. Ask them how the children are feeling (bored).

3 🔊 **9.9** Play the recording so that students can read and listen to the first part of the story. Put students in pairs to answer the questions. If students ask about vocabulary in the story, try to help them guess from context. Ask students if they have ever been in a situation such as the one in the story.

Answers
1 One hour.
2 Three children with their aunt, and a young man.
3 Because they are bored, hot, and tired.
4 That he had chosen the wrong carriage.
5 Lots of 'why' questions.
6 To keep them quiet.
7 Probably not.

🔊 **9.9** See SB p94.

4 🔊 **9.10** Play the second part of the story. Were they surprised by the aunt's lack of success with her story? Why didn't the children like the story? Students work in pairs to match the first and second parts of the sentences. Check in whole-class feedback. Ask volunteers to read the lines rather than simply saying the number/letter combination.

Answers
1 c   2 e   3 a   4 b   5 f   6 d

🔊 **9.10** See SB p95.

5 Put students in pairs. They look at the pictures of the story the man tells and predict what it will be about. Tell them to tell the story to each other beginning with *Once upon a time, there was a …* . They can organize it so that they take turns telling parts of the story (i.e. Student A begins with picture 1, Student B continues with picture 2, etc.). Once they have come up with their story, put them with another pair to compare stories. Ask the students if they think the children will like the man's story.

Listening

6 🔊 **9.11** Play the recording. How similar was it to the story the students came up with? Put students in pairs to answer the questions. Play the recording again if needed for students to answer the questions.

Answers
1 Because it started in the same way as the aunt's story.
2 She worked hard at school and she was never late, never dirty or untidy, never rude, and she never told lies.
3 Because it was unusual and they liked how it sounded.
4 Three: never late, always polite, best-behaved child in town.
5 Because of her clean white dress.
6 He could hear her medals clinking together.

🔊 9.11 The young man's story
'Once upon a time, a long time ago, there was a little girl called Bertha, who was very, very good.'
The children looked disappointed. They had hoped for a better story from him.
'She was always well-behaved, and worked hard at school because she wanted to please her parents and teachers. She was never late, never dirty or untidy, never rude, and she never told lies.'
'Was she pretty?' asked the small girl.
'Not as pretty as you', the young man said. 'But she was horribly good.'
The children were suddenly interested. Using the word 'horribly' with 'good' was unusual, and they liked how true it sounded.
'Bertha was so good that she'd won three medals for it – one said 'Never late', one said 'Always polite', and the third said 'Best-behaved child in town'. She wore them every day as she walked around town, so that everyone knew how good she was.'
'Horribly good,' Cyril reminded him.
'Yes. Well, the King had heard how good this girl was, and he invited Bertha to tea at the Royal Palace. Bertha wore her best dress, which was very white and clean, put on her medals, and walked through the woods towards the King's palace. But in the woods, there lived a big hungry wolf. He quickly saw Bertha's clean white dress through the trees. "Aha!" thought the wolf. "Lunch!" He moved quickly and quietly through the trees towards Bertha. Bertha saw the wolf and ran, but it was difficult to run fast because of the medals. She hid in some bushes, but she was shaking with fear, and the wolf could hear the medals clinking together. He caught her, and ate every bit of her – except for the medals, of course.'

7 🔊 **9.12** Tell students to read and listen to the last part of the story. Discuss the questions as a class. Ask students why they think the man's story was more interesting to the children than the aunt's. Find out if students know of other stories where the ending is not what's expected.

🔊 **9.12** See SB p95.

VIDEO In this unit students can watch a video about Roald Dahl, the successful children's author, and find out why his stories are so special. You can play the video clip on the Classroom Presentation Tool or download it from the Teacher's Resource Centre together with the video script, video worksheet, and accompanying teacher's notes. These notes give full guidance on how to use the worksheets and include a comprehensive answer key to the exercises and activities.

Additional material
For teachers
Photocopiable activity – Video worksheet: *Roald Dahl*
For students
Online Practice – *Look again*
Online Practice – *Practice*

Vocabulary and speaking SB p96

Feelings

In this section, students learn that words can sometimes have either a positive or a negative connotation. An example from Unit 8 were the words *slim* and *thin* – *slim* being positive and *thin* being negative when describing a person. Discussing positive and negative feelings is a good introduction to connotation.

1 Refer students to the words in the box. Drill the pronunciation of each, and ask students to categorize them under their stress pattern:

Oo	*angry*, *nervous*, *lonely*, *jealous* /ˈdʒeləs/, *homesick*
oOo	*delighted*
ooOo	*disappointed*
oO	*upset*, *amazed*
O	*stressed*, *proud*, *scared*

Allow students to use a dictionary to find the meaning of the words, then categorize them as positive or negative. Ask students to add the words to their vocabulary notebook and note down words with double letters (disa**pp**ointed, stre**ss**ed), silent letters (deli**gh**ted), and words with *ea* (j**ea**lous). Teach the relevant phonemes as needed.

Answers
positive = delighted, proud, amazed
negative = angry, nervous, stressed, disappointed, upset, homesick, jealous, scared, lonely

2 Students match the feelings to the pictures and discuss their choices in pairs. Ensure they understand that there is more than one possible answer sometimes. In class feedback, check students' pronunciation of the adjectives.

Answers
A homesick
B delighted, amazed
C nervous, stressed, scared
D stressed
E delighted, jealous, amazed
F delighted, proud, amazed
G angry, stressed, upset
H angry, upset, jealous
I angry, upset
J disappointed, upset

3 🔊 9.13 Students complete the sentences with their own ideas. They don't have to be true. Fast finishers can choose one to two more adjectives from the list in exercise 1 and write sentences with them. Pairs read their sentences to each other. Play the recording. Ask students *Why was I (scared/jealous/etc.)?* to elicit the answers from the recording. See how many they can recall.

Answers and audioscript

🔊 **9.13 How did you feel?**
1 I was scared because **the lights had gone out**.
2 I was jealous because **my sister got the biggest bedroom**.
3 I was nervous because **I hadn't sung in public before**.
4 I was upset because **my best friend had forgotten my birthday**.
5 I was disappointed because **the restaurant wasn't very good**.
6 I was proud because **my photo won first prize**.

4 🔊 9.14 Students match lines A and B. Check they understand the phrase: *You'll manage* (you'll succeed in finishing the work). Play the recording for students to check their answers. Put students in pairs. They first practise all the conversations, then they choose one or two to build into a bigger conversation, making changes as needed. Set a two-minute challenge: Tell students to carry on their conversations for one minute. Use a timer to keep track of the time.

Answers
1 d 2 e 3 a 4 b 5 c

🔊 **9.14 Talking about feelings**
1 A Sometimes I feel really homesick.
  B I'm sure you do. What do you miss the most?
2 A I've got too much work to do!
  B You'll manage. You're just stressed right now.
3 A I'm worried about my driving test.
  B It's normal! I was nervous when I took mine.
4 A We're going to have a baby!
  B Oh, that's fabulous! I'm delighted for you both!
5 A I get upset when people are so horrible.
  B Well, remember that people can be really nice, too!

SUGGESTION Elicit the adjectives in exercise 1 that can be used with *get*: *get angry/nervous/stressed/upset/homesick/jealous/scared/lonely/disappointed*. Students can practise the phrases by talking about themselves, e.g. *I get stressed when (I have a driving lesson). I get upset when (people are cruel to animals).*

Additional material
For teachers
Photocopiable activity – Vocabulary: *Feelings* pp218–9
For students
Online Practice – *Look again*
Workbook p62, exercises 1–3
Online Practice – *Practice*

Everyday English SB p97

Exclamations with *so* and *such*

Possible problems
The rules for using *so* and *such* are fairly straightforward, but students often confuse the words, especially in free speaking.
– *so* + adjective/adverb: *so cold*
– *such a/an* + adjective + singular noun: *such a nice man*
– *such* + adjective + plural or uncountable noun: *such lovely people*
– *so many* + plural noun: *so many friends*

128 Unit 9 • What a story!

– *so much* + uncountable noun: *so much fun*
Common mistakes:
*I have never known so cold weather. (Correction: *I have never known such cold weather.*)
*She's such nice person. (Correction: *She's such a nice person.*)
*It was a such good film. (Correction: *It was such a good film.*)
The rules are set out in Grammar reference 9.3 on p150 of the Student's Book.

1 🔊 **9.15** Refer students to the photo. Ask them how they think the people are feeling in the photo. Play the recording as students read the sentences. Play it again and ask students to repeat with the same stress and intonation as the speakers. Which word has the most stress?

Answers
such, so

🔊 **9.15** See SB p97.

2 🔊 **9.16** Play the recording so students can listen and repeat, copying the stress and intonation of the speakers. Ask *What do you notice about the punctuation at the end of each sentence?* (exclamation mark) *What is an exclamation?* (an expression of surprise, pain, or strong emotion).

🔊 **9.16** See SB p97.

3 This is a guided discovery exercise. Students look at the sentences to work out the rules. One way to support this is to ask them to identify the parts of speech that come after *so, such*, etc. Do the first together as a class.
I was so surprised! (= *so* + adjective). Ask students to look at Grammar reference 9.3 on p150 to check. Check as a class.

Answers
so + adjective *(surprised)* or adverb *(beautifully)*
such a + noun *(shock)*
such a/an + adjective + noun *(awful day)*
such + adjective + plural noun *(crazy ideas)*
such + adjective + uncountable noun *(terrible weather)*
so many + plural noun *(people)*
so much + uncountable noun *(work)*

4 Students may find this exercise easier if they first identify what kind of words come after the gap. Go through each quickly, then ask students to fill in the gaps with the words from the box.

Answers
1 such a
2 so
3 such
4 so many
5 so
6 such a
7 so much
8 such an

5 🔊 **9.17** Students match the sentences in exercise 4 with those in exercise 5. They compare answers in pairs. Play the recording so that students can check their answers to exercises 4 and 5. Play the recording again, if there is time, so that students can listen and repeat. Tell them to listen and mark the stressed words (*so/such*). Put them in pairs to do the activity. Make sure they stress *so* and *such* when they practise the conversations.

Answers and audioscript
🔊 **9.17**
1 This is such a good novel! You must read it!
 Do you want to borrow it now?
2 Don't watch that film on your own! It's so scary!
 I had my eyes closed for a lot of it!
3 Susie and John are such nice people!
 They're always so friendly and helpful.
4 There are so many pizzas to choose from!
 I can't decide which one to order!
5 Why are you driving so fast?!
 We're not in any hurry!
6 Oh! You've made such a mess in the kitchen!
 Come and clean it up now!
7 I've spent so much money this week!
 I should leave my credit card at home!
8 That was such an amazing experience!
 It's the first time I've been to an IMAX cinema!

6 Give students about ten minutes to write their conversation. They then practise it in pairs. Once each pair feels confident with their conversation, ask them to recite it to another pair or to the whole class.

SUGGESTION If you haven't had a vocabulary spelling revision in a while, try this: Ask students to make a 4x4 grid on their paper. Starting at the second row in the first column, they write *adjective, noun, verb*. Along the top row starting with the second column, they write a letter (students will all have different letters. Tell them to avoid X, Y, Z, and Q). Give them one minute to try to think of an adjective, noun, and verb starting with each letter they wrote in the top row. Who was able to complete their table? Students swap papers to check each other's spelling using their books or dictionaries if needed.

An example of the grid:

adjective			
noun			
verb			

Additional material
For teachers
Photocopiable activity – Communication: *Guess what I did!* pp220–1
For students
Online Practice – *Look again*
Workbook p63
Online Practice – *Practice*

Writing SB p98

Reviewing a book or film

Referring back in a text

The aim of this *Writing* section is to write a review of a book or film. The writing skill covered is understanding pronoun referencing, including subject, object, and relative pronouns. Students start by discussing films that are popular, then analyse the referencing in a model paragraph. Students discuss what they know about the story of Frankenstein and then read and analyse a model text, before making notes for their own book or film review. If you are doing extensive reading with your students, they can write their review on the graded reader they are reading. Ask them to give it a star rating and post the reviews around the room. Students read the reviews to help them decide on the next book to read for their three-book challenge.

About the text

The book chosen for the model text in this section is *Frankenstein* written by the British novelist Mary Shelley (1797–1851) and published in 1818. Mary, her husband, the Romantic poet, Percy Bysshe Shelley, and two other writers decided they would have a competition to see who could write the best horror story. After thinking about possible storylines, Mary had a dream about a scientist who created life and was horrified by what he had made. This became the basis of the plot for the novel. The novel has had a considerable influence across literature and popular culture. Some of the most iconic images of the monster are taken from the 1930s films starring English actor Boris Karloff.

1 Lead in to the topic by telling the students about a film you have seen recently, using the questions and sentence frames in your description. Put students in groups of three or four to discuss films they have seen.

2 Ask students to read the paragraph and answer the question. Do the first one together as an example. Ask them to draw a line to what each pronoun refers to. Tell students we use pronouns in this way to avoid repeating ourselves over and over.

Answers
It = the really good film
They = the friends the speaker went with
it = the film
which = the acting
That = the fact that the friends didn't like the acting
it = the acting
this = the film they saw last week

3 Refer students to the picture of the monster Frankenstein /ˈfræŋkənstaɪn/ created. Have they seen this film or a similar one? Discuss the questions as a class.

4 Ask students what they think a *review* is. What kinds of reviews have they read? Do they read books/see films based on reviews? What do they expect to find out from a review? Tell students to read the review of the novel *Frankenstein*, and check answers to exercise 3. Does the review contain the information they expected? Was there anything else they think should go into the review?

Answers
1 *Frankenstein* is both a book and a film.
2 It is a horror story, with elements of science fiction and romance.
3 (Victor) Frankenstein is a scientist.
4 Victor Frankenstein makes a human being from dead bodies, but it is huge and ugly and scares people. The monster wants Frankenstein to make it a wife. Frankenstein refuses, the monster kills various people, and is chased by Frankenstein. Both Frankenstein and the monster die in the end.
5 No, the ending is sad.

5 Students read the review again to find what each pronoun refers to. Discuss answers as a class.

Answers
It = the story of Frankenstein
They = people
it = the monster
He = Captain Robert Walton
these = bodies
it = the monster
This = making a wife for the monster
his = Victor Frankenstein's
itself = the monster
The first = the first Frankenstein film
which = the character of the monster

6 Ask students what kind of information they expect to find in a review. Try to elicit the terms in the headings. Ensure students understand *plot*. Refer students to the headings in exercise 6. Students look at the text to find the information and make notes under each heading. Check answers as a class.

Answers
Title and author: *Frankenstein*; Mary Shelley
Type of book/film: horror/science fiction
The period or date: 1818
Characters: Captain Robert Walton (an explorer), Victor Frankenstein (a scientist), the monster, Frankenstein's brother, Frankenstein's friend, and Frankenstein's wife (Elizabeth)
Plot: Frankenstein has discovered the secret of life and makes a human being from dead bodies, but it is huge and ugly and it scares people. The monster feels lonely and wants Frankenstein to make it a wife. Frankenstein refuses, the monster kills various people, and is chased by Frankenstein. Both Frankenstein and the monster die in the end.
People's reaction: frightened, sad

7 Before setting the writing task, brainstorm some types of books/films: *comedy, mystery, horror, documentary, biography, sci-fi, fantasy, romance,* etc. Ask students to use the headings and write their review. If students have been doing extensive reading, they could write their review on their graded reader. This could form part of their graded reader portfolio, and would help others choose a graded reader they would like to read next. Ask them to give the book or film a star rating (e.g. four or five stars for a positive review, one or two stars if they think it's boring/terrible). Ideally, they would write their reviews using a word processor. In this way they can print them out. Post them around the room and allow students to walk around reading the reviews. Ask students to choose one book or film they would like to read/see based on the reviews.

Additional material
For students
Online Practice – *Practice*
Workbook p63, *Review*, exercises 1–2
Online Practice – *Check your progress*

10 All-time greats

Introduction to the unit

The theme for this unit is all-time greats – number one games, inventions, football teams, and habits.

In the *Grammar* section, a reading about the best-selling video game ever is used to contextualize and teach passives, in present, past, present perfect, and future forms, and passives are further practised in the context of inventions that changed the world.

In the *Vocabulary and speaking* section, students focus on common *noun + noun*, *verb + noun*, and *adverb + adjective* collocations, e.g. *computer program*, *send a text*, *well-dressed*.

In the *Reading and speaking* section, students skim read a text about Manchester United to find information, then scan the text to find answers to questions. They form groups to ask questions about why others in their group like or dislike sport.

The *Listening and speaking* section features a radio programme about the history of the world's most common habit. Students survey the class as an introduction, then they listen for specific information. The skills practised are listening closely to correct false information and listening for answers to questions.

Everyday English practises useful telephone language, including how to say telephone numbers. Students roleplay a phone call to practise. There is scope here for discussion about phone etiquette and cultural norms related to phoning.

The *Writing* section focuses on planning and linking ideas in a pros and cons essay on the topic of social media. Students learn useful linking words to make their essay more cohesive.

Language aims

Grammar

Passives – all tenses

This section introduces passive forms in four main tenses: *Present Simple, Past Simple, Present Perfect,* and future with *will*, as well as the *Present Infinitive Passive*, passives with modals, and question forms. Passives are introduced in the context of where things are made or grown, then students get more exposure in an article about a popular video game, and in a practice activity about inventions that changed the world. In the practice exercises, students read active sentences and find the corresponding passives in the text, they then choose the correct active or passive verb to complete sentences. Further practice on form includes a gap-fill activity and an exercise in which students write questions in the passive. Finally, there is a freer speaking activity which reviews the language covered in the section.

Vocabulary

Words that go together

This section focuses on different forms of collocations: *noun + noun*, *verb + noun* and adjectives formed from *adverb + past participles*.

Students improve dictionary skills by using a bilingual dictionary to help them find common collocations. They practise using them in sentences.

Everyday English

On the phone

This section has two main aims: to ensure students can say phone numbers correctly and with good intonation, and to teach common phrases used in phone calls which students will use in a roleplay.

Additional material

Workbook

The theme of inventions and how they affect modern life is continued in a text which students complete using passive forms, in present, past, and future tenses. There is a task focusing on positive and negative passive forms, and another on questions using passives. Students then have to decide where to use active or passive forms. This is extended into working on past participles used as adjectives. Vocabulary concentrates on compound nouns and collocations using adverbs and adjectives. There is further practice of phone language and a final Grammar review.

Photocopiable activities

There are photocopiable activities to review grammar (*Passives quiz*), vocabulary (*Would you rather … ?*), and communication (*You're breaking up!*) at the back of the Teacher's Guide as well as on the Teacher's Resource Centre. There is also a worksheet to accompany the video on the Teacher's Resource Centre.

Notes on the unit

Unit opener page

Choose from these activities to engage your students with the topic and target language of this unit.

- Talk about the title
- Talk about the unit goals (*Grammar*, *Vocabulary*, …)
- Talk about the photo
- Watch the video
- Look at the bottom banner
- Do the activity

Refer students to the photo on p99. Ask students to think about great people from history. Elicit only the ones that are considered really great by a majority of the population (e.g. Pele – great footballer; Einstein – great scientist, etc.). Refer students to the unit title 'All-time greats'.

Ask students if they know where the person is (at the London 2012 Olympics – he has a British flag around his neck beside the Jamaican one). Do they know which sport he does? (athletics – 100 metres, 200 metres race) What do they think has just happened? (he was just won a race) Why do they think he has one gold shoe? (he has already won Olympic Gold medals in Beijing in 2008).

If you don't have time to watch the video introduction to the unit, go through the unit goals below the title: *Grammar, Vocabulary, Everyday English, Reading, Listening, Writing*. Give examples or use translation for unknown words.

Video (2 minutes approximately): The video gives a step-by-step overview of the unit. Play the video, pausing where necessary – especially for students to answer any questions, e.g. *What do you think is the the most common habit round the world?* This makes it a more interactive experience. Highlight the option of practising online.

As shown in the bottom banner, don't forget that there are many exercises to consolidate and practise the target language of the unit in the Workbook as well as online. There are links to these exercises on the relevant pages of the Student's Book and they can be done in class time or you can set them for homework.

Summary: If you're short of time, use the title and the photo to help students understand and engage with the topic, and then move straight on to the activity so that they can discuss the theme in more detail. If you have any more time, try to watch the video together. It is a clear and interesting introduction to the different parts of the unit.

Notes for activity:

Put students in pairs. Ask them to look at the photo and discuss their answers to the questions. Ask them to justify their choices where possible.

> **Suggested answers**
> 1 He is Usain Bolt, a Jamaican sprinter who has won eight Gold medals at three Olypmic Games, and eleven World Championship Gold medals, in the 100 metres, 200 metres, and 4 x 100 metres relay races.
> 2 They want to be associated with success, winners.
> 3 Students' own answers.

Grammar SB p100

Passives – all tenses

Possible problems

1 This will likely be the first time students will have studied the passive. The focus is mostly on form, and typical problems will include:
   – Omitting or misusing the verb *be*:
   Our car repaired last week. (Correction: *Our car was repaired last week*.)
   – Not using the past participle:
   Our car was repair last week.
   Our car was repairing last week.
   – Choosing the wrong form of *be*:
   Our car already be repaired.
   (Correction: *Our car has already been repaired.*)
   – Including the agent in the sentence as the subject:
   The mechanic has been repaired our car. (Correction: *Our car has been repaired.*)

2 Use of passive does not generally pose a problem for students, though you will need to point out that passive is used when the action is more important than the doer of the action (the agent).
   - *Our car was repaired last week.* (We are more interested in the repair of the car.)
   - *That new Dutch mechanic repaired our car last week.* (We are more interested in who repaired the car.)
   When we want to specify the agent in passive sentences, we use the *by* phrase:
   - *Our car was repaired last week by that new Dutch mechanic.*
   Only transitive verbs can be used in the passive:
   She arrived early. NOT: *She was arrived early.*

3 The text contains one other type of passive that is not explicitly taught – the Perfect Infinitive Passive: *Minecraft is the only other video game to have sold over 100 million units*. This is here to give information about another game, and shouldn't cause misunderstanding, though students may ask about it. Another way to say this same sentence: *Minecraft is the only other video game where over 100 million copies have been sold.*

STARTER SB p100

As a lead-in to the topic, bring in a box of tea, or some coffee. Show the students and ask them if they know where it comes from. Ask questions about how it is produced to elicit the word *grow* (*They grow tea in China./They grow coffee plants in Brazil.*) Say, *Ah! So tea is grown in China!*

Refer students to the *Starter* section – ask them if they know where these other things are made or grown. To add a competitive element to the activity, ask students to work in teams of three or four to make true sentences using the positive and negative verbs in the chart – no looking up answers on the Internet! Give them three or four minutes to make their sentences, then ask them to swap papers with another group for checking. The team with the most right answers, 'wins'.

Answers
Toshiba cars are made in Japan.
Champagne is made in France.
Coffee is grown in Brazil.

132 Unit 10 • All-time greats

Rolex watches are made in Switzerland.
Rice is grown in China.
Whisky is made in Scotland.
(Many negative sentences are possible, e.g. Toshiba cars aren't made in France. Champagne isn't made in China. Coffee isn't grown in Scotland. Rolex watches aren't made in Japan.)

About the text

The text is about a popular game called Tetris. In the game, players move or spin falling coloured blocks of different shapes (called tetrominoes) into place so that they fill a horizontal row. If the row is filled, it disappears. The pieces continue to fall, and players continue to position them to form the row. If the shapes reach the top of the screen, the game is over. There are different levels. At the lowest level, the shapes are simpler and easier to manipulate into place. As players go up in level, the pieces get more complicated and harder to slot in and fall faster. Tetris is a simple but addictive game which could increase spatial cognition. The article also briefly mentions Minecraft. This game, a type of 'sandbox' game, is a creative game for one or more players. There is no 'winning' the game; players essentially build things in it with 3D cubes of various materials (dirt, stone, water, lava, tree trunks, ore, diamonds, etc.). There are different biomes (grasslands, deserts, forests, etc.) and terrains (mountainous, rocky, sandy, etc.) and in-game night and day cycles, and non-player characters such as animals and villagers, spiders, and skeletons. There are also different modes – survival, creative, adventure, spectator, and multiplayer. Minecraft is increasingly being used in schools for a number of reasons such as teaching maths concepts, 3D building, or to support creativity and collaboration.

The best video game ever!

1 Discuss the questions as a class. If you have students who play video games, ask them to describe some of them. If students have played Tetris /ˈtetrɪs/, ask them how it is played and if they think it's the best ever video game. If you have a class with a mix of age groups, find out if they have played Tetris on different devices. Allow students to voice their opinion on video games, even if they don't like or play them! If no one has played Tetris, ask them to look at the photos and guess how it might be played. Tell students they are going to read to find out why Tetris is still popular after many years.

2 Give students a moment to read the questions, then ask them to read the first part of the article to find the answers. Check understanding of: *artificial intelligence (AI), colleague, exported.* Check answers in whole-class feedback.

Answer

It's over 35 years old.
Alexey Pajitnov – he worked at the Russian Academy of Science, in Moscow.
It spread to Budapest, and then on to Britain and the US.

3 🔊 **10.1** You may need to pre-teach/check: *puzzle, mastered, simplicity, doubt* /daʊt/. Tell students to read the sentences which all contain false information. Play the recording as they read the text. Give them a few minutes to correct the false information in pairs before checking as a class. Discuss the article further as a class: *Did you find any of the information new or surprising? Do you think the game will continue to be popular? Why/Why not?* Elicit reasons if possible.

Answers

1 Over 495 million games have been sold worldwide.
2 It was discovered by a Russian Artificial Intelligence Researcher, Alexey Pajitnov.
3 Tetris was the game enjoyed the most by his colleagues.
4 The game is made up of coloured squares.
5 It is simple enough to be played by children.
6 It can be played in any country.
7 The Nintendo Game Boy was the first hand-held computer.
8 There is little doubt that Tetris will be downloaded in the future.

🔊 **10.1** See SB p100.

GRAMMAR SPOT SB p101

1 Write these two sentences on the board:
- *Tetris is played all over the world.*
- *Everyone in the world plays Tetris.*

Ask *Does the first sentence tell us who plays it?* (no) *What about the second?* (yes) *What's the difference?* (the first is passive – we use passive when the doer of the action is not important. In sentence 1, the fact that Tetris is played everywhere is more important than who plays it. In sentence 2, the emphasis is on the fact that everyone plays it). Ask students to notice the underlined verbs. See if they can work out the rule for using passive. Draw their attention to where Tetris is in each sentence. In the passive sentence, Tetris is the subject, but not the *agent*, or *doer* of the action. Refer students to the *Grammar spot* box to read and answer the question. If needed, refer them to Grammar reference 10.1 on p151 to read the rules.

Answers

We form the passive with the appropriate form of the verb *be* and the past participle.

2 Ask students to find one or two passive examples for each tense in the text.

Possible answers

Present Simple: is played, is said, is mastered
Past Simple: was created, were enjoyed, was discovered, was launched
Present Perfect: have been sold
***will* future**: will be downloaded

Active to passive

4 This exercise focuses primarily on form. The sentences in the exercise are all in the active voice. Read the first sentence together as a class. Ask students to find the corresponding passive sentence in the text. Put students in pairs to complete the exercise. Ask them to write the passive sentences out in full. Draw students' attention to the difference in meaning between the passive and active: *Why is it better to say, for example, Tetris is played all over the world rather than They play Tetris all over the world?* (the emphasis is on the playing of Tetris – who plays it is not important in this case). When checking answers, draw students' attention to sentences 4, 5 and 8. These sentences contain the *by* phrase. Ask students why they

think it makes sense to include the *by* phrase here and not in the other sentences. (In these sentences, it's interesting or important to know who created it, who initially enjoyed it, and who will be downloading it. Compare: *It is still played all over the world by them.* Here, who plays is not as important as the popularity of Tetris. The *by* phrase allows us to know the agent – *Alexey Patjinov, his colleagues, our children and grandchildren* – even in the passive construction. Using a mixture of passive and active in writing can make it more interesting to read.) If students have problems with number 2, explain that *It* is used to replace the entire noun clause – *that it's difficult to find a video game player who has never heard of Tetris*. You could also teach this as a lexical phrase similar to others: *It is said/known/thought/felt that …*

Answers
1 Tetris/It is still played all over the world.
2 It is said that it's difficult to find a video game player who has never heard of Tetris.
3 Over 495 million have been sold worldwide.
4 It was created by Alexey Patjinov in Russia, in 1984.
5 Many of the games were enjoyed by Patjinov's colleagues.
6 It can be played on any computer.
7 Nintendo Game Boy was launched in Japan in 1989.
8 Many years from now, it will be downloaded by our children and grandchildren./It will be downloaded by our children and grandchildren many years from now.

Check it
5 This exercise mixes passive sentences with active ones to check that students understand when to use each. If students are struggling with this, ask them to think about who does the action. In sentence 1, for example, we don't know who made the shoes, but in sentence 4, we know that the newsagent is the one who sells stamps. In sentence 2, we do know who gave the watch, but the agent, *my aunt*, is in the *by* phrase, not the subject position (*My aunt gave me the watch.*), so this means that the most important thing is me being given the watch, hence the use of passive. Students work alone to complete the exercise, then compare answers in pairs. When checking as a class, ask students if the sentence is active or passive.

Answers
1 were
2 by
3 has been
4 sells
5 don't carry
6 drunk
7 been eaten

SUGGESTION Practise short answers with passives using the sentences from exercise 4, e.g.
  Teacher: *Is Tetris played all over the world?*
  Students: *Yes, it is*.

Practice SB p102
1 🔊 10.2 As a lead-in, before opening books, ask students to brainstorm inventions that they think have changed the world. See if they can say when the inventions were invented as a review of saying dates. (e.g. *nineteen oh one, fourteen forty*, etc.). Ask them to look at the photos on p102 to see if any of the inventions they mentioned in the brainstorm are pictured there. If they have problems identifying each invention, tell them they are listed in the exercise below. Read the instructions as a class. Students work together to decide which is the oldest/newest and to match them with the person and date. Monitor and encourage students to use the language presented in the sentence frames in their discussion. Before listening to check the answers, ask students what nationality they think the people listed are, and what their jobs were. Play the recording for students to check. After listening, ask students if they heard any surprising or new information. Were they right about the nationality and job of each person?

Answers
paper – T'sai Lun – 105 AD
printing press – Johannes Gutenberg – 1440
telephone – Alexander Graham Bell – 1876
radio – Guglielmo Marconi – 1901
television – John Logie Baird – 1924
ballpoint pen – László Bíró – 1938
Apple PC – Steve Jobs & Steve Wozniak – 1976

🔊 **10.2 Inventions that changed the world**
1 Paper was invented by a Chinese government official, called T'sai Lun, in 105 AD. The first paper was made from a mixture of plants and cloth. Since the 18th century, paper has been made of wood because it is much stronger than cloth.
2 The printing press was invented in 1440 by a German printer called Johannes Gutenberg. Today, everything is done by computer and more words are printed every second than were printed every year in the 15th and 16th centuries.
3 Alexander Graham Bell invented the telephone in 1876. Bell was born in Scotland, but he moved to America and became a scientist and teacher of the deaf. He worked with his assistant, Thomas Watson, and the first sentence he ever sent was 'Watson, come here; I want you.'
4 Guglielmo Marconi was an Italian physicist. He invented the radio in 1895. In 1909 he was awarded the Nobel Prize for Physics. The company he founded, The Marconi Company Ltd., was bought by the Swedish firm, Ericsson, in 2006.
5 Television was invented by a Scottish engineer, John Logie Baird, in 1924. The first BBC television broadcasts in 1929 were made with Baird's system. In 2006, Logie Baird was named one of the ten greatest Scottish scientists in history.
6 The first ballpoint pen was invented by the Hungarian journalist, László Bíró, in 1938. Many other ballpoint pens have been designed over the years, but in the UK they are still called Biros.
7 The Apple PC was invented by two American computer engineers, Steve Jobs and Steve Wozniak, in 1976. The name Apple was chosen because it was Jobs' favourite fruit. Apple computers have always been highly praised for being both user-friendly and beautifully designed.

Discussion
2 This activity provides a good opportunity to revise comparatives/superlatives and *because* for giving reasons. Ask students if they agree that all these inventions are important. Working alone, they rank them from most important (number 1) to least important. Discuss rankings as a class. Ask students to give reasons for their choices. To support the discussion, write sentence frames on the board: *I think … is more important than … because ….; … is the most important because …*. Take a class vote on the three most important inventions. See if students think there is another invention that is even more important than the ones listed.

Forming the passive

3 🔊 **10.3** This exercise focuses on the form of passives, but also shows students that passives are often used to report statistics. Pre-teach/Check *statistics*, and check that students know how to say percentages (e.g. *sixty per cent*). Ask them how many zeros are in a *billion* (nine) and *trillion* (12). Note that *Airbnb* is pronounced *Air b and b*. Read the instructions together and do the first statistic as an example to ensure students know they should first put the verb into the passive, and then choose the statistics. Play the recording for students to check. Write the passive verbs on the board for students to check spelling.

> **Answers and audioscript**
> 🔊 **10.3 Statistics worldwide**
> 1 **60%** of video games **are bought** by men and **40%** by women.
> 2 Nearly **75 trillion** emails **are sent** every year.
> 3 Over **40,000** questions **are answered** by Google every second.
> 4 eBay **was invented** in **1995**.
> 5 Facebook **has been translated** into **76** languages since it began.
> 6 The first Twitter message **was sent** in **2006**.
> 7 Airbnb **was founded** in San Francisco in **2008**.
> 8 Amazon.com **was founded** in **1994**.

EXTRA IDEA Students could conduct a class survey, then use the statistics to make a class report such as the one in exercise 3.

Draw the table below onto the board and ask students to copy it. Put students in small groups. Members of the group should each choose three different students from the rest of the class to ask the questions and write their names at the top of the columns. Make sure students from the same group have all chosen different people to 'interview'. They then ask those students the questions and make notes of the answers.

When they have asked the questions, they go back to their groups and compare their answers. Then they add up the numbers and report the statistics they calculated to the rest of the class.

Video games were bought by … % of students we asked.
Twitter is used by … % and Instagram is used by … % of students. … % of students shop online.

	1	2	3
How many video games do you buy every year?			
Which social network sites do you use? (Twitter, Facebook, Instagram, etc.)			
Which online shopping places do you use?			
What brand of laptop/tablet do you prefer?			

4 🔊 **10.4** Students work in pairs to make the questions. Read the example question together. This exercise is a little more challenging, so monitor to give support. Play the recording so that students can check their answers, then allow them to ask and answer the questions in pairs. To increase the challenge, see if students can remember the statistics without looking!

> **Answers and audioscript**
> 🔊 **10.4 Questions and answers**
> 1 A **How many video games are bought by men and women?**
>   B 60% are bought by men, 40% by women. And did you know the average age of a video game player is 38?
> 2 A **How many emails are sent every year?**
>   B Nearly 75 trillion. The average office worker receives 121 emails a day.
> 3 A **How many questions are answered by Google every second?**
>   B Over 40,000 a second! About 15% of these have not been asked before.
> 4 A **When was eBay invented?**
>   B In 1995. Pierre Omidyar was 28 when he invented it – he was a billionaire by the time he was 31.
> 5 A **How many languages has Facebook been translated into?**
>   B 76. There are now over 2 billion Facebook users – of these 83 million are fake profiles.
> 6 A **When was the first Twitter message sent?**
>   B In 2006, by Jack Dawsey. Now 500 million tweets are sent every day by 328 million users.
> 7 A **Where and when was Airbnb invented?**
>   B In San Francisco in 2008. It is now used by 150 million people in 191 countries.
> 8 A **When was Amazon.com founded?**
>   B In 1994. Jeff Besoz started it from his garage. It is now the world's greatest online shopping company with over 300 million customers.

Project

5 This exercise provides a good opportunity for students to do a research project. Some of the facts in exercise 3 may have changed, so as a small project, students can research to find out the new statistics. They share their findings in a class discussion. To turn this into a larger project, put students in pairs or small groups to find some information and statistics about one or more important inventions. They could use their ideas from the brainstorming session in exercise 1. Ask them to find out:

- why it's so important
- when it was invented
- who it was invented by
- the nationality of the inventor
- other interesting statistics

Ask them to create a poster or infographic with the information, using complete sentences and adding illustrations or graphs. Post these around the room and invite the class to walk around and read the posters, making a note of new or surprising information. As an alternative, ask them to make a short video documentary to present their information. Set aside class time to view the documentaries, or put them onto a class website.

Unit 10 • All-time greats   135

Additional material
For teachers
Photocopiable activity – Grammar: *Passives quiz* pp222–3
For students
Online Practice – *Look again*
Workbook pp64–7, exercises 1–12
Online Practice – *Practice*

Vocabulary and speaking SB p103

Words that go together

Noun + noun

This section focuses on common collocations, or words that go together. Mistakes in collocations make students' English sound awkward, and it's particularly common at this level to make mistakes with *make* and *do*:

*I made my homework.

*I do a lot of mistakes.

It's a good idea to show students how to use dictionaries to find collocations. If you can, bring in a set of *Learner's Dictionaries*, or *Collocations Dictionaries*. These are specially designed to highlight collocations and support collocation learning. Online learner's dictionaries are another option if you don't have access to paper dictionaries. In either case, it's worth spending some time teaching students how to find collocations on their own.

1 **10.5** Write *video game* on the board and ask students what part of speech each word is. Ask them if they know what it's called when two nouns are together to form a new word (compound noun). Refer them to the box on p103 to find out. Point out that some compound nouns stay as two words, but others go together to form one word. When in doubt, they should check the dictionary. Ask students to say the words and think about which word is stressed. Play the recording. Students listen and repeat. Point out that in all compound nouns, the first noun is stressed.

Answers
The first word is stressed.

10.5 See SB p103.

2 **10.6** See how many compound nouns students can make from the lists. Allow students to use paper or online dictionaries to find combinations. Note that *football game* is more common in American English (in British English, it's generally a *football match*). Play the recording for students to listen and check. Play it again so they can listen and repeat. See if students found any other combinations.

Possible answers
business: card, deal, call, game
football: game, ground, team, card
phone: card, number, call
computer: game, virus, program

10.6 Noun + noun
business call
business card
business deal
football team
football ground
football game
phone number
phone call
computer program
computer game
computer virus

Verb + noun

3 Explain that some verbs and nouns go together, and others don't. The reason for this is based on convention rather than grammar. If you are in a monolingual class and speak the students' language, give some examples of *verb + noun* collocations in the language. If not, give common English examples, e.g. we say *play football,* not *do football,* and *do exercise,* not *play exercise.* Refer students to the boxes and check that they understand the instructions. Put them in pairs to complete the exercise. When checking answers as a class, check that students understand: *send your love* (used in letters for example: *Send her my love.*), *take a pill* (medicine), *win a trophy* (an award such as the FA cup).

Answers
2 take: a big breakfast x
3 make: an invention x
4 do: a photo x
5 play: yoga x
6 win: a team x

4 Students work alone to write one sentence with each verb + one of the nouns from the group. In a small class, students can read their sentences to the class; in a larger group, ask them to share sentences with two or three other students. As an alternative or extension activity, ask each student to write a sentence as instructed, but leave a gap where the verb would go (e.g. *I've just _____ you a text message.*). They then swap papers with another student who fills in the gap with the right verb. As an added challenge, see if students can write at least one of their sentences in the passive.

Adverb + past participle

5 **10.7** Refer students to the third set of words that go together to learn about how to use the adverbs *well* and *badly* with past participles to form adjectives. Ask students what they think *well-known, well-paid,* and *badly-behaved* mean. What spelling convention do they notice with all three words? (They are hyphenated when they come before a noun. Note that after the verb *be,* they are not hyphenated, e.g: *Justin Bieber is well known.*) Elicit a sentence to illustrate each, e.g. *Justin Bieber is a well-known pop star. Teaching isn't a well-paid job. Students in this class are never badly behaved.* Ask students to use the past participles in the box plus either *well-* or *badly-* to complete the sentences. Play the recording. Ask students which word in the collocation has the most stress. Point out that although both words do carry some stress, it's the second that carries the most (primary) stress. Play the

recording again so that students can listen and repeat the sentences. Refer students to the picture on page 103. What does it show? (*badly-behaved dogs*)

Answers
1 well paid
2 badly written
3 well-dressed
4 well equipped
5 badly behaved
6 well done
7 well-known

The stress is on the second word.

🔊 10.7 Adverb + past participle
1 She has a wonderful job. She's very well paid.
2 I didn't enjoy that novel. It was really badly written.
3 You don't need to spend a lot of money on clothes to look well dressed.
4 Our office is really well equipped. We have all the latest machines.
5 I hope they don't bring their dogs. They're so badly behaved.
6 Can I have my steak very well done, please? I don't like it rare.
7 Surely you've heard of Ed Sheeran. He's a really well-known singer.

Talking about you
6 🔊 10.8 This section brings together language and topics from the previous sections. Set this up as an interview. Student A interviews Student B and takes notes on the answers. Students then swap roles so that each student has the opportunity to ask and answer questions. Put pairs together to share information: each interviewer tells the others about his/her partner. Play the recording. Do any of the answers in the recording match answers provided by the students in their interviews?

🔊 10.8 Talking about you
1 A Do you ever play computer games?
   B No, but my nephew does, all the time.
2 A Do you send a lot of text messages?
   B Of course I do. Doesn't everybody? I text all the time.
3 A Do you take a lot of photos?
   B I do. I have hundreds on my phone, too many really. I put them on Facebook sometimes.
4 A Who does the most housework in your home?
   B Not me or my dad! My mum always says: 'Oh I'll do it, you're too slow.'
5 A How do you like your steak?
   B Medium rare. I don't like it well done.
6 A Is your school well equipped?
   B It's OK – we have a lot of technical equipment – trouble is, it sometimes breaks down – the teacher can't fix it – but there's a tech genius in our class who usually can.
7 A What do you think is the most important discovery ever made?
   B Mmmm! A difficult one. There are so many. The discovery of DNA is pretty important I think.

SUGGESTION Revise words that go together (collocations) with a game. Create a set of cards for each group of three or four students – one word per card. Make sure that each card has a matching word/collocation that goes with it. It's OK to have more than one possible match, as long as there is a match for every word (e.g. *badly + behaved*; *badly + paid*; *badly + written*). Students deal out seven cards each, and put the rest in a pile face down. One student puts down a card for the others to see. If another student has a card that collocates, then they put it down, say the words, and keep the set. They then take a card from the upside down pile.

The aim of the game is to get the most sets of words. You can easily make multiple sets of cards by creating a table with a word processor. Print the page out and laminate it if possible, then cut out the cards. You could bring in word combinations from previous units to revise these as well, e.g. *for + half an hour*; *since + 2003*; phrasal verbs from Unit 5 p56, amount + item combinations from Unit 4 p46, and collocations from Unit 2 p23.

Additional material
For teachers
Photocopiable activity – Vocabulary: *Would you rather … ?* pp224–5
For students
Online Practice – *Look again*
Workbook p68, exercises 1–3
Online Practice – *Practice*

Reading and speaking SB p104

The world's most loved football team!

About the text

The text is about Manchester United – the older of Manchester's two rival football teams (the other is Manchester City). Since 1910, Manchester United football club has been based in Old Trafford, a borough two miles south-west of the city centre that was, in ancient times, a crossing point over the River Irwell. Old Trafford Stadium was dubbed *The Theatre of Dreams* by one of England's great football players, Sir Bobby Charlton. Manchester United is a premier league club that has been very successful and has had a number of successful and high-profile players, including Northern Irishman George Best, known as one of the greatest footballers of all time. The club colours are white, red, and black, and the official anthem of the team is *Glory, Glory, Man United*. Some important competitions to know in association with football include:

UEFA Champions League – tournament organized by the Union of European Football Associations and open to all European teams.

English Premier League – the top level of English football leagues.

Emirates FA cup – the oldest football tournament; open to top English League clubs (includes around 740 clubs).

1 If it is football season, lead in to the topic by talking with students about the latest match. You could also ask students, *What sport is known as 'the beautiful game'?* Put students in pairs to discuss the questions, then open up the discussion to the whole class. Find out who is a football fan and which is their favourite or least favourite team.

2 Refer students to the title and introduction. Ask for a show of hands: *Who agrees that most people round the world have heard of Manchester United?* Find out what students know about the club in a quick brainstorm.

3 Tell students to read the first part of the article to find the information to complete the gapped sentences. Check answers as a class. Note that careful reading is needed to answer the first question – the information needed is found in the second paragraph. (54,000 is the number surveyed, but 659 million is the number of fans worldwide.) Ask students to look at the photo of Old Trafford Stadium. Find out if they know about the stadium and if anyone has been to a match there. Find out if anyone has heard the team anthem, *Glory, glory Man United*. If possible, find a version on the Internet to play to the students. Check that students understand *glory*.

Answers
1 **659 million**
2 **Man U** and **The Red Devils**.
3 **English people**

4 Pre-teach/Check: *railway, trophies, brand, logo, ups and downs*. Read the questions together as a class, then give students a few minutes to read *Man. U – a brief history* and answer the questions. They compare answers in pairs before checking as a class.

Answers
1 The first players for the club all worked for a local railway company.
2 It was named Manchester United.
3 The football ground – Old Trafford.
4 He brought a lot of young players into the team.
5 Because eight players were killed in a plane crash in Munich in 1958.
6 Alex Ferguson – the club won 25 major trophies during his time at the club.
7 Because the team sells about two million shirts a year.
8 They put their logos on the shirts.

5 Before reading the last part of the text, ask students why they think the club is so popular. Give them a few minutes to read the text and find four possible reasons for its popularity. As a final task, ask students to find and highlight or underline all the passives in the text.

Answers
Reasons for the club's popularity:
1 They've won a great many trophies.
2 A number of talented players have played/play for the team.
3 They have lots of famous fans.
4 Old Trafford is a 'theatre of dreams' where players and fans can find fairy-tale glory and make their dreams come true.

Talking about you

6 Ask students to look at the chart and say whether they are A – I like sport or B – I don't like sport. Ask for a show of hands for A, then for B. Put students in groups with a mix of As and Bs in each. For the discussion, tell students who don't like sports to ask the questions in column A. The students who do like sports ask the questions in column B.

SUGGESTION If your students are interested in sport, ask them to prepare a short presentation on their favourite team. Ask them to think about: team colours, league, nickname, games won, players, and especially, why they like the team or any personal stories, e.g. a memorable time they saw them play. Students could prepare a poster which includes statistics, photos with captions, and wear their team scarf or T-shirt when they give the presentation. In large classes, students present to a group.

VIDEO In this unit students can watch a video about how football can change people's lives. You can play the video clip on the Classroom Presentation Tool or download it from the Teacher's Resource Centre together with the video script, video worksheet, and accompanying teacher's notes. These notes give full guidance on how to use the worksheets and include a comprehensive answer key to the exercises and activities.

Additional material
For teachers
Photocopiable activity – Video worksheet: *The Homeless World Cup*
For students
Online Practice – *Look again*
Online Practice – *Practice*

Listening and speaking SB p106

The world's number one habit!

1 Ask students if they have any good or bad habits as a lead-in to the topic. Refer them to the photos and discuss them as a class. Do they recognize any of the brands of gum? Ask students if they know that chewing gum is the most common habit in the world. Write the questions from exercise 1 on the board. Ask students to stand up and ask at least three people the questions. They should talk to people they don't usually work with. If they find someone who never chews gum, tell them to find out why.

2 Ask students to tell the class what they found out from their interviews. Collate the answers to the questions on the board as statistics (e.g. 80% of the class chews gum). Point out the stress pattern difference in the compound noun *chewing gum* /ˈtʃuːɪŋˌɡʌm/ and the verb form *(be) chewing gum* /ˈtʃuːɪŋ ˈɡʌm/. Note that *bubble gum* is a particular type of chewing gum specially formulated for bubble blowing. Chewing gum is also called *gum*.

3 Read the questions together and pre-teach/check *rubber, skeleton, tree sap, freshened*. Ask students to predict whether the statements are true or false.

Answers
1 ✓
2 ✗ It isn't made of rubber.
3 ✗ The habit of chewing gum goes back nine thousand years.
4 ✓
5 ✗ It was made of tree sap and honey.
6 ✓ They also thought it was good for their health.
7 ✗ They wrapped it in leaves.

4 ◆ 10.9 Play the recording. Students compare answers in pairs. Play the recording again if needed for students to correct false statements and answer the question. Check as a class. See if students remember other information from the listening, and if any of the facts surprised them.

10.9 Part 1 – The world's number one habit – chewing gum!

P = Presenter   I = interviewer   LW = Lilian Wood
A = girl interviewee   B = boy interviewee

P This week on *Worldly Wise* we look at the world's most common habit … chewing gum! Yes, chewing gum! – every year 374 trillion sticks of chewing gum are made, and we chew 100,000 tons of it. So why do we do it and how many of us know what it's made of?
I Excuse me, I see you are chewing gum.
A Yeah.
I And … er … do you have any idea what it's made of?
A Made of? Nah – I've never thought about it.
I What about you? Do you know?
B Er … no idea – rubber maybe.
I And … er … do you know who invented it?
A Erm … the Americans?
B Yeah – the Americans – I bet it was invented in the US.
I And finally, tell me – why do you chew it?
A & B Why?!
A Er … I dunno – it's cool … it's cool to chew gum.
B It's something to do.
P Cool or not – chewing gum isn't made of rubber and it wasn't invented by the Americans. It was invented by the Swedes. The Swedes!? I hear you say. But listen to Lilian Wood, a chewing gum expert. Lilian, welcome!
LW Thank you. Well, the history of chewing gum goes back thousands of years. In Sweden in 1993 a skeleton of a teenage boy was found – this boy was 9,000 years old and in his mouth was some gum. It was made of tree sap and honey – and this is the first known chewing gum.
P That's amazing. Perhaps we've always needed to chew things. After all babies are born wanting to chew – they put everything into their mouths. So, Lilian, why do we chew gum?
LW We chew to clean our teeth and freshen our breath, but also just because we like chewing – it keeps us calm.
P Yeah – 'Keep calm and chew gum!'
LW Yes – the ancient Greeks chewed a gum called mastica – it's a type of tree sap. The Greeks thought it was good for the health and it made the breath sweet-smelling. We also know that in the first century AD the Mayan Indians in South America enjoyed chewing gum – they chewed a tree sap called chiclay. They wrapped it in leaves and put it in their mouths …
P The first packet of chewing gum!
LW Yes indeed – the first packet of gum.

5 🔊 **10.10** Read the questions as a class. Tell students that *chum* is an old word that means *friend* or *pal* in this context. If you think your students might struggle to write all the information, put them in pairs and assign Student A the odd-numbered questions and Student B the even-numbered ones. Play Part Two of the radio programme. Students compare answers in pairs before checking as a class.

Answers
1 Thomas Adams was an American inventor who introduced chewing gum to the US (from Mexico) and William Wrigley was a business genius who decided chewing gum was the thing of the future.
2 He was the first to use advertising to sell his products.
3 He hired hundreds of pretty girls and they walked up and down the streets of New York and Chicago, handing out free chewing gum.
4 During the Second World War.
5 The US army.
6 Children said it to American soldiers.
7 The recipe is a secret.
8 More than £10 million a year.

10.10 Part 2 – The history of modern chewing gum
P = Presenter   LW = Lilian Wood

P So, what's the history of modern chewing gum? Well, in 1871 Thomas Adams, an American inventor, introduced chewing gum from Mexico to the US … and it became popular very quickly with American kids.
LW Yes, but it was in 1892 when a very clever young man called William Wrigley decided chewing gum was the thing of the future. He was a business genius – he was the first to use advertising to help sell his products.
P Really? What did he do?
LW He hired hundreds of pretty young girls – he called them, 'The Wrigley girls', and they walked up and down the streets of New York and Chicago handing out free chewing gum. Millions of pieces were given away.
P Very clever, very modern!
LW Yes, he also had huge electric billboards made – one billboard was a mile long and ran along the side of a train track. So, of course, Wrigley's gum soon became very popular all over the US.
P But how did the rest of the world get to love chewing gum?
LW Well, during the Second World War, American soldiers were given Wrigley's gum to help them stay calm. In fact, in 1944 all chewing gum production went to the US Army and they took it overseas and gave it to children. Soon they were followed everywhere with the cry, 'Got any gum, chum?' So, of course, it spread worldwide.
P Yes, I believe it's even taken into space by the astronauts. So, Lilian, what is it made of?
LW Well, the strangest thing about gum today is that nobody knows exactly what it's made of – the recipe is secret!
P Hah! Thank you Lilian. That's all fascinating … but there's a problem with gum. It's a favourite habit, but when the flavour has gone and we finish chewing, what do we do? We throw it away – chewing gum litter covers the streets of all our towns. Did you know that the cost of cleaning it from the streets of London is more than £10 million a year?! Now that's a fact worth chewing on!

What do you think?

Put students in small groups to discuss the questions. As an extension, tell them to interview friends and family to find out who chews gum. They could also do some Internet research to find out about other worldwide habits and facts. For example, chewing gum is largely illegal in Singapore and chewing gum scraped off the streets in Amsterdam is being used to make shoes! They share their findings with the class.

Additional material
For students
Online Practice – *Practice*

Everyday English   SB p107

On the phone

Possible problems

1 Telephoning is a more difficult means of communication because callers can't rely on visual cues. Although students will know numbers 0–9, they may not know the convention of saying phone numbers as individual numbers (*one four nine*, NOT *one hundred and forty-nine*), including the grouping of parts of the phone number and the use of *oh* (/əʊ/) instead of *zero* in British English.
2 While national conventions for writing phone numbers vary, they are nonetheless divided into parts. Mobile phones often start with a similar prefix (e.g. 077), and

Unit 10 • All-time greats   139

free phone numbers are identifiable by the 0800 prefix. Parts of a phone number are grouped together with a falling intonation and pause after each: 0800/142/2466.

oh eight hun<u>dred</u>, one four <u>two</u>, two four double <u>six</u>

3 We also tend to use *double* or *treble* when a number is repeated. In the UK, 0800 indicates a free phone number while 0900 indicates a number charged at a high rate. They are said *oh* /əʊ/ *eight/nine hundred*.
4 The expressions in this section are idiomatic, so some of them may need an explanation, though the contexts should give students clues to meaning.

1 **10.11** Lead in to the topic with a show of hands: *Hands up if you have a mobile phone. Hands up if you have a landline phone. Hands up if you have ever used a public telephone.* Refer students to the telephone numbers in exercise 1. Ask them why there are spaces between some of the numbers. (They are grouped to make it easier to read and say them.) Play the recording. Students listen and repeat. Play it again if needed. Refer students to the list of numbers and elicit how they were expressed. Repeat these in a choral drill. Put students in pairs to practise saying the numbers. Monitor to check intonation and convention.

Answers
0	= /əʊ/
00	= double /əʊ/
99	= double nine
0800	= /əʊ/ eight hundred

10.11 See SB p107.

2 Elicit the numbers from students as a class. Note that the exercise is not asking for their entire phone number, but for the part of the number that identifies a landline, mobile, or country. To illustrate this, you could give the example of a number from the UK:

country = +44
city code = (0)161
phone number = 4960413

+44 (0)161 4960413 (Landline numbers in the UK start with 01, 02, or 03. Note that the 0 is only used when the country code is not.)

Note that in the EU, the international emergency numbers are 911 or 112, and in the UK it's 999. Emergency numbers can generally be dialled without a SIM card or even on a locked phone.

Find out how many phone numbers students know by heart. Whose are they? Ask students to recite the ones they remember. If students are interested and if there is class time, continue the discussion about phones and phone numbers. Find out who has had experience telephoning abroad or who has travelled abroad – what problems or issues came up? Has anyone had to dial an international operator? Does anyone remember making phone calls in the days before mobile phones? Students might be interested to know that at the start of the 1970s, only 35% of the population of Britain had landlines in their homes – most people had to use public pay phones.

3 **10.12** Refer students to the chart to read the information they will be listening for. Play the recording, pausing after each conversation so that students can fill in the chart. Allow students to compare notes, then play the recording again. Elicit the answers from a range of students. Encourage them to give you complete sentence answers. Check students understand the contexts of each conversation.

Answers
Conversation 1
1 Pat is speaking to John.
2 Pat is on a mobile. We don't know about John.
3 Pat is at the train station. We don't know about John.
4 Pat wants to rearrange a meeting.
5 They know each other well.

Conversation 2
1 Emma is speaking to John.
2 We don't know.
3 We don't know.
4 John wants to speak to Patrick. He asks Emma to take a message.
5 They know each other well. John and Emma's husband are friends.

Conversation 3
1 Harriet is speaking to the receptionist, Chantal, and then to Patrick's secretary, Teresa.
2 They're on a landline.
3 The receptionist and secretary are in the office. Emma is at Digby and Moss Associates.
4 Harriet wants to speak to Patrick. He isn't available at first and then his secretary puts her through.
5 They know each other.

Conversation 4
1 Teresa is speaking to Emma.
2 Teresa is on a landline. We don't know about Emma.
3 Teresa is in the office and Emma isn't.
4 Emma wants to speak to Patrick. He isn't available and she leaves a message.
5 They know each other well.

10.12
1 **Patrick and John**
P Hi, John? It's Pat.
J Hi, Pat! Where are you?
P I'm at the station on my way home from work.
J I thought I could hear a lot of noise in the background.
P I'll be quick 'cos my train's due. I just wanted to ask you …
J Sorry, you're breaking up. I couldn't hear that.
P I know, it's not a good signal. But, listen, I'm calling because I can't make it on Thursday.
J What's that?
P I said, I can't make Thursday.
J You can't make Thursday?
P Yeah. Are you free on Friday instead?
J Friday? I'm not sure. Can I get back to you?
P Sure. That's fine. Oh, there's my train! Speak later!
J Yeah! Speak to you later, then. Bye!

2 **John and Emma**
E Hello.
J Hello, Emma, it's John. I'm trying to get hold of Patrick.
E I'm afraid he's not in. Have you tried his mobile?
J Yeah. I tried that first, but he's not answering.
E It's probably switched off. He's at the cinema with Richard.
J Oh, OK. Can you give him a message then?
E Of course.
J Just tell him Friday's fine.
E OK, I'll tell him as soon as he's back.
J Thanks, Emma. Anyway, how are you? Why aren't you at the cinema?
E Oh, I was tired and I had to finish some work.
J Well, tell that husband of yours I'll see him Friday straight after work.

140 Unit 10 • All-time greats

E I'll do that. Hope to see you soon, John.
J You too. Bye.
E Bye.

3 Chantal, Harriet, Patrick, and Teresa
C Good morning. Wells and Marriot International. Chantal speaking. How can I help you?
H Hello, could I speak to Patrick Doyle, please?
C I'm afraid his line's busy. Would you like to hold?
H Yes, please.
C It's ringing for you now.
H Thank you.
T Hello. Patrick Doyle's office. Teresa speaking.
H Hello. Can I speak to Patrick Doyle, please?
T Who's speaking, please?
H This is Harriet Smith from Digby and Moss Associates.
T Oh, good morning, Ms Smith. I'll put you through immediately.
H Thank you.
T It's Harriet Smith on the line for you, Patrick.
P Harriet! Good to hear from you!. Are you back from that conference in New York?
H Yes, and I wondered …

4 Teresa and Emma
T Hello. Patrick Doyle's office.
E Hi Teresa, it's Emma
T Oh, hello, Mrs Doyle.
E Can I speak to Patrick, please?
T Oh, I'm afraid he has someone with him at the moment, Mrs Doyle. Is it urgent? Do you want me to interrupt him?
E No, no, it's not urgent. It can wait until this evening. I've got a meeting myself in a few minutes. Just tell him I rang and I'll see him this evening at home.
T Will do. I hope there isn't a problem.
E No, no, not a problem. Good news, actually. Bye, Teresa.
T Ooh? Bye, Mrs Doyle.

4 Refer students to the gapped conversations in exercise 4. See if they can fill in any of the gaps before playing the recording again. Pause to let students complete the expressions and compare answers. Draw attention to the expressions by asking students to circle them. Check students understand the expressions by asking questions: *What does John mean when he says 'you're breaking up'? What's a 'signal'? What does Patrick mean when he says 'I can't make it'? What does 'Can I get back to you' mean?*, etc. Ask students to practise the conversations in pairs.

Answers
1 breaking, signal, make, instead, back, later
2 hold, tried, answering, switched, message
3 busy, hold, ringing, speaking, This, through
4 afraid, someone, urgent, rang, do

SUGGESTION Write the expressions from the conversation on the board on one side. On the other side, write the synonymous expressions, but mix them up. Ask a student to come to the board – they draw a line to connect the expressions that match. Draw a line under the stressed words in the new expressions. Remind students of the rules for stress: content words like nouns and verbs are stressed. In the case of phrasal verbs, the verb includes the preposition.

you're breaking up = the phone signal is bad
I can't make it = I can't come
can I get back to you = can I tell you later
to get hold of = to contact
his line's busy = he's already on the phone
to hold = to wait
I'll put you through = I'll connect you

Roleplay

You may want to write the expressions on the board for students to refer to during the roleplay. Read the instructions with the students. Put them in pairs and direct each student to the appropriate page in the Student's Book. Before they start their roleplay, ensure each student understands what to do. Model one of the conversations if needed. Give them some time to think about what they will say. Ask students to sit back-to-back for the roleplay so that they have to rely on careful listening instead of visual cues. You could ask the class to stand back-to-back in a line, or line up the chairs, or students could just turn in their seats. Another option is to do the roleplays using students' mobile phones. Check that students are comfortable sharing their mobile number with their partner, and that they are not being charged for the call. After the roleplays, find out how students felt doing them. Was it harder when they couldn't see the other student? What did they decide to do in each situation?

SUGGESTION If your students are interested in the topic, you could get them to discuss mobile etiquette in their country. Write some prompts on the board to help focus the students' ideas:

Where can mobiles be used?
Where shouldn't they be used?
What annoys you about other mobile users?
Have you ever been asked to turn your phone off? When?
Would you like mobiles to be banned in some situations?

Additional material
For teachers
Photocopiable activity – Communication: *You're breaking up!* pp226–7
For students
Online Practice – *Look again*
Workbook p69
Online Practice – *Practice*

Writing SB p108

Discussing pros and cons

Social media sites

The aim of this writing section is to help students write a discursive essay using linking words. The writing skills covered include planning and organizing notes, understanding the main purpose of each paragraph, and using linking words correctly.

1 Lead in by talking about your own use and opinion of social networking sites. Brainstorm a list on the board. Read the instructions as a class and ask students to write down their likes and dislikes of these sites. Ask students to share their ideas with a partner, and then with the class.

2 Pre-teach/Check *advantages/pros* and *disadvantages/cons*. Check students understand that in the text they are going to write it's important to have a balance of positive and negative points. Give students time to read the notes. Check comprehension of *flooded with requests*, *private life*, *tagged* (another user has included an image of you that might be available across the network), and *addicted*.

Unit 10 • All-time greats   141

Ask students how many of their ideas are included in the notes and elicit further pros and cons from the class as appropriate, e.g. *It's good fun. It can help build businesses. People can write false/nasty things about you. It can be difficult to delete content.* Check which pros and cons students think are the most important.

3 Ask students to read the text and discuss the purpose of each paragraph in pairs. *Which paragraph shows the advantages? The disadvantages? What does the third paragraph express?*

Answers
Paragraph 1: expresses advantages/pros
Paragraph 2: expresses disadvantages/cons
Paragraph 3: expresses personal view

4 This stage highlights the use of linking words often used in discursive essays. Linking words add cohesion to a text; without them, paragraphs sound choppy and it can be unclear how the information links together. Ask students if they think the information in the paragraphs hangs together well. They may say that it does – this is fine for now, because they can compare this essay to the way it is after they complete the exercise.

Elicit where the first two linkers go as an example. Put students in pairs to discuss where to put the rest of the linking words. Monitor and help as necessary. With weaker students, you could do the first paragraph as a class stage, with students working in pairs for paragraphs 2 and 3. Get students to read out sections of the text with the linkers in place. Remind them to give any changes in punctuation. Write up on the board any sections that the students disagree on. Go through these with the class, helping students understand the use and/or position of the linkers (see Overview of linkers in Answers below). Ask them to compare the essay with linkers to the essay before the linkers were added – *Does the essay feel like it fits together better now?*

Draw students' attention to the first sentence in each paragraph – the *topic sentence*. Point out that topic sentences are general sentences that introduce the paragraph. The rest of the paragraph supports the topic sentence.

Answers
THE PROS AND CONS OF SOCIAL MEDIA SITES
Social media sites, such as Facebook, **clearly** have many advantages. **First of all,** they are an excellent way of keeping in touch with people in your life, **both** friends and family, **and** they are a great way of finding old friends. **Also**, you can communicate with these people at any time you want and in many ways, **for example** you can share your photos or your favourite music and videos with them. **Another advantage is that** you can join groups with similar interests to yourself, **such as** sports, hobbies, and your work.
However, social media sites **also** have many disadvantages. **Firstly,** you are often flooded with requests from unknown or unwanted 'friends'. **Secondly,** friends and family may find out too much about your private life, and **what is more**, you may hear about boring events in their lives. You can **also** be tagged in pictures that you don't want others to see. **Finally, perhaps** the biggest problem is that you can waste too much time on Facebook. Some people can **even** become addicted to it.
Despite the disadvantages, social media sites are definitely here to stay. They are now one of the main means of communication worldwide. **The fact is** that we can't imagine our lives without them.

Overview of linkers
Listing information:
- *First of all/Firstly, Secondly, Another (advantage) is that, Finally,* – used when listing a number of similar points; usually go at the start of a sentence, followed by a comma.

Addition:
- *Also,/also* – introduces a new piece of information; can go at the beginning of a sentence, followed by a comma, or goes before a main verb, after the verb *to be*, and after a modal.
- *, and* – used to link two clauses to give more information, preceded by a comma when linking two independent clauses.
- *what is more,* – used to introduce an additional point; often goes at the start of a sentence, followed by a comma.

Example:
- *for example,* – introduces one or more examples; can link two clauses or go at the beginning of a sentence, followed by a comma.
- *such as* – introduces one or more examples; goes in the middle of a sentence before a noun.

Contrast
- *however,* – introduces a contrast; often goes at the start of a sentence, followed by a comma.
- *despite* – introduces a contrast; goes before a noun or an -*ing* form.

Emphasis
- *even* – used to give emphasis; goes before a main verb, after the verb *to be,* and after a modal.
- *The fact is that* – used to give emphasis to the statement that follows; goes at the start of a sentence.
- *clearly* – adverb used to emphasize that what you are saying is true; goes after an auxiliary verb or the verb *be,* or before a main verb.

Other
- *both* – used to show that your point refers to two things; goes before a noun.
- *perhaps* – used to say that you are not certain about something; can go at the start of a sentence, after the verb *to be*, or before a main verb.

5 Give students time to add in any additional ideas to the text, working in pairs. Monitor and help, checking that students use an appropriate linker to join the new ideas to the existing text.

6 Ask students to choose one of the topics and brainstorm the advantages and disadvantages. Students can then work in pairs to check and help each other with further ideas. Monitor and help as necessary.

Give students time to write their essay in class or set it for homework. When you check the students' work, circle errors, but allow students to self-correct. Try to limit correction to major problems to avoid demoralizing the students. Ask students to correct their work, then display it in the classroom or on a class blog so that students can read each other's work. If appropriate, ask students to vote on the most interesting essay.

Additional material
For students
Online Practice – *Practice*
Workbook p69, *Review*
Online Practice – *Check your progress*

11 People with a passion

Introduction to the unit

The theme of this unit is people – their passions and big life moments. Music, science, and people's passions are covered in the themes. Present Perfect Simple and Present Perfect Continuous are reviewed in the *Grammar* section, with two texts for context – one is about physicist, astronomer and TV presenter Brian Cox, and the other is about Martha Lane Fox, co-founder of lastminute.com.

In the *Listening and speaking* section, students listen to three people talk about hobbies they are passionate about and share their own passions with the class. The listening skills practised here include inferring meaning from context, note-taking, and paraphrasing.

In the *Reading and speaking* section, students read about some unusual things people are passionate about collecting and discuss the pros and cons of collecting things. Students do close reading to find the answers to questions and look for synonyms in the text for new vocabulary words and phrases.

The *Vocabulary and listening* and *Everyday English* sections are linked by practising the vocabulary of birth, marriage, and death, and the language of giving and reacting to good and bad news. The vocabulary section introduces key terms for stages of life, while the Everyday English section introduces ways of talking about these stages.

The *Writing* section focuses on the useful skill of note-taking while listening to a talk. Two different note-taking methods are introduced: linear and mind-mapping. Students use their notes to write a summary.

Language aims

Grammar

Present Perfect Simple and Continuous, tense review

This section reviews Past Simple and Present Perfect Simple in a reading text in which Present Perfect Continuous is also introduced. Students answer questions about the text using these tenses. They focus on the difference in meaning of each in the *Grammar spot*, then match questions with responses as a review of time clauses. Students then practise choosing the right tense in statements and questions in a variety of controlled and freer practice exercises. In *Questions with How long … ?* students think of a question and response to a statement. They then complete questions with the right tense and interview their partner. In the *What have they been doing?* section, students review giving reasons with *because* while practising the Present Perfect Continuous. They then complete sentences with Present Perfect Simple and listen to the conversations that tie the tenses together. Finally, they review all three tenses again in a reading text where they choose the right verb tense and make questions with the appropriate tense.

Vocabulary

Life's big moments

This section looks at three important parts of many people's lives: birth, marriage, and death. Students learn vocabulary associated with each of these stages and read or hear them in realistic contexts.

Everyday English

Finding the right words!

This section links to the *Vocabulary* section, bringing in the vocabulary and themes. Students learn language for discussing good and bad news related to birth, marriage, divorce, and death.

Additional material

Workbook

Students complete a text using Present Perfect Simple and Continuous. They then do several discrimination tasks, deciding where to use the Simple or Continuous forms of the Present Perfect. Students do vocabulary work on the stages of life, and practise reacting to life events. The Grammar review is an interview with a famous actress.

Photocopiable activities

There are photocopiable activities to review grammar (*Present Perfect picture race*), vocabulary (*Birth, marriage, and death*), and communication (*Say the right thing!*) at the back of the Teacher's Guide as well as on the Teacher's Resource Centre. There is also a worksheet to accompany the video on the Teacher's Resource Centre.

Notes on the unit

Unit opener page

Choose from these activities to engage your students with the topic and target language of this unit.

- Talk about the title
- Talk about the unit goals (*Grammar, Vocabulary, …*)
- Talk about the photo
- Watch the video
- Look at the bottom banner
- Do the activity

Tell students to look at the photo and unit title on p109. Ask *How is the title connected to the photo? What is the man's passion?* Note that here, *passion* means something people like more than anything else. Teach the word *gnomes* /nəʊmz/. Explain that in the UK, many people put gnomes in their garden as decorations, and the tradition dates back to ancient Rome. Some people think they bring luck or fertility for their garden, as they are considered to be spirits of the earth. Find out if students have ever seen figures like this or if they would put one in their garden! Find out if students think they could ever have a passion for collecting gnomes.

Video (2 minutes approximately): The video gives a step-by-step overview of the unit. Play the video, pausing where necessary – especially for students to answer any questions, e.g. *What's your passion?* This makes it a more interactive experience. Highlight the option of practising online.

As shown in the bottom banner, don't forget that there are many exercises to consolidate and practise the target language of the unit in the Workbook as well as online. There are links to these exercises on the relevant pages of the Student's Book and they can be done in class time or you can set them for homework.

Summary: If you're short of time, use the title and the photo to help students understand and engage with the topic, and then move straight on to the activity so that they can discuss the theme in more detail. If you have any more time, try to watch the video together. It is a clear and interesting introduction to the different parts of the unit.

Notes for activity:

Put students in pairs. Ask them to look at the photo and discuss their answers to the questions. Ask them to justify their choices where possible.

> **Suggested answers**
> 1 He collects them.
> 2 Students' own answers.
> 3 Students' own answers.

Grammar   SB p110

Present Perfect Simple and Continuous

SUGGESTION For a deductive approach to learning this grammar, you could ask students to read Grammar reference 11.1 on the Present Perfect Continuous for homework before beginning this presentation. They don't need to spend more than five to ten minutes on it, and tell them not to worry if they don't understand it all.

Possible problems

1 The tenses covered in previous units and reviewed here are:
   - Present Simple, Present Continuous – Unit 2 (TG p31)
   - Past Simple – Unit 3 (TG p44)
   - Present Perfect Simple – Unit 6 (TG p81)

   In Unit 6, several uses of the Present Perfect Simple were presented and practised. Your students should be familiar with the form of the Present Perfect Simple by now, but they are still likely to make mistakes in the different uses of the tense.

2 In this unit, the Present Perfect Continuous is dealt with relatively lightly. This is because at Pre-intermediate level, it is unrealistic to expect students to perceive all the differences of meaning between Present Perfect Simple and Present Perfect Continuous.
   Common mistakes of form:
   *I been learning English for three years.
   *I've learn English for three years.
   *I've been learn English for three years.
   (Correction: *I've been learning English for three years.*)

3 The concepts expressed by the Present Perfect Continuous are often expressed in other languages by either a present tense or a form of the Present Perfect Simple. Many languages manage without the need to express the ideas inherent in the continuous aspect, but it is used very naturally in English, e.g. *I've been learning English for three years.* sounds much more natural than *I've learned English for three years.* But *I've lived here all my life.* sounds better than *I've been living here all my life.*, because the continuous aspect often implies a temporary action. When the Present Perfect refers to an activity with a result in the present, it can be difficult to know whether to use the simple or continuous form. The following two sentences refer to the same action, but mean very different things:
   - *I've painted the bathroom.* (a completed action and the result is that the bathroom painting is finished)
   - *I've been painting the bathroom.* (a recent activity which may or may not be finished)

   If a completed quantity is stated, the Present Perfect Simple must be used, not the Present Perfect Continuous. This is because of the idea of activity in progress in the continuous and the idea of completion in the simple, e.g.
   *I've been writing three letters today. (Correction: *I've written three letters today.*)
   *I wait here for two hours. (Correction: *I've been waiting here for two hours.*)
   *I'm hot because I've run. (Correction: *I'm hot because I've been running.*)

4 Finally, students may need reminding that some verbs, e.g. *know, like*, etc. are not used in the continuous form.
   Common mistakes of use:
   *I've been knowing her for a long time. (Correction: *I've known her for a long time.*)

144   Unit 11 • People with a passion

STARTER SB p110

1 Set this up as a milling activity. Write all four questions about learning and teaching English from exercises 1 and 2 on the board. Students stand up and move around the class asking the two questions. They should ask at least five different people the first two questions and ask you the third and fourth questions as well. You could give an extra piece of information about your teaching to some of the students, e.g. *My first teaching job was in Spain; I taught primary school children.*, etc. As a class, compare information the students learned about each other to determine who has been studying English the *longest* and the *shortest* amount of time. Students can also discuss what they learned about you.

A passion for music and science

About the text

Brian Cox is a professor of particle physics in the School of Physics and Astronomy at the University of Manchester and he spends a lot of time working with the Large Hadron /ˈhædrɒn/ Collider at CERN in Geneva, Switzerland. He is also a popular TV presenter who specializes in teaching people about science. He has an engaging style full of passion for his subject, and he breaks down very complex concepts so that audiences can understand. He started out working in television for the BBC (British Broadcasting Corporation), but found that people were keen to hear him speak live, so he now tours the UK and Europe giving interactive lectures. He encourages questions, and in his live shows audience members are invited to tweet questions for him to answer. He is also a musician who played the keyboard in the pop bands *Dare* and *D:ream*. *D:ream* had a hit single, *Things Can Only Get Better,* which was later used as a New Labour election anthem in the 1990s. Cox has gained many achievements. The Lord Kelvin Award, an award granted in recognition of exceptional and impactful long-term achievements, was granted to him in 2006. Brian was made OBE (Officer of the Most Excellent Order of the British Empire) by Queen Elizabeth II in 2010 for his efforts in publicizing science. He is known as the country's best-loved physicist.

1 Refer students to the photos of Brian Cox. Ask *What does each photo show? Where do you think he is in each? Who else can you see?* (The photo at the bottom of the chart shows Stephen Hawking.) Ask them to read the introduction to the article. Read and answer the questions in exercise 1 as a class. Has anyone ever heard of Brian Cox? Check understanding of *physicist* /ˈfɪzɪsɪst/ (someone who studies matter and energy and the relationships between them, i.e. physics), *astronomer* (someone who studies astronomy – the sun, moon, stars, planets, etc.) and *passionate*. You could also show the different word forms on the board: <u>phy</u>sicist (person); <u>phy</u>sics (subject); <u>phy</u>sical (adj); <u>phy</u>sically (adv); a<u>stron</u>omer (person); a<u>stron</u>omy (subject); astro<u>nom</u>ical (adj); astro<u>nom</u>ically (adv); <u>pas</u>sionate (adj); <u>pas</u>sion (noun); <u>pas</u>sionately (adv).

2 This is a scanning exercise, so give students a short amount of time to scan the chart to find three jobs he has had in his life. Set a timer for one minute so that students can read the text quickly to find the information.

Answers
Scientist (physicist / astronomer), TV presenter, musician

3 Give students a moment to read the questions, then put them in pairs to find the answers in the text. Note that the date of the moon landing is not in the text – check students know when it happened so they can do the maths for question 2 (it was 1969). Check answers as a class.

Answer
1 In Oldham /ˈəʊldəm/, north of England, in 1968.
2 He was 1 (they landed on the Moon in 1969).
3 He read his book.
4 Because he discovered music.
5 Two – DARE and D:ream.
6 Since he was 35. He has one son and one stepson.
7 Yes, many.
8 He's touring Europe and Australia, giving a series of lectures.

4 🔊 11.1 This exercise focuses students' attention on question forms in the three tenses, and possible answers with different phrases. To support weaker students, first ask students to identify and underline the tense in each sentence. Draw students' attention to the question words *When* and *How long* and corresponding tense (e.g. *When?* – Past Simple; *How long?* – Present Perfect, Present Perfect Continuous). Give students a few minutes to match the questions and answers in pairs. Play the recording for students to check their answers. Ask *What do you notice about the tense of the question and the answer?* to help them make the connection between tense and choice of *when, since, for,* and *in*. Students work in pairs. Student A has book closed. Student B chooses four questions from the exercise and asks Student A. Can they remember the right answer? Students swap roles so that Student B asks and Student A answers.

Answers and audioscript

🔊 **11.1 Brian Cox – from pop star to professor**
1 A When did he start being interested in the stars?
 B **When he was three.**
2 A How long has he been interested in the stars?
 B **Since he was three.**
3 A When did he start doing research at CERN?
 B **When he was 29.**
4 A How long has he been doing research at CERN?
 B **For over 20 years.**
5 A When did he make his first TV programme?
 B **In 2005.**
6 A How long has he been making TV programmes?
 B **Since 2005.**
7 A How many programmes has he made?
 B **A great many.**
8 A Where has he been touring recently?
 B **All over Europe and Australia.**

GRAMMAR SPOT SB p111

1 Read the three sentences together. Ask students which tense is in each one. Give them a moment to work in pairs to answer the two questions. Check answers with the class. Ask students what the difference is between *He's been making ….* and *He's made ….* . (*He's been making* has a sense that he has been doing this again and again. There's a feeling of continuous making. *He's*

Unit 11 • People with a passion 145

made gives the idea of completed actions or a number of actions).

Answers

He **made** his first TV programme in 2005. = Past Simple (a single action in the past)

He**'s been making** programmes since 2005. = Present Perfect Continuous (an activity which began in the past and continues to the present/has been repeated many times)

He**'s made** over 40 programmes so far. = Present Perfect Simple (completed up to now – 'so far' suggests that he may make more)

2 Students complete the questions in pairs. Ask confident students to read their questions to the class.

Answers

When **did** he **make** his first TV programme?
How long **has** he **been making** TV programmes?
How many programmes **has** he **made** so far?

EXTRA IDEA If there is time, ask students to turn to Grammar reference 11.1 on p151 to find:

- two uses of the Present Perfect Continuous:
  1 to express an activity which began in the past and continues to the present – *He's been teaching music for years.*
  2 to refer to an activity with a result in the present – *I'm hot because I've been running.*
- an example of when the Present Perfect Continuous and the Present Perfect mean the same thing: *How long have you worked/been working here?*
- five verbs that have the idea of a long time: *wait, work, learn, travel, play*. These are often in the Present Perfect Continuous.
- seven verbs that don't have the idea of a long time and so are not usually found in the Present Perfect Continuous: *find, start, buy, die, lose, break, stop*
- four state verbs that aren't usually used in the Present Perfect Continuous: *like, love, know, have*
- which tense is used if there is a number or quantity: Present Perfect Simple

SUGGESTION Practise using state verbs with the Present Perfect: Write a list of state verbs on the board, e.g. *like, love, know, have, hate, believe*. Give each student a slip of paper. They write a true sentence about themselves using a state verb and the Present Perfect – they shouldn't let anyone see what they write! Give an example: *I've liked Brian Cox since I first saw him on TV.* Collect the slips, then redistribute them so that every student has someone else's slip. They walk around to try to find the student who wrote the slip, but must do it by changing the sentence to the question: e.g. *Have you liked Brian Cox since you first saw him on TV?* In feedback, students can report back, using the third person, e.g. *Susan has never liked chocolate.*

Practice SB p111

Discussing grammar

1 Do the first sentence together as a class. Ask students to work alone to complete the exercise, then compare answers in pairs. This is a challenging exercise, so when checking as a class, ask students why the tense is used.

Draw students' attention to the 's in number 2. 's can be a contraction of *is* or *has* – ask students which it is. (*has*)

You could also do some pronunciation work here, since these forms of the verb have unstressed parts that are hard to hear. Ask students to note how the auxiliary verb is not stressed in the sentences, but the main verb is:

How <u>long</u> have you been (sounds like /əvjuːbɪn/) <u>waiting</u>?
<u>Jo</u>'s been <u>looking</u> (/dʒəʊzbɪn/)
… have been (/əvbɪn/) <u>going</u> <u>out</u>
How <u>long</u> have you had (/əvjuː(h)æd/)
<u>Tom</u> has been (/tɔːmzbɪn/) <u>working</u>
<u>Sue</u> has been (/suːzbɪn/) <u>talking</u>
<u>She</u>'s (/ʃiːz/) <u>spoken</u>

Answers

1 have you been waiting (begins in past, continues to present)
2 been looking (begins in past, continues to present)
3 have been going out (begins in past, continues to present)
4 bought (finished action in the past)
5 have you had (the action begins in the past and continues to the present, but *have* is a state verb here as it means possession)
6 has been working (begins in past, continues to present)
7 has been talking (begins in past, continues to present)
8 has spoken to (continuous is not possible because the number of friends (six) is given)

Questions with *How long … ?*

2 🔊 **11.2** This activity brings together the question *How long … ?* using either the Present Perfect Simple or the Present Perfect Continuous and possible responses in a freer and more creative way. Do the first sentence together as an example. Give students a few minutes to think of the questions and possible answers. In pairs, Student A reads the statement, Student B asks the question, then Student A responds. They then swap with Student B saying the same statement but adding *too: I'm training to run the marathon, too!* Student A then asks the question and Student B provides an answer. Ask pairs of students to perform their dialogues to the class. Gently make corrections if needed. Play the recording so that students can compare their questions and answers.

Answers and audioscript

🔊 **11.2 Questions with *How long … ?***
1 A My sister's working in New York.
  B How long has she been working there?
  A Only a couple of months.
2 A I'm training to run the marathon.
  B How long have you been training?
  A Since Christmas. Wish me luck!
3 A My boss is on holiday.
  B How long has he been away?
  A Two weeks. It's great without him!
4 A I'm learning how to drive.
  B How long have you been learning?
  A Nearly two years. I've failed my test three times already.
5 A I know Maria very well.
  B How long have you known her?
  A Since we were at school together.

146 Unit 11 • People with a passion

6 **A** I have the new iPhone.
  B **How long have you had it?**
  A I only got it yesterday.

Talking about you

3 Put students in pairs to complete the exercise. Monitor and support if needed. Ask fast finishers to write one or two more gapped questions. They give their questions to another pair of fast finishers to complete. Check answers before students ask and answer the questions in pairs. As an extension, ask pairs to work together to try to find five things they have been doing longer than their partner – they have to ask questions in the Present Perfect Simple or Present Perfect Continuous, e.g. *How long have you been living here?/How long have you known Pedro?*, etc.

Answers
1 How long **have** you **been coming** to this school?
2 How long **have** you **been using** this book?
3 Which book **did** you **use** before this one?
4 How long **have** you **known** your teacher?

What have they been doing?

4 This exercise practises Present Perfect Continuous to refer to an activity with a result in the present. Refer students to the pictures on p112. Ask students to say what the pictures show. Draw students' attention to the captions. Ask *Why are the students in picture 1 bored?* Elicit possible reasons. Encourage students to use Present Perfect Continuous in their reason, and ensure they use the word *because*. Put students in pairs to ask *Why?* questions about the pictures and reply with *because* and a reason. Monitor and support as needed. Check that students are using *have got* for pictures 4 and 6. In whole-class feedback, ask *Why?* questions about each picture and elicit responses from a range of students. Ask students why Present Perfect Continuous is a good tense to use in this situation (because it refers to an activity with a result in the present – we see the evidence in the photos; the use of the continuous tense emphasizes the duration of the past action).

5 🔊 **11.3** Tell students that in the next activity, they will give more information about each person using Present Perfect Simple. Look at the first sentence together, then ask students to complete the exercise. Play the recording to check. Put students in pairs to repeat exercise 4, but this time giving more information using the Present Perfect Simple as in the recording. Do a quick review of the Past Simple verbs in the exercise – focusing on pronunciation:

Teacher: *win* → Students: *won*;
Teacher: *spend* → Students: *spent*;
Teacher: *plant* (one syllable) → Students: *planted* (two syllables); etc.

Answers and audioscript

🔊 **11.3 What have they been doing?**

1 **A** Why are the students bored?
  B Because the teacher's been talking for hours and they **haven't understood** a word.
2 **A** Why are they so tired and dirty?
  B Because they've been playing rugby, but they're happy because they**'ve won** the match.
3 **A** Why is she hot and tired?
  B Because she's been cooking all morning. She**'s made** two huge chocolate cakes for the party.
4 **A** Why has he got backache?
  B Because he's been digging the garden. He**'s planted** six rows of cabbages.
5 **A** Why is she covered in paint?
  B Because she's been decorating her flat. She**'s painted** two walls already.
6 **A** Why have they got no money left?
  B Because they've been shopping. They**'ve spent** over £200!

SUGGESTION As a way to practise Present Perfect Continuous for present result, you could do a drama activity. Write some activities on slips of paper, e.g. watching a sad film, attending a boring lecture, eating a big meal, painting the house, watching your team win the world cup, etc. Put these together into a bag or hat. Ask a confident student to come take a slip. The student must mime how s/he is feeling and try to give clues about why. The student can draw on the board or mime an action, but not speak. The rest of the class try to guess: *Are you sad? Have you been watching a sad film?*

Tense review – simple and continuous

Who is Martha Lane Fox?

About the text

A *life peer* is a person who has been given the title of *peer* (Lord or Lady). Like some hereditary peers, *life peers* can sit in the House of Lords, the upper house of Parliament in the UK, and make laws. However, a life peerage is not passed on to children as is the case in hereditary peerage. A chancellor of a university is the ceremonial head. The Open University is a public distance learning University that offers undergraduate and postgraduate degrees, diplomas, certificates, and continuing education. In 2019, it will celebrate its 50th anniversary.

6 Lead in to the topic by asking students if they have ever decided to go on holiday somewhere at the last minute, so they've had to book something really quickly. How did they arrange the travel? Find out if anyone has heard of lastminute.com. Ask students to look at the photo and read the introduction about Martha Lane Fox. Ask and answer the questions as a class. Check that students understand *dotcom millionaire* and *tragedy*. Note that a *golden girl* is a successful/popular woman. We can also use the term *golden boy*, but we don't use the term, *golden man* or *golden woman*.

Answers
Because she's very successful – she's a dotcom millionaire – she's the co-founder of lastminute.com. She's passionate about Internet access being for everyone – young and old.

7 Ask students to read the article and tell you what her tragedy was and what negative impact it had on her life. Check students have understood *surrogate mother* (a woman who gives birth to a baby for another woman who is unable to have a baby herself). They then read the article again and choose the correct verbs. If some students are struggling with this, help them by pointing out words such as *while, in + date, since*, and state verbs.

Unit 11 • People with a passion   147

Students discuss their choices in pairs before checking as a class. Get students to say why the tense choice is the right one in the context.

Answers
1 studied
2 has been working
3 was working
4 sold
5 was driving
6 has never fully recovered
7 has been doing
8 has had
9 has been
10 has

8 🔊 **11.4** Do the first question together as a class. Ask students why Past Simple is used in the question. Put students in pairs to write the rest of the questions. Play the recording so that students can check. Play it a second time if needed. In pairs, Student A chooses four questions to ask Student B, then they swap roles with Student B asking the last four questions. As a follow-up, ask the class what they think of Martha. If students are interested in her work in making technology accessible, responsible, and fair, ask them to go online to find out more about Martha's work, or they can find out about other dotcom millionaires. They can share what they found in the next lesson in a short presentation in groups. Ask students if they think it's still possible to become a dotcom millionaire and if there is another trend that is making people rich currently (e.g. the bitcoin trend).

Answers and audioscript

🔊 **11.4 Martha Lane Fox – co-founder of lastminute.com**

Tense review
1 Q **Where did she study?**
   A At Oxford University.
2 Q **How long has she been working in digital technology?**
   A Since 1994, when she joined an IT company called Spectrum.
3 Q **Who did she meet while she was working at Spectrum?**
   A Brent Hoberman. She founded lastminute.com with him.
4 Q **How much did they sell lastminute.com for?**
   A £577 million in 2005.
5 Q **Where was she driving when she had a car crash?**
   A In Morocco.
6 Q **Has she fully recovered from the accident?**
   A No, she hasn't. She still walks with a stick.
7 Q **What has she been doing since 2007?**
   A She's been doing a lot of work for charities.
8 Q **How long has she been director of Twitter? How many followers does she have?**
   A Since 2016. She has over 186,000 followers.

SUGGESTION Ask students to use the Internet to research someone famous. They write ten things about that person using Past Simple, Present Perfect Simple, and Present Perfect Continuous. They work in small groups. Student A reads the list until the other students can guess the famous person. You could give an example to get them started:

She has been on TV.
She has met the Queen of England.
She hasn't had a baby.
She has been travelling a lot since she got married.
She married a royal.
(etc.)
Answer: Meghan Markle

Additional material

For teachers
Photocopiable activity – Grammar: *Present Perfect picture race* pp228–9

For students
Online Practice – *Look again*
Workbook pp70–3, exercises 1–12
Online Practice – *Practice*

Listening and speaking SB p113

My kind of thing!

About the text
In this listening text, three people talk about the things they are passionate about and why. Each person gives information about what it is that makes them love the thing they love.

1 Read the question together, then ask students to read the three quotes and guess what they are talking about. Allow students to discuss in pairs for a few minutes, then feedback with the whole class. What words gave them clues?

2 🔊 **11.5** Refer students to the chart. They should make notes for each speaker in the spaces provided. For weaker classes, put students in pairs – Student A completes column 1 and Student B completes column 2. They compare answers to ensure they have all the information. Play the recording once without stopping. Were the students' guesses correct? Play the recording again, pausing if needed so that students can complete their notes. Check answers as a class.

Answers
Paula
Her passion is horse-riding.
She likes it so much because she's always liked horses – they're so big and powerful, and also beautiful. Riding is physically demanding and she's learning how to give clear instructions. She likes the fact that horses have 'moods' as it shows they have their own personalities.
Andrew
His passion is poetry.
He likes it so much because he's heard other poets read their poetry aloud and he felt the power of the words. He likes the fact that you can say a lot with only a few words – each word has to work hard. He also thinks a poem can help you when you feel tired or depressed.
James
His passion is the British weather.
He likes it so much because he enjoyed rainy holidays as a child. He thinks the rain makes you appreciate the sunshine more, and he likes the fact that the English weather is so changeable.

🔊 **11.5 My kind of thing!**
1 **Paula**
My passion at the moment is horse-riding – it's strange to hear myself say that 'cos I've only been doing it for about a year, and I never thought I'd love it so much. It all happened because I was talking to someone who rode horses, and I said that stupid thing people often say 'Oh, I've always wanted to do that', and she said 'Why don't you then?'. And I thought, 'why not?' I've always liked

horses, they're so big and powerful, but so beautiful when you see them racing round a field or a track. Riding's very physically demanding – your body has to move with the horse, and, of course, I've fallen off a few times, but amazingly the more you fall the less it hurts. I've been learning how to give really clear instructions – you have to understand your horse – they have moods, you never know what a ride is going to be like – a horse you had a fantastic ride on one week, can be slow and miserable the next week. I like that about horses – they have personalities.

2 Andrew

I'm passionate about poetry. I studied English Literature at university, but it wasn't until after I graduated that I really saw the point of poetry and started writing it myself. I've been trying to write for about ten years now – I'm not sure it's any good, but I keep trying. I've met some other hopeful poets, like me, and I've heard them reading it aloud – it was amazing – I felt the power of the words. The thing I like so much about it is that you can say so much with just a few words – a little means a lot. Each word, each noun, verb, adjective, preposition has to work hard. There's a poem by Simon Armitage called *To His Lost Lover* – it's a poem of regret, about not saying the things you wish you had said to a past lover. This poem really speaks to me – poetry's all about saying what often goes unsaid and with passion. It can be such a help in your life. If you feel tired or depressed, you can always find a poem that will help.

3 James

The thing I'm passionate about, and this may surprise many people, is … um … British weather. I've been interested in it ever since I was a child. I loved all our rainy holidays by the English seaside. I know everyone complains about the weather, but I love it. It means there's always something to talk about, and it's a great way of starting a conversation at a bus stop. Also, you know, it's the rain that gives us our green, green fields. I think if you live somewhere like California and there are 365 days of sunshine, it's boring. But here … perhaps it's been raining all morning, and then suddenly the sun comes out, and you really appreciate that sunshine. It's magic – raindrops are like diamonds in the sun. And it's not true that it rains all the time in Britain, it doesn't – it just rains quite a lot. You know that joke – 'if you don't like English weather – wait ten minutes' – that's why it's always interesting.

3 Read the questions together. Play the recording, pausing after each person. Answer the questions as a class.

Answers

1 Paula has had her passion for about a year.
Andrew has had his since he graduated from university.
James has had his since he was a child.
2 Paula's interest was created when she was talking to someone who rode horses and she said, 'I've always wanted to do that', and the other person said, 'Why don't you, then?'.
Andrew's interest was created when he started writing it himself after he graduated and then when he heard other poets reading their poems aloud.
James' passion started due to the rainy holidays he enjoyed as a child and the fact that the weather is always a good conversation starter.

What do you think?

Put students in groups of three or four to discuss the questions. Assign a group leader who ensures everyone has the opportunity to discuss their ideas. As a follow-up, you could ask students to prepare a presentation about their passion. In the presentation they should answer the questions:
• What is your passion?
• Why do you like it so much?
• How long have you had your passion?
• What was it that first created your interest?

Students can present their passion to the class, or prepare a slide show or infographic that they print out and post around the room or on a shared class webpage.

Additional material

For students

Online Practice – *Practice*

Reading and speaking SB p114

The collectors

1 If you collect anything, lead in to the topic by talking with the students about your collection. Read the instructions and example responses as a class. Ask the class if they have ever collected anything. As an alternative, you could do this as a milling activity. First, ask students to write down something they have collected, or something that someone they know has collected. They shouldn't show anyone what they write. Collect these up and write them on the board in a random order. Tell students they are going to walk around the class and interview the other students to find the person who collects each of the items on the board. They should ask *Have you ever collected … ?* and *Has anyone you know ever collected … ?* Stop the activity after about five minutes or when all the people have been found. Do a quick round up discussion of the collections.

2 Refer students to the photos. Answer the questions in exercise 2 as a class.

Answers

Jan Hugo collects royal memorabilia.
Davide Andreani collects Coca-Cola cans.
Bettina Dorfman and Jian Yang collect Barbie dolls.

3 Look at the numbers in question 8. Ensure students can say them. Check the stress pattern in *90* and *2016*. (*NINEty, twenty sixTEEN*). Divide the class into three groups. Group A reads *The Royal Memorabilia Collector*, Group B reads *The Coca Cola Can Collector*, and Group C reads *Two Barbie Collectors*. They work in pairs in their groups to answer the questions. Monitor and support as needed. Fast finishers can help the others in their group to find the information. Alternatively, they can find one more interesting piece of information to share.

4 Students find partners from the other groups, A/B/C, and make a group of three so that they can share the information. Give them time to tell each other about the other collectors, then ask the class what they think about each of the collectors/collections. Would they want to collect any of the items in the articles?

Answers

Group A

Royal Memorabilia Collector

1 Since 1981.
2 Over 10,000 pieces.
3 Her passion started by chance when she and her husband were given a commemorative coin for Prince Charles and Diana's engagement.
4 In four rooms in her home.
5 Yes – a doll of newborn Prince George.
6 Her husband – he calls himself her royal servant and he takes tour groups around their home.

Unit 11 • People with a passion   149

7 They have spent over £100,000 on the collection and they have turned their home into a museum.
8 4: the number of rooms in Jan's house filled with her collection; 5,800: the number of beer cans David has collected; 100,000: the amount of money they have spent on the collection; 2013: the year Prince George was born.

Group B
Coca-Cola Can Collector
1 Since he was 15.
2 Over 22,000.
3 When he was five – he was given his first can of Coke.
4 In his house and garage.
5 Yes – the cans made of gold and silver.
6 His father – he bought unusual cans home with him from his business trips abroad.
7 He uses a website to swap and search for the rarest cans worldwide.
8 5: his age when his passion started; 90: the number of countries the cans come from; 400: the amount in dollars that the silver and gold cans can be worth; 1979: the year his father brought his first can from Germany; 2013: the year Davide received the Guinness World Record award for the 'largest Collection of Soft Drink cans'.

Group C
Two Barbie Collectors
1 Bettina = since she was ten, Jian Yang = when he was a child.
2 Bettina = over 17,000, Jian = over 6,000.
3 Bettina – she was given a Barbie when she was ten, during a stay in hospital; Jian – he wasn't allowed one when he was a little boy.
4 Bettina – all over her house and she also has a special room called 'Barbie's Kingdom' for her favourite dolls; Jian = not known.
5 Bettina – many, one of which is from 1959 – the year Barbie was 'born'; Jian = not known.
6 Bettina – her daughter, Melissa – she wanted her to share her passion, but Melissa prefers table tennis; Jian = his parents didn't allow him to have a Barbie when he was little.
7 Bettina – she's also a Barbie Doctor and repairs broken dolls from all over the world; Jian = his girlfriends feel that they have to compete with the beauty of the Barbies.
8 2: Barbie Doll collectors; 10: when Bettina started collecting Barbie dolls; $5,000: what the original Barbie is worth; 300,000 the amount in dollars that Bettina's Barbies are worth; 1959: when Barbie was born and the oldest Barbie Bettina owns.

Vocabulary

5 This exercise helps students identify synonyms. Read the instructions as a class, then ask students to find the words in the article. Check as a class and drill pronunciation as needed.

Answers
1 by chance
2 lifelike
3 never-ending
4 swap, rarest
5 repairs
6 an original one
7 wasn't allowed to

What do you think?

Put students in groups for the discussion. Ask them to choose a group leader, a group writer who will take notes, and a group presenter who will share the group's ideas with the rest of the class. Monitor and help students think of pros and cons of collecting. In whole-class feedback, ask the presenter in each group to summarize what the group said and share the list of pros and cons.

VIDEO In this unit students can watch a video about *parkrun* – a 5km race for people with a passion for running. You can play the video clip on the Classroom Presentation Tool or download it from the Teacher's Resource Centre together with the video script, video worksheet, and accompanying teacher's notes. These notes give full guidance on how to use the worksheets and include a comprehensive answer key to the exercises and activities.

Additional material
For teachers
Photocopiable activity – Video worksheet: *Passion for parkrun*
For students
Online Practice – *Look again*
Online Practice – *Practice*

Vocabulary and listening   SB p116

Life's big moments!

This vocabulary section practises the words associated with three key stages of many people's life. This language is, of course, easily personalized, though care is needed not to make students feel uncomfortable by asking them to talk directly about sensitive topics.

Birth

1 Lead in to the topic by giving an example of your own birth date and time. Check students know how to say times and dates. Put students in groups of three or four to discuss the questions. Monitor and help as necessary. If your classroom size allows it, ask students to stand in a line in order of birth. This means that they will have to communicate with each other to find out when everyone was born. Establish which two students are closest in age. Correct any mistakes with times and dates.

2 Focus attention on the photos. Ask *What's happened to Laura in the second picture?* (She's had her baby.) Focus attention on the example. Then give students time to complete the information about Laura. Let students check their answers in pairs before checking with the class. Make sure students can pronounce the words correctly: point out the silent *g* in *weighed* /weɪd/ and you may need to check the vowel sounds in *birth* /bɜːθ/, *born* /bɔːn/, and *due* /djuː/. If students are having problems with the /θ/ sound in *birth*, ask them to put their forefinger up to their lips when they say the word. Their tongue should come out far enough to wet their finger for the /θ/ sound. If appropriate, get students to talk about the birth of a baby in their own family or circle of friends. Or they can talk about the baby of someone in the public eye.

Answers
2 expecting   5 born
3 due   6 weighed
4 birth

Unit 11 • People with a passion

Marriage

3 Give an example of a wedding that you have been to or read about. Elicit other examples from the class and build up a set of relevant vocabulary on the board, e.g. *bride, groom, guests*, etc. Ask the students to share wedding customs in their country: *Are marriages arranged in their culture? What colour does the bride wear? Are there any particular wedding customs? Is there a civil and religious service?*, etc. Focus attention on the pictures and elicit the correct word for number 1. Give students time to complete the task, working individually. Check the answers, checking pronunciation as you go. Students may need help with *marriage* /ˈmærɪdʒ/ (vs *married* /ˈmærɪd/), *widowed* /ˈwɪdəʊd/, and *engaged* /ɪnˈɡeɪdʒd/. Ask students to use the words to talk about people that they know or people in the public eye. If students ask, you could mention that the terms for a woman whose husband has died is a *widow* /ˈwɪdəʊ/, and a man whose wife has died is a *widower* /ˈwɪdəʊə(r)/. The term for an unmarried man is a *bachelor* /ˈbætʃələ(r)/ and an unmarried woman is *spinster* /ˈspɪnstə(r)/. These two terms, however, have very different connotations – a bachelor implies young and carefree, while spinster implies old and past her best years! Other terms that may come up include *bride* /braɪd/, *groom* /ɡruːm/, and *fiancé* /fɪˈɒnseɪ/.

Answers
1 single
2 engaged
3 married
4 divorced
5 widowed

SUGGESTION From a cultural perspective, the topic of marriage can be an interesting one. In a multicultural class, you could have a class discussion to share marriage traditions. For example, in the UK many people get married in a church, the bride traditionally wears a white dress, and both the bride and groom give each other a wedding ring, which is worn on the left ring finger (closest to the heart). In other countries, the wedding ring is worn on the right hand or not at all.

4 Focus attention on the photos of Harry and Nina, and Harry and Laura. Ask students to predict what happened. Put them in pairs to order the events in Harry's life. Check understanding of *honeymoon* and *split up* and pronunciation of *colleague* /ˈkɒliːɡ/. See which students have been able to calculate Harry's age now. (Hint: he was 20 in 2007.)

Answers
1 Harry met Nina at school when they were 16.
2 They got engaged when they were 19.
3 They got married a year later in 2007.
4 They couldn't afford a honeymoon.
5 After a few years, the marriage started to go wrong.
6 They split up. Nina left Harry.
7 They finally got divorced in 2012.
8 Harry remarried in 2017. He married Laura, a colleague from work.
9 They went to Venice on honeymoon.
10 It's their anniversary today! They've just had a baby boy.

Death

5 Focus attention on the missing words and elicit the answer to number 1 as an example. Then give students time to complete the sentences. Let students check their answers in pairs before checking with the class. Make sure students can pronounce the words correctly. You may need to check the vowel sounds in *died* /daɪd/, *alive* /əˈlaɪv/, and *funeral* /ˈfjuːnərəl/. To assess if your students feel happy using this vocabulary, talk about people in your own family or people in the public eye. Let students volunteer any personal information to be sure they are comfortable talking about the topic. Note that RIP on the grave stone in the picture stands for *Requiescat in pace*, Latin for *Rest in Peace*.

Answers
1 die
2 alive, died
3 death
4 died of, funeral
5 dead, miss

My life in a nutshell!

6 🔊 **11.6** This listening brings together the three themes of birth, marriage, and death, revisiting the vocabulary related to each. Refer students to the photo of Alison. Ask *How old do you think she is?* Look at the title of the section and explain that *in a nutshell* means *in brief*, or *in very few words*. Read the questions as a class. Ask students to choose one or more questions they want to listen for. Play the recording. Students discuss answers in pairs before checking as a class.

Answers
1 Ben is Alison's husband. Ellen is their first baby. Tessa and Tom are their twins.
2 They were born in 2015, so answer depends on the current year.
3 They got divorced when she was 13. Her dad died last year of a heart attack – she misses him a lot. Her mum helps out with the kids.
4 She hasn't been divorced. She has small children.

🔊 **11.6 Alison's life**
I didn't marry until quite late. I met my husband Ben when I was 30, and we didn't marry until I was 33 – that was in 2012. We got married in a church near where my mum lives. Ben and I had a great honeymoon, we toured America, we were away for three weeks. And soon after that I found I was pregnant. That was Ellen, our first baby. She was born the year after we got married, and two years after that, in 2015, we had the twins, Tessa and Tom. They've been keeping us busy ever since! I'm exhausted most of the time, but they're great fun. I'm really glad I married Ben – he's a great dad. I want it to be forever. My mum and dad divorced when I was just 13, and I don't want us to do that. My mum helps me with the kids, but my dad died last year – he had a heart attack. I miss him a lot.

> **Additional material**
>
> **For teachers**
> Photocopiable activity – Vocabulary: *Birth, marriage, and death* pp230–1
>
> **For students**
> Online Practice – *Look again*
> Workbook p74, exercises 1–2
> Online Practice – *Practice*

Everyday English SB p117

Finding the right words!

Knowing the right thing to say in conversations involving good or bad news is an important skill. This section links to the topics of birth, marriage, and death on p116 and recycles some of the vocabulary from that section. If you have time, it would be a good idea to cover both these pages in the same lesson. If you do them in different lessons, you could briefly review some of the key words that are recycled here (*weigh, get engaged/married, wedding, split up*).

1 Lead in to the topic by asking students if they have heard any good or bad news recently. As with the *Vocabulary* section, let students volunteer to tell any bad news or personal information to be sure they are comfortable talking about the topic. Focus attention on the photos and elicit which give good and bad news.

> **Answers**
> **1 & 2** Good news
> **3 & 4** Bad news

2 🔊 **11.7** Ask students to work with a partner to complete the conversations. Ask them to speculate on who is talking to whom in each of the conversations. Check students understand the vocabulary. Check pronunciation of *weigh* /weɪ/. Play the recording so they can check their answers. Ask concept check questions: *What does it mean, 'They've been having a tough time at the moment'? What does she mean by 'What a shame!'*, etc. (see below).

How are they doing? – always used in the continuous form to ask about a person's health or general situation

a tough /tʌf/ *time* – a difficult time

What a shame! /ʃeɪm/ – used to show that some news makes you feel sad or disappointed

We lost .... – used as a kinder way of saying that someone died. Ask students if they can use the equivalent of *lose* in the same way in their language.

to be fond /fɒnd/ *of someone* – to like and care about someone very much

coping /ˈkəʊpɪŋ/ – dealing with a situation that is difficult

> **Answers and audioscript**
>
> 🔊 **11.7 Finding the right words**
> 1
> A Helen **had** the baby last night.
> B Wow! Oh! **Congratulations!** Was it a boy or girl?
> A A boy.
> B How much did he **weigh**?
> A 4.1 kilos.
> B Ooh! A big boy! What's he **called**?

> A William James, after both of our fathers.
> B That's nice. How are mother and baby **doing**?
> A They're fine.
> B That's wonderful. **Give Helen my love** when you see her.
> A I will do. Thanks.
> 2
> A Alfie and I have got **engaged.**
> B That's **fantastic news**! Congratulations!
> A Do you like my **ring**?
> B Wow! Diamonds! It's **beautiful**. When's the **wedding**?
> A We're thinking of getting married next spring.
> B I hope I'm invited.
> A Of course you are. I want you to be a **bridesmaid.**
> B Really? I'd love that. I've never been one before.
> 3
> A Have you heard about Bill and Josie?
> B No! **What's happened**?
> A Well, they've been having a **tough time** recently.
> B I know, they haven't been **getting on well** at all.
> A Mm. Well, they've finally decided to **split up**.
> B I'm so **sorry to hear** that. What a **shame**!
> A Yes, I always thought they were so good together.
> 4
> A We lost Grandpa last week.
> B I know. Your dad told me. I'm **so sorry**. He was such a **lovely man**. Everyone was really **fond of him**.
> A He and Grandma were **together** over 60 years.
> B That's incredible. How old was he?
> A Eighty-eight.
> B And how's your Grandma **coping**?
> A She's OK. She's got her family around her.
> B Well, I'm sure you all have wonderful **memories** of him.

3 Pairs choose two of the conversations to practise and try to memorize. They can act them out in class or, in large classes, they can act them out in small groups.

EXTENSION Ask students to write their own good news/bad news dialogues. Encourage them to use vocabulary and expressions from this section and the *Vocabulary and listening* section on p116. They can perform them for the class or in groups. Ideally, they would record themselves and listen to how they sound – are they using appropriate intonation and stress for the situation they are presenting?

> **Additional material**
>
> **For teachers**
> Photocopiable activity – Communication: *Say the right thing!* pp232–3
>
> **For students**
> Online Practice – *Look again*
> Workbook p74
> Online Practice – *Practice*

Writing SB p118

Note-taking

Note-taking is an important skill for students aiming to attend university, and the mental processes that people undergo when note-taking improve understanding. In the process, listeners are gathering and processing the information in order to note down the important information, so multiple parts of the brain are working simultaneously. Note-taking can be hard at first, but with practice, gets easier. The second skill practised here is using notes to write a summary. Writing from notes helps students put ideas into their own words, which is important in avoiding plagiarism.

My vision for the 21st century

1 **11.8** Ask students briefly what their vision of the future is – is it positive or negative? Elicit *optimistic* and *pessimistic*. Put students in pairs and tell them to think of two positive things and two negative things about the future. Get some feedback from the pairs, but don't agree or disagree with any of their ideas at this point. Tell them they are going to listen to a talk by Professor Ivan Gregor about his vision of life in the future. Ask them to predict what they might hear, e.g. what language he will use, and what topics he might talk about. (e.g. *He's a professor, so it might be some sort of lecture.; He may give factual information.; He will use perfect and future tenses.; He might talk about world population or technology.*; etc.) Play the recording. Give students a moment to think about what kind of person Professor Gregor is, and three things they remember from the talk. They share in a whole-class discussion.

Answer
He is optimistic.

11.8 My vision for the 21st century – Part 1: Reasons to be optimistic

Although the world is facing many serious problems at the moment, I am generally optimistic about the future. We've been worrying about the end of civilization for over a hundred years now, but we've always found ways to deal with the problems we face, and I believe we can do the same in the future. Life could actually become much better for us all with improvements in healthcare and technology. We've already made big improvements in life expectancy. People have been living longer and longer lives since the 1950s, when most Americans lived for about 50 years. Nowadays, life expectancy is nearly 80 years, and in future, most people will live to be 100. People often say that they don't want to live to be 100, but that's because they imagine living in an old and broken body. We've already discovered how to grow new cells to repair parts of the body, and when we can grow new hearts, kidneys, and livers outside of the body, we'll be able to use them like the spare parts of a car, keeping our bodies fit and healthy until we die.

People worry about world population becoming an even bigger problem if people live longer. However, when people become more educated and richer, they don't need or want to have so many children. The challenge therefore is to use the technology we have to educate people better and to use robots to create wealth that we can share more equally.

In recent times, many people have been demanding independence and wanting more control of their own countries. I think we need to go the other way. I strongly believe that there will be a world government in future because our problems and resources will have to be managed at a global level.

EXTRA IDEA Students work with a partner. Give them some or all of these definitions and ask them if they can remember the words Professor Gregor used in his talk. Play the talk again, pausing, if necessary for students to hear how each word is used.

1 the culture and way of life in any human society (*civilization*)

2 the service of providing medical care in a country (*healthcare*)

3 the length of time someone can hope to live (*life expectancy*)

4 the smallest unit of living beings – all plants and animals are made up of these (*cells*)

5 a new part that you buy to replace a broken part in a car (*spare parts*)

6 all of the people who live in one area, a town, a city, a country, etc (*population*)

7 something that a country or group of people has and can use, especially to make life more comfortable or to make people richer (*resources*)

2 Refer students to the two sets of notes taken by two students. In pairs, students use the notes to help them remember more of the talk and say which style of note-taking they prefer and why. Play the recording again if students want to listen again as they read the student notes. Ask students what they think of Professor Gregor's ideas. Which ideas do they agree with and which do they disagree with?

3 **11.9** In this exercise, student will complete the part of the talk which is more pessimistic. They choose either Student 1's or Student 2's notes, depending on which style they prefer. Ask them to choose one style. Ensure they understand that they should take notes as they listen, not afterwards. Play the second part of the talk.

4 **11.9** Students compare notes. Play the second part of the talk again so that students can fill in any missing information. Check answers as a class. Discuss the second part of the talk as a class.

Answers
Pessimistic
- people will remain the same: selfish and greedy
- people don't understand – have to look after our world
- people who think money = everything – fight wars
- have technology, but need wisdom

11.9 My vision for the 21st century – Part 2: Reasons to be pessimistic

There are reasons to be pessimistic. There have always been selfish and greedy people, and there always will be. These people will refuse to accept that we need to look after our planet and use our resources carefully. They won't be interested in finding ways to live happily without spending money on more and more material things. These people will always want to fight wars to get what they want. We have the technology to make our lives better, but we need the wisdom to go with it. The big question is – how can we stop the most selfish and greedy people being in the positions of power in the world?

5 Ideally, students should work alone to write a summary of the talk using the notes as a guide. It is strongly suggested that students write their summaries in class – this is a challenging task and they may need your support. If you find that some students are struggling, working in pairs may be the better option. You could put sentence frames on the board to help students get started:

Professor Ivan Gregor is optimistic about the future because ... .

However, he said there are reasons to be pessimistic, too, because ... .

Unit 11 · People with a passion   153

Or write the first part of the summary together as a class:

Professor Ivan Gregor is optimistic about the future because, although there are serious problems in the world, we have always found ways to deal with problems and we can do the same in the future. Life could even become better because healthcare and technology are getting better. In addition … .

Remind students of the useful linking words from Unit 10. Write these on the board for students to reference.

When students have finished writing their summaries, tell them to work with a partner to compare summaries. Each student reads the other's summary. They compare what information their partner has put in the summary and decide if they think each summary gives all the main points, and excludes any extra or unnecessary details.

EXTRA IDEA Many students find writing summaries daunting and don't know where to start. For weaker classes, you could scaffold the activity further by creating a summary frame like the one below. Students use the frame and the notes in the SB to write their summary.

Once they have written their summary, ask them to compare summaries with another student or another pair. Tell them to say one thing they like or think is good about the other student's summary.

You could hand out the sample summary in the next column. However, it is just an example and there will be many good ways to write a summary, so ensure students know this is not the 'right' way. Ask them to find one thing in the example summary that they would like to do in their own writing in the future. You could also ask them to highlight or underline all the linking words to draw their attention to how these are used to create a cohesive piece of writing.

Summary frame for weaker classes

Professor Ivan Gregor is optimistic about the future. There are many reasons. Firstly, there are … , but we have always found … . We can … . Life could even become better because … . Secondly, big improvements have already been made in … . The fact is that people are living longer. In the past, people only lived … , but now we … . In the future, … . In addition, scientists are finding ways to … , so people can stay … longer.

… is another big problem. If people live longer, it might be a bigger problem. However, as people become … , they … . What is more, we can use … to educate people better and use … to create wealth so we can … .

One good idea is to have a … because many … , so they need another direction. Perhaps … can be managed at a global level.

Professor Gregor also has some reasons he is … . First of all, there are selfish people. They will not … . They also will not want to find ways to be happy without … . Another problem is that these people will fight … because they want more and more things. Professor Gregor thinks that we need … . We must think about how we can use technology to stop … .

Possible summary:
Professor Ivan Gregor is optimistic about the future. There are many reasons. Firstly, there are serious problems in the world, but we have always found ways to deal with problems. We can do the same in the future. Life could even become better because healthcare and technology are getting better. Secondly, big improvements have already been made in life expectancy. The fact is that people are living longer. In the past, people only lived to be 50, but now we live to be 80. In the future, we may live to be 100. In addition, scientists are finding ways to grow new body parts, so people can stay fit and healthy longer.

World population is another big problem. If people live longer, it might be a bigger problem. However, as people become more educated and richer, they don't need or want so many children. What is more, we can use technology to educate people better and use robots to create wealth so we can share more equally.

One good idea is to have a world government because many people are demanding independence, so they need another direction. Perhaps problems and resources can be managed at a global level. Professor Gregor also has some reasons he is pessimistic. First of all, there are selfish people. They will not look after the planet or use resources well. They also will not want to find ways to be happy without a lot of money. Another problem is that these people will fight wars because they want more and more things. Professor Gregor thinks that we need wisdom. We must think about how we can use technology to stop greedy and selfish people.

Additional material
For students
Online Practice – *Practice*
Workbook p75, *Review*
Online Practice – *Check your progress*

12 You never know ...

Introduction to the unit

The theme for this unit is thinking about the future and what will or might happen. This provides the context for the two grammar presentations, starting with the First Conditional and *might*, and moving on to the Second Conditional.

In the *Listening and speaking* section, three people talk about being at a crossroads in their life, and discuss what big decisions they have to make. The skill focus here is on listening for specific information. Students also say what they would do in a similar situation which brings in contextualized practice of the Second Conditional from the grammar point.

In the *Reading and speaking* section, students read about risk, probability, and coincidence. The skills practised are close reading to decide if statements are true or false, and deciphering vocabulary from context. In the *What do you think?* section, students practise giving their viewpoints in a group discussion.

Opposites *bring* and *take,* and *come* and *go* are introduced and practised in the *Vocabulary and speaking* section, and this is a good opportunity to revise other collocations from previous units. In *Everyday English*, students learn conversational gambits for saying *thank you* and *goodbye* in a range of situations.

The *Writing* section is a review of grammar from the course. The skill focused on is correcting mistakes using a correction key. Students first work on using the key to highlight and correct mistakes in sentences and a text. They then write their own text, swap papers, and use the correction key to identify mistakes in their partner's writing.

Language aims

Grammar

First Conditional, Second Conditional

In this unit, the First Conditional is presented along with *might* in the first grammar presentation, followed by the Second Conditional on p122. The use of *will* to express a future intention/decision made at the moment of speaking was presented in Unit 5. *Going to* for plans and Present Continuous for future were also practised there. These are recycled in this section. First Conditional is presented in context, then the rules for forming it are presented. Students then use the First Conditional and *might* to talk about plans for the weekend, to give advice based on a listening text and finally in the context of advice, warnings, offers, and threats. Second Conditional is presented in the context of *What if ... ?* to instil its hypotheical meaning. Students practise controlled and freer practice exercises ending in a roleplay.

Vocabulary

bring and take, come and go

Bring and *come, take* and *go* follow a similar pattern – the first pair meaning *here, to me*, and the second pair meaning *away, to someone else*. The section uses a guided discovery approach to introduce the meanings, then students use them to complete a set of gapped dialogues. In the *Words that go together* section, students learn some common collocations with the four words, then use them in their own sentences.

Everyday English

Thank you and goodbye!

This section provides a nice way to wrap up the course with expressions for saying thank you and goodbye. Students complete gapped conversations of everyday phrases. They then learn one which they act out for the class.

Additional material

Workbook

Students complete a text using the First Conditional and practise making questions. There is a task on the Second Conditional on someone's dreams and aspirations. Students continue working on discriminating where to use First and Second Conditionals, and *might*. The focus moves to the difference between sentences using *if* and *when*. The vocabulary task is on phrases which use *bring* and *take*, and *come* and *go*, and there is an exercise on prepositions. Everyday English focuses on saying thank you and goodbye.

The third and last *Stop and check* progress test completes the Workbook.

Photocopiable activities

There are photocopiable activities to review grammar (*Would you do the same?*), vocabulary (*Draw it, act it!*), and communication (*Thank you and goodbye*) at the back of the Teacher's Guide as well as on the Teacher's Resource Centre. There is also a worksheet to accompany the video on the Teacher's Resource Centre.

Notes on the unit

Unit opener page

Choose from these activities to engage your students with the topic and target language of this unit.

- Talk about the title
- Talk about the unit goals (*Grammar*, *Vocabulary*, …)
- Talk about the photo
- Watch the video
- Look at the bottom banner
- Do the activity

Refer students to the photo on p119 and ask them to say what it shows. Some words that may come up include: *stargazing/ sunrise/sunset/Milky Way/light pollution*. Find out if students like to look at the sky – do they prefer the sky at night or in the daytime (e.g. with big, white fluffy clouds)? Elicit other things you might see in the sky (stars, planets, constellations /ˌkɒnstəˈleɪʃnz/, sun, moon, satellites, meteors /ˈmiːtɪə(r)z/, falling stars, planes, hot air balloons, UFOs, etc.).

Ask students to think about how the title of the unit relates to the photo. Elicit an ending to the sentence, e.g. *You never know, one day the sky might fall. You never know, one day you might live on Mars.* Put students in pairs to write an ending. Pairs share their sentences with the class.

Video (2 minutes approximately): The video gives a step-by-step overview of the unit. Play the video, pausing where necessary – especially for students to answer any questions, e.g. *What would you do if you won the lottery?* This makes it a more interactive experience. Highlight the option of practising online.

As shown in the bottom banner, don't forget that there are many exercises to consolidate and practise the target language of the unit in the Workbook as well as online. There are links to these exercises on the relevant pages of the Student's Book and they can be done in class time or you can set them for homework.

Summary: If you're short of time, use the title and the photo to help students understand and engage with the topic, and then move straight on to the activity so that they can discuss the theme in more detail. If you have any more time, try to watch the video together. It is a clear and interesting introduction to the different parts of the unit.

Notes for activity:
Put students in pairs. Ask them to look at the photo and discuss their answers to the questions. Ask them to justify their choices where possible.

> **Suggested answers**
> 1 In a field, or in the countryside. He is looking at the sky.
> 2 Students' own answers.
> 3 He might feel calm and relaxed. There is nobody else around and so he might be enjoying the peace and quiet.

Grammar SB p120

First Conditional: *if + will/might*

> **Possible problems**
> **First Conditional**
> 1 Although most students find the meaning of First Conditional fairly easy to understand, they often have difficulty with the form. The problem seems to be that there are two clauses to get right – *will* is used in the result clause, but is not used in the condition clause, even though it too often refers to future time. In many languages, a future form is used in both clauses.
> Common mistakes:
> **If it will rain, we'll stay at home.*
> **If it rains, we stay at home.*
>   (Correction: *If it rains, we'll stay at home.*)
> 2 This section also contains examples of time clauses with *when*. This presents the same problems as in the First Conditional, i.e. a future verb form is not used in the time clause, even though it might refer to future time.
> Common mistakes:
> **When I will arrive, I'll phone you.*
> **When I arrive, I phone you.*
>   (Correction: *When I arrive, I'll phone you.*)
> 3 Speakers of Germanic languages confuse *when* and *if*, as they are translated by the same word.
> **I'll meet you there when I finish before 6.00.*
>   (Correction: *I'll meet you there if I finish before 6.00.*)
> **If I get home, I'll have a shower.*
>   (Correction: *When I get home, I'll have a shower.*)
>
> **Second Conditional**
> There may be confusion with meaning and form here. This may be due to the use of the past tense in the secondary clause which students can confuse for past instead of unreal meaning. Some confusion over the use of the subjunctive *were* with *I may* occur: *If I were you, I'd …* . There are very few cases where the subjunctive verb form differs from the past indicative form in English, so you might want to teach *I were …* as a fixed phrase. Students may hear *If I was you …* , and this form is fine in everyday speech.
> Common mistakes:
> **If I would have more time, I would play tennis.*
>   (Correction: *If I had more time, I would play tennis.*)
>
> **might**
> The use of *might* is very common in English, but tends to be avoided by learners of English, who often prefer to use *maybe/perhaps + will* to express lack of certainty about the future, e.g.:
> - *Maybe she will come.*
> - *Perhaps I will play tennis this afternoon.*
>
> These are not incorrect, but it sounds much more natural to say:
> - *She might come.*
> - *I might play tennis this afternoon.*

> **STARTER** SB p120
>
> The aim of the *Starter* section is to lead in to the presentation of the First Conditional in a context that students are familiar with. Start by telling the students what you might do at the weekend, using the examples in the *Starter* as a guide. If there is a holiday coming up, talk about what you might do then. Be sure to include *It depends on …* so that students get the idea that you aren't sure. Put students in small groups to talk about possible plans for the upcoming weekend. Ask a few students to share their plans with the class. Find out what the plans depend on.

It all depends …

1 🔊 **12.1** Give students a moment to read the instructions and questions. Play the recording so that students can

answer the questions. Check the answers, then play the recording again for students to complete the conversation. Check as a class by asking two confident students to read the conversation with the answers. Play the recording again so that students can focus on the stress, rhythm and intonation. Pause so they can repeat, with particular focus on question intonation, stress on the word *think*, and pronunciation of *I'll*.

Answers
1 He's not sure.
2 She will if it doesn't rain, but she won't if it does rain.

Answers and audioscript
12.1 It all depends
H = Holly   L = Lewis
H What are you doing this weekend?
L Er, I think my brother's coming home from university for the weekend, but he's not sure. If he **comes**, I'll go to the football with him on Saturday. If he doesn't come, I'll probably **play** video games with Oliver at his house. What about you?
H It depends on the weather. If it's nice on Sunday, I **might** go to my uncle's with my parents. He's having a barbecue. But I **won't** go if it rains – I might just stay at home. I don't like typical English barbecues – with umbrellas!
L Yeah, I know what you mean!

GRAMMAR SPOT SB p120
This *Grammar spot* uses a guided discovery approach to help students:
- understand the form of First Conditional sentences
- understand the difference in the use of *might* or *will* in First Conditional

1 Read the first part of the *Grammar spot* together. Ask students to identify the verb tense in the first and second parts of the sentences. Ask them which sentence needs a comma. Elicit the rule and write it on the board:
If + Present Simple, *will* + infinitive without *to*
will + infinitive without *to* + *if* + Present Simple
Elicit one example sentence for each and write it on the board.
Refer students to Grammar reference 12.1–12.2 on p152.
Refer students back to the sentences in the *Grammar spot*. Ask students how likely it is that these things will happen.

Answers
Present Simple comes after *if*. The other verb form is *will* + infinitive.
It's fairly likely that these things will happen.

2 Read the examples together. Check students understand *might*. Ask *What's another word for* might? (*maybe, perhaps, may, could, possibly*)

Answers
In the first sentence the speaker is surer.

2 **12.2** This exercise is an accuracy exercise which focuses on First Conditional sentences and good stress, rhythm and intonation in asking and responding to the question. Weaker students may feel more confident if they write out the sentences before having the conversations.

You could also get them to think about which words are stressed in the sentences. Say the first sentence together so that students notice the stressed words and rhythm: *If the WEATHER's GOOD, I'll GO to the BEACH*. Drill the stress and intonation for the question. Give them some time to think about or write the sentences using the prompts, then ask them to roleplay the conversations, swapping roles so that each has the opportunity to ask and answer. Play the recording. Go through each of the prompts and elicit full sentences as a class. Allow for options, e.g. *If the weather's good I'll go/I might/I'll probably go to the beach*.

Answers and audioscript
12.2 What are you doing this weekend?
1 What are you doing this weekend?
   If the weather's good, I'll go to the beach.
2 What are you doing this weekend?
   If I have time, I'll meet friends for coffee.
3 What are you doing this weekend?
   If it doesn't rain, I'll do some gardening.
4 What are you doing this weekend?
   If it rains, I won't go out. I'll stay in and watch TV.
5 What are you doing this weekend?
   If I don't have any work to do, I'll spend a day in London.
6 What are you doing this weekend?
   If there's a good film on, I'll go to the cinema.

3 Ask students to think about the conversations they had at the beginning of the lesson. Refer students to the examples in the speech bubbles. Put students in small groups with people they didn't work with before. They discuss their plans using *will* and *might*.

Practice SB p121
1 **12.3** This section focuses on *might* for expressing uncertainty and reviews *going to* for future plans. Read the instructions as a class. Play the recording. Answer the two questions in a whole-class discussion.

Answers
She's sure that she's going to go to university and she's going to have a gap year. She's going to travel in South America. She's going to look for work while she's travelling.
She isn't sure which university she's going to go to and she isn't sure what kind of job she'll do.

12.3 Holly's plans
H = Holly   L = Lewis
L Have you decided which university you're going to yet?
H Mmm, I'm still not sure. I might go to Liverpool, or I might go to Manchester. I'm definitely going to have a gap year though. I need a break from studying.
L Great! What are you going to do?
H I'm going to travel round South America.
L Sounds great! Is that just travelling, or working?
H I'd like to just travel, but I'm going to look for work, because I'll need the money! I might get a job picking fruit, or I might teach English somewhere.

2 Students need to remember Holly's plans in order to do this exercise, so you may want to play the recording once again before they start. Allow students to refer to the audioscript on p140 if needed. Put students in pairs to complete the exercise. Check as a class, eliciting the full sentence.

Unit 12 • You never know …   157

> **Answers**
> She might go to Liverpool University or she might go to Manchester University.
> She's definitely going to have a gap year.
> She's going to travel round South America.
> She's going to look for work.
> She might get a job fruit picking.
> She might teach English somewhere.

3 🔊 **12.4** In this exercise, students use First Conditional to give advice to Lewis. Students work in groups of three. They take it in turns to play the role of Lewis, Student A, and Student B. Look at the first sentence together. Ask a student to be Student A and choose a confident student to be Student B. Read Lewis' part. Student A looks at the prompt and example, and responds. Student B looks at the prompt and sentence frame, and responds. Put students in groups of three. Ask them to decide who is Lewis, who is Student A, and who is Student B. Check they understand they should swap roles for each sentence. Weaker students may need to write out the sentences before trying to do the roleplay. In this case, ask the whole class to write out the sentences using the prompts, then put them in groups of three to do the conversations.

> **Answers and audioscript**
> 🔊 **12.4 Giving advice**
> 1 L I can't decide what to study at university, French or economics.
>   A **If you study French, you'll have to spend a year in France!**
>   B **If you study economics, it might be more useful in life.**
> 2 L I'm not sure where to go, Bristol or Edinburgh.
>   A **If you go to Bristol, you'll be nearer home.**
>   B **If you go to Edinburgh, it'll be a new experience!**
> 3 L I don't know whether to live on campus, or in the city.
>   A **You'll get to know more people if you live on campus.**
>   B **You might learn more about real life if you live in the city.**
> 4 L I don't know whether to get a part-time job or take out a big loan.
>   A **If you get a part-time job, you'll have less time to study.**
>   B **If you take out a big loan, it might take a long time to pay it back.**
> 5 L I'm wondering whether to start next year or have a gap year.
>   A **You won't forget what you've learned at school if you start next year**
>   B **You'll have a wonderful break from studying if you have a gap year.**

4 This exercise pulls together First Condicionals, *might*, and *will* for degrees of likelihood. Put students in pairs to complete the exercise. Note that *I might tell*, in sentence 1 is possible, though less likely, and sounds like a threat. You could discuss this point and give an example context where *might* would work, e.g.:

   A *What are you going to do?*
   B *If I see Jack, I might tell him I saw you.*
   A *No! Don't do that! He doesn't know I'm in town.*

If students are struggling with this exercise, remind them which part of the sentence contains the Present Simple and which part contains the *will* or *might* + infinitive without *to*, or refer them to the Grammar reference. Check as a class. Ask for full-sentence responses.

> **Answers**
> 1 I'll tell   5 I get
> 2 I have   6 I won't say
> 3 I might go   7 you fall
> 4 I'll collect   8 I'll decide

Advice, warnings, offers, threats

5 This exercise shows students four more contexts for when First Conditionals are used. Check that students understand the terms *warnings* and *threats*, and elicit an example of each. Students complete the sentences with the verbs in brackets. They compare answers in pairs before checking as a class. Ask students to think of a response to each sentence, then roleplay the situations in pairs. As an extension, ask pairs to write four more mini conversations, one each for advice, warning, offer, and threat in the First Conditional. They can act these out for the class or to another pair. You could also collect these mini conversations for checking.

> **Answers**
> 1 do, 'll feel (advice)
> 2 eat, 'll be (warning)
> 3 don't have, 'll lend (offer)
> 4 don't stop, 'll send (threat)

EXTENSION Tell students to work in pairs and come up with *if* sentences for advice, warnings, offers, and threats, e.g.:

- advice: for passing exams, for someone who is going to live abroad, for someone who is starting a new job
- warning: for someone who drives too fast, for someone who often forgets to lock their door, for children playing near the road
- offer: to drive someone going to the train station (give someone a lift), to cook dinner for someone, to help someone with a maths problem
- threat: boss to employee who often comes to work late, parent to child who won't stop playing video games, sister who has an exam to teenage brother who is listening to very loud music

But what if? SB p122

Second Conditional: *if* + *would*

Possible problems

1 There may be confusion with meaning and form here. This may be due to the use of the past tense in the secondary clause, e.g. the *if*-clause, which students can confuse for past instead of unreal meaning. The use of a past tense in the *if*–clause to express an unreal present or improbable future often seems strange to students, especially as in many languages unreality is expressed by separate subjunctive verb forms.
2 In fact, English once used subjunctive, but it has largely disappeared. It does, however, still exist in the use of *were* in all persons of the verb *to be* in the Second Conditional:
   - *If I were you, I'd ….*
   - *If he were here, he'd ….*
   - *If she were rich, she'd ….*
   This use of the subjunctive is becoming less common nowadays, and it is now common to hear *If I was you …* , etc. in everyday speech.

Common mistakes:
*If I would have more time, I would play tennis.
(Correction: If I had more time, I would play tennis.)
3 The contraction of would to 'd can also be a problem, not only in terms of pronunciation, but also because 'd can also be a contraction for the auxiliary had.

1 🔊 12.5 As a lead-in to the topic, you might play a game of What would you do if … ? Think of a few hypothetical situations, e.g. you discovered buried gold in your back garden; you found a wallet belonging to Donald Trump; you had superpowers; your mother was an alien, etc. Ask students What would you do if … ? Tell them what you would do so that students have a model, and elicit responses. Keep it light and fun. The idea is that students are responding with I would … ./I'd … . without thinking about the grammar. Refer students to the photo and ask them how old they think the men are. Read the questions as a class, then play the recording. Check answers. Make sure students understand the context well – for Robert, he feels that there is a real possibility he will lose his job. His company is not doing well. For Scott, it's unlikely. This distinction is important in understanding the difference between First and Second Conditionals.

Answers
Robert is worried because he might lose his job – his company are losing money and making a lot of cuts.
Scott isn't worried about his job because his company is doing really well.
Robert can't get a job with Scott's company because he's not in sales.

🔊 **12.5 Why is Robert worried?**
S = Scott   R = Robert
S Hi, Robert! How's it going?
R Not good, Scott. My company's losing money, and they're making a lot of cuts.
S Oh, no! Is your job safe?
R No, not at all. I'm really worried. If I lose my job, what will I do?
S Well, it's not always the end of the world, you know.
R Oh, easy for you to say – your company's doing really well. But what if it were you? If you lost your job, what would you do?
S Well, that's very unlikely – we're looking for new people at the moment! But if it happened, …, I'd start my own business.
R Mmm. I can't do that. It's a shame – if I were in sales, your company would probably give me a job.
S Oh they would, for sure! If I were you, I'd retrain!

2 🔊 12.5 Play the recording again so that students can complete the sentences. Ask students what the difference in meaning is between sentence 1 and 2, 3, 4. (Robert is likely to lose his job, so he uses will. He asks Scott what he would do, but it's not a real situation/it's an improbable condition.) Tell students that this is called the Second Conditional and it's used when the situation is unreal. Draw students' attention to the short form I'd. Write I would → I'd on the board. Drill pronunciation of each.

Answers
1 lose, will
2 lost, would, do
3 happened, 'd start
4 were, 'd

GRAMMAR SPOT SB p122
1 This Grammar spot introduces Second Conditional in a guided discovery approach. Students notice the forms and work out the rules. Read number 1 together and answer as a class.

Answers
Past Simple, would + infinitive

2 Read number 2 to the students. Ask them if they have heard sentences with I were/I was. Explain that most people use If I/he/she were, … but that many people also say If I/ he/ she was … . Were is still the preferred word in writing.

3 Check that students understand the difference in the two sentences. Ask Which sentence is asking about an unreal/improbable situation? (question 2)

Answer
The first sentence is more likely to happen than the second sentence

Tell students to read Grammar reference 12.3 on p152.

3 🔊 12.6 Refer students to the photos. How old is the boy? What do you think his dream is? What about the woman? What is her dream? Play the recording so that students can complete the texts. After listening, see how close the students were in their predictions. Ask students if they could hear the 'd. Play the recording again so students can fill in any spaces missed and also focus on the 'd sound. When checking answers, check understanding of lie-in and point out that instead of would, Charlie uses could. Just as in First Conditional, it's possible to substitute might for will, in Second Conditional it's possible to substitute could for would.

Answers and audioscript
🔊 **12.6**
Charlie's dream
I'd like to be bigger. I play rugby, and if I **were** bigger and stronger, and **I'd be** in the first team. And if I **played** really well, I **might be** captain. And then if I **trained** really hard, maybe one day I **could play** for England, and I **would take** my dad to meet the team. He **would be** so proud of me!
Jessica's dream
I love my kids, but I'd really like to have more time to myself. If I **had** a weekend without kids, I**'d have** a long lie-in. If there **was** a good film on, I**'d go** to the cinema in the afternoon, with a friend. On Sunday, if the weather **was** nice, I**'d have** a nice long walk somewhere, maybe on my own. Heaven!

4 In this exercise students focus on what is real and what is unreal. Do the first one together as an example. Ensure students understand that Charlie's dream is unreal because he isn't big and strong (yet!). Put students in pairs to discuss Jessica. As an extension, ask students if they have any advice for Charlie and for Jessica – this will revise using should/shouldn't for giving advice from Unit 8.

Answers
Charlie isn't big and strong, if he were bigger and stronger he'd be in the first team at rugby. If he played really well, he'd be captain. Then if he practised really hard, maybe one day he could play for England. His dad would be so proud of him.
Jessica doesn't have any time to herself. If she had a weekend without kids, she'd have a long lie-in. If there was a good film on, she'd go to the cinema in the evening with a friend. On Sunday, if the weather was nice, she'd have a nice long walk somewhere, maybe on her own.

Talking about you

5 Students work alone to write down three dreams, using the sentence frames in the examples. Put them in groups of three or four to share their dreams. Do any students share the same dreams? Ask students if they have any advice to give each other to make their dreams come true. Elicit some dreams and advice in whole-class feedback.

Practice SB p123

1 This exercise gets students practising positive and negative Second Conditionals in a controlled way. Put students in pairs. They take turns making sentences orally with phrases from the chart. As an extension, ask them to make some negative sentences, and try to say a bit more, e.g. *I wouldn't live in Paris if I were French. I'd live in Nice. If I were you, I wouldn't stop working. I'd wait until I found another job first.*

> **Possible answers**
> If I were French, I'd live in Paris.
> If I had the time, I'd help you.
> If I knew the answer, I'd tell you.
> If I didn't know the time, I'd ask someone.

2 Read the instructions together. Students look at the likelihood of each sentence as expressed as a percentage in brackets at the end of the sentence. Complete the first sentence together as an example. When checking answers as a class, ask students if there is a low or high probability.

> **Answers**
> 1 won, I'd give
> 2 go, will
> 3 had, would
> 4 would, lived
> 5 'll, is
> 6 stole, wouldn't
> 7 doesn't rain, we'll
> 8 Wouldn't, had

3 🔊 **12.7** Refer students to the photo of Dan. Tell them he needs to make some lifestyle changes – elicit ideas for what those changes might be (e.g. eat more healthily, exercise more, etc.) Read the instructions and questions to the students. Play the recording and ask students for their answers to the questions as a class. Tell the class that Dan makes a lot of *excuses* – reasons for why he won't change. Play the recording again so that students can note down his excuses. Elicit these in feedback and write them on the board for students to refer to in the roleplay in exercise 4.

> **Answers**
> No, he doesn't want to change and he probably won't.

🔊 **12.7 Dan**
The doctor says I need to do more exercise. I hate doing exercise.
And I'm not interested in cycling to work – I like driving.
I can't drink less coffee. I need ten cups a day.
I don't want to eat less junk food. I like junk food.
I can't cook, and I don't want to learn.
Why should I watch less TV? It's my only hobby!
I like going to bed really late.
I am not going to meditate! It's really boring!

---

4 Give students a few minutes to write sentences from the prompts. Check as a class. Put students into pairs to roleplay the conversation, using the excuses on the board from exercise 3. Students take it in turn to be Dan. Do the first as an example:

Student A *I hate exercising!*
Student B *But Dan, if you did more exercise, you'd feel great!*

> **Answers**
> 1 If you did more exercise, you'd feel great.
> 2 If you cycled to work, you'd get fit, and get there quicker! If you didn't drive to work, you would save money on petrol.
> 3 If you drank less coffee, you wouldn't have so many headaches.
> 4 If you ate less junk food, you'd have more energy.
> 5 If you learned to cook, you'd eat more fresh food.
> 6 If you didn't watch so much TV, you'd find some new hobbies.
> 7 If you didn't go to bed so late, you wouldn't feel so tired in the morning.
> 8 If you meditated, you wouldn't feel so stressed.

SUGGESTION As a way to wrap up First and Second Conditionals, look online for songs which contain First and Second Conditionals (e.g. *A Little Help from my Friends* by The Beatles, *If I could Turn Back Time* by Cher, *I'll be There* by The Jackson 5, *If I had a Million Dollars* by the Barenaked Ladies). Create a worksheet with the lyrics, leaving a few gaps for students to fill in. Play the song for them to complete, then play it for them to sing!

Additional material
For teachers
Photocopiable activity – Grammar: *Would you do the same?* pp234–5
For students
Online Practice – *Look again*
Workbook pp76–9, exercises 1–14
Online Practice – *Practice*

Listening and speaking SB p123

At a crossroads in life

About the text

This skills section carries through the theme of wondering about the future with a focus on three people who are at a crossroads in their life. This also gives the opportunity of further practice of the Second Conditional and *might*.

The section opens with a brief task on what it means to be at a crossroads in life. Students then listen to three people, Jamie, Sylvia, and Donna, talking about their lives and answering specific questions. The second listening task tests understanding of the main idea, with three short monologues, given by Jamie, Sylvia, and Donna a year later. Fluency practice comes in the form of a discussion activity on a range of dilemmas. Some of the vocabulary is new, so be prepared to pre-teach/check the following items, especially with lower-level classes: *band, pub, to sell out, gigs* (=a live performance by musicians), *make money from downloads, to drop out of university, to go crazy* (= to be very angry about something), *most senior person, retire, partner in a law firm, the clock is ticking fast* (= time is running out to have the chance to have a baby), *to regret something, to get a flat, granny flat* (= part of a house that is made into a living space for an elderly relative).

1 Ask students what they think the expression means. Explain what the literal meaning of a *crossroads* is (= where two roads cross each other). Ask them what you usually have to do when you get to a crossroads (make a decision). See if they can guess what it means *to be at a crossroads in one's life*. Elicit some examples.

Answer
A crossroads is literally where two roads cross each other. A crossroads in life is a time when you must choose which direction to take in life. Examples include choosing which university to go to after school, getting a first job, choosing who to marry, moving house, changing career, having children, deciding what to do when you retire.

2 🔊 **12.8** Refer students to the photos of Jamie, Sylvia, and Donna. Ask them to predict what the crossroads are that each are facing. Use this as an opportunity to work in some of the key vocabulary from the listening. Tell students to listen to the big decisions each person needs to make. Play the recording. Allow students to discuss in pairs. Check any vocabulary difficulties and play the recording again if needed.

Answers
Jamie has to decide whether to continue his studies, or leave university to focus on his band.
Sylvia has to decide whether to have a baby or to push forward in her career and become a partner at her law firm.
Donna has to decide whether to sell her house and then whether to move into her own flat or move in with her daughter.

🔊 12.8 At a crossroads in life
Jamie
I'm in my second year at university. I'm doing Physics, and I like my course. But the thing is, I sing and play guitar, and I joined a local band in my first year. The other band members aren't students – I met one of them in a pub. And, I love playing in the band – I'm discovering I'm more of a musician than I thought I was, and … well, we're actually pretty good, and our last few concerts sold out completely. So, the other guys want to give up their jobs and try to make a living from it. It might not be much of a living, but if we were prepared to go on the road and travel, we'd get plenty of gigs in pubs and local halls. And if we recorded some of our songs, we could put them online and make some money from downloads. But obviously, I'd have to drop out of university, and … my parents would go crazy! I don't know how easy it would be to get back onto a course later, so … it feels like it would be a stupid thing to do really.

Sylvia
I'm a lawyer, and I've been with the same law firm for 11 years now. It's difficult work sometimes, but I love it, and I'm doing very well. Although I'm only 37, I'm one of the most senior people here. I know that if I continue in this job, when a certain person retires next year, I'll probably become one of the partners in the firm. That would be amazing. But … well, I've never been sure whether I really want to have children – it's never seemed the most important thing to me. That's probably because it would mean giving up work for a year or two – I wouldn't want to go back to work too soon and try and do this job, and deal with a baby. But now that the clock is ticking fast, it's time to make a final decision. If I left now to have a baby, I don't think I'd get the partnership in the firm. I think they'd give it to someone else next year. But if I decided not to have children, I wonder if I'd really regret it later.

Donna
My husband died three years ago. He'd been very ill for a long time, so it wasn't a shock, but it hasn't been easy. We were married for 41 years. I couldn't imagine life without him when it happened, but … here I am, and I need to decide what to do with my life now. I'm thinking of selling this house. It's nice that it's full of nice memories of our lives together, but I wouldn't lose those memories if I moved out. It's way too big for me really, and I think I'll feel happier and more relaxed if I live somewhere smaller. If I get a flat in the right area, in town, there'll be lots of people around, and I'd like that. But, my daughter really wants me to go and live with them – she says she could make part of their house a 'granny flat'. It's kind of them, and I love being around my grandchildren, but, oh, granny flat! That sounds so horrible! I'm still young – I'm only 68! And if I lived with them, I wouldn't feel independent any more.

3 Give students a few minutes to answer the questions in pairs. Play the recording again if needed. Ask fast finishers to compare their answers with another pair.

Answers
1 That he's more of a musician than he thought he was.
2 They could put them online and make money out of downloads.
3 He doesn't know how easy it would be to get back onto a course later.
4 She's experienced, is doing very well, and someone is retiring next year.
5 She's never been sure if she really wants them.
6 She wouldn't want to go back to work too soon and try to do the job as well as dealing with a baby.
7 Because he'd been ill for a very long time.
8 Happier and more relaxed.
9 She wouldn't feel independent any more.

What do you think?

4 The aim of this exercise is to get students using the Second Conditional and *might*. Give students a few minutes to read the instructions and think of what to say. If needed, do a couple of examples together on the board, e.g. *If I were Jamie, I'd stay in school. If he stopped, he might not make any money in the future. I'd keep working if I were Sylvia. She might lose her opportunity*. You might introduce the expression, *If I were in his/her shoes …* (= *If I were him/her …*). Put students in pairs to say what they would do and what the consequences might be. Monitor and check for accurate use of Second Conditional. In class feedback, elicit a range of advice from the students.

5 🔊 **12.9** Tell students they are going to hear each person talking about what they decided to do one year later. Play the recording. As a class, elicit a summary of what each person did. Ask students if they think they made the best decision.

🔊 12.9 What happened next?
Jamie
Well, I surprised myself! The scientist in me told me to continue with my course, but, the artist in me suddenly felt stronger, so I dropped out! I know I'll be able to get back onto a course somehow if I change my mind, and I felt I'd really regret it if I didn't try this weird and wonderful life I'm living. We're doing OK, just. And who knows, if we start selling a lot more downloads, we might make the big time!

Sylvia
It was an easy decision in the end. Nature is clever, and I started having really strong feelings about wanting to have a baby! I don't know how I'd live without little Oscar now – he's gorgeous! They've been great at work – they gave the partnership to someone else, but they say there'll be another one coming up in a few years, and I'll be first in line for that one.

Donna
I sold the house and decided to buy a flat. It's not in town, but it's not far away, so I can easily go there if I feel like I need to be among people. And it's not very far from my daughter's either, so she's

Unit 12 · You never know … 161

happy that I'm close. She often comes round and brings the children to visit me. And I go to theirs for dinner a couple of times a week, but I still feel very independent.

6 Elicit from students how they might ask for advice using the Second Conditional (*What would you do if you were me?/What should I do?*). Put students in groups of three or four for the discussion. If students are not at a crossroads or don't know anyone who is, suggest they think about crossroads they or someone they know were at in the past. As an alternative, ask them to think about or even take on the persona of someone else – a fictional character or someone in the public eye. What would they do in their situation? What advice would they give?

Additional material

For students

Online Practice – *Practice*

Reading and speaking SB p124

Risk and chance

About the text

The text aims to clarify issues around risk, probability, and coincidence, and provides a good example of the importance of critical thinking when reading the news. It starts with a discussion of risk as related to probability. Risk is the possibility of something bad happening. Probability is the likelihood of something (good or bad) happening. The article says that in order to understand how risky something actually is (not just perceived danger), we need to understand how probable it is that it will happen. The article goes on to show that statistics reported in news articles may not give enough factual information to be of serious consideration and that correlation does not imply causation (just because two things appear to be connected doesn't mean they are). Coincidences can be explained by calculating probability, and probability tells us that there is an equal chance that something will or won't occur – as illustrated in the case of a coin flip. Probability is related to statistics – statistics often uses probability distributions in its analysis. Statistics is notoriously deceptive. As Mark Twain, American writer and humorist once famously said, *There are three kinds of lies: lies, damned lies, and statistics.*

1 As a lead-in to the topic, tell students that you are going to toss a coin. If it lands on heads, they will have a test tomorrow. If it lands on tails, they won't. Ask *Do you want to take the chance?* Discuss the *risk* as a class and elicit *chance* and *possibility*. Now say you are going to put 99 pink balls and one white ball into a bag. If you pull out the white one, there will be a test, but if you pull out a pink one, there won't be. Ask the class if they would accept this *risk*. Again, discuss in terms of *chance* and *probability*. Tell them they are going to learn more about risk, chance, and probability. Find out if there are any mathematicians in the classroom – they can be your resident experts! Ask students to look at the photos in the text. Ask *What do the photos have to do with chance, possibility, and risk?* Elicit a range of responses. Refer students to the questions in the exercise. Check to see if there are any vocabulary questions before putting them in pairs to discuss and answer the questions. In whole-class feedback, see if students can agree on a ranking for question **A** and write it on the board. What chances did they choose for questions **B** and **C**? Discuss reasons as a class.

2 This is a scanning exercise – the aim is for students to scan the article quickly to find which questions in exercise 1 are answered in the text, and what each of the listed numbers refers to. You might want to set a timer for this – three minutes to start and then if students need more, a further minute. Reassure them that they will have time to read the article more carefully in the next exercise. Check answers as a class and refer students to p157 to find the correct ranking for the things in question 1. Compare it to the ranking they did earlier. How similar are they? Review how to say large numbers and percentages if needed.

Answers

Questions B and C are answered – the chance of landing on either heads or tails in a coin toss is always 50%; there is a 95% chance of two people having the same birthday if there are 48 people in a room. Part of question A is answered – both accident deaths occur every day in the US, and shark attack deaths happen once a year in the US.
1 in 5,000 refers to the chances of dying in a car crash.
1 in 300,000 refers to the chances of being killed by lightning.
1 in a million refers to the chances of a coin landing on heads 20 times in a row.

3 Give students time to read the article again to decide if the statements are true or false, and to correct the false ones. At this point, don't worry too much about the highlighted vocabulary – tell students they will look at that in the next exercise. Allow them to discuss their answers in pairs or small groups before checking as a class. If you have any mathematicians in the group, ask them what they think about probability and coincidence. Ask students if they were surprised by any of the information.

Answers

1 ✗ 1,600 people died as a result of driving rather than flying after the 9/11 plane attacks.
2 ✓
3 ✗ Americans should worry more about having baths.
4 ✓
5 ✗ A 100% increase in risk is not always a big problem – not if the risk was very small in the first place.
6 ✗ Friday 13th is no more dangerous than any other day.
7 ✓
8 ✗ There's a 95% chance of someone with the same birthday as you being in a group of 48 people.

Vocabulary

4 This exercise focuses on the highlighted vocabulary in the text, which students may have been able to guess from context. Tell them to work in pairs to find the words in the text to match to the definitions. Check answers and pronunciation as a class. Difficult words may include: *average* /ˈævərɪdʒ/, *gambler* /ˈɡæmblə(r)/, *confuse* /kənˈfjuːz/, *coincidence* /kəʊˈɪnsɪdəns/. As a way to practise the vocabulary further, see if students can write a paragraph in pairs that includes all or most of the vocabulary. In the next class, put students in pairs to revise the vocabulary together. One student reads a definition, and the other says the word. They swap roles and repeat.

Answers

1 in a row	6 gambler
2 doubled	7 flip
3 lack of	8 coincidence
4 risky	9 on average
5 logical	10 confuse

What do you think?

There are a number of interesting questions in this section for discussion, and the focus is on fluency rather than accuracy. Give students a few minutes to read the questions and coincidences, and think about what they want to say about them. Put students in groups of three or four for the discussion. Appoint a discussion leader. Monitor and prompt groups as needed. Once students have finished, elicit responses in a class discussion.

VIDEO In this unit students can watch a video where people describe how their life would be different if they had more free time, more money, or if they could do any job in the world. You can play the video clip on the Classroom Presentation Tool or download it from the Teacher's Resource Centre together with the video script, video worksheet, and accompanying teacher's notes. These notes give full guidance on how to use the worksheets and include a comprehensive answer key to the exercises and activities.

Additional material
For teachers
Photocopiable activity – Video worksheet: *What if … ?*
For students
Online Practice – *Look again*
Online Practice – *Practice*

Vocabulary and speaking SB p126

bring and *take*, *come* and *go*

The choice of *bring/take* or *come/go* often depends on where the speaker is. We use *bring* and *come* for movement to the place where the speaker is. *Please bring me a coffee. Maria, can you come here, please?* We use *take* and *go* for movement away from the place where the speaker is. *Take out the rubbish, please. I'm going on holiday to Spain.*

1 Ask students to look at the examples and decide which mean *here to me* or *away, to someone else*. See if students can explain their choices.

Answers
Here, to me = come, bring
Away, to someone else = take, go

2 The aim of this exercise is to contextualize the four verbs so that students perceive them in the rigth context. Put students in pairs. Tell them to underline the verbs, then ask and answer the questions with a partner.

Answers
1 come
2 bring
3 go
4 take
5 come, bring

3 Refer students to the picture. Discuss the difference in verb choice between the two speakers. Note that both speakers are in Britain. One is going away to France from Britian, and the other has travelled from France to Britain. Check that students understand that in the first context, the person is referring to France – *away, to somewhere else*. In the second, the person is in Britain, so the meaning is *here, to me*. Ensure students understand that the choice of verb depends on the *context*, not grammar.

4 **12.10** This exercise requires that students understand the context of the conversations. Tell students to read the conversations, then put the verbs in the correct form in the gaps. They compare answers in pairs. Play the recording to check. Check comprehension of *boomerang* /ˈbuːməræŋ/, *to toast* (to drink to someone's health), *Guinness* /ˈgɪnɪs/ (a stout beer which originated in Dublin, Ireland). Put students in pairs to read the conversations together.

Answers and audioscript

12.10 *Bring* and *take*, *come* and *go*

1 A Bye everyone! I'm **going** on holiday tomorrow.
  B Where are you **going**?
  A Australia. I'm **taking** my kids to meet their cousins in Sydney.
  B Lucky you! When you **come** back, will you **bring** me a boomerang?

2 A OK class, it's nearly time to **go** home. Don't forget to **bring** your money for the school trip tomorrow. We're **going** to the Natural History Museum.
  B Oh, Miss Jones, can't you **take** us somewhere more exciting?

3 A Jake, you were very late last night. What time did you **come** home?
  B It was before midnight, Mum, honest! Ryan **brought** me home in his car.

4 A I've got a new flat. You must **come** and visit soon. And **bring** Emma and Dan with you. I'll cook you a meal.
  B Great! We'll **bring** some champagne to toast your new home!

5 A I'm **going** to Ireland tomorrow. Deirdre's **coming** round this evening – she's **bringing** a present she wants me to **take** to her sister in Dublin.
  B Have a good trip! **Bring** me a bottle of Guinness back!

Words that go together

5 **12.11** The aim of this exercise is to introduce common collocations with *bring*, *take*, *come*, and *go*. Tell students to match the pairs of expressions with one of the verbs. Explain that *takeaway food* is food that you take away from the restaurant to eat at home. It is commonly used as a noun: *Let's get a take-away tonight. I don't feel like cooking.* Check *to go crazy* (= to become very angry or upset – *My parents will go crazy if they find out.*; to become bored or impatient – *If I have to do any more homework, I'll go crazy.*; to become very excited – *The fans went crazy when their team scored.*), *to come first/last* (= to be the most important/least important thing – *My family comes first before work./ Work should come last in my opinion.*; to win a competition – *He came first/last in the race.*), *to come true* (= something that you dream of really happens).

Unit 12 • You never know … 163

Answers
1 take
2 bring
3 go
4 come

🔊 12.11 Words that go together
1 I usually order a takeaway on Friday evenings – I like the ones from my local Indian restaurant.
2 I had to take the jumper I bought back to the shop because it had a hole in it.
3 I sing in a choir, and I think music is a great way to bring people together.
4 I don't know if it's possible to bring peace to the world – some people seem to love fighting.
5 Colin went a bit crazy when his girlfriend left him.
6 I find it difficult to go to sleep if the room isn't completely dark.
7 I always came last in sports competitions at school.
8 When we took little Marc to Disneyland he thought his dreams had come true!

Additional material

For teachers
Photocopiable activity – Vocabulary: *Draw it, act it!* pp236–7

For students
Online Practice – *Look again*
Workbook p80, exercises 1–3
Online Practice – *Practice*

Everyday English SB p127

Thank you and goodbye!

In this section, students learn and practise expressions used when saying goodbye.

1 Refer students to the photos. Ask *What's happening in each of the photos? Where are the people? What are they doing?* Put students in pairs to complete the sentences with words from the boxes.

2 🔊 **12.12** Play the recording for students to listen to the conversations and check their answers. Go through the conversations to check that students understand the expressions: *My pleasure!/Don't mention it!* (= another way to say *You're welcome!*); *I'm glad* (= I'm happy); *I'm grateful for your …* (= I'm thankful for …); *give her my love* (= tell her hello); *Who's picking you up?* (= Who is collecting you from the airport at the other end of your journey); *Thanks for having me.* (= thank you for letting me stay with you); *I'd better get on.* (= here it means: I should get on the train now; It can also mean I should go now.); *take care* (= keep yourself safe). Note that *We must be going now.* in conversation 1 is more common and less formal than *We must go now.* We might also say, *We've got to go now.*, or *We have to go now.* The use of *must be going* in this case suggests that the speaker is being quite firm with herself, but also very polite to her host. Ask students how similar these conversations are to the way they say goodbye in their culture. Play the recording again so that students can focus on intonation.

Answers and audioscript

🔊 **12.12 Thank you and goodbye!**

1 A It's late! We must **be going now**. Thank you **so much** for a lovely evening.
  B **Our pleasure!** Thank you for **coming**.
  C The meal was fantastic!
  B I'm **glad** you liked it! Bye! Drive safely!
  A I will. Bye! And thanks again!

2 A Thanks so much! It's so **kind** of you.
  B That's OK.
  A I'm so **grateful** for all your help.
  B Don't **mention** it! It's been fun.
  A Well, er, would you **mind** helping me with just one more thing?
  B Of course **not**! No problem!

3 A I hope you have a good **flight**. Who's **picking** you up?
  B My sister, Lara.
  A Well **give** her my love.
  B Will do. OK, I'd better go **through** security now. It takes ages. Bye!
  A Goodbye! Look after **yourself**!

4 A Thanks for **having** me. I've really enjoyed my stay.
  B You're very **welcome**! It's been a **pleasure**. Come back and see us again soon!
  A That's very **kind** of you. Maybe next year!
  B That would be lovely!

5 A Have a safe **journey**!
  B Thanks. I'll text you when I **arrive**.
  A And **say** hello to your parents from me.
  B I will. OK, I'd better get on.
  A OK. Bye! Take **care**!
  B And you! See you soon. Bye!

6 A Goodbye! Thanks for **everything**! It's been great **fun**!
  B Thank you! I've really enjoyed being your teacher!
  C Well, we've learned so much with you!
  B I'm glad to hear it. Good **luck** with your English in future! And **keep** in touch!
  A We **will**! Bye!

3 Students choose a conversation that they would like to memorize in pairs. Give them some class time to practise. Monitor and help students with pronunciation as needed. If possible, allow them to record themselves and listen back to themselves to self-assess their fluency and pronunciation. If possible, ask students to act out their conversations to the class.

EXTENSION Ask students to write their own dialogue using expressions from the example conversations.

Additional material

For teachers
Photocopiable activity – Communication: *Thank you and goodbye* pp238–9

For students
Online Practice – *Look again*
Workbook p81
Online Practice – *Practice*

Writing SB p128

Correcting common mistakes

Language review

This section reviews grammar, spelling, and punctuation, and aims to help students become more independent in finding and correcting mistakes. Students work towards a peer review in which they help their partner find mistakes in their work. Students may be unfamiliar with this kind of collaboration. They may think it's the teacher's job to correct mistakes. You may need to tell them that the teacher is not always around, so it's important to be able to identify your own mistakes. Peers can help, too, by being a fresh set of 'eyes' before turning work in because it can be difficult to spot your own mistakes. This is collaborative learning.

1 As a lead-in to this section, ask students what kinds of mistakes they make when they write. Elicit a range of responses. Refer them to the list of mistake types in the exercise. Is there anything there that they didn't mention? Tell them to work in pairs to find the mistakes in the sentences, correct them, and say what kind of mistake each is. Do the first together as a class. Check as a class, and elicit the rule where possible. Ask students if they found it difficult or easy to find the mistakes. Did they see any mistakes that they sometimes make? Elicit common mistakes from the students, e.g. *will* vs *going to*; which preposition to use; which article to use, etc.

Answers

2 She's **a** doctor. (word missing – missing article; use *a* with professions)
3 They went **to** Italy on holiday. (wrong word – we go *to* a place)
4 I have two **younger brothers**. (word order – adjective before the noun)
5 The wine is **from** France. (wrong word – use preposition *from*)
6 He **arrived** yesterday. (tense – use past tense)
7 They**'ve eaten** the two packets of biscuits. (tense; Present Perfect for present result/don't use Perfect Continous with quantities)
8 The dog has lost **its** collar. (punctuation – *it's* is a contraction of *it is/it has*; *its* is the possessive)
9 **Who is** coming for dinner? (wrong word – *whose* is a determiner/pronoun; you need the question word (*who*) + verb (*is*) here)

2 Divide the class into A and B groups. Each group finds the mistakes in their sentences, circles them, and writes what kind of mistake they are **without correcting it**.

3 Students find a partner from the other group so that there is an A-group and B-group student in each pair. They swap books and correct the sentences. Check answers as a class. Ask *Was it easier to correct the mistake once you knew what kind it was?*

Answers

A
1 I like Rome because **it** is a beautiful city. (missing word)
2 She studied psychology **for three years**. (word order)
3 **He speaks** French, German and Spanish. (tense)
4 I watched TV **then** I went to bed. (spelling)
5 Did you **buy** any bread at the supermarket? (wrong word/spelling)
6 I'll text you as soon as **I arrive**. (tense)

B
1 I lost **all my** money. (word order)
2 What did you **do** last night? (missing word)
3 He **doesn't believe** a word I say. (tense)
4 My town is **quiet** at the weekend. (wrong word/spelling)
5 I **want to** pass the exam. (wrong word)
6 She's married **to** Peter. (wrong word)

4 Refer students to the photo and the title of the student writing. Ask *What is this writing going to be about?* In pairs, students find and correct the mistakes. As a class, go through the text. Ask a student to read a sentence, say what the mistake is and say what the correction is. Do the first as an example: *My best friend was my best man at my wedding. The mistake is spelling. 'Best man' is not in capitals.* Use the board if needed to correct spelling of words.

Answers
My best man and best friend
My best friend was my **best man** at my wedding, when I **got** married two **years** ago. **His** name is Flavio and we met **at** university in Bologna. In fact**,** we met on our very first day **there**. Flavio was **the** first person I spoke **to,** and we discovered that we were both studying Spanish and that we were both football fans. When we left university we went travelling **together for** six months. We **had** a fantastic time touring **North** and **South** America.
When we were in Mexico we met two sisters **from** Chicago, Tamsin and Tanya. Now I'm married **to** Tanya and next year Flavio and Tamsin **are** going to get married.
I like Flavio because he **is** very funny, and I'm never **bored** when we are together. **I'm moving/I'm going to move** to a different town soon, but I'm sure we will often text or email **each other**.

5 Give students time to think about who they would like to write about. Put them in pairs to discuss and ask each other questions about the person they have decided to write about so they can generate some ideas about what to say. If needed, write some prompts on the board: *When did you meet? How did you meet? What do you have in common? What is the person like? What do you like doing together? Why do you like this person?* Give students time to write in class if possible. If you think students won't be able to read each other's hand writing, you could ask them to type up their papers – with the spelling and grammar check turned off!

6 This may be the first time that students have been asked to peer review each other's work, but the work they have done before should give them an idea of how useful it is. Ask students to swap papers. They should look for mistakes, circle them, and write the kind of mistake, but should not correct them. They give the papers back and correct their own papers.

EXTENSION As a fun way to end the term, ask students to create a poster with photos/pictures of the person they wrote about, and the corrected text they wrote. Put these on the wall. Divide the class into three groups. Group A stands next to their poster. Groups B and C find people in Group A and ask them about the person they wrote about. Students in Group A can read their paper or tell the others about what they wrote. Swap so that Group B stands next to their poster and Groups A and C move around. Do this one more time with Group C standing by their poster and Groups A and

B moving around. If possible, encourage students who are listening to say thank you and goodbye, e.g. :

> B *Thank you for telling me about your friend. She sounds interesting.*
> A *My pleasure. Thank you for listening.*
> B *Goodbye!*

SUGGESTION 1 As a fun way to review grammar and vocabulary from the unit, you could hold a grammar auction. First prepare a list of 10–15 sentences, between four and seven of which are correct, but the rest all contain a mistake. This works best if the sentences contain mistakes that the students are still making. Mistakes could be mistakes in grammar, spelling, or word choice. Students work in teams of three or four. They give themselves a team name. Each team starts out with £1,000. Write all the team names across the board in separate columns along with the amount of money they have to spend. The idea is that they buy good sentences. Tell students that if they buy a correct sentence, then they keep the money they bid, but if they buy an incorrect sentence, then they lose the amount they bid. The team with the highest number of good sentences and the most money at the end of the auction is the 'winner'. Hand out the worksheet with the list of sentences, and give students 10–15 minutes to decide which sentences they want to buy. Don't tell them how many are good/bad. You could allow students to look in their notebooks, but don't let them refer to the book. Keep the time pressure high. Start the auction. Start with sentence one and say *How much will you pay for this sentence? Shall we start with £25? Who will pay £25?* Allow students to bid. Close the bidding when no one will go higher. 'Sell' the sentence to the highest bidder – write the sentence number down under the team name and substract the amount they paid from their £1,000. Continue in this way until you have sold (or tried to sell) all the sentences, then reveal which ones are good/bad. This is a good way to wrap up the term and show students what they need to revise for the end of year exam.

SUGGESTION 2 A way to review grammar and vocabulary from the whole course is to set up revision teams. You need to do this a few lessons before the last lesson to give students time to prepare their revision activities.

Divide the class into groups, or pairs. Then give each group/pair a unit of the course to review, or if it is a small class two or three units. Tell them to look at each section in the unit and to think of ways to revise the language, grammar, vocabulary, etc. They choose the grammar, vocabulary, and other language point from their unit or units. They can write sentences with gaps or alternative forms to choose the correct one. They make dialogues for students to complete or put in the correct order. They can use word games, like anagrams, word searches, crosswords, or noughts and crosses to revise vocabulary. The group gives clues or definitions of the words in the puzzle. (You can find word search and crossword programs online for them to make the games.) Set a limit of three exercises or activities each group can present.

Each group presents its revision activities for the rest of the class to do either on the board or on a computer with an interactive whiteboard. Each presentation should only last ten to fifteen minutes.

Additional material
For students
Online Practice – *Practice*
Workbook p81, *Review*; *Stop and check* Units 9–12, pp82–3
Online Practice – *Check your progress*

Unit 1   Grammar
A game of past, present, future → SB p10

Headway 5th edition
Pre-intermediate

Three in a row

How many languages / teacher speak?	Where / meet your best friend?	Married?	How / teacher / travel to work?	Where / 7 p.m. yesterday?	Who / live with?
What type / mobile / have?	Where / go / holiday / next summer?	Who / favourite teacher / school?	How many friends / have on Facebook?	What / the last film / see?	Where / go / last summer?
Why / choose / to study English?	What / favourite meal?	How often / use / Internet?	Have / pet / when / a child?	What / like about your hometown?	What / do / next weekend?
Know how / use chopsticks?	Where / buy / shoes?	What / cook / tonight?	What / get / last birthday?	Can / play / instrument?	How much water / drink every day?
Which / favourite room / your house?	Where / parents / from?	When / learn / read?	Whose hair / longest / in your class?	Where / born?	What / wear / tomorrow?
How many texts / best friend / send a day?	What / average salary / your country?	How often / make mistakes / English?	How often / chat / friends online?	How old / grandfather?	What / eat / breakfast / this morning?

Headway © Oxford University Press 2019

Photocopiable

Unit 1 Grammar Teacher's notes
A game of past, present, future → SB p10

5th edition
Headway
Pre-intermediate

Aim
To practise asking and answering questions about the present, past, and future

Language
Question formation with Present Simple, Past Simple and *going to*
Question words

Skills
Speaking and Listening

Materials
One copy of the worksheet for each group of four students

Pre-activity (10 minutes)
- Write *Where?* on the board. Elicit more question words from the class, and write them on the board as a list.
- Write short answers to the questions in a jumbled order, e.g.:

    1 *Where?*   *Because I was tired.*
    2 *What?*   *Last week.*
    3 *Why?*   *A lot.*
    4 *When?*   *Two.*
    5 *How?*   *A bicycle.*
    6 *How many?*   *Every day.*
    7 *How much?*   *By car.*
    8 *How often?*   *Barcelona.*

- As a whole-class activity, students make questions with the question words and match them to the answers.

Procedure (20 minutes)
- Put students in groups of four and divide the groups into pairs. Hand out one copy of the worksheet to each group.
- Students are going to play the game *Three in a row*. The aim is for each pair of students to ask and answer three adjacent questions correctly, each with a follow-up question and answer.
- Explain that there are four 3X3 game boards on the worksheet, so students can play up to four rounds. Before the first round, you might want to assign different game boards to groups to start off with.
- Pairs within a group can toss a coin to decide who goes first. The students in the first pair choose a question to ask and answer from the game board, e.g.:

    A *Where did you go on holiday last summer?*
    B *I went to Italy.*
    A *Who did you go with?*
    B *I went with my family.*

- If the questions and answers are correct, the pair puts a cross (**✗**) next to the chosen question on the game board and it's the other pair's turn to choose a question. If they ask and answer correctly, they draw a circle (**O**) next to the question on the game board.

| How many friends / have on Facebook? ✗ | What / the last film / see? ✗ | Where / go last summer? O |

- If either pair gets three questions correct in a row horizontally, vertically, or diagonally, they 'win' those questions and can cross them out – the other pair may now not use these crossed out questions.
- The game is over when there are no questions left to ask. The winning pair is the one who has the most sets of 'three in a row'. Students can then move on to the next game board and play another round.
- Go around checking that students are using question forms correctly. Make a note of any common errors.
- At the feedback stage, ask students to correct the errors.

Extension (10 minutes)
- Ask pairs to choose a question from the game and write a 10-line dialogue. They can then perform it in front of the class.

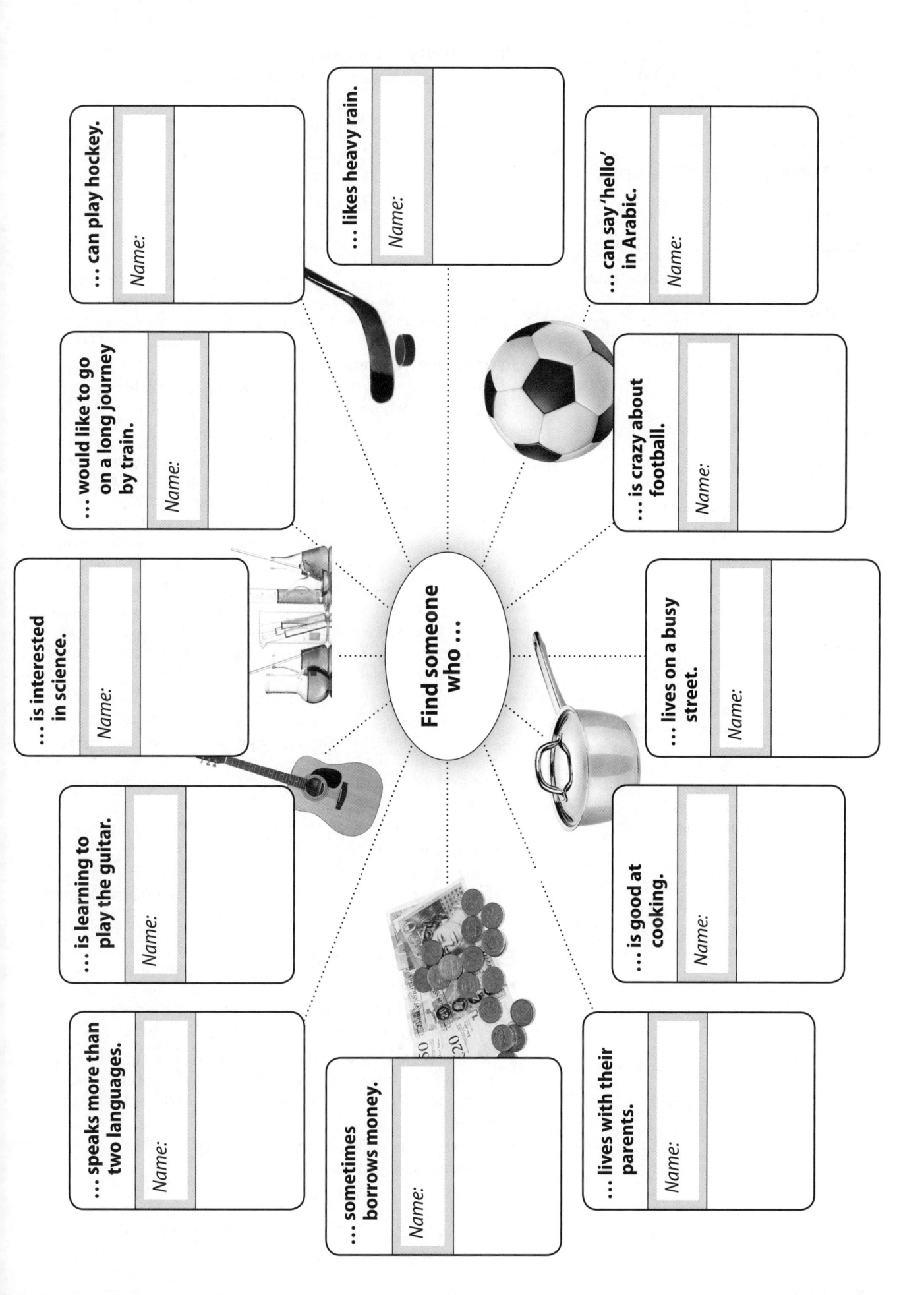

Unit 1 Vocabulary
Find someone who ... → SB p16

Headway 5th edition
Pre-intermediate

- ... can play hockey. Name:
- ... likes heavy rain. Name:
- ... can say 'hello' in Arabic. Name:
- ... would like to go on a long journey by train. Name:
- ... is crazy about football. Name:
- ... is interested in science. Name:
- **Find someone who ...**
- ... lives on a busy street. Name:
- ... is learning to play the guitar. Name:
- ... is good at cooking. Name:
- ... speaks more than two languages. Name:
- ... sometimes borrows money. Name:
- ... lives with their parents. Name:

Headway © Oxford University Press 2019

Photocopiable

Unit 1 Vocabulary Teacher's notes
Find someone who … ➔ SB p16

5th edition
Headway ››
Pre-intermediate

Aim
To have personalized conversations with different classmates and get to know them better

Language
Collocations (verb + noun, adjective + noun, adjective + preposition, verb + preposition)

Skills
Reading, Writing, Listening, and Speaking

Materials
One copy of the worksheet for each student

Answers

Pre-activity
1 say hello
2 speak two languages
3 crazy about something
4 interested in something
5 good at something
6 long journey
7 heavy rain
8 busy street

Procedure
Starting from the top and going clockwise:

Do you like heavy rain?
Can you say 'hello' in Arabic?
Are you crazy about football?
Do you live on a busy street?
Are you good at cooking?
Do you live with your parents?
Do you sometimes borrow money?
Do you speak more than two languages?
Are you learning to play the guitar?
Are you interested in science?
Would you like to go on a long journey by train?
Can you play hockey?

Pre-activity (10 minutes)

- Write these jumbled collocations on the board:
  1 say   two languages
  2 speak   in something
  3 crazy   journey
  4 interested   street
  5 good   at something
  6 long   hello
  7 heavy   rain
  8 busy   about something

- Put students in pairs and give them two minutes to match the jumbled parts. Check answers with the whole class.

Procedure (25 minutes)

- Tell students they're going to do a speaking activity. First, demonstrate how it works. Write on the board:
  Find someone who has a heavy bag today. Name: _____

- Explain that you need to find someone in the class and write their name. Ask the question *Do you have a heavy bag today?* until someone says 'yes' (asking a different question if no one does). Write their name on the board, and ask some questions to get more information, e.g. *What's in your bag? Why do you need those things? How often do you carry a heavy bag?* Write the student's answers in note form on the board.

- Give one worksheet to each student in the class. Put students in pairs and give them five minutes to look at the worksheet and prepare the 12 *Yes/No* questions they need to ask. Go round as students work, giving help and support where necessary. Check the correct answers with the class. Drill the questions for pronunciation.

- Explain that students need to ask their questions to as many different people as possible. They can ask the questions in any order, but they can only ask three questions to one person and then they need to move on. When they find someone who says 'yes', they must write their name on their worksheet, ask for some extra information and make notes.

- Tell students to get up and mingle. Allow about 15 minutes for them to complete the task.

- At the feedback stage, find out who's got the most names on their sheet. Then invite students to share anything interesting or surprising that they've learnt.

Extension (10 minutes)

- Write on the board:
  It was a very high mountain.   *It was a delicious meal.*
  I met an important person.   *I paid a high price.*

- Tell students to choose ONE of the sentences on the board. Give them five minutes to write a short paragraph about it and tell them to include two or three collocations. The paragraph can either be true or false.

- In small groups, students take turns to read out their story. The others in the group guess if it's true or false.

Unit 1 Communication
Can I help you? → SB p17

Headway 5th edition — Pre-intermediate

Hi, how are you?	Thank you so much for helping me yesterday.	Can you help me with something?	Sorry I'm late.	Excuse me! Is this table free?
Can I help you?	Cheers!	I'm so sorry. I can't come on Saturday night.	Good afternoon!	How do you do?
Very well, thanks. How about you?	You're welcome. It was no problem at all.	Of course. What's the matter?	Never mind. Better late than never!	Yes, sure. Go ahead!
No, thank you. I'm just looking.	Cheers! Happy birthday!	No worries. Perhaps another time.	Afternoon! Terrible weather, isn't it?	How do you do? Lovely to meet you!

Headway © Oxford University Press 2019

Unit 1 Communication Teacher's notes
Can I help you? ➔ SB p17

Headway 5th edition
Pre-intermediate

Aim
To play a memory game based on typically occurring conversation pairs

Language
Social expressions

Skills
Speaking and Listening

Materials
One copy of the worksheet for every four or six students, cut into 20 cards

Answers

Pre-activity
1 Hi, how are you?
2 How do you do?
3 Excuse me, is this seat free?
4 Cheers!
5 Sorry I'm late.

Procedure
Hi, how are you?
Very well, thanks. How about you?

Thank you so much for helping me yesterday.
You're welcome. It was no problem at all.

Can you help me with something?
Of course. What's the matter?

Sorry I'm late.
Never mind. Better late than never!

Excuse me! Is this table free?
Yes, sure. Go ahead!

Can I help you?
No, thank you. I'm just looking.

Cheers!
Cheers! Happy birthday!

I'm so sorry. I can't come on Saturday night.
No worries. Perhaps another time.

Good afternoon!
Afternoon! Terrible weather, isn't it?

How do you do?
How do you do? Lovely to meet you!

Pre-activity (10 minutes)
- Review the topic by giving students these social situations and eliciting some typical expressions:
  1. You meet a friend in the street.
  2. You meet a new boss at work.
  3. You're on a crowded train.
  4. You're starting a meal and everyone's got a drink.
  5. School starts at 9 o'clock. You arrive at 9.10.
- Write the expressions on the board, model and drill them. Draw attention to the fact that it sounds more friendly if you say these expressions with stress (making key words longer and louder) and intonation (up and down movement in the voice). Contrast saying *Bye!* in a low, quiet voice with flat intonation and saying it in a higher, louder voice with falling intonation.

Procedure (20 minutes)
- Explain that students are going to use some conversation cards to play a memory game. Divide students into groups of four (or six) and divide each group into two (or three) AB pairs. Give each group a set of cut-up cards.
- Each group lays all 20 cards out on the table, face down.
- Student A in Pair 1 turns over a card. Student B in Pair 1 turns over a second card. If the cards don't match to make a conversation, they should turn the cards back over and it's Pair 2's turn. If the two cards match to make a conversation, they should say the conversation using appropriate stress and intonation, and then keep the cards. They can then turn over another two cards to see if they match.
- The pair with the most conversation pairs wins the game.
- Allow students 10–15 minutes to play the game. Go round the class giving help where necessary and checking students are using and pronouncing the expressions naturally.

Extension (10 minutes)
- In small groups, students play a different game using just the cards which contain the starting line of the dialogue. They put all the cards in a pile, face down on the table. Player 1 takes the first card and says it to the group. The first person to give an appropriate response wins the card. HOWEVER, if Player 1 quickly says an appropriate third line to continue the conversation, he/she can keep the card. It's then Player 2's turn, and so on. The player with the most cards at the end wins the game.

Unit 2 Grammar
Spot the difference → SB p20

5th edition
Headway »
Pre-intermediate

Picture A

Picture B

Headway © Oxford University Press 2019

Photocopiable 173

Unit 2 Grammar Teacher's notes
Spot the difference ➔ SB p20

Aim
To play a 'spot the difference' information exchange game

Language
Present tenses and *have/have got*
State verbs

Skills
Speaking, Listening, and Writing

Materials
One copy of the worksheet cut in half per pair of students

Answers

Pre-activity
1 My friend **is working** at a café at the moment.
2 Cafés serve food and drink. ✓
3 He **has (got)** a new bike.
4 I **don't understand** this question.

Procedure
1 In Picture A, it's snowing but in Picture B it's raining.
2 In Picture A, the old man likes the sandwich but in Picture B he doesn't like it.
3 In Picture A, the woman near the window is listening to music but in Picture B she isn't listening to music.
4 In Picture A, the café isn't serving hot food today but in Picture B the café is serving hot food.
5 In Picture A, the boy is reading a Harry Potter book but in Picture B he's reading *Hunger Games*.
6 In Picture A, the boy isn't eating anything, but in Picture B he's eating chips.
7 In Picture A, the man hasn't got a bowl of soup on the table, but in Picture B he has got a bowl of soup on the table.
8 In Picture A, the waitress is wearing a tie but in Picture B she isn't wearing a tie.
9 In Picture A, the waitress doesn't know the New Theatre but in Picture B she knows the New Theatre.
10 In Picture A, the waitress is carrying a notebook under her arm, but in Picture B she isn't carrying a notebook.
11 In Picture A, the old woman has got a dog but in Picture B she hasn't got a dog.
12 In Picture A, the young woman with glasses studies/is studying at Manchester University but in Picture B she studies/is studying at Oxford University.

Extension
Example answer
I like this café. I don't see many people every day and the people here are very friendly. The food isn't expensive. I often have lunch here but today I'm just having something cold. I'm feeling happy because my grandchildren are coming to see me this afternoon.
(the old man eating a sandwich)

Pre-activity (5 minutes)
- Introduce the topic and review present tenses by writing these sentences on the board:
  1 *My friend works at a café at the moment.*
  2 *Cafés serve food and drink.*
  3 *He's having a new bike.*
  4 *I'm not understanding this question.*
- Tell students that some of the sentences are correct and some aren't. Put students in pairs to find the mistakes and correct the sentences.
- Check the answers with the whole class.

Procedure (20 minutes)
- Briefly hold up Pictures A and B. Explain that both pictures show the same café. The pictures are very similar but there are twelve differences between them. Students must work in pairs to find the differences by talking together without looking at each other's pictures.
- Divide the class into AB pairs. Give Student A Picture A and Student B Picture B. Make sure students don't look at each other's pictures.
- Give students 10–15 minutes to compare the pictures and find as many differences as they can by talking together. When they find a difference they must circle it on their worksheet. Go round the class as the students work, giving help and support where necessary.
- Stop the activity after 10–15 minutes, or when most students have finished. Check the answers by eliciting the twelve differences from the class.

Extension (15 minutes)
- Make sure students can see Pictures A and B. Read the **Example answer** to the students and see if they can identify the speaker (the old man eating a sandwich).
- Tell students to choose one of the people in the picture and imagine that person's life. Then give them 5-10 minutes to write a short paragraph about that person without naming them.
- In groups, students read out their pieces and the others guess which person it is.

Unit 2 Vocabulary
Who's like me? → SB p23

Worksheet A

Me	Others
• I *sometimes / never* go for long walks with my friends. • I like taking photos of *people / places / animals* best. • I usually meet friends for a drink *in the morning / in the afternoon / in the evening*. • I like *having a lie-in more than going to the gym / going to the gym more than having a lie-in*. • When I have a barbecue, I cook lots of *meat / fish / vegetables*.	

Worksheet B

Me	Others
• I like *doing nothing / singing / dancing* when I listen to music. • I like visiting other cities *in my country / in other countries / in my country and in other countries*. • I *sometimes / often / never* watch dramas on TV. • I *don't like chatting on the phone / often chat on the phone / chat on the phone all the time*. • I *never / sometimes / often* do puzzles.	

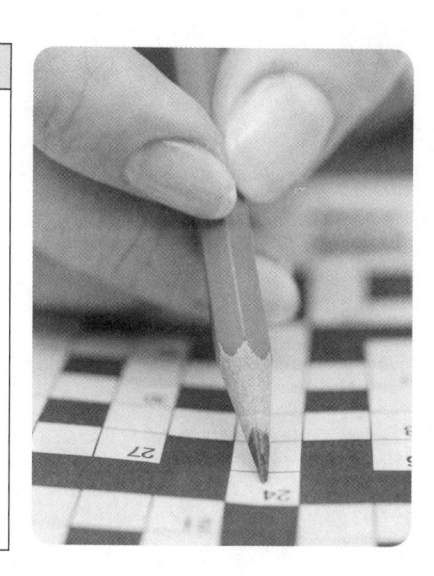

Worksheet C

Me	Others
• I *like / love / hate* doing nothing. • I play games on my phone *every day / when I'm bored*. • I *hate shopping for clothes / like shopping for clothes with friends / like shopping for clothes alone*. • I *usually / always / sometimes / never* go out for a meal on my birthday. • I *never read magazines / only read magazines when I'm waiting for something / love reading magazines*.	

Unit 2 Vocabulary Teacher's notes
Who's like me? → SB p23

Aim
To do a survey about free time activities

Language
Verb + noun phrases: things you like doing

Skills
Reading, Speaking, and Listening

Materials
One copy of the worksheet for every three students, cut into three along the dotted lines

Pre-activity (5 minutes)
- Say some true things about your likes, dislikes and habits to the class, e.g.:
  I like eating chocolate. How about you?
  I don't like going to the supermarket. How about you?
  I never eat in expensive restaurants. How about you?
- Elicit some responses. Find a student who feels the same way as you and say: *You're like me!*
- Write on the board: *I like you. ≠ I'm like you.* Check students understand the difference, i.e. *I like you.* = ☺; *I'm like you.* = *I'm similar to you.*

Procedure (30 minutes)
- Check students understand *survey* (= asking the same questions to different people to get and compare information). Write *Who's like me?* on the board and tell them they're going to do a survey with this title. Divide the students into ABC groups. Give Student A Worksheet A, Student B Worksheet B and Student C Worksheet C.
- First, give students five minutes to read through their worksheet and circle the answers that are true for them.
- Then, get students to do their surveys within their ABC groups by reading out their sentences to their groupmates and asking *How about you?* Every time a classmate feels the same way as them about something, they should write that classmate's name in the right-hand column of their worksheet.
- Finally, get students mingling around the classroom, talking to as many different people as possible.
- After about 15 minutes, tell students to come back to their seats. Give them 5–10 minutes to write two or three sentences that answer the question *Who's like me?*, e.g. *Maxim's like me because he likes taking photos of people, he likes going to the gym more than having a lie-in and when he has a barbecue he cooks lots of meat.*
- At the feedback stage, ask *Was it easy to find people who are like you?* Invite a few students to read out their sentences to the whole class.

Extension (10 minutes)
- Elicit (or supply) ways of making suggestions, e.g. *I'd like to …*, *Let's …*, and *Shall we … ?* and write them on the board. Elicit a few example sentences.
- Put students in small groups and tell them they're going to spend a weekend together. Give them five minutes to make some plans for the weekend, using vocabulary from the worksheet and/or their own ideas.
- Invite one student from each group to report their plans to the class, using *We're going to…* . Students listen and decide which weekend sounds most interesting.

Unit 2 Communication
Keep talking → SB p27

What terrible weather!	I'm going into town. Do you want to come?	Are you enjoying the party?	I'm not feeling very well.
I'm bored.	My uncle's opening a shop in town.	Did you have a good weekend?	Is that a new phone?
Do you eat meat?	How's your brother these days?	I'm really busy this week.	I like your jacket.
If you want any help, just ask.	I'm getting a tattoo tomorrow.	I'm starting a new job next week.	What are you doing at the weekend?
I don't want to cook tonight.	I'm hungry.	I've got new neighbours.	We're getting a dog!
You look smart! Where are you going?	Have you got any plans for this evening?	Hi, it's me. I'm calling from the hospital.	I need to go home.

Unit 2 Communication Teacher's notes
Keep talking → SB p27

Aim
To play a speaking game

Language
Making conversation

Skills
Speaking and Listening

Materials
One copy of the worksheet for every four (or six) students, cut into 24 'conversation starter' cards

Answers

Pre-activity
1 That's interesting.
2 Oh, no! That's a shame.
3 Oh, really?
4 Thank you very much.
5 What's the matter?
6 Lucky you!
7 Me too!

Procedure
Example answer:
A How's your brother these days?
B He's very well, thanks. He's got a new job and he's really enjoying it.
A Oh, what does he do?
B He's a manager. He started a new job at a big shoe shop a few weeks ago.

Pre-activity (10 minutes)
- Write these jumbled responses on the board:
  1 That's   very much.
  2 Oh no! That's a   too!
  3 Oh,   shame.
  4 Thank you   the matter?
  5 What's   really?
  6 Lucky   interesting.
  7 Me   you!
- Put students in pairs and give them a minute to match the jumbled responses. Check answers with the whole class. Drill the responses, making sure students are using correct stress and intonation.

Procedure (25 minutes)
- Tell students they're going to play a speaking game in pairs. To win the game, they and their partner must try to keep conversations going for as long as they can.
- Divide students into groups of four (or six) and divide each group into two (or three) AB pairs.
- Give a set of 'conversation starter' cards to each group, face down. Demonstrate how to play the game with a strong/confident member of the class.
- Student A in Pair 1 takes a 'conversation starter' card, reads it aloud and places it face up on the table so his/her partner can see it. Student B responds with a comment or question, and then both students must try to keep the conversation going for as long as they can.
- Then Student A in Pair 2 takes a new card and has a conversation with Student B. The game ends when all the cards have been used. The pair with the highest total score wins the game.
- Pairs win points as follows:
  1 point for one exchange (one extra question and answer)
  2 points for two exchanges
  3 points for three exchanges
- Allow 20 minutes for the groups to play. If a group finishes quickly, they shuffle the cards and play again.
- Close the activity by finding out which pair in each group won. You could also then invite the winning pair in each group to take part in a final round in front of the whole class so that an overall winner can be declared.

Extension (10 minutes)
- Get the pairs to write six more conversation starter cards, which they pass to another group to use in a few more rounds of the game.
- Alternatively, for written practice, ask pairs to choose one of their conversations and write it out as a dialogue. They can then perform it in front of the whole class.

Unit 3   Grammar
The birthday present   SB p30

Headway
5th edition
Pre-intermediate

Unit 3 Grammar Teacher's notes
The birthday present → SB p30

5th edition
Headway
Pre-intermediate

Aim
To put a picture story in order, then retell the story

Language
Past Simple and Past Continuous

Skills
Speaking

Materials
One copy of the cut-up worksheet for each pair of students

Answers
Suggested order: c, f, i, a, e, l, b, d, k, h, j, g

A married couple was window-shopping in a fashionable shopping mall when the woman saw a beautiful hat that she really liked in a designer shop.

It was her birthday the following day, so her husband decided to buy her the hat.

He also bought them tickets to the theatre to see a popular show.

His wife was very happy when she received her birthday presents: the beautiful hat and the theatre tickets.

They were having dinner at home when the man looked at his watch and realized they were late for the theatre.

They arrived at the theatre just in time to catch the start of the show – they barely had time to check in their clothes at the cloakroom.

They sat comfortably and watched the show.

Afterwards, the man quickly checked out their clothes from the cloakroom, but the cloakroom attendant didn't give him the beautiful new hat!

His wife was really upset, and she cried while her husband was having an argument with the cloakroom attendant.

They waited until the cloakroom was empty but there was no sign of the new hat.

The same evening, the man took his wife back to the designer shop just before it was closing. He bought her another hat.

When they got home, they realized the birthday present was still on the table so now she had two new hats!

Pre-activity (5 minutes)
- Ask students what's the most expensive thing they have ever bought in a shop. Ask them if they bought it for themselves or as a present.
- Ask them how they felt about buying it, and if they still have the object.

Procedure (20 minutes)
- Explain that students are going to put some pictures from a story about a birthday present into the correct order and then retell the story. Write *The birthday present* on the board.
- Pre-teach/Check the following key vocabulary: *window-shopping, designer shop, gift box, queue, box office, cloakroom, cloakroom attendant*.
- Divide the students into pairs and give each pair a jumbled set of picture cards. Tell students that the letters *a–l* do not give the correct order.
- Ask students to try and put the pictures into the correct order. Ask them as a class to say which they think is the first picture (*c*).
- Explain that they need to talk in detail about what happens in the story. Allow up to 10–12 minutes for them to do this.
- Go around helping students where necessary. Encourage them to use both the Past Simple and Past Continuous forms, and linking words (*but, although, however, so,* and *because*).
- Ask students to work with another pair. Each pair should retell their story. The pairs can then discuss/debate any similarities or differences between their stories.
- The teacher should choose a pair who have the correct story and ask them to retell it to the whole class. If there are any interesting variations on the story, you may like to elicit those as well.

Extension (10 minutes)
- Put students in small groups and ask them to tell each other about the best birthday party they have had and the best present they have received.
- Have a group feedback session and invite a few students to share the most interesting stories they heard.

Unit 3   Vocabulary
Think of ...   → SB p36

Headway 5th edition
Pre-intermediate

Team name _____

		ANSWER
1 ... an event which you shouldn't arrive late for.		
2 ... a person who is famous because they can write or paint well.		
3 ... a place where or a time when you should speak quietly.		
4 ... something which most six-year-old children can do well.		
5 ... a place where you should always drive slowly.		
6 ... a person who is famous because they can run, swim or cycle fast.		
7 ... a situation when it's important to speak clearly.		
8 ... a way to contact someone if you need to speak to them urgently.		
9 ... a country where most people speak Spanish fluently.		
		TOTAL SCORE

Unit 3 Vocabulary Teacher's notes
Think of ... → SB p36

5th edition
Headway »
Pre-intermediate

Aim
To play a 'categories' game
Language
Adverbs
Skills
Speaking and Listening
Materials
One copy of the worksheet for every two to four students

Pre-activity (5 minutes)
- Write these sentences on the board. Put students in pairs and ask them to finish each sentence using an adverb:

    Sleep _____!

    Listen _____!

    Don't work too _____!

- Elicit answers from the whole class. (Most likely answers: *Sleep well!; Listen carefully!; Don't work too hard/late!*) If students have other suggestions, listen and decide whether or not they are acceptable.

Procedure (25 minutes)
- Explain that students are going to play a team game. Demonstrate how the game works. Divide the class into teams of two to four. Ask the teams to write down the name of a country where people speak French fluently (There are 29 countries with French as an official language, including: France, Canada, Monaco, Belgium, Haiti, Madagascar, Cameroon, etc.) Tell them to try and come up with an answers the other teams might not think of. Give the teams one minute to write down their answer. Check the answers with the whole class, awarding points as follows:

    0 points for an empty box or an incorrect/unacceptable answer. You will have to be the final judge if there is any disagreement.

    3 points for a correct/acceptable answer which one or more team has also got.

    5 points for a correct/acceptable answer no other team has got.
- The team with the highest total score wins the game.
- Give one worksheet to each team and ask them to think of a team name. Write the team names on the board and tell students to write their team name on the worksheet. Allow the teams ten minutes to complete the worksheets. Tell the teams to pass their worksheet to the team on the right for scoring.
- Go through the answers one by one. Allow the teams time to write the score for each answer in the small boxes, and to calculate and write the total score in the column on the right.
- The team with the highest overall score wins the game.

Extension (10 minutes)
- Write on the board: *run fast, do something well, sleep badly* and *arrive late for something*. Put students in pairs and ask them to tell each other about a time when they did the things on the board.
- Have a group feedback session, inviting students to report back on one of the stories their partner told them.

182 Photocopiable

Headway © Oxford University Press 2019

Unit 3 Communication
Guess when … → SB p37

5th edition
Headway »
Pre-intermediate

My birthday is _____.

My favourite date is _____.

I started learning English _____.

I last took an important exam _____.

I like to go on holiday _____.

Last year I went on holiday _____.

I usually relax with friends or family _____.

My family usually has a big meal together _____.

I went to bed _____ last night.

I got up _____ this morning.

I last looked at my phone _____.

I listened to the news _____.

Headway © Oxford University Press 2019   Photocopiable   183

Unit 3 Communication Teacher's notes
Guess when ... ➔ SB p37

5th edition
Headway ≫
Pre-intermediate

Aim
To talk about times, days and dates

Language
Saying when

Skills
Speaking and Listening

Materials
One copy of the worksheet for each student.

Answers
Pre-activity
1 *the evening* because we say **in** *the evening*, but **on** *April 16* and **on** *Monday*
2 *Friday afternoon* because we say **on** *Friday afternoon*, but **in** *1995* and **in** *winter*
3 *June* because we say **in** *June*, but **at** *six o'clock* and **at** *the weekend*
4 *the 1980s* because we say **in** *the 1980s* but *(--) last night* and *(--) the other day*

Pre-activity (10 minutes)
- Write these days, dates and times on the board:
   1 *April 16, Monday, the evening*
   2 *1995, Friday afternoon, winter*
   3 *six o'clock, June, the weekend*
   4 *last night, the other day, the 1980s*
- Put students in pairs to find the 'odd one out' in each line. To get them started, ask: *Which preposition goes before 'April 16'? Which preposition goes before 'Monday'?*
- After a couple of minutes check the answers with the whole class.

Procedure (25 minutes)
- Explain that students are going to think and talk about days, dates and times in their lives.
- Give each student a copy of the worksheet. Give them ten minutes to read and complete the 12 sentences by adding a preposition (if necessary) and a time expression in each gap. Tell them that every answer must be different. Go round the class as the students work, checking that they are using the correct prepositions.
- When students have finished, ask them to copy their 12 times, days and dates into the shapes at the bottom of the worksheet, but in a different order. Tell students to fold and tear their worksheets along the dotted line (you can demonstrate with one student's worksheet), and to keep the 'sentences' part of their worksheet hidden by turning it over.
- Put students into pairs. Students look at the 'shapes' half of each other's worksheets. They take turns to point to a shape and guess why their partner wrote the sentence, e.g.:

   (ten minutes ago)

   A *I think you last looked at your phone ten minutes ago.*
   B *Yes, that's right. / No, I last listened to the news ten minutes ago.*
- Student B can look at the 'sentences' part of their worksheet discretely if they need to check a complete sentence, but must continue to keep it secret from Student A. When the correct answer has been established, Student A can ask Student B for more information about their answer, e.g. *Why did you look at your phone?* It's then Student B's turn to guess something about one of Student A's shapes, and so on.
- After 10–15 minutes, have a class feedback session, inviting pairs to tell the whole class anything surprising or interesting they found out about their partner.

Extension (10 minutes)
- Write on the board: *I usually ... , I last ... , I went ... , I ate ... , I was ...*
- Students complete the sentences with their own ideas and time expressions, but two of their sentences must be false. They then read their sentences to a partner, who must try to identify which of the sentences are false.

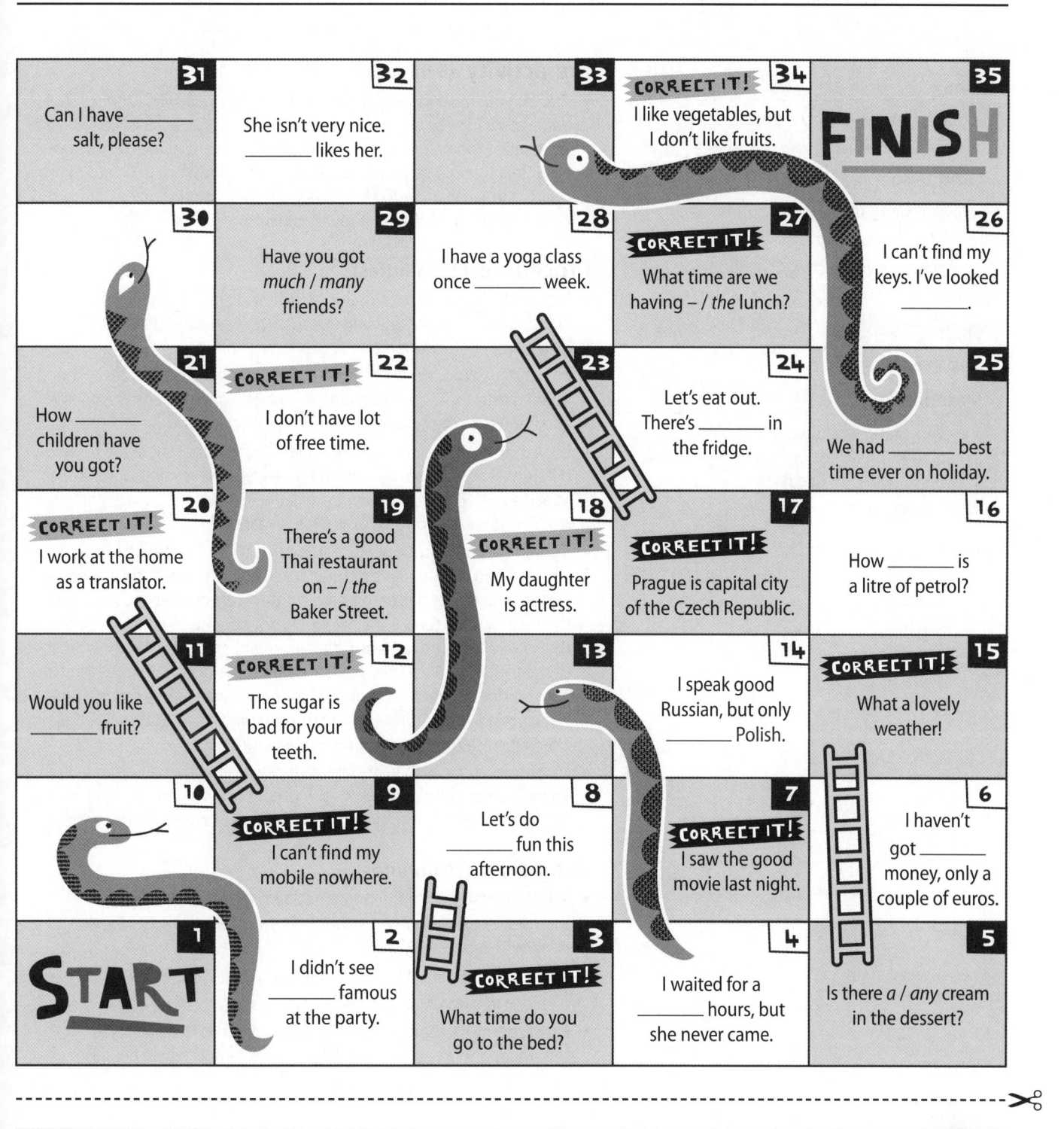

Unit 4 Grammar
Snakes and ladders → SB p40

Headway 5th edition
Pre-intermediate

31 Can I have _____ salt, please?

32 She isn't very nice. _____ likes her.

33 (snake)

34 CORRECT IT! I like vegetables, but I don't like fruits.

35 FINISH

30 (snake)

29 Have you got *much* / *many* friends?

28 I have a yoga class once _____ week.

27 CORRECT IT! What time are we having – / *the* lunch?

26 I can't find my keys. I've looked _____.

21 How _____ children have you got?

22 CORRECT IT! I don't have lot of free time.

23 (snake/ladder)

24 Let's eat out. There's _____ in the fridge.

25 We had _____ best time ever on holiday.

20 CORRECT IT! I work at the home as a translator.

19 There's a good Thai restaurant on – / *the* Baker Street.

18 CORRECT IT! My daughter is actress.

17 CORRECT IT! Prague is capital city of the Czech Republic.

16 How _____ is a litre of petrol?

11 Would you like _____ fruit?

12 CORRECT IT! The sugar is bad for your teeth.

13 (snake)

14 I speak good Russian, but only _____ Polish.

15 CORRECT IT! What a lovely weather!

10 (snake)

9 CORRECT IT! I can't find my mobile nowhere.

8 Let's do _____ fun this afternoon.

7 CORRECT IT! I saw the good movie last night.

6 I haven't got _____ money, only a couple of euros.

1 START

2 I didn't see _____ famous at the party.

3 CORRECT IT! What time do you go to the bed?

4 I waited for a _____ hours, but she never came.

5 Is there *a* / *any* cream in the dessert?

Answers

2 anyone/anybody
3 go to bed
4 few/couple of
5 any
6 a lot of/much
7 a good movie
8 something
9 anywhere
11 some
12 Sugar

14 a little/a little bit of/a bit of
15 What lovely
16 much
17 the capital city
18 an actress
19 –
20 at home
21 many
22 a lot of/much
24 nothing

25 the
26 everywhere
27 –
28 a
29 many
31 the/some
32 No one/Nobody
34 fruit

Headway © Oxford University Press 2019   Photocopiable   185

Unit 4 Grammar Teacher's notes
Snakes and ladders → SB p40

Aim
To play a board game by completing and correcting sentences

Language
Countable and uncountable nouns
some/any, much/many
some/any/no/every + thing/where/one/body
Articles

Skills
Speaking

Materials
One copy of the worksheet (A3 if possible) for each group of three or four students (with 'Answers' section removed)
Dice and counters

Pre-activity (5 minutes)
- Ask: *Do you ever play games with your friends and family? What kind of games do you play? What games do you enjoy?* Elicit a variety of answers. Try to elicit the names of some well-known board games, e.g. *Scrabble*. Elicit/Teach *board game* and explain that students are going to play a board game called *Snakes and ladders* to practise the grammar from Unit 4. Ask if any students know this game.

Procedure (20 minutes)
- Pre-teach/Check the expressions students will need to play the game: *Throw/Roll the dice; It's my/your turn; I'm/You're next; That's right/wrong; Go up the ladder; Go down the snake; I am the winner!*
- Put students into groups of three or four, and hand out copies of the board game, the dice, and counters. Appoint one student as a referee and hand them a copy of the Answers from the bottom of the worksheet.
- Look at the board game with the class. Explain that there are three different types of questions in the game: *Say the missing word*, e.g. squares 2, 4, 6; *Correct the sentence* (labelled *Correct it!*), e.g. squares 3, 7, 9; *Choose the correct answer*, e.g. squares 5, 19, 27.
- Explain the rules: students take it in turns to throw the dice, move the counter, and do the task on the square they land on. If the answer is correct, the player has earned the right to stay on that square and it's the next player's turn. If the answer is not correct, the player returns to the square they moved from. If a player lands on a ladder, they move to the top, but only if they have answered the question at the bottom of the ladder correctly. If a player lands on a snake, they move to the bottom and wait until their next turn before throwing the dice again. The first student to reach 'Finish' is the winner.
- Monitor and check that students are playing the game correctly. Try to encourage students to check each other's answers, but be prepared to be the final judge if the groups don't have a referee with the answers.

Extension (10 minutes)
- Ask students to write three true and two false sentences about themselves using *some/any, much/many, some/any/no/every + thing/where/one/body*, e.g.:
  I bought some strawberries yesterday.
  I didn't go anywhere at the weekend.
- Put students in small groups. Students take turns to read their sentences and guess which of them are true and which are false.

Unit 4 Vocabulary
What do you need? → SB p46

Headway 5th edition
Pre-intermediate

Shopping list — Uncountable / Countable — Total

Shopping list — Uncountable / Countable — Total

Shopping list — Uncountable / Countable — Total

Shopping list — Uncountable / Countable — Total

GRAND TOTAL

✂ -

Shopping list — Uncountable / Countable — Total

Shopping list — Uncountable / Countable — Total

Shopping list — Uncountable / Countable — Total

Shopping list — Uncountable / Countable — Total

GRAND TOTAL

Headway © Oxford University Press 2019 — Photocopiable — 187

Unit 4 Vocabulary Teacher's notes
What do you need? → SB p46

5th edition
Headway ›››
Pre-intermediate

Aim
To list things you need for a variety of situations

Language
Countable and uncountable nouns
Food vocabulary
A piece of …

Skills
Writing

Materials
One copy of the cut-up worksheet for each pair of students

Pre-activity (5 minutes)
- Write the headings *Countable nouns* and *Uncountable nouns* on the board. Ask students to imagine that they are going to buy their weekly food and to brainstorm items they need.
- As students call out the items, ask them to say which heading they go under, e.g. *Countable nouns: tomatoes, olives, biscuits; Uncountable nouns: cheese, pasta, sugar*. Ask students to think of expressions of quantity for each item, e.g. *a kilo of tomatoes, a packet of biscuits,* etc.

Procedure (25 minutes)
- Explain that students are going to race each other to write lists of things they need in different situations.
- Divide the students into pairs and give each pair a copy of the worksheet.
- Choose a situation from below (or one of your own) and write the question on the board, e.g. *What do you need for … (a picnic)?* Students complete the heading in the first box of their worksheet, under *Shopping list,* then brainstorm words for that same situation under the *Countable* or *Uncountable* headings, e.g. *sandwiches, fruit, crisps, orange juice.*

  Situations
  - a picnic
  - your national dish
  - your favourite meal
  - a birthday party
  - a healthy meal
  - a cake

- In their pairs, students brainstorm as many ingredients or foods as they can in three minutes.
- After three minutes shout *Stop!* Pairs call out their answers around the class spelling words as they go, and identifying whether they are countable or uncountable nouns. They receive one point for every answer correctly spelt, correctly categorized as countable or uncountable, and correct for the situation. They receive an extra point for every expression of quantity they can add, e.g. *a slice of cheese.* Pairs record their totals at the bottom of the box.
- Repeat the procedure for the three other boxes. At the end, students calculate their grand total and the pair with the highest score wins.

Extension (10 minutes)
- In pairs, students think of a new situation and make a list of things they need, both countable and uncountable nouns, for that situation.
- In groups of four, pairs take it in turns to read out their list of things and the other pair tries to guess the situation.

188 Photocopiable Headway © Oxford University Press 2019

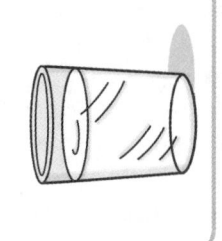

Unit 4 Communication
Can I get anyone a drink? → SB p47

5th edition
Headway ≫
Pre-intermediate

OFFER	OFFER	OFFER
A sweet? *(would)*	A lift to the station? *(would)*	Some chocolate? *(anyone)*
A drink? *(can)*	An ice cream? *(anyone)*	A biscuit? *(would)*
Some water? *(can)*	A coffee? *(can)*	Some cheesecake? *(would)*

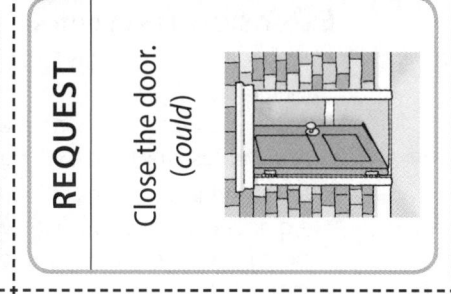

REQUEST	REQUEST	REQUEST
Open the window. *(mind)*	Close the door. *(could)*	Give me a lift to the airport. *(possibly)*
Lend me some money. *(possibly)*	Pass me the salt. *(would)*	I want some orange juice. *(can)*
I want to see the menu. *(could)*	Lend me a pen. *(could)*	Tell me where the toilets are. *(can)*

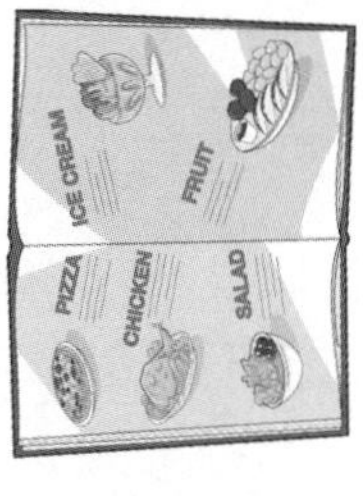

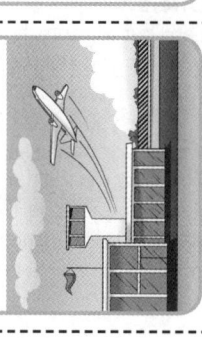

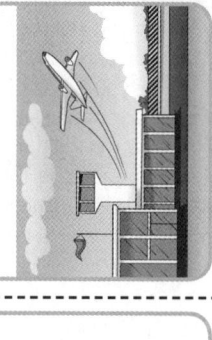

Headway © Oxford University Press 2019

Photocopiable 189

Unit 4 Communication Teacher's notes
Can I get anyone a drink? → SB p47

5th edition
Headway >>>
Pre-intermediate

Aim
To practise making and responding to offers and requests to individuals and groups

Language
Making offers and requests

Skills
Speaking and Listening

Materials
One copy of the worksheet for every three students, cut up into cards

Answers

Requests
Could I see the menu, please?
Could you possibly lend me some money?
Would you mind opening the window?
Could you lend me a pen, please?
Would you pass me the salt, please?
Could you close the door, please?
Can you tell me where the toilets are?
Can I have some orange juice, please?
Could you possibly give me a lift to the airport?

Offers
Can I get you some water?
Can I get you a drink?
Would anyone/you like a sweet?
Can I get you a (cup of) coffee?
Would anyone like an ice cream?
Would you like a lift to the station?
Would you/anyone like some cheesecake?
Would you like a biscuit?
Would anyone like some chocolate?

Pre-activity (5 minutes)
- Ask students when was the last time they had guests over and what was the occasion.
- Elicit a few requests and offers people use when they are guests or hosts, e.g.:
  Can/Could I have a glass of water?
  Would anyone like more dessert?
- Model and drill the requests, helping students pronounce them as naturally as possible.

Procedure (20 minutes)
- Give each student six cards, making sure everyone has a mix of offer and request cards. Allow students a few minutes to look at their cards and to think about how they will make each offer/request.
- Tell students they can choose how they want to respond to the requests and offers they hear, but they can't say *No* every time. When someone responds with a *Yes* answer, the student must give their card to that person, and that person must give one of their cards to the student who made the offer/request.
- Get students up and moving around the room with their cards, making offers and requests to different people and swapping their cards.
- After about ten minutes, stop the activity. Put students into groups of four and get them to make offers and requests to the whole group. Monitor students as they work, making sure they aren't just talking to individuals.
- To close the activity, ask a few students, *Who offered you something nice? Who made a difficult request?*

Extension (15 minutes)
- Put students in pairs and give them two minutes to list as many different kinds of food, drink and objects people might provide at a dinner party (e.g. fish, plates, wine) as possible. After a minute, elicit a few suggestions from each pair and write them on the board.
- Put students in groups of four or five. Tell them to imagine they're at a dinner party and to decide who the host is. Using the ideas on the board, they should write a short dinner party dialogue with lots of requests and offers.
- Get the groups to practise reading their dialogues, then invite one or two groups to perform theirs in front of the class.

Unit 5 Grammar
Verb patterns quiz → SB p50

Headway 5th edition
Pre-intermediate

Worksheet A

Right ✓ or wrong ✗?

1. ☐ I like to go on a cycling holiday next summer.
2. ☐ I'm looking forward to going somewhere special this weekend.
3. ☐ I'm planning to go abroad after I finish this English course.
4. ☐ I enjoy to meet new people when I go travelling.
5. ☐ I've decided to go to university next year.
6. ☐ I'm fed up having a stressful job – I need to apply for a new one.
7. ☐ I like sleep late when I have a day off.
8. ☐ I'm thinking to have a party to celebrate my next birthday.
9. ☐ I'd love to go camping for my next holiday.
10. ☐ I always forget to return books to the library on time.

-- ✂

Worksheet B

Right ✓ or wrong ✗?

1. ☐ I'd like to go on a cycling holiday next summer.
2. ☐ I'm looking forward going somewhere special this weekend.
3. ☐ I'm planning go abroad after I finish this English course.
4. ☐ I enjoy meeting new people when I go travelling.
5. ☐ I've decided going to university next year.
6. ☐ I'm fed up with having a stressful job – I need to apply for a new one.
7. ☐ I like to sleep late when I have a day off.
8. ☐ I'm thinking of having a party to celebrate my next birthday.
9. ☐ I love to go camping for my next holiday.
10. ☐ I always forget return books to the library on time.

Headway © Oxford University Press 2019

Photocopiable 191

Unit 5 Grammar Teacher's notes
Verb patterns quiz → SB p50

5th edition
Headway ≫
Pre-intermediate

Aim
To identify and correct grammar mistakes

Language
Verb patterns

Skills
Speaking

Materials
One copy of Worksheet A for Student As, and one copy of Worksheet B for Student Bs

Answers
Pre-activity
1 ✗ want to apply
2 ✓

Procedure

Worksheet A	Worksheet B
1 ✗	1 ✓
2 ✓	2 ✗
3 ✓	3 ✗
4 ✗	4 ✓
5 ✓	5 ✗
6 ✗	6 ✓
7 ✗	7 ✓
8 ✗	8 ✓
9 ✓	9 ✗
10 ✓	10 ✗

Pre-activity (5 minutes)
- Explain to students that they are going to do an activity which will practise the verb patterns from Unit 5.
- Write the following sentences on the board and explain that students need to decide whether they are correct or incorrect.
  1 *I want apply for a new job.*
  2 *I'd love to have a drink because I'm so thirsty.*
- Elicit the answers. Ask students to correct the wrong sentence. Highlight the pattern *want + to*-infinitive.

Procedure (20 minutes)
- Explain that students are going to decide if sentences are correct or incorrect.
- Divide students into two groups - A and B. Give Group A Worksheet A, and Group B Worksheet B. Pre-teach/Check any difficult vocabulary.
- Students work through the sentences on their worksheet in pairs or small groups to decide whether the verb patterns in the sentences are correct or incorrect. Students mark any incorrect sentences with a cross, and then correct the sentence.
- After ten minutes, stop the activity. Ask each person in Group A to find a partner from Group B to compare their answers. Point out that for each sentence, one worksheet shows the correct verb pattern. Students score a point for every sentence that has been corrected accurately on their worksheet.
- Have a class feedback session, eliciting from students the correct verb pattern for each sentence and writing it on the board.

Extension (10 minutes)
- In pairs, students discuss whether the ten statements on the worksheets are true for them or not. Ask students to give more information after making their statement. e.g. *I'd like to go on a cycling holiday next summer. I'd like to cycle around France and visit some of my French friends.*

Unit 5 Vocabulary
Phrasal verbs pair-up → SB p56

Headway 5th edition
Pre-intermediate

pick up	take off	try on
run out of	give up	throw away
look up	turn off	get on well with
put on	look after	fall out with

Headway © Oxford University Press 2019   Photocopiable   193

Unit 5 Vocabulary Teacher's notes
Phrasal verbs pair-up → SB p56

Aim
To match phrasal verbs to pictures illustrating their meanings

Language
Phrasal verbs

Skills
Speaking and Writing

Materials
One copy of the worksheet cut up for each pair or group of three students

Answers
Pre-activity
1 up
2 down
3 back

Pre-activity (5 minutes)
- Explain that students are going to play a game in which they match phrasal verbs with pictures. Briefly review common phrasal verbs by writing gapped sentences on the board and eliciting the missing adverb/preposition:
  1 *I grew _____ in a big city.*
  2 *I don't feel too well. I need to lie _____.*
  3 *I lent her some money, but she didn't pay me _____.*

Procedure (15 minutes)
- Pre-teach/Check the expressions students will need to play the game: *It's my/your turn; I'm/You're next; That's right/wrong; That picture matches/doesn't match the verb.*
- Put students into pairs or groups of three. Give each pair/group a set of jumbled phrasal verb cards and a set of jumbled picture cards. Tell students not to look at the phrasal verbs or the pictures. Get them to lay out each set of cards separately, face down on the desk.
- Demonstrate the game with one pair/group. Students take turns to turn over one picture card and one phrasal verb card. If the cards match, the student then has to make a sentence using the phrasal verb in a meaningful context. Provided the sentence is accurate, the student keeps the cards and has another turn. If the sentence isn't accurate, or if the cards don't match, the student turns the cards over again, and play moves on to the next student. Emphasize that students mustn't change the position of the cards at any time in the game, as it is a memory game.
- Students play the game in their pairs/groups. Monitor and check that students are playing the game correctly. Try to encourage them to check each other's sentences, but be prepared to be the final judge if the pairs/groups disagree.
- Students play until all the cards have been matched. The student with the most cards is the winner.

Extension (15 minutes)
- Students continue working in their pairs or groups and use the phrasal verbs to write a story. The stories can be as realistic or as silly as you think appropriate. Students use as many of the verbs as possible in their story. Monitor and help with vocabulary as necessary. Students can then read their stories to the class and vote for the best one.

Unit 5 Communication
Anything's possible! → SB p57

Headway 5th edition
Pre-intermediate

Worksheet A

	Opinion 1	Opinion 2	Opinion 3
1 Do you think you will ever _____ ?			
2 Do you think _____ is a good age to get married?			
3 Are you going to _____ next year?			
4 Is _____ the most popular sport in the world?			
5 Do you think people in the US _____ ?			
6 Were people happier _____ ago?			

Worksheet B

	Opinion 1	Opinion 2	Opinion 3
1 Do you think you will _____ one day?			
2 Do you think _____ is a good age to retire?			
3 Are you going to _____ in the next five years?			
4 Is _____ the most powerful country in the world?			
5 Do you think people in Australia _____ ?			
6 Was music better _____ ago?			

Worksheet C

	Opinion 1	Opinion 2	Opinion 3
1 Do you think you will _____ next year?			
2 Do you think _____ is a good age to have children?			
3 Are you going to _____ in the next 12 months?			
4 Are _____ the most dangerous animals on Earth?			
5 Do you think people in the UK _____ ?			
6 Were people healthier _____ ago?			

Unit 5 Communication Teacher's notes
Anything's possible! → SB p57

Headway 5th edition
Pre-intermediate

Aim
To prepare and conduct an opinion survey

Language
Expressing doubt and certainty

Skills
Reading, Speaking, Listening, and Writing

Materials
One copy of the worksheet for every three students, cut into Worksheet A, B, and C

Answers
Pre-activity

(1) ✓✓✓	(2) ?	(3) ✗✗✗
Defi<u>nite</u>ly.	Per<u>haps</u>.	<u>Defi</u>nitely <u>not</u>.
Abso<u>lute</u>ly.	I'm <u>not</u> <u>sure</u>.	<u>No</u> <u>chance</u>.
Of <u>course</u> it is.	<u>Any</u>thing's <u>possible</u>.	Not a <u>chance</u>.
Of <u>course</u> it will.	Mmm … <u>may</u>be.	
	I <u>might</u>.	
	I <u>think</u> so.	
	I <u>doubt</u> it.	
	I <u>don't</u> think so.	

Pre-activity (10 minutes)
- Draw this table on the board:

(1) ✓✓✓	(2) ?	(3) ✗✗✗

- Say these phrases and ask students to tell you which column to write them in:

  Perhaps. Anything's possible. I think so.
  Definitely. I doubt it. Of course it is.
  Definitely not. Absolutely. Of course it will.
  No chance. Mmm … maybe. Not a chance.
  I'm not sure. I might. I don't think so.

- Write the phrases into the table. Elicit and underline the stressed words/syllables.
- Drill the phrases column by column, making sure the phrases in column 1 and 3 are pronounced emphatically.

Procedure (25 minutes)
- Explain that students are going to prepare and conduct a short opinion survey.
- Pre-teach/Check *retire*, *powerful* and *healthier*.
- Divide students into three groups, A, B and C. Give a copy of Worksheet A to each student in Group A, a copy of Worksheet B to each student in Group B, and a copy of Worksheet C to each student in Group C.
- Give students five to ten minutes in their groups to discuss and complete the six questions on their worksheet. If the groups are very large, put students in pairs within the groups.
- Go round the class as the students work, giving help and support where necessary.
- When everyone's ready, regroup the students into ABC groups to conduct their surveys. They should record their answers using the ✓✓✓ / ? / ✗✗✗ symbols. Encourage them to ask one or two follow-up questions and to make note of the answers they get.
- When students have finished, they return to their original groups and compare what they found out.
- To close the activity, invite groups to report back to the class anything that they found interesting or surprising.

Extension (15 minutes)
- Each student chooses one of the questions they asked and writes a short report about it. After a short introduction, they should give their own opinion, with reasons, and explain how other students replied to it.
- If there is time, one or two students can read out their reports to the whole class.

Unit 6 Grammar
How long have you … ? → SB p60

Headway
5th edition
Pre-intermediate

How long have you … ?

	NAME	For …	Since …
… (*be*) a student of English			
… (*work/study/live*) where you are now			
… (*be*) able to swim			
… (*be*) able to drive			
… (*have*) an Internet connection or mobile phone			
… (*wear*) glasses/make-up			
… (*be*) on Facebook			
… (*know*) your closest friend			
… (*be*) interested in your favourite hobby			
… (*have*) your favourite childhood possession			
… (*be*) awake today			

Headway © Oxford University Press 2019   Photocopiable   197

Unit 6 Grammar Teacher's notes
How long have you … ? → SB p60

Aim
To do a class survey

Language
Present Perfect with *for* and *since*

Skills
Speaking

Materials
One copy of the worksheet for each student

Pre-activity (5 minutes)
- Review the use of *for* and *since* with time expressions. Call out the following time expressions and ask students to repeat with *for* or *since*, e.g. *March (since March); three weeks (for); a very long time (for); last weekend (since); half an hour (for); the beginning of the class (since); I was born (since); Christmas (since).*

Procedure (20 minutes)
- Explain that students are going to do a class survey to find out how long people in the class have had, been, or done certain things. Hand out a copy of the worksheet to each student. Pre-teach/Check *be awake, have an Internet connection, be able to* (used to talk about ability when *can* isn't possible, e.g. *How long have you been able to speak English?*).
- Give students a few moments to read through the prompts in the first column and deal with any other vocabulary queries.
- Demonstrate the activity with the class. Write *For* and *Since* on the board. Now ask a student the first question *How long have you been a student of English?* If the student gives an answer with *for*, write the answer under *For* on the board. Ask the same student the question again, but this time elicit the answer with *since* and write it under *Since* on the board.
- Explain that each question should be asked to a different student, and they should record the student's name, and their *For* and *Since* answer. If one of the questions isn't relevant to a student, the person asking should move on and ask another classmate. Students stand up and walk around the classroom, interviewing each other, and writing the relevant names and answers.
- When students have finished, elicit examples from the class, e.g. *Loukas has worked for a marketing company for a year. He's worked there since last September.*

Extension (10 minutes)
- Put students in groups of four to six. Choose two or three of the questions and get students to work out who has been, had, or done different things for the longest, e.g. *Who has been a student of English for the longest?* or *Who has known their best friend for the longest?*
- When they have finished, ask them to share their findings with the class.

Unit 6 Vocabulary
I'd love to be famous! → SB p63

1 -er   -or   -ist   -ant   -ian

1 account____
2 act____
3 archaeolog____
4 chocolate tast____
5 doct____
6 electric____
7 event plann____
8 farm____
9 histor____
10 invent____
11 journal____
12 make-up art____
13 music____
14 photograph____
15 politic____
16 racing car driv____
17 reception____
18 scient____
19 scuba diving instruct____
20 shop assist____
21 teach____
22 TV present____
23 video game design____
24 writ____

- I'd like to be _____.
- I wouldn't like to be _____.
- Someone in my family is _____.
- One of my friends is _____.
- When I was a child, I wanted to be _____.
- If you work as _____ in my country, you don't get paid much.
- If you work as _____ in my country, you can earn a lot of money.

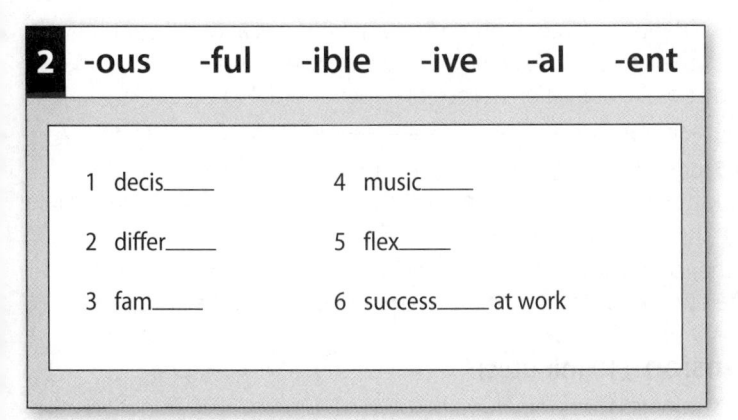

2 -ous   -ful   -ible   -ive   -al   -ent

1 decis____
2 differ____
3 fam____
4 music____
5 flex____
6 success____ at work

- I'd really like to be _____.
- I know someone who's _____.

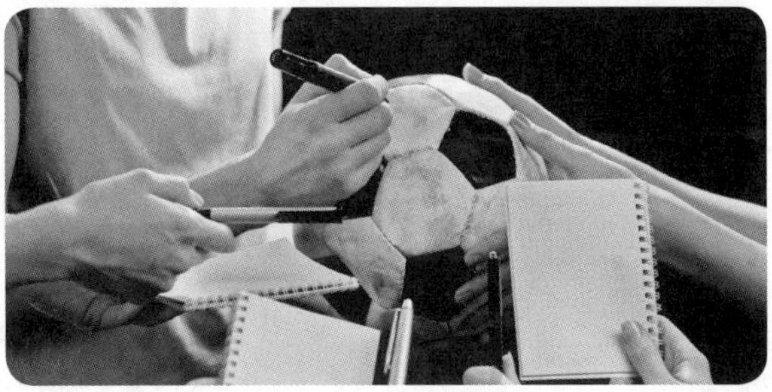

3 Adjectives and nouns

1 ambitious – _____
2 happy – _____
3 famous – _____
4 healthy – _____
5 successful – _____
6 wealthy – _____
7 kind – _____
8 honest – _____
9 beautiful – _____

- I think _____ is more important than _____.
- I think _____ is more important than _____.
- I think _____ and _____ are the most important things in life.

Unit 6 Vocabulary Teacher's notes
I'd love to be famous! → SB p63

5th edition
Headway ≫
Pre-intermediate

Aim
To take part in a discussion about work and values

Language
Suffixes (to form nouns and adjectives)

Skills
Speaking and Listening

Materials
One copy of the worksheet for every student

Answers

1

1	accountant	13	musician
2	actor	14	photographer
3	archaeologist	15	politician
4	chocolate taster	16	racing car driver
5	doctor	17	receptionist
6	electrician	18	scientist
7	event planner	19	scuba driving instructor
8	farmer	20	shop assistant
9	historian	21	teacher
10	inventor	22	TV presenter
11	journalist	23	video game designer
12	make-up artist	24	writer

2

1	decisive	4	musical
2	different	5	flexible
3	famous	6	successful

3

1	ambition	6	wealth
2	happiness	7	kindness
3	fame	8	honesty
4	health	9	beauty
5	success		

Pre-activity (10 minutes)

- Write *noughts and crosses* on the board. Check students know the aim of the game (to get three noughts or crosses in a row).
- Copy these suffixes into an empty grid on the board: -ness, -er, -ous, -ility, -ist, -tion, -ment, -ian, -ive
- Divide the class into two teams – noughts and crosses. Toss a coin to see which team goes first.
- The first team have ten seconds to say a word with a suffix from the grid. If the word is correct, replace the suffix in the square with a nought or a cross.
- The members of the other team then take their turn, and so on, until one team wins or there is a draw.
- If you have time, play another round, replacing some of the suffixes, e.g. -ant, -al, -y, -ence, -sion, -ment.

Procedure (30 minutes)

- Give each student a copy of the worksheet. Put students in pairs and ask them to complete the names of the jobs in the first box and the adjectives in the second box by adding suffixes. Then ask them to make nouns from the adjectives in the third box. Pre-teach/Check *wealthy* and *honest*. When they've finished, ask students to work individually and complete the sentences on the right-hand side of the worksheet about themselves and the people they know by using the nouns and adjectives in the boxes. Remind students to use the indefinite article *a/an* with the names of the jobs.
- Tell students you want them to find out how similar or different they are to their partner. Draw this scale on the board and ask each student in the class to copy it on a piece of paper or in their notebook:

  very similar ←————————→ very different

- Put students into pairs to compare and discuss the answers on their worksheets. When they've finished, they should mark a cross on the line with their and their partner's initial.
- At the feedback session, ask students to report back on how similar/different they are to their partner, giving reasons for their answers.

Extension (10 minutes)

- Ask students *What's important to you in a partner?* Check students understand *partner* (= boyfriend/girlfriend/husband/wife). If you think this is not appropriate for your class, ask *What's important to you in a friend?*. Elicit a few answers and write them on the board.
- Ask students to look at the third box on their worksheets and rank the items in the table from 1 (most important) to 9 (least important). Then put students in pairs to compare and discuss their answers. To extend the discussion, put pairs into bigger groups.
- At the feedback session, see if the class can agree on three important factors and three factors that aren't important.

Unit 6 Communication
Question tags — SB p67

Headway — 5th edition — Pre-intermediate

Statement	Tag	Response
You take lovely photographs,	don't you?	Thanks, I won this camera in a photography competition.
We haven't got any homework this evening,	have we?	No, we haven't. The teacher said we needed to rest.
There are lots of similarities between Paris and Rome,	aren't there?	In some ways, yes, they are similar.
You don't work full-time,	do you?	No, I don't. I've got a part-time job.
Life is more stressful these days,	isn't it?	Yes, it is. We have to work much harder.
He hasn't been married for very long,	has he?	No, he hasn't. He only got married a few months ago.
We've known each other for ages,	haven't we?	Yes, we have. We were at primary school together.
She's got beautiful blue eyes,	hasn't she?	Yes, she has. She's inherited her father's good looks.
You went to bed late last night,	didn't you?	Yes, I did. I only had a few hours' sleep.
He wasn't very well-behaved,	was he?	No, he wasn't. I thought he was quite rude.
You weren't at school yesterday,	were you?	No, I wasn't. I had a bad headache.
He didn't earn much money in his last job,	did he?	No, he didn't. He's on a much higher salary now.

Headway © Oxford University Press 2019 — Photocopiable

Unit 6 Communication Teacher's notes
Question tags ➔ SB p67

Headway 5th edition
Pre-intermediate

Aim
To practise identifying and using question tags asking for agreement

Language
Question tags

Skills
Reading and Speaking

Materials
One copy of the worksheet for each pair

Pre-activity (5 minutes)
- Explain that students are going to do a matching activity to practise question tags.
- Pre-teach/Check any vocabulary from the worksheet, e.g. *primary school, inherited, well-behaved*.
- Draw three boxes on the board. In the first box, write: *She's a hotel receptionist*, and in the third box, write: *Yes, she is. She works at the Hilton*.
- Elicit the question tag *isn't she?* and write it in the second box.

She's a hotel receptionist,	**isn't she?**	Yes, she is. She works at the Hilton.

- Ask students if the intonation goes up or down at the end of these question tags, and draw a line to show the falling intonation above *isn't she?* Check that students understand that falling intonation means that the speaker wants the other person to agree with him/her.

Procedure (20 minutes)
- Explain that students are going to make mini dialogues similar to the example on the board.
- Tell students that you will give them three sets of cards – a set of question openings, a set of question tags, and a set of reply cards. Explain that they will need to match them up correctly.
- Divide students into pairs. Give each pair the three sets of cards, cut up.
- Students make 12 mini dialogues with each one laid out clearly in front of them. Go around the class checking and monitoring.
- When most pairs are finished, go through the answers with the class. Ask pairs of students to read the mini dialogues aloud to check their answers. Focus on falling intonation in the questions tags, if necessary.
- Ask students to turn over the question tag cards so they can't see them. In pairs, practise the mini dialogues again still using the appropriate question tag.

Extension (10 minutes)
- Ask students to make their own questions and answers using the question tags provided.
- Invite pairs to perform their new dialogues in front of the class.

Unit 7 Grammar
What's it like? → SB p70

5th edition
Headway
Pre-intermediate

START

- What / your best friend / like?
- What / your home / like?
- **GO BACK ONE SQUARE**
- What / weather like / today?
- What / weekend activities / you like?
- How / your parents?
- What / your oldest relative / look like?
- **MISS A GO**
- What / your boss or teacher / like?
- How / things in general?
- What / your favourite actor / look like?
- **HAVE ANOTHER GO**
- What / bands / you like?
- What / weather like / in December in your country?
- What / your best friend / look like?
- What / your capital city / like?
- What / your doctor / like?
- What / your favourite food / like?
- **GO FORWARD TWO SQUARES**
- What / weather like / in May in your country?
- What / people / like / in your hometown?
- What / food / you like?
- **GO BACK ONE SQUARE**
- What / your neighbours / like?
- What / your mobile phone / look like?
- How / your best friend?
- What / places in Europe / you like?
- **GO BACK ONE SQUARE**

FINISH

BONUS WORDS AND PHRASES

- modern and cosmopolitan
- hot and humid
- Just ordinary, really.
- OK, but a bit stressed.
- friendly and helpful
- attractive
- a bit miserable
- home-made
- hardworking and successful
- wet and windy
- dark hair and eyes
- warm and sunny
- short, but good-looking
- amazing, a really good place
- hot and spicy

Headway © Oxford University Press 2019   Photocopiable

Unit 7 Grammar Teacher's notes
What's it like? → SB p70

Aim
To play a board game by asking and answering questions correctly

Language
Questions with *like*
Adjectives for describing people and things

Skills
Speaking

Materials
One copy of the worksheet for each group of four students
Dice and counters

Pre-activity (5 minutes)
- Ask students what questions with *like* they can remember. Elicit the question forms *What is he like? What does he like? What does he look like?* and write them on the board. Add the question *How is he?* Then check that students understand the differences between the questions by eliciting some typical answers to each.

Procedure (20 minutes)
- Explain that students are going to play a board game to practise these questions.
- Pre-teach/Check the expressions students will need to play the game: *Throw/Roll the dice; Go back/forward one square; Miss a go; Have another go; It's my/your turn; I'm/You're next; That's right/wrong; We are the winners!*
- Put students into groups of four and explain that each group has two teams of two. Hand out one copy of the board game, and dice and counters to each group.
- Look at the board game with the class. Explain that most of the squares have a prompt for a question, many of them containing the word *like*.
- Some of the prompts are 'open' and can be interpreted in two ways, e.g. *What / your best friend like?* can be *What is your best friend like?* or *What does your best friend like?* Explain that students need to listen carefully to the questions asked in the game and word their answer accordingly.
- Explain the rules: students play the game in their teams of two and take turns to throw the dice and move around the board. If a pair lands on a square with a prompt, the student who threw the dice forms the question and the other student gives an answer. If they both get it right, they move forward one square. If they get either the question or answer wrong, their turn ends, and play moves on to the other team.
- Focus attention on the Bonus Words and Phrases in the middle of the page. Explain that if students use any of the bonus words/phrases correctly in their answers, they get to move forward two squares, instead of one.
- Students should cross out the words/phrases in the Bonus Words and Phrases chart as they use them. The first pair to reach 'Finish' are the winners.
- Monitor and check that students are playing the game correctly. Try to encourage students to check each other's answers, but be prepared to be the final judge if the groups disagree.

Extension (5 minutes)
- Get students to say some of the descriptions they used in the game to the rest of the class. Other students can either guess who or what they have described, or can guess which question from the game board they were answering.
- For extra practice, get students to answer questions from the board game again.

Unit 7 Vocabulary
I think ... → SB p76

5th edition
Headway ›»
Pre-intermediate

Survey sheet A

good	large	miserable
fast	dirty	frightened
easy	rude	fascinating
glad	terrible	well-known

I think ...

... *everybody* / _____ *people* / *nobody* here had a **terrible** day yesterday.

... *everybody* / _____ *people* / *nobody* here *finds* / *find* it **hard** to stay calm when people are **rude** to them.

... *everybody* / _____ *people* / *nobody* here *has* / *have* got a pair of **dirty** shoes at home.

Survey sheet B

good	large	miserable
fast	dirty	frightened
easy	rude	fascinating
glad	terrible	well-known

I think ...

... *everybody* / _____ *people* / *nobody* here *thinks* / *think* politics is **fascinating**.

... *everybody* / _____ *people* / *nobody* here *is* / *are* **glad** that they're learning English.

... *everybody* / _____ *people* / *nobody* here had a **good** holiday last year.

Survey sheet C

good	large	miserable
fast	dirty	frightened
easy	rude	fascinating
glad	terrible	well-known

I think ...

... *everybody* / _____ *people* / *nobody* here *has* / *have* got **fast** Internet on their phone.

... *everybody* / _____ *people* / *nobody* here *is* / *are* feeling **miserable** today.

... *everybody* / _____ *people* / *nobody* here had a **large** breakfast this morning.

Survey sheet D

good	large	miserable
fast	dirty	frightened
easy	rude	fascinating
glad	terrible	well-known

I think ...

... *everybody* / _____ *people* / *nobody* here *has* / *have* met someone **well-known**.

... *everybody* / _____ *people* / *nobody* here *finds* / *find* English pronunciation **easy**.

... *everybody* / _____ *people* / *nobody* here *is* / *are* **frightened** of snakes.

Unit 7 Vocabulary Teacher's notes
I think ... → SB p76

5th edition
Headway >>
Pre-intermediate

Aim
To make guesses about the class and conduct a class survey to see if those predictions are correct

Language
Synonyms and antonyms

Skills
Reading, Speaking, and Listening

Materials
One copy of the worksheet for every four students, cut along the dotted lines into four survey sheets

Answers
Pre-activity
1 S, A
2 A, S
3 S, A, S
4 A, S, A
5 S, A, S, S

Pre-activity (10 minutes)
- Write these adjective chains on the board:
  1 *intelligent – clever – stupid*
  2 *wrong – correct – right*
  3 *fantastic – amazing – awful – terrible*
  4 *strange – normal – usual – unusual*
  5 *sad – miserable – happy – glad – pleased*
- Put students in pairs to discuss how each adjective is connected to the one before it. Is it a synonym (S) or an antonym (A)? Do the first one as an example. Check the correct answers with the class.

Procedure (25 minutes)
- Write on the board:
  I think ...
  ... everybody / _____ people / nobody here is / are happy.
  Circle *everybody* or *nobody*, or write a number in the gap, and underline the correct verb form.
- Conduct a short class survey to check your guesses. Keep a tally of answers, including your own, and ask some follow-up questions. Briefly draw attention to the singular verb (*is*) after *everybody* and *nobody*.
- Tell the class they're going to do a similar survey. Put students into groups of four and divide the groups into pairs. Give each group a copy of the cut-up worksheet so each pair has two survey sheets. For each adjective in the box, ask pairs to write a synonym and an antonym (they will need to use some of these when answering the questions in the survey). When they have finished, ask pairs to compare their answers with the other pair in their group.
- Ask students to work individually and read the *I think ...* statements on their sheets. For every question, they should guess the answer (circle *everybody* or *nobody*, or write in a number), choose the correct verb form and write the question they need to ask the other students in order to check their assumptions. They should also think of some follow-up (*Wh-*) questions to ask. With weaker classes, you could put students into AA, BB, CC, and DD pairs to write the questions, but make sure students return to their groups to do the survey.
- Tell students that when answering the questions in the survey they must use synonyms and antonyms in their answers. Write this example question on the board:
  A *Did you have a terrible day yesterday?*
  Elicit these answers and write them on the board, too:
  B *No, I had a fantastic day.*
  C *Yeah, I had an awful day.*
  Underline the synonyms and antonyms in the dialogue (*terrible, fantastic, awful*).
- Ask students to conduct their surveys in their groups. They should interview each member of the group, one at a time. Remind them to keep a tally and ask follow-up questions.
- At the feedback stage, ask a few pairs *How many correct guesses did you make?*

Extension (10 minutes)
- Tell students to think of a quiet place in this town/city, an amazing film, an interesting job, a stupid idea and a difficult question. Put students in pairs or small groups to compare and discuss their ideas.
- Conduct class feedback. Do students agree or disagree?

206   Photocopiable   Headway © Oxford University Press 2019

Unit 7 Communication
I don't want to do that! → SB p77

5th edition Headway Pre-intermediate

PART 1: Conversations

1

A I think it sounds great. There are lots of famous paintings.
A From 9.00 till 5.00.
A Well, would you like to go to an art exhibition at the Riverside Gallery?
A What shall we do today?
A £20.50.
A How about going to a concert in the park?

B I'm not sure. How much is it?
B Is it any good?
B Oh, I can't – I'm a student, I don't have much money. Sorry!
B I'm not sure.
B Mmm, I don't know. What time is it open?
B Mmm, I don't really feel like listening to live music.

2

C Mmm, I don't really feel like watching sport.
C There's a horror film on at the Odeon.
C Good idea! Let's stay in.
C It sounds really funny. It's a comedy!
C OK, how about *Padman* then?
C It's on at 3 o'clock.
C Shall we go to the cinema on Saturday?

D I don't know. What's on?
D What time is it on?
D Right, shall we stay at home and make pizza?
D I'm not sure. Is it any good?
D I don't know. I'd prefer to watch the football at the Sports Café.
D Mmm ... Not my kind of thing. What else?

PART 2: Ideas

go to a basketball game	go to the cinema	go to a nightclub	go to the ballet *Romeo and Juliet*
stay at home	go to a jazz concert	go to a modern art exhibition	go to the musical *Mamma Mia!*

Unit 7 Communication Teacher's notes
I don't want to do that! → SB p77

Aim
To practise making and responding to suggestions

Language
Making and responding to suggestions

Skills
Reading, Listening, and Speaking

Materials
One copy of the worksheet for each pair of students, with the eight idea cards removed and cut up

Answers

Conversation 1
- A What shall we do today?
- B I'm not sure.
- A How about going to a concert in the park?
- B Mmm, I don't really feel like listening to live music.
- A Well, would you like to go to an art exhibition at the Riverside Gallery?
- B Is it any good?
- A I think it sounds great. There are lots of famous paintings.
- B Mmm, I don't know. What time is it open?
- A From 9.00 till 5.00.
- B I'm not sure. How much is it?
- A £20.50.
- B Oh, I can't – I'm a student, I don't have much money. Sorry!

Conversation 2
- C Shall we go to the cinema on Saturday?
- D I don't know. What's on?
- C There's a horror film on at the Odeon.
- D Mmm … Not my kind of thing. What else?
- C OK. How about *Padman* then?
- D I'm not sure. Is it any good?
- C It sounds really funny. It's a comedy!
- D I don't know. I'd prefer to watch the football at the Sports Café.
- C Mmm, I don't really feel like watching sport.
- D Right, shall we stay at home and make pizza?
- C Good idea! Let's stay in.

Pre-activity (5 minutes)
- Elicit the names of a film, an art exhibition, a show, a sporting event, etc., which are being shown or happening in your town or city, and write them on the board.
- In pairs, students discuss which event they would like to go to.
- Have a brief feedback session. Ask students which event they would like to go to, and when and where it is on. Leave the events on the board so students can refer back to them during the Extension activity.

Procedure (30 minutes)
- Explain to students that they are going to put the lines from two conversations in order.
- Divide students into pairs. Give each pair Part 1 of the worksheet, and ask them to put the lines in the conversations in order. As students complete their worksheets, monitor and help if necessary.
- Stop the activity when most students have finished and check the answers as a class.
- Ask students to practise the dialogues in pairs for a few minutes. Then ask students to turn over their worksheets so they can't see the dialogues. Students have to try and remember the conversations with their partner.
- Explain that students are now going to try and decide what to do this weekend. Give each pair a set of *Ideas* from Part 2, placed in a pile face down on the table. One student suggests an activity from one of the cards and asks their partner to give an answer.

    - A *Shall we go to a basketball game?*
    - B *I'm not sure. How much is it?*
    - A *£8.00 per ticket.*
    - B *Oh no – sorry, I haven't got any money!*

- Go around the class listening to their conversations and making a note of any common errors.
- Have a feedback session and discuss any common language problems you noted.

Extension (5 minutes)
- Put students into new pairs. With their new partner, students look at the activities written on the board during the Pre-activity. They take turns to suggest going to each of these events.

Unit 8 Grammar
Do you agree? → SB p80

1. 'People who are scared of heights shouldn't go skydiving.'
   DISAGREE — AGREE

2. 'Women shouldn't compete against men in sports.'
   DISAGREE — AGREE

3. 'You have to go to the gym regularly if you want to stay fit.'
   DISAGREE — AGREE

4. 'Children shouldn't start sports until the age of 12.'
   DISAGREE — AGREE

5. 'Karate should be a school subject.'
   DISAGREE — AGREE

6. 'People over 50 should stop doing dangerous sports.'
   DISAGREE — AGREE

7. 'You shouldn't do exercise straight after eating.'
   DISAGREE — AGREE

8. 'You don't have to be very fit to do yoga.'
   DISAGREE — AGREE

9. 'All football players should wear helmets.'
   DISAGREE — AGREE

10. 'Gymnasts have to be very skinny to be successful.'
    DISAGREE — AGREE

Unit 8 Grammar Teacher's notes
Do you agree? → SB p80

Aim
To discuss opinions about sports and fitness

Language
should/shouldn't, have to/don't have to
Sports vocabulary

Skills
Speaking

Materials
One copy of the worksheet for each student

Pre-activity (5 minutes)
- Write the following activities on the board:
  - skydiving   surfing
  - karate   scuba-diving
  - gymnastics   motor racing
  - skateboarding   horse riding
- Put students in pairs and ask them to decide which activity is the hardest, the most dangerous/expensive, etc.
- Ask a few pairs to share their answers with the class. For each statement, ask the other students in the class if they agree or disagree, and ask them to tell you why.

Procedure (20 minutes)
- Explain that students are going to do a discussion activity to practise *should/shouldn't, have to/don't have to*.
- Hand out a copy of the worksheet to each student. Explain that the ten statements deal with different aspects of sports and fitness. Pre-teach/Check *scared of heights, skinny, compete*. Give students a few moments to read through the ten statements and deal with any other vocabulary queries.
- Explain that students need to record their response to each statement on the tinted bar underneath. If they strongly agree, they put a cross very close to *Agree* and if they strongly disagree, they put a cross very close to *Disagree*. They can also put their cross at any position between the two extremes to indicate where their opinion falls. Give students time to work through the statements and record their response to each one. Monitor and help as necessary.
- Put students into groups of three or four for the discussion stage. Pre-teach/Check expressions students can use in their discussion, e.g. *What do you think? I completely agree/disagree with this; Yes, me too/I'm not sure; I don't really know about this one; It doesn't make any difference to me, I think people can/must/should ...*
- Put students from different cultures/age groups together to ensure a range of opinions. Encourage students to give examples from their own experience wherever possible.
- Monitor and help as necessary. Note down common errors in the use of *should/have to*, but don't give feedback on these until after the task.
- Bring the class back together and ask groups to share their opinions on one or two of the statements.

Extension (15 minutes)
- Get students to think about their own attitude to sports and fitness, and prepare a short speech. Ask questions to prompt students' ideas, e.g. *What do you do to keep fit? How often do you do sports? How do you feel about extreme sports/competitive sports? Do you think professional sports have become too commercial? Do you think sports play an important role in international relations?* etc. Give students time to make a few notes to help them with their speech.
- Students give their speeches to the class, or to their classmates in small groups.

Unit 8 Vocabulary
What shall I wear? → SB p86

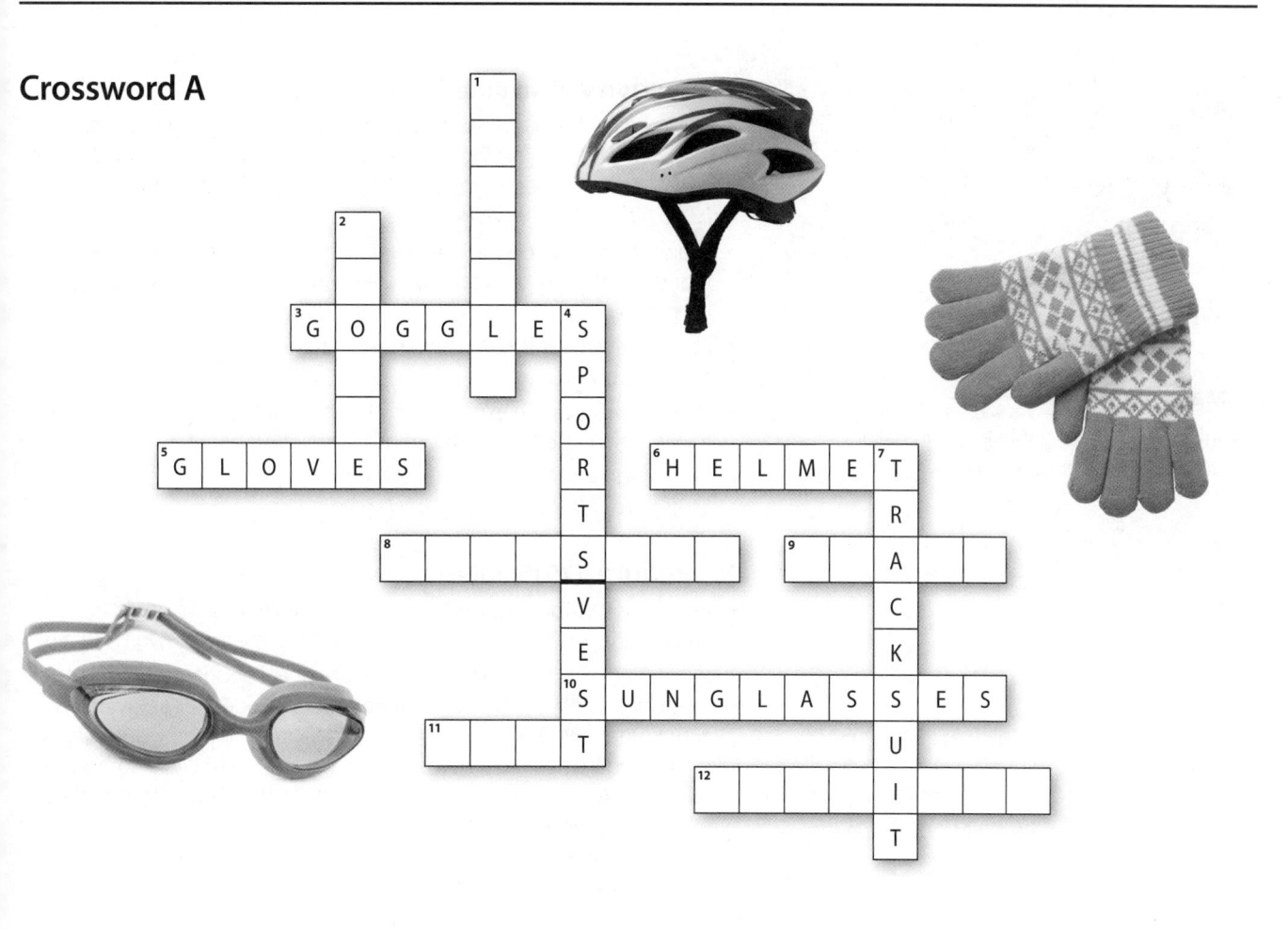

5th edition
Headway »»
Pre-intermediate

Crossword A

3 across: GOGGLES
5 across: GLOVES
6 across: HELMET
7 down: TRACKSUIT
10 across: SUNGLASSES
4 down: SPORTSVEST

Crossword B

1 down: SANDALS
2 down: HOODIE
8 across: SWIMSUIT
9 across: SCARF
11 across: BELT
12 across: LEGGINGS

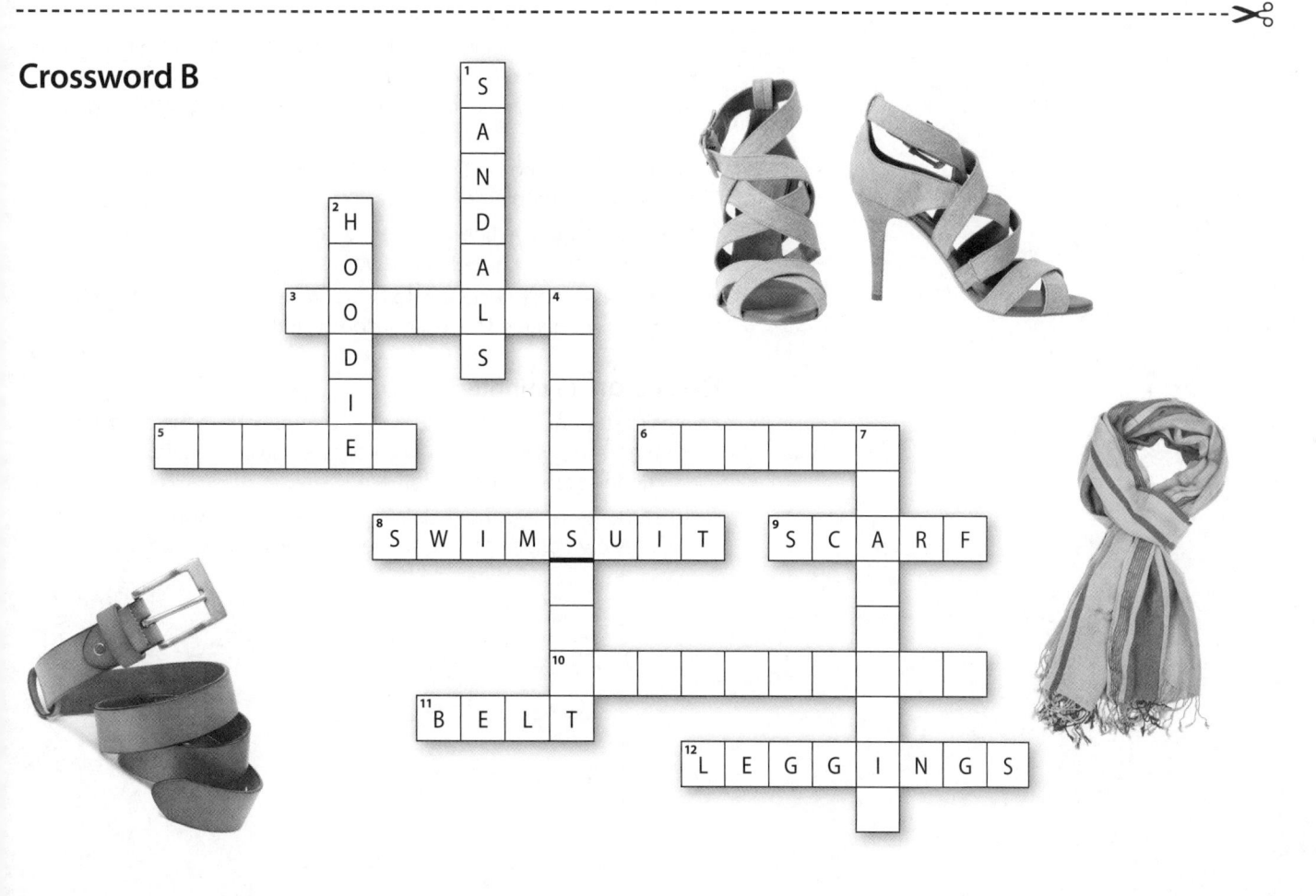

Headway © Oxford University Press 2019   Photocopiable   211

Unit 8 Vocabulary Teacher's notes
What shall I wear? → SB p86

Headway 5th edition
Pre-intermediate

Aim
To complete a crossword by asking for and giving definitions for clothes words

Language
Clothes vocabulary

Skills
Speaking, Listening, and Writing

Materials
One copy of the worksheet cut in half for each pair of students

Pre-activity (5 minutes)

- Ask students *What am I wearing today?* Elicit the language to describe your items of clothing. Or, alternatively, bring in some items of clothing and elicit the names for these. Ask *What is it made of? When do we wear it? Do men or women wear it?*
- Draw a crossword on the board and elicit the word *crossword*. Explain that students are going to play a game to complete a crossword together.
- Check that students can make the questions *What's one down? What's three across?*
- Pre-teach/Check the expressions students will need to play the game and write these expressions on the board:
  - You start.   It's my/your turn.
  - Shall I start?   Whose turn is it?

Procedure (20 minutes)

- Explain that students are going to write definitions for clothes vocabulary, which they will then use to complete a crossword in pairs.
- Put students in pairs and give each student a worksheet so that Student As are working with Student As and Student Bs are working with Student Bs. Ask students to write definitions for the words already completed in their crosswords. Encourage them to include some of the following details: the material the item of clothing is usually made of, who usually wears it, and the situation where it is usually worn, e.g. *They are often made of cotton, both men and women wear them, we usually wear them in bed.* (= pyjamas)
- Monitor while they work. Make sure that their definitions are accurate and will be understood by students in the other group.
- Put students in new pairs so that Student As are working with Student Bs. Tell students not to show each other their crosswords. They take turns to ask their partner for definitions of the missing words, e.g. *What is one down?*
- Go around listening to students and helping when necessary. Note any pronunciation problems.
- When students have finished, they can check their answers are correct by looking at their partner's crossword.
- Have a class feedback session to focus on any common pronunciation problems connected to the language of clothing.

Extension (5 minutes)

- In pairs, students take turns to describe somebody in the class. Tell them not to say who it is, but their partner must guess from the description of this person's clothes.
- Ask students to describe their favourite outfit to the class. This can be one they own or one they have seen on a well-known person.

Unit 8 Communication
What seems to be the matter? → SB p87

5th edition Headway Pre-intermediate

Worksheet A

| Tom Martin | Bella Smith | Mike Lewis | Paula Field | Sam Green |

Labels visible: Vicky Turner, Adam White, Kate Walker, Lily Ball, Jack Butcher

Worksheet B

| Adam White | Kate Walker | Jack Butcher | Vicky Turner | Lily Ball |

Labels visible: Paula Field, Bella Smith, Mike Lewis, Sam Green, Tom Martin

Headway © Oxford University Press 2019 — Photocopiable — 213

Unit 8 Communication Teacher's notes
What seems to be the matter? → SB p87

Headway 5th edition
Pre-intermediate

Aim
To take part in an information exchange activity

Language
At the doctor's

Skills
Speaking and Listening

Materials
One worksheet for every two students, cut into Worksheet A and Worksheet B

Answers
Procedure
1 What seems to be the matter?
2 Any sickness/diarrhoea/temperature/headache?
3 Have you got a temperature/sore throat/headache/earache/stomach ache?
4 Do you feel hot/tired/sick?
5 Does it hurt when you swallow/walk on it/use it?
6 Can I look at your throat/finger/ears/knee?

Pre-activity (10 minutes)
- Draw an outline of a body on the board. Draw lines to the following body parts and elicit the words for these:
  1 head   4 wrist
  2 throat   5 ankle
  3 stomach   6 the whole body
- Put students in pairs and give them a few minutes to think of the different health problems someone might have with numbers 1–6.
- Check the correct answers with the whole class.

Procedure (30 minutes)
- Explain that students are going to take turns to be doctor and patient.
- Working with the whole class, elicit/review questions doctors often ask patients by providing the sentence beginnings below:

    What seems … ?   Do you feel … ?
    Any … ?   Does it hurt when … ?
    Have you got a … ?   Can I look at your … ?

- Divide students into AB pairs. Give Student A Worksheet A and Student B Worksheet B. Tell students not to look at each other's worksheets.
- Explain that students need to match the five names at the top of their worksheets to five of the people in their picture. To do this, they must take turns to be doctor and patient. Student A starts by being 'doctor'. He/She 'calls' one of the patients at the top of their worksheet (e.g. *Tom Martin, please!*). Student B finds Tom Martin on his/her worksheet and takes on this role. They then roleplay a short doctor-patient conversation, during which Student A looks at his/her worksheet, deduces who Tom Martin is in the picture and draws a line between the name and the patient. It's then Student B's turn to be the doctor, and so on.
- When students have finished, they compare worksheets to see if they have matched the names to the patients correctly.

Extension (10 minutes)
- Write these health problems on the board:
    flu
    a very sore throat
    a very high temperature
    food poisoning
    a sprained ankle/wrist/knee/shoulder
- Put students in pairs to ask and answer *Have you ever had … ?* questions about them. Encourage students to use follow-up questions like *What happened? What did you do?* to keep the conversations going, but only if students feel comfortable talking about their health.
- Have a quick whole class feedback session.

Unit 9 Grammar
Two news stories → SB p90

5th edition Headway >>
Pre-intermediate

Worksheet A

Story 1

Edyta Kowalska, a Polish teacher, was shocked when she saw her dog walking up her garden path. Why?

On September 25, 2012, Edyta was in [1]_____ (*Where ... ?*) for the day. She had taken her dog, Cherry, with her because [2]_____ (*Why ... ?*). Edyta had had Cherry for [3]_____ (*How long ... ?*) and she loved her very much. While Edyta and Cherry were [4]_____ (*What ... ?*), a car suddenly stopped near them. Three men jumped out of the car. They were all wearing [5]_____ (*What ... ?*). They grabbed Cherry and they drove away. Edyta felt [6]_____ (*How ... ?*) because she thought they were going to hurt Cherry. She called [7]_____ (*Who ... ?*), but they didn't seem very interested. Edyta started putting photos and messages on social media [8]_____ (*When ... ?*), but nobody had any information about Cherry. After six months, Edyta thought she would never see Cherry again. Then, [9]_____ (*How many ... ?*) years later, Cherry came home! Edyta was looking out of her kitchen window when she saw the dog coming up her garden path. 'I couldn't believe it,' Edyta says. 'She looked very [10]_____ (*What ... like?*), but she was OK and she had got home. That was all that mattered.'

Story 2

Heidemarie Schwermer, a German grandmother, says she's been much happier since she gave up cash more than 10 years ago. Here's her story.

15 years ago, Heidemarie Schwermer was living in Dortmund. She had lived in a small town since she was a child, but then she had moved to the city after her marriage ended. She was shocked because lots of homeless people were living on the streets of Dortmund, so she decided to do something about it. She opened a shop called *Give and Take*, where people could trade goods and services. Soon, Heidemarie decided that she owned too many things and that she wanted to live a simpler life. She sold her apartment and kept just €200 of the money. She gave the rest of it to other people. Now she owns just a suitcase of clothes, a laptop and a mobile phone, and she travels around the world exchanging work for food and accommodation. In 2001, she received a large amount of money because she had written a book about her lifestyle. She gave the money to charity, saying 'It can make many people happy instead of just one.'

Unit 9 Grammar
Two news stories → SB p90

Headway 5th edition
Pre-intermediate

Worksheet B

Story 1

Edyta Kowalska, a Polish teacher, was shocked when she saw her dog walking up her garden path. Why?

   On September 25, 2012, Edyta was in Warsaw for the day. She had taken her dog, Cherry, with her because she didn't want to leave her at home. Edyta had had Cherry for two years and she loved her very much. While Edyta and Cherry were crossing a bridge, a car suddenly stopped near them. Three men jumped out of the car. They were all wearing masks. They grabbed Cherry and they drove away. Edyta felt terrified because she thought they were going to hurt Cherry. She called the police, but they didn't seem very interested. Edyta started putting photos and messages on social media as soon as she got home, but nobody had any information about Cherry. After six months, Edyta thought she would never see Cherry again. Then, two years later, Cherry came home! Edyta was looking out of her kitchen window when she saw the dog coming up her garden path. 'I couldn't believe it,' Edyta says. 'She looked very thin, but she was OK and she had got home. That was all that mattered.'

Story 2

Heidemarie Schwermer, a German grandmother, says she's been much happier since she gave up cash ¹_____ (When … ?). Here's her story.

   15 years ago, Heidemarie was living in ²_____ (Where … ?). She had lived in a small town ³_____ (How long … ?), but then she had moved to the city ⁴_____ (When … ?). She was shocked because lots of homeless people were living on the streets of Dortmund, so she decided to do something about it. She ⁵_____ (What … ?) where people could exchange goods and services. Soon, Heidemarie decided that she owned too many things and that she wanted to live a ⁶_____ (What kind of … ?) life. She sold ⁷_____ (What … ?) and kept just ⁸_____ (How much … ?) of the money. She gave the rest of it to other people. Now she owns just a suitcase of clothes, a laptop and a mobile phone, and she travels around the world exchanging work for food and accommodation. In 2001, she received a large amount of money because she ⁹_____ (Why … ?). She gave the money to ¹⁰_____ (Who … ?), saying 'It can make many people happy instead of just one.'

216 Photocopiable

Headway © Oxford University Press 2019

Unit 9 Grammar Teacher's notes
Two news stories → SB p90

5th edition
Headway »
Pre-intermediate

Aim
To exchange information and complete a text

Language
Narrative tenses – Past Simple, Past Continuous, Past Perfect
Joining words

Skills
Reading, Speaking, Listening, and Writing

Materials
One copy of the worksheet for each pair of students, cut into two along the dotted line

Answers

Worksheet A
1 Where was Edyta on September 25, 2012? (Warsaw)
2 Why had she taken her dog, Cherry, with her? (because she didn't want to leave her at home)
3 How long had she had Cherry? (two years)
4 What were Edyta and Cherry doing when a car stopped near them? (crossing a bridge)
5 What were the men wearing? (masks)
6 How did Edyta feel? (terrified)
7 Who did she call? (the police)
8 When did Edyta start putting photos and messages on social media? (as soon as she got home)
9 How many years later did Cherry come home? (two)
10 What did Cherry look like? (very thin)

Worksheet B
1 When did Heidemarie give up cash? (more than 10 years ago)
2 Where was Heidemarie living 15 years ago? (Dortmund)
3 How long had she lived in a small town? (since she was a child)
4 When had she moved there/to Dortmund? (after her marriage ended)
5 What did Heidemarie do (to help the homeless)? (opened a shop called *Give and Take*)
6 What kind of life did she want? (a simpler life)
7 What did she sell? (her apartment)
8 How much money did she keep? (€200)
9 Why did she receive a large amount of money in 2001? (because she'd written a book about her lifestyle)
10 Who did she give the money to? (charity)

Pre-activity (10 minutes)
- Tell students that they are going to read two news stories. Write these key words on the board and check students understand them all.
  Story 1: dog, car, garden path
  Story 2: cash, homeless, travel
- Put students in pairs or small groups to discuss what they think each story might be about. Elicit ideas and suggestions from the pairs/groups in a whole class discussion, but don't say yet whether or not any of them are correct.

Procedure (30 minutes)
- Tell students they are going to read and complete the two news stories by asking each other questions to find the missing information.
- Check/Pre-teach *shocked, mask, to grab, to exchange, goods, services, charity* and *lifestyle*.
- Put students in pairs and give each student a worksheet so that Student As are working with Student As and Student Bs are working with Student Bs. Give them a few minutes to read the texts alone and then work with their partner to prepare the ten questions they need to ask in order to find out the missing information. They should write their questions on a separate piece of paper. Go around the class as the students work, giving help and support where necessary. Make sure that each student has ten correctly formed questions.
- Regroup the students into AB pairs. Tell them not to look at each other's worksheets. Students take turns to ask questions and complete their texts.
- When all the pairs have finished, ask the whole class *Were they good news or bad news stories?* (good news).
- Finally, ask students *Which story did you like best? Why?* and elicit a few opinions.

Extension (10 minutes)
- Write on the board:
  a time you sold something
  a time you lost something
  a time you found something
  a time you exchanged something with someone
  a time someone stole something from you
- Put students in pairs to talk about their personal experiences for a few minutes.
- Have a class feedback session. Invite one or two students to report back any interesting stories that they heard.

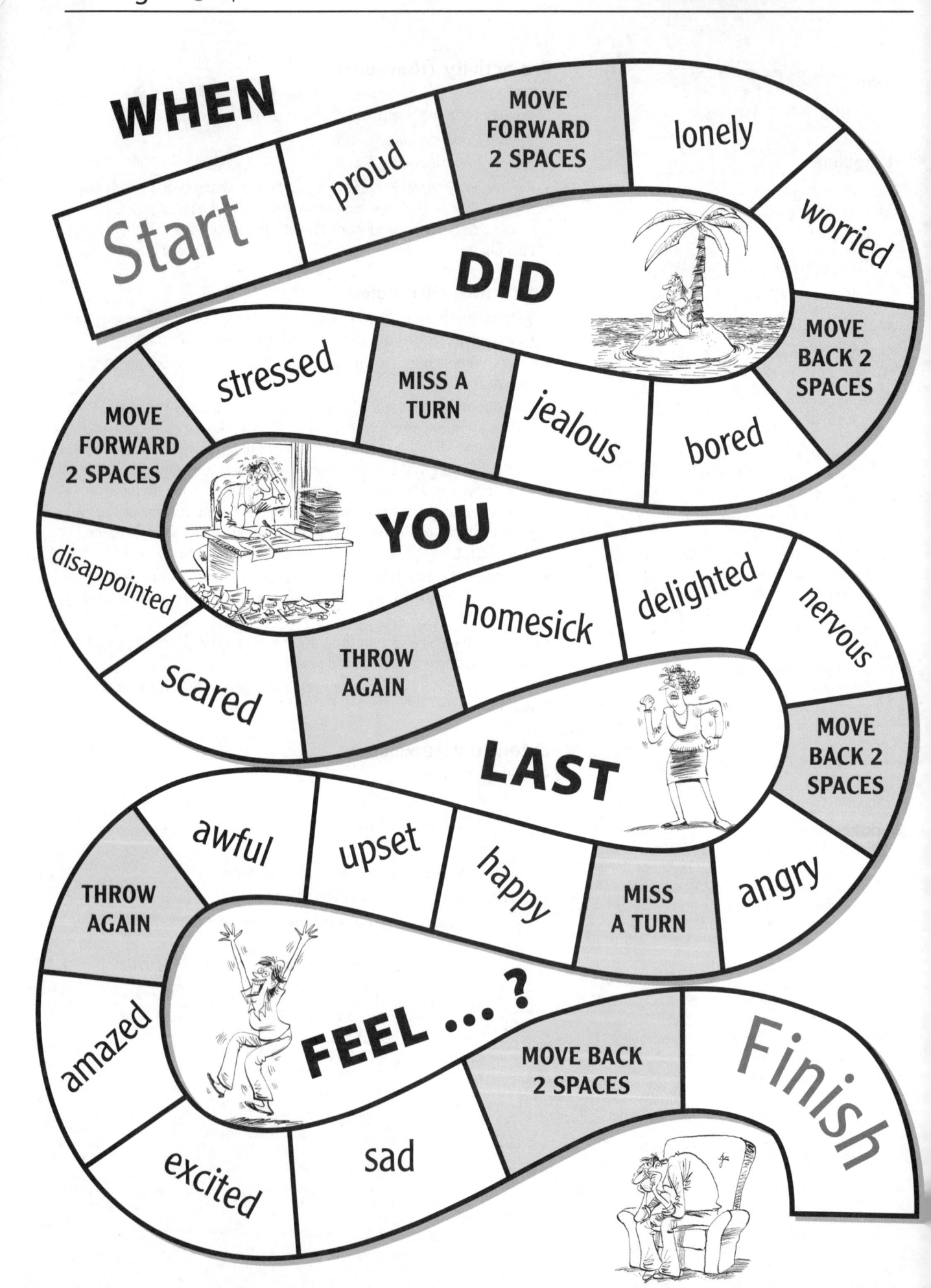

Unit 9 Vocabulary
Feelings → SB p96

5th edition
Headway »
Pre-intermediate

WHEN DID YOU LAST FEEL …?

Start → proud → MOVE FORWARD 2 SPACES → lonely → worried → MOVE BACK 2 SPACES → bored → jealous → MISS A TURN → stressed → MOVE FORWARD 2 SPACES → disappointed → scared → THROW AGAIN → homesick → delighted → nervous → MOVE BACK 2 SPACES → angry → MISS A TURN → happy → upset → awful → THROW AGAIN → amazed → excited → sad → MOVE BACK 2 SPACES → Finish

218 Photocopiable

Headway © Oxford University Press 2019

Unit 9 Vocabulary Teacher's notes
Feelings ➔ SB p96

5th edition Headway
Pre-intermediate

Aim
To complete a speaking activity practising vocabulary for feelings

Language
Adjectives to describe feelings

Skills
Speaking, Listening, and Writing

Materials
One copy of the worksheet for each group of three or four students
Coins and counters

Pre-activity (5 minutes)
- Explain that students are going to play a game to revise adjectives describing feelings from Unit 9. Write on the board *When did you last feel … ? Why?*
- Mime two feelings, e.g. *sad* and *nervous*, and elicit the adjectives to describe these feelings.
- Ask students to work in pairs to list as many adjectives to describe feelings as they can. After one minute, stop the activity and ask students to call out their adjectives. List them on the board making sure you include the following: *angry, nervous, delighted, stressed, upset, homesick, jealous, proud, scared, amazed, lonely,* and *disappointed*. Check pronunciation if necessary.

Procedure (20 minutes)
- Divide the class into groups of three or four and give each group a copy of the board game, some counters, and a coin to flip.
- Pre-teach/Check expressions students will need to play the game, e.g., *It's your turn; It's my turn; Move the counter; Flip the coin; It's heads/tails.*
- Explain that students will flip their coin in order to move their counter forward. (heads = one square, tails = three squares)
- Students take turns to move around the board. When they land on a square with a feeling, e.g. *lonely*, they need to answer the question *When did you last feel (lonely)?* If they answer the question correctly, they can take another turn.
- Tell students that those listening must ask the speaker follow-up questions in order to get more information. Explain that they will need to listen to each other carefully because they will be asked to remember some of the information.
- As students play, go around monitoring, noting any common errors or pronunciation problems.
- The first player to get to the finish square wins the game.
- Bring the class back together and ask groups to share some interesting information they found out about each other.

Extension (10 minutes)
- Students write a paragraph about one of the feelings they didn't answer a question for in the board game. Go around monitoring and helping with vocabulary where necessary.

Unit 9   Communication
Guess what I did! → SB p97

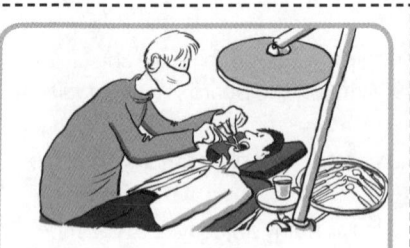

Headway
5th edition
Pre-intermediate

I went to the dentist.	I went ice-skating.	I went to the cinema.
I went shopping in the town centre.	I met an old friend for lunch.	I was in bed with flu.
I got a new car.	I was at the beach.	I started a new job.
I broke my phone.	I did an exam.	I was late for work.
I had a holiday in London.	I gave a presentation.	I had breakfast at a café.

Unit 9 Communication Teacher's notes
Guess what I did! → SB p97

Aim
To prepare and play a guessing game

Language
Exclamations with *so* and *such*

Skills
Writing, Speaking, and Listening

Materials
One worksheet for every three or five students, cut into 15 game cards

Answers
Pre-activity
Example answers:
☺ I was so happy/proud/delighted/excited.
☹ I was so sad/angry/nervous/stressed/disappointed/upset/homesick/jealous/scared/lonely.
I had so many friends/books/problems.
I had so much homework/money/time.
I had such a good idea/an awful day/fun/interesting conversations.

Pre-activity (5 minutes)
- Write these sentence stems on the board and put students in pairs to think of possible endings:
    ☺ I was so …
    ☹ I was so …
    I had so many …
    I had so much …
    I had such …
- Elicit and collate the pairs' suggestions on the board. Drill all the sentences, making sure students are stressing *so* and *such*.

Procedure (25 minutes)
- Explain that students are going to prepare and play a guessing game. Do an example with the whole class. Pretend you have a card which says *I flew over the city in a helicopter*. Make a show of keeping it secret from the class. Write the following on the board:
    I _____ _____ _____.
    (what?) (where?) (how?)
  Say slowly and clearly:
    We travelled so fast!
    It had such big windows!
    The cars and houses looked so small.
- If necessary, repeat the sentences. The first person to guess your sentence wins a point. If nobody guesses, tell them the answer.
- Divide students into groups of three or five and give each student five or three cards. Tell them to keep their cards secret from the other students. Give them about ten minutes to write two or three exclamations with *so* or *such* for each of their cards without using any of the words on that card. Go around the class as the students work giving help and support as necessary and checking that they are using *so* and *such* correctly.
- When all the students are ready, they play the game in their groups. Player 1 chooses one of their cards, keeps it secret, and reads out their two or three exclamations. The other students listen and guess what the sentence on Player 1's card is. If nobody guesses, Player 1 should show the card to the group, then put it to the bottom of their pile and use it again later to see who can remember the answer first. It's then Player 2's turn, and so on. The first student to guess correctly wins the card. The student with the most cards at the end wins the game.

Extension (10 minutes)
- Working in the same groups, students look through the cards together and talk about their real experiences of doing the things on the cards, or similar things. Encourage students to use some exclamations with *so* and *such* if they can. Also, remind them to use narrative tenses.
- Invite students to report back to the class anything interesting they learned about their classmates.

Unit 10 Grammar
Passives quiz → SB p100

5th edition Headway Pre-intermediate

Worksheet A

Quiz

1 When / the first Harry Potter book / write?
   a 1997   b 2001   c 2005

2 Where / Welsh / speak / outside Wales?
   a Peru   b Portugal   c Patagonia

3 When / antibiotics / introduce?
   a 1920s   b 1950s   c 1930s

4 Where / the Olympics / hold / in 2008?
   a Tokyo   b Beijing   c Seoul

5 When / the credit card / invent?
   a 1950   b 1960   c 1970

6 Where / Volvo cars / make?
   a Switzerland   b Slovenia   c Sweden

7 When / Nelson Mandela / set free from prison?
   a 2001   b 1990   c 1986

8 Where / ice cream / first / produce?
   a China   b Italy   c the US

9 When / the Burj Khalifa / build?
   a 1990   b 1999   c 2009

10 Where / the Internet / first / develop?
   a the US   b Russia   c the UK

Worksheet B

Quiz

1 Where / the first underground / build?
   a New York   b Paris   c London

2 When / eBay / launch?
   a 1994   b 1995   c 1996

3 Where / Ducati motorbikes / make?
   a Italy   b Spain   c Romania

4 When / the euro / introduce?
   a 1992   b 2002   c 2004

5 Where / *The Lord of the Rings* / film?
   a Iceland   b New Zealand   c Russia

6 When / the printing press / invent?
   a 1430s   b 1530s   c 1830s

7 Where / 'haggis' / eat?
   a Turkey   b Poland   c Scotland

8 When / Facebook / create?
   a 2004   b 2005   c 2008

9 Where / World Cup / hold / in 2010?
   a Australia   b South Africa   c Mexico

10 When / aspirin / first / use?
   a 12th century
   b 17th century
   c 4th century BC

Unit 10 Grammar Teacher's notes
Passives quiz → SB p100

Aim
To do a general knowledge quiz

Language
Passive forms

Skills
Writing and Speaking

Materials
One copy of the worksheet cut in half for each pair of students

Answers
Wording for questions plus answers

Student A
1 When was the first Harry Potter book written? a
2 Where is Welsh spoken outside Wales? c
3 When were antibiotics introduced? c
4 Where were the Olympics held in 2008? b
5 When was the credit card invented? a
6 Where are Volvo cars made? c
7 When was Nelson Mandela set free from prison? b
8 Where was ice cream first produced? a
9 When was the Burj Khalifa built? c
10 Where was the Internet first developed? a

Student B
1 Where was the first underground built? c
2 When was eBay launched? b
3 Where are Ducati motorbikes made? a
4 When was the euro introduced? b
5 Where was *The Lord of the Rings* filmed? b
6 When was the printing press invented? a
7 Where is 'haggis' eaten? c
8 When was Facebook created? a
9 Where was the World Cup held in 2010? b
10 When was aspirin first used? b

Pre-activity (5 minutes)
- Briefly review Present Simple and Past Simple passives by writing the following prompts and possible answers on the board:
  Where / oranges / grow?
  a Hungary b Belgium c Spain
  When / the radio / invent?
  a 1745 b 1895 c 1901
- Elicit the questions in the correct tense and get students to tell you the answers:
  Where are oranges grown? Spain.
  When was the radio invented? 1895.

Procedure (20 minutes)
- Explain that students are going to do a quiz to practise passive forms of the Present Simple and Past Simple.
- Put students into AB pairs and hand out the relevant worksheet to each student. Pre-teach/Check *Welsh/Wales, antibiotics, credit card, to launch, printing press, haggis* (a traditional dish made from the organs of a sheep, onion, oatmeal, and seasonings – don't mention that this is a Scottish dish, as this will give away the answer).
- Give students time to read through their prompts and then deal with any other vocabulary queries. If necessary, explain that the Burj Khalifa is one of the tallest buildings in the world and is located in Dubai.
- Point out that students will need to use the Present Simple and Past Simple passives in the questions, and then circle the correct answer. With weaker classes, you could put all Student As and all Student Bs into separate groups and get them to prepare the questions together.
- Demonstrate the activity with two students. Student A asks Question 1 and gives the three possible answers. Student B gives the answer he/she thinks is correct. Explain that students get one point for each correct answer. Students do the quiz in their pairs. Monitor and help as necessary. Also check for accurate formation of the passive forms.
- When most students have finished, bring the class together. Go through the questions and answers, and ask students to make a note of their score. The student with the highest score wins the game.

Extension (10–15 minutes)
- Students can write their own passive questions and three possible answers. This can be done as a class quiz, with the students in teams, or in pairs with students working with a new partner.

Unit 10 Vocabulary
Would you rather … ? → SB p103

5th edition
Headway
Pre-intermediate

1 Would you rather _____ … ?
   a the piano quite well
   b baseball very well

2 Would you rather _____ your friend a … ?
   a birthday email
   b birthday card

3 Would you rather _____ a … ?
   a match as part of a team
   b trophy just for you

4 Would you rather _____ a complaint … ?
   a over the phone
   b in person

5 Would you rather _____ … ?
   a the housework for an hour
   b yoga for two hours

6 At a conference, would you rather _____ … ?
   a notes
   b photos of the slides

7 Would you rather _____ a … ?
   a lot of money
   b very important discovery

8 Would you rather _____ a … ?
   a £1000 cash prize
   b five-night holiday in New York

9 Would you rather be smart and _____-… ?
   a known
   b paid

10 Would you rather have a kitchen that's modern but _____-… ?
   a designed
   b equipped

Photocopiable   Headway © Oxford University Press 2019

Unit 10 Vocabulary Teacher's notes
Would you rather … ? → SB p103

5th edition Headway
Pre-intermediate

Aim
To complete collocations in a series of personal questions and then to compare and discuss answers to the questions.

Language
Words that go together: verb + noun, adverb + adjective

Skills
Speaking

Materials
One copy of the worksheet for each student

Answers

Pre-activity
1. play
2. send
3. well

Procedure
1. play
2. send
3. win
4. make
5. do
6. take
7. make
8. win
9. well
10. badly

Pre-activity (5 minutes)
- Write on the board:
  1. _____ football for two hours or tennis for 45 minutes
  2. _____ your best friend your love or an expensive present
  3. have a _____-equipped kitchen or office
- Elicit the missing word in each phrase and leave the phrases on the board.
- Write *Would you rather X or Y?* on the board and check the meaning of *rather* (= *prefer to*). Use the words on the board to elicit some questions, e.g. *Would you rather play football for two hours or tennis for 45 minutes?*
- Invite pairs of students to ask and answer questions across the classroom. Encourage them to ask *Why?* as a follow-up question.

Procedure (20 minutes)
- Tell students they are going to discuss ten more *Would you rather … ?* questions. Explain that they will first need to complete the questions by adding the missing words.
- Give each student a worksheet. Give students five minutes to add the missing words, working individually. Then put students in pairs to compare their answers. Check the correct answers with the whole class.
- Put students in different pairs to discuss the ten questions, taking turns to read out the question. Remind them to ask each other *Why?* about each of their answers.
- When a pair finishes talking, join them with another pair so that students can compare and discuss their answers in bigger groups.
- At the feedback session find out which questions created the most discussion, and get a show of hands so everyone can see how the different questions were answered.

Extension (10 minutes)
- Write *Have you ever … ?* on the board.
- Put students into new pairs and tell them to ask each other *Have you ever … ?* questions about items 3–8, e.g. *Have you ever made a complaint over the phone?* Remind students to ask follow-up questions using the Past Simple if their partner says *Yes, I have*.
- At the feedback session, ask students to tell the class anything interesting or surprising they found out about their partner.

Unit 10 Communication
You're breaking up! → SB p107

5th edition
Headway
Pre-intermediate

Who's speaking to who?

- ⚀⚁ a friend to a friend
- ⚂⚃ a husband to his wife / a wife to her husband
- ⚄⚅ a businessperson to a businessperson

Where is the caller?

- ⚀ at home
- ⚂ at work
- ⚁ on the train
- ⚃ at the beach
- ⚄ at a library
- ⚅ at an airport

What's the conversation about?

- ⚀⚁ changing a plan
- ⚂⚃ asking for some information
- ⚄⚅ giving some good/bad news

Good or bad signal?

- ⚀⚁⚂ good
- ⚃⚄⚅ bad

226 Photocopiable

Headway © Oxford University Press 2019

Unit 10 Communication Teacher's notes
You're breaking up! → SB p107

Aim
To prepare and take part in telephone roleplays

Language
On the phone

Skills
Speaking and Listening

Materials
One worksheet and one dice for each pair of students

Answers

Pre-activity
1 S
2 S
3 D
4 D
5 S
6 D

Pre-activity (10 minutes)

- Write these pairs of sentences on the board:
  1 *You're breaking up. / It's not a good signal.*
  2 *This is Sue. / Sue speaking.*
  3 *The line's busy. / It's ringing for you.*
  4 *I'll see you on Friday. / I can't make it on Friday.*
  5 *She's not answering. / I can't get hold of her.*
  6 *Can I get back to you? / Would you like to hold?*

- Put students in pairs for a few minutes to discuss whether the sentences have a similar (S) or different (D) meaning. Check the correct answers with the whole class. Drill all the sentences, helping students to pronounce them as naturally as possible.

Procedure (25 minutes)

- Tell students they're going to roleplay conversations on the phone. Hold up a dice and a copy of the worksheet and explain that for each phone call, they first need to roll the dice to establish some important things.

- Do an example with the class. Roll the dice once to establish who's speaking to who and write that on the board (e.g. a friend to a friend). Then roll it again to establish where the caller is. Again, write that on the board. Keep going until all the factors are on the board. Pick a strong and/or confident student to roleplay the phone conversation with you.

- Put students in pairs. Give a worksheet and a dice to each pair and give students a few minutes to prepare their first roleplay. Go around the class as they work, giving help and support where needed.

- When pairs are ready, they conduct their first roleplay. Once they've finished, they can then start preparing their second one. Whoever started the first call should answer the second one. If there's time, pairs can prepare and conduct a third or even a fourth call.

- When all the pairs have done at least two roleplays, get them to choose one to practise in preparation for performing to the class.

- When they're ready, invite one pair to perform their roleplay so that the rest of the class can hear. As they listen, the other students should look at their worksheets and work out which options from each block the pair started with. They can then check whether or not they guessed correctly before you invite another pair to speak.

Extension (10 minutes)

- Write these questions on the board:
  How many phone calls have you made today/this week/this month?
  Do you like talking on the phone? Why/Why not?
  Have you ever made a phone call in English? Did you find it easy or difficult? Why?

- Put students in pairs or small groups to discuss the questions for a few minutes, then get some feedback from the whole class.

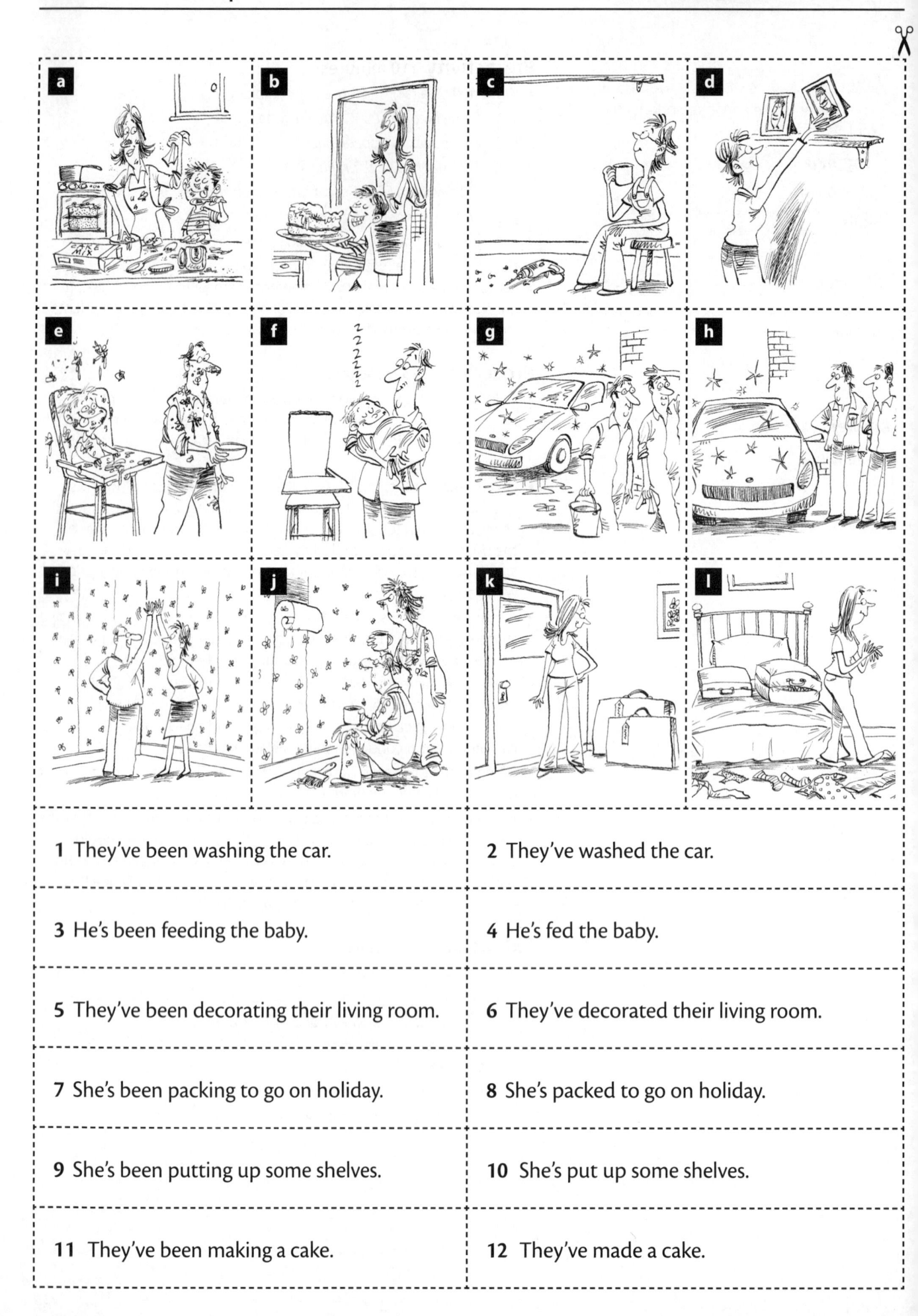

Unit 11 Grammar
Present Perfect picture race → SB p110

Headway 5th edition
Pre-intermediate

1 They've been washing the car.

2 They've washed the car.

3 He's been feeding the baby.

4 He's fed the baby.

5 They've been decorating their living room.

6 They've decorated their living room.

7 She's been packing to go on holiday.

8 She's packed to go on holiday.

9 She's been putting up some shelves.

10 She's put up some shelves.

11 They've been making a cake.

12 They've made a cake.

228 Photocopiable

Headway © Oxford University Press 2019

Unit 11 Grammar Teacher's notes
Present Perfect picture race → SB p110

Headway 5th edition
Pre-intermediate

Aim
To match pictures to sentences using the Present Perfect Simple and Present Perfect Continuous

Language
Present Perfect Simple and Present Perfect Continuous

Skills
Speaking

Materials
One copy of the worksheet cut up for each pair of students

Answers
Procedure
1 g
2 h
3 e
4 f
5 j
6 i
7 l
8 k
9 c
10 d
11 a
12 b

Pre-activity (5 minutes)

- Briefly review the Present Perfect Simple and Present Perfect Continuous by writing the following jumbled sentences on the board:
  he's / his / He's / because / happy / room / tidied / been / tired / he's / tidying / room / because / He's / his
- Elicit the sentences with the words in the correct order and check the names of the tenses. Also briefly check the use of the tenses (Present Perfect Continuous focuses on an activity in progress that started in the past, Present Perfect Simple focuses on the completed action). *He's happy because he's tidied his room.* (Present Perfect Simple) *He's tired because he's been tidying his room.* (Present Perfect Continuous)

Procedure (10 minutes)

- Explain that students are going to have a race to see who can be the first to match a set of pictures with a set of sentences in order to practise the Present Perfect Simple and Present Perfect Continuous.
- Put students into pairs and hand out a set of jumbled pictures and a set of jumbled sentences to each one. Pre-teach/Check *to feed a baby* and *to pack*. Tell students that they need to match the pictures to the sentences as quickly as possible and write the letters that correspond to the pictures next to the sentences.
- Say *3, 2, 1, go!* and get students to lay out the pictures and sentences face up. Students match the sentences with the pictures and write the correct letter. Monitor and check students are matching correctly. If they make a mistake, get them to review the pairings but don't tell them the correct answer at this stage.
- The first pair to match all the pictures and sentences correctly are the winners. Then check the answers with the class.

Extension (10 minutes)

- Get students to put the sentence cards to one side and to put the picture cards face down on the desk in a pile. Students take it in turns to turn over a picture and make a new sentence about the image in the Present Perfect Simple or Present Perfect Continuous, e.g. *She's been using a drill. She's put a vase on the shelf.* Monitor and help with vocabulary. Also check for accurate use of the Present Perfect Simple or Present Perfect Continuous.

Unit 11 Vocabulary
Birth, marriage, and death → SB p116

Crossword A

Across:
2. ENGAGED
8. DEAD
10. FUNERAL
11. HONEYMOON

Down:
1. (6 letters)
3. A...
4. (letters)
5. (letters)
6. SINGLE
7. (letters)
9. DIVORCED

Crossword B

Across:
2. E_ _ _
6. SPLIT UP
8. (E_ _)
10. (word)
11. (word)

Down:
1. MARRIED
3. ALIVE
4. WIDOWED
5. BIRTH
7. PREGNANT
9. (word)

230 Photocopiable

Headway © Oxford University Press 2019

Unit 11 Vocabulary Teacher's notes
Birth, marriage, and death → SB p116

Headway 5th edition
Pre-intermediate

Aim
To complete a crossword puzzle by asking for and giving definitions for words related to birth, marriage, and death

Language
Vocabulary related to birth, marriage, and death

Skills
Speaking

Materials
One copy of the worksheet cut in half for each pair of students

Pre-activity (5 minutes)
- Sketch a crossword on the board and elicit the word *crossword*. Use the crossword to elicit the words *across* and *down*.
- Pre-teach/Check the expressions students will need to complete the crossword:
  You start.
  Shall I start?
  It's my/your turn.
  Whose turn is it?

Procedure (15 minutes)
- Explain that students are going to write definitions for vocabulary related to birth, marriage, and death, which they will then use to complete a crossword in pairs.
- Put students in pairs and give each student a worksheet so that Student As are working with Student As and Student Bs are working with Student Bs. Ask students to write definitions for the words already completed in their crosswords. Encourage students to define their words as clearly as possible, e.g. *This is when you are in a legal relationship with someone as their husband or wife.* (married)
- Put students in AB pairs. They take turns to ask their partner for definitions of the missing words, e.g. *What's one across? What's two down?*, etc. to gradually complete their crosswords.
- Go around monitoring and helping where necessary. Check for pronunciation errors.
- Have a class feedback session to make sure everyone completed the crossword correctly. Go over any common errors.

Extension (10 minutes)
- Write the following questions on the board, and get students to discuss them in small groups.
  How long do you think a couple should be engaged before they get married?
  How many guests do you think should go to a wedding?
  Have you been to a wedding recently? If so, describe it.
  What gift would you buy for a new baby?
  Should there be a limit on the number of times a person can get married/divorced?

Unit 11 Communication
Say the right thing! → SB p117

Headway 5th edition
Pre-intermediate

Role sheet A

Roleplay 1: Giving news

☺ Good news: Your sister's had a baby.

Guess what? My sister's …

Think about …
- Boy or girl: _____
- Name: _____
- Weight: _____

Roleplay 2: Responding to news

Listen and respond to your friend's bad news.

I'm so sorry to hear that. I know you were very fond of him/her.

Roleplay 3: Giving news

☹ Bad news: Clem and Lucy have split up.

Have you heard about … ?

Think about …
- When: _____
- Why: _____
- Who ended it: _____

Roleplay 4: Responding to news

Listen and respond to your friend's good news.

Wow! Diamonds!

I hope I'm invited!

Role sheet B

Roleplay 1: Responding to news

Listen and respond to your friend's good news.

How much did he/she weigh?

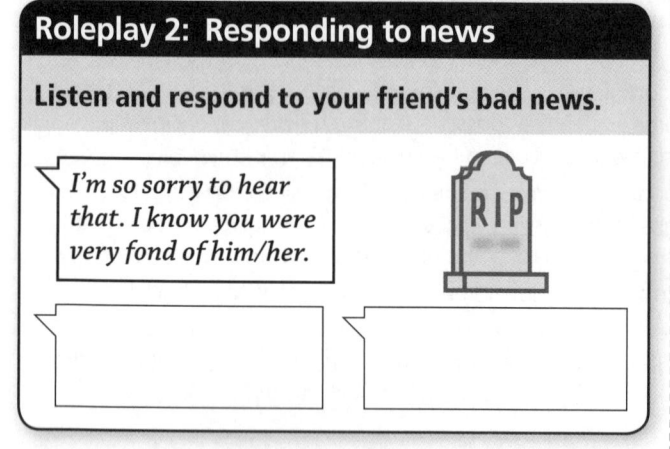

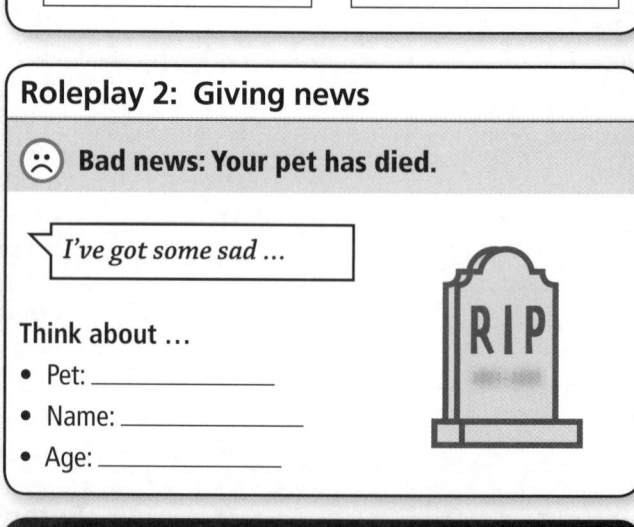

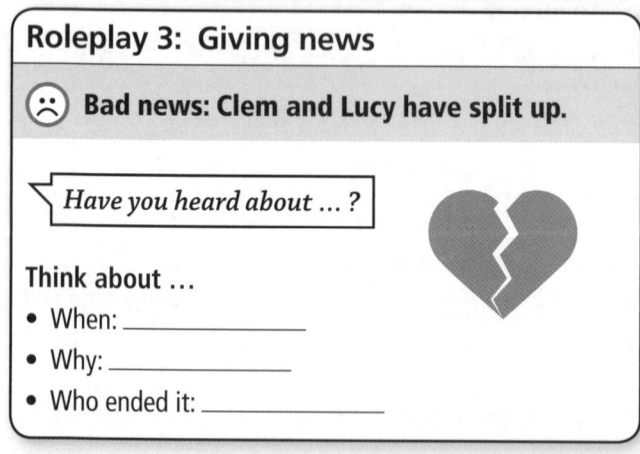

Roleplay 2: Giving news

☹ Bad news: Your pet has died.

I've got some sad …

Think about …
- Pet: _____
- Name: _____
- Age: _____

Roleplay 3: Responding to news

Listen and respond to your friend's bad news.

No!

What a shame!

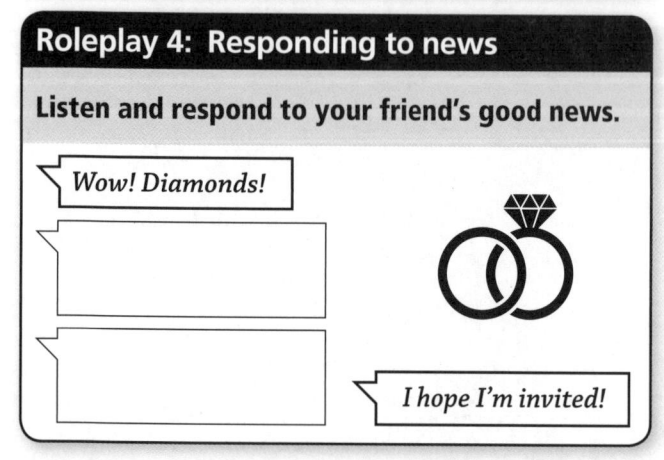

Roleplay 4: Giving news

☺ Good news: You and Alex are engaged.

I've got some exciting …

Think about …
- Date of the wedding: _____
- Location: _____
- Honeymoon: _____

Unit 11 Communication Teacher's notes
Say the right thing! → SB p117

5th edition
Headway
Pre-intermediate

Aim
To complete five role cards and take part in five short roleplays

Language
Finding the right words

Skills
Speaking and Listening

Materials
One worksheet for every two students, cut into two role sheets

Answers

Pre-activity
1 got, E
2 heard, B
3 sad, B
4 call, E
5 touch, E
6 what, B

Pre-activity (10 minutes)

- Write the following on the board. Put students in pairs to work out the missing words.
    1 I'm really sorry, but I've g_____ to go now.
    2 Have you h_____ about … and … ?
    3 I've got some s_____ news.
    4 I'll c_____ you this evening.
    5 I'll be in t_____.
    6 Guess w_____?

- Elicit the answers, and add them to the sentences. Then ask *Do these sentences come from the beginning (B) or end (E) of a conversation?* Check the correct answers with the whole class. Drill all the sentences, helping students to pronounce them as naturally as possible.

Procedure (30 minutes)

- Tell students they're going to take part in four short roleplays. Explain that in some of them they will give news while in others they will respond to news. For the 'giving news' roleplays they need to think of some information in advance. For the 'responding to news' ones they need to think of expressions they can use and questions they could ask to find out more information.

- Divide students into AB pairs. Give Role sheet A to Student As and Role sheet B to Student Bs. Give them five to ten minutes to read through their role sheets and complete the missing information for the 'giving news' roleplays and write responses and questions for the 'responding to news' ones. Encourage students to look in the SB if they're stuck for ideas.

- Choose a strong and/or confident student and get them to do one of the roleplays with you as an example for the whole class. Explain that students will need to work with a different partner for each roleplay. If possible, sit them in two lines facing each other, with Student As on one side and Student Bs on the other, or create a 'wheel' with Student As forming an outer circle facing in and Student Bs forming an inner circle facing out. Alternatively, get students moving about the classroom so they can keep finding new partners to work with.

- Stop the students after about three minutes, reminding them to close the conversation politely. Then get students to work with a new partner for Roleplay 2. Repeat until all the roleplays have been done.

- Invite one or two pairs to perform one of their roleplays in front of the class.

Extension (10 minutes)

- Write on the board:

    Telling someone … you're sad / you're happy / you're angry with them / you have made a mistake

    Asking someone for … money / help / information / advice

- Put students in small groups to discuss which conversations they find easier and which they find more difficult, and why.

- Invite students to report back to the class. Were their opinions similar or different?

Unit 12 Grammar
Would you do the same? → SB p122

5th edition
Headway
Pre-intermediate

Lily was at the hairdresser's. The hairdresser started cutting her hair. Then, after about 15 minutes, he went to make a drink. Lily didn't like how her hair looked so got up and walked out of the shop. She didn't pay.

- What would you do if you didn't like a haircut?
- Would you ever walk out of a shop or restaurant without paying?
- If your friend had a new haircut that you didn't like, what would you say?

Luke got home late and his parents were asleep in bed. He didn't have a key or a phone with him. All the windows were closed. It was a warm night so he decided to sleep in the garden.

- Would you ever sleep outdoors? If so, in what situation?
- What would you do if you needed to get into your house or flat but you didn't have your key with you?
- In what situation would you break a window to get into or out of a building?

Ellie was at her boyfriend's house. His parents had cooked a special meal and everybody was eating it together. Suddenly, Ellie's phone started ringing. She answered it and had a long conversation at the dinner table.

- What would you do if you were in the same situation?
- Would you be angry if a friend answered a call when you were at the dinner table together?
- Would you ever switch off your phone for 24 hours? Why/Why not?

Henry passed a homeless man in the street every day for six weeks. The man always asked Henry for money, but Henry never gave him any. Then, one day, Henry invited the man to come to his house for lunch.

- Would you ever give money to a stranger? Why/Why not?
- Would you ever invite a stranger into your house for lunch? Why/Why not?
- If you were the homeless man in the story, would you accept Henry's invitation? Why/Why not?

Sam was at the cinema with her friends. The film made her feel sad so she cried very noisily. One of her friends offered her a tissue.

- What would you do if a film made you feel very sad?
- If someone was sad at the cinema, would you offer them a tissue? Why/Why not?
- Would you ever walk out of a cinema in the middle of a film? Why/Why not?

Freddie bought a magazine which cost £4.50. He gave the shop assistant a £5 note. The shop assistant thought it was a £10 note and gave Freddie £5.50 change. Freddie took the money and left the shop.

- What would you do if you were given too much change?
- If you saw someone accept too much change in a shop, would you say anything? Why/Why not?
- What would you do if you were the shop assistant in the story and you realized your mistake after Freddie left the shop?

Unit 12 Grammar Teacher's notes
Would you do the same? → SB p122

Headway 5th edition
Pre-intermediate

Aim
To take part in a personalized discussion activity
Language
Second Conditional
Skills
Reading, Speaking, and Listening
Materials
One copy of the worksheet for every six students, cut into story situation cards

Answers
Pre-activity
1 swam
2 'd drive
3 ate

Pre-activity (5 minutes)
- Write these sentences on the board:
  1 I'd be worried about sharks if I _____ (swim) in the sea.
  2 I _____ (drive) at 200 kph all the time if my car was good enough!
  3 If I _____ (eat) less junk food, I'd have more energy.
- Put students in pairs and give them a couple of minutes to add the missing verbs. Check the correct answers with the whole class.

Procedure (35 minutes)
- Tell the class they're going to work in groups and discuss how they would behave in different situations.
- Remind students of useful language for leading a discussion, e.g. *What do you think, Sergei? Marco, how about you?*
- Put students in groups of six and give each group a set of story situation cards. Students take a situation card each, read it and think about their answers to the questions.
- After a few minutes, start the speaking stage. Students take turns to tell their stories and to use the questions beneath it to lead a short discussion with their group. Allow about 25 minutes for this.
- Conduct a class feedback session and ask students to share with the whole class which 'story situation' created the most discussion.

Extension (10 minutes)
- Write on the board:
  What / you / do if a friend/stranger/family member …?
- Then below it write:
  … give / you / _____ (What?)
  … want / borrow / your / _____ (What?)
  … want / discuss / _____ (What?) / with you
- Put students in pairs. Give them five minutes to write three questions like the ones on the story strips, using the prompts on the board and their own ideas. Elicit an example from the whole class first, e.g. *What would you do if a stranger wanted to borrow your phone?*
- Put students in new pairs to ask and answer the questions, reminding them to ask follow-up questions. Get some feedback from the whole class at the end.

Unit 12 Vocabulary
Draw it, act it! → SB p126

go first	take lunch to school	take a friend to the airport
order a takeaway meal	bring people together	go on holiday
Go away!	take your books back to the library	bring me a present
come to my party	come home	go last
take a gift to a friend's house	bring your books to school	take some shoes back to the shop
Come here!	go home	go to sleep

Unit 12 Vocabulary Teacher's notes
Draw it, act it! → SB p126

Headway
5th edition
Pre-intermediate

Aim
To play a game of charades in which teams compete against each other to define as many phrases as possible by drawing them or acting them out but without saying anything

Language
Verbs: *come, go, bring, take*

Skills
Speaking and Listening

Materials
One copy of the worksheet for every group of four or five students, cut into 18 cards
One envelope for every group.
Some plain paper for students to draw on

Answers
Pre-activity
1 come
2 bring
3 go
4 take, bring

Pre-activity (10 minutes)
- Write these questions on the board:
    1 *How did you _____ to school today?*
    2 *Did you _____ any food or drink with you?*
    3 *What time will you _____ home?*
    4 *Will you _____ anything home that you didn't _____ with you?*
- Put students in pairs to discuss the missing words, then check the correct answers as a class.
- Put students in pairs again to discuss their answers to the questions. Conduct a quick class feedback session.

Procedure (20 minutes)
- Put students in teams of four or five. Demonstrate how the game works. Tell students you're thinking of a phrase with *come, go, bring* or *take*. Without saying *come* or *back*, use mime and/or drawing to demonstrate and elicit the phrase *come back*. Students should watch you and call out the phrase when they know what it is.
- Hold up the envelopes of cards. Explain that the cards have phrases with *come, go, bring* or *take*. Students have to draw or act the phrases for their team members to guess. They have 12 minutes to guess as many of the phrases as they can.
- Give each team an envelope of 18 cards. Player 1 takes a card from the envelope and looks at the phrase on it without letting his/her teammates see it. He/She then places it on the table face down. Without speaking at all, he/she must try to get his/her teammates to say the phrase. He/She can do this by acting it out or drawing it on a piece of paper.
- As soon as one of the members of the team says the phrase, Player 1 can turn the card over and the team has won the point. If no one can say the phrase, Player 1 must put the card back in the envelope. It's then Player 2's turn, and so on. The team with the most points wins the game.
- Go around the class as the teams play, making sure nobody's speaking when they should be just drawing or acting.
- When time is up and the winning team has been established, ask *Which phrases were easy to draw? Which phrases were easy to act? Which were difficult?*

Extension (10 minutes)
- Write on the board:
    Talk about a time you …
    … went to sleep somewhere strange.
    … took something back to a shop.
    … came to class late.
    … brought someone a gift from somewhere.
- Put students in small groups to talk for five minutes about these situations. Then discuss for a few minutes with the whole class.

Unit 12 Communication
Thank you and goodbye → SB p127

A Well, it's too late. I must be going now. Thank you so much for a lovely party.

B Was my pleasure!

A And the food was very wonderful!

B I'm glad you enjoyed it. I hope you don't get home all right. Bye!

A Bye! And thanks you again!

A Thanks for your having me. I really enjoyed spending the week with you.

B You're welcome. It was a pleasure. Come back another and visit again sometime!

A That's very kind. Maybe the next summer!

B That would to be great!

A Have you a safe trip!

B Thanks. I'll ring you when I will arrive.

A Say the hello to your family from me.

B I will to. Oh! The bus is leaving!

A OK! Bye! Take care of!

B See you too soon! Bye!

Unit 12 Communication Teacher's notes
Thank you and goodbye → SB p127

5th edition Headway
Pre-intermediate

Aim
To correct sentences and order them to form conversations

Language
Expressions for saying thank you and goodbye

Skills
Speaking

Materials
One copy of the worksheet cut up for each group of three or four students.

Answers

Conversation 1
- **A** Well, it's ~~too~~ late. I must be going now. Thank you so much for a lovely party.
- **B** ~~Was~~ my pleasure!
- **A** And the food was ~~very~~ wonderful!
- **B** I'm glad you enjoyed it. I hope you ~~don't~~ get home all right. Bye!
- **A** Bye! And thanks ~~you~~ again!

Conversation 2
- **A** Thanks for ~~your~~ having me. I really enjoyed spending the week with you.
- **B** You're welcome. It was a pleasure. Come back ~~another~~ and visit again sometime!
- **A** That's very kind. Maybe ~~the~~ next summer!
- **B** That would ~~to~~ be great!

Conversation 3
- **A** Have ~~you~~ a safe trip!
- **B** Thanks. I'll ring you when I ~~will~~ arrive.
- **A** Say ~~the~~ hello to your family from me.
- **B** I will ~~to~~. Oh! The bus is leaving!
- **A** OK! Bye! Take care ~~of~~!
- **B** See you ~~too~~ soon! Bye!

Pre-activity (5 minutes)
- Ask: *In what situations do people say thank you and goodbye?* Elicit a range of situations, e.g. *at the end of a party, after staying in someone's house, at the end of a course,* etc. Elicit some different ways of saying goodbye in these different situations.

Procedure (10 minutes)
- Explain that students are going to do a correction and sentence ordering task to practise saying thank you and goodbye.
- Put students into groups of three or four. Hand out a set of jumbled conversations to each group. The task can also be done as a mingle exercise, in which case give students one or two of the conversation lines, depending on how many students you have.
- Explain that the set of lines form three conversations in which people say *thank you* and *goodbye*. On each line, there is an extra word that students have to find and cross out. Write one of the lines on the board and elicit the extra word, e.g. *Have you a safe trip!* (Have ~~you~~ a safe trip!)
- Ask students to work through the lines, and find and cross out the extra words. Emphasize that they can do this in random order. If necessary, set a time limit of about three minutes to discourage students from focusing on the order of the lines at this stage. Check the answers.
- Ask students to put the lines in the correct order to form the three conversations. Tell students that each conversation has a different number of lines.
- Ask students to read out the conversations to check they have put the lines into the correct order. Students then practise the conversations in pairs within their groups.

Extension (10 minutes)
- Students can work in pairs and write a longer conversation for one of these situations:

    Saying thank you and goodbye …
    … to a host family.
    … when emigrating to another country.
    … when leaving a job.

OXFORD
UNIVERSITY PRESS

Great Clarendon Street, Oxford, OX2 6DP, United Kingdom

Oxford University Press is a department of the University of Oxford.
It furthers the University's objective of excellence in research, scholarship,
and education by publishing worldwide. Oxford is a registered trade
mark of Oxford University Press in the UK and in certain other countries

© Oxford University Press 2019

The moral rights of the author have been asserted

First published in 2019

2023 2022
10 9 8 7 6 5

All rights reserved. No part of this publication may be reproduced, stored
in a retrieval system, or transmitted, in any form or by any means, without
the prior permission in writing of Oxford University Press, or as expressly
permitted by law, by licence or under terms agreed with the appropriate
reprographics rights organization. Enquiries concerning reproduction outside
the scope of the above should be sent to the ELT Rights Department, Oxford
University Press, at the address above

You must not circulate this work in any other form and you must impose
this same condition on any acquirer

Links to third party websites are provided by Oxford in good faith and for
information only. Oxford disclaims any responsibility for the materials
contained in any third party website referenced in this work

Photocopying

The Publisher grants permission for the photocopying of those pages marked
'photocopiable' according to the following conditions. Individual purchasers
may make copies for their own use or for use by classes that they teach.
School purchasers may make copies for use by staff and students, but this
permission does not extend to additional schools or branches

Under no circumstances may any part of this book be photocopied for resale

ISBN: 978 0 19 452791 0   Teacher's Guide
ISBN: 978 0 19 452793 4   Teacher's Resource Centre
ISBN: 978 0 19 452792 7   Teacher's Resource Centre Access Card
ISBN: 978 0 19 452790 3   Pack

Printed in China

This book is printed on paper from certified and well-managed sources

ACKNOWLEDGEMENTS

Cover image: Getty Images (man on bicycle/Philipp Nemenz).

Back cover photograph: Oxford University Press building/David Fisher

Illustrations by: Ian Baker pp.218, 228; Gill Button pp.193, 207, 230; Simon
Cooper p.197; Dylan Gibson pp.173, 213, 215, 216; Ned Jolliffe p.185; Oxford
University Press pp.181 calendar (Sophie Rohrbach/The Organisation),
skiing (Lisa Hunt/Bright Agency), clock (Nancy Carlson), 189 menu (Andy
Hamilton), money (Andy Hamilton), open window (Alan Rowe), water (Mena
Dolobowsky), fizzy drink (Kiera P), sweets (Martina Farrow), pen (Oxford
University Press), salt (Oxford University Press), door (Anna Iosa), coffee
(Oxford University Press), ice cream (Oxford University Press), train station
(Q2A Media Services), loo (Q2A Media Services),), juice (Oxford University
Press), airport (Andy Hamilton), cake (Shutterstock), biscuit (Oxford University
Press), chocolate (Paul Gibbs); Roger Penwill pp.220, 226, 234; Gavin Reece
p.179, Mark Ruffle p.232.

The publisher would like to thank the following for permission to reproduce photographs:
123RF p.199 (archaeologist/microgen); Alamy p.169 (money/Chris Howes/
Wild Places Photography); Oxford University Press pp.167 (Alamy),
205 (old sneakers/Shutterstock/Cbenjasuwan) (woman with snake/Alamy)
(cooked breakfast/Joe Gough), 209 (karate/Mikhail Kondrashov fotomik/
Alamy), (skydiving/Shutterstock/Mauricio Graiki) (gymnast/Shutterstock),
224 (baseball/123rf/betochagas) (trophy/Getty/Brand X Pictures), (yoga/
LatinStock Collection/Alamy); Shutterstock pp.169 (beakers, ice hockey, soccer
ball, saucepan, guitar), 175 (all), 181 (all), 199, (autograph/Africa Studio), (man
eating/RossHelen), 205 (beach hammock/Vixit), 211 (all), 224 (spinning fortune
wheel/MicroOne), 232 (broken hear/musemellow).